MW00448246

THE DORK SIDE OF THE GOON
THE COLLECTED DORK TOWER, VOLUME VII

By John Kovalic

DORK STORM PRESS

OTHER BOOKS BY JOHN KOVALIC

Dork Covenant: The Collected Dork Tower Volume I
(Issues 1-6 of the comic book)

Dork Shadows: The Collected Dork Tower Volume II
(Issues 7-12 of the comic book)

Heart of Dorkness: The Collected Dork Tower Volume III
(Issues 13-17 of the comic book)

Livin' la Vida Dorka: The Collected Dork Tower Volume IV
(previously uncollected comic strips from national magazines and dorktower.com)

Understanding Gamers: The Collected Dork Tower Volume V
(Dork Tower 18, the Lord of the Rings special, plus previously uncollected comic strips)

1d6 Degrees of Separation: The Collected Dork Tower Volume VI
(Issues 19-24 of the comic book)

The Dork Side of the Goon: The Collected Dork Tower Volume VII
(Issues 25-29 of the comic book)

Go, Dork, Go: The Collected Dork Tower Volume VIII
(previously uncollected Dork Tower comic strips) (Spring 2005)

DORK STORM PRESS
PO Box 45063
Madison, WI 53744
http://www.dorkstorm.com

Marketing, sales and advertising inquiries
sales@dorkstorm.com

Editorial and other inquiries
john@kovalic.com

Interior design and layout: Jeff Mackintosh

PRINTED IN CANADA • FIRST PRINTING • November 2004 * ISBN 1-930964-85-4

Story and Art © John Kovalic. All rights reserved. No portion of this publication save for brief review excerpts may be reproduced without the express consent of the copyright holder. This is a work of fiction: any similarities to any actual persons or gamers save for the purpose of satire is purely coincidental. No muskrats were harmed in the making of this book. Published by Dork Storm Press, PO Box 45063, Madison, WI 53744, where all Jelly Babies, Cheese Twisties and bottles of Gulden Draak may be sent. E-mail: john@kovalic.com. Advertising: sales@dorkstorm.com. And the public gets what the public wants/But I want nothing this society's got.

To Jon Leitheusser, Phil Prange,
Tommy Boyd and Marty Devine.

Founding members of
the Army of Dorkness.

INTRODUCTION

By Steve Marmel

Producer/Writer ("Fairly Oddparents,"
"Danny Phantom," "Johnny Bravo"): stand-up
comedian: Cheesehead expatriate.

4

Cosmo © & T 2004 Viacom International, Inc.

t was when we both stopped being dorks that John and I stopped being friends.

I met John at the same time I met parachute pants, Michael Jackson and alcohol. He was a dorkish young cartoonist at **The Daily Cardinal**, the left-leaning (he said politely) newspaper (he said politely) at the University of Wisconsin – Madison.

I was a dorkish young columnist at the **Badger Herald**, the right-leaning (he said politely) newspaper. Each of us had our goals.

John was working his way up the cartoonist ladder, and eventually started selling cartoons to real newspapers. I ended up goofing my way into being student body president – a job that paid $10,000 a year.

Basically, John and I were acquaintances – running into each other at parties, always enjoying each other's' company in that "hey, we're both trying to be funny, in print, for a living" sort of way.

But something had happened in that final year of my six-year stint at the UW. (Yes. Six. Shut up.) I had become "a public official." Student government – as ludicrous as this sounds – constituted that.

We had a six-million dollar budget and - while we might have spent that on Jell-O, Halloween parties (that ALSO ended in riots back then), bands, comedians and filling parking meters so students wouldn't get tickets – some people felt we needed to be accountable.

At the same time, I continued writing my student column, because – as I said - I was a big, fat hypocrite. A lot of it went to my head. And, like most stand-up comedians, I have a large head. Not ego…size-wise.

That same year, one of the geniuses in the Fraternity System decided to throw a "Ghetto Party." And by "Ghetto," that meant a bunch of spoiled Caucasian rich kids in loincloths, with spears. I can't say I'm the most sensitive person on Earth, but even *I* knew that was ridiculous.

So I wrote a column, later that week, making fun of whitey. And in those days (of beer and bourbon, cheese and late bar times, underage drinking and underage thinking) I had a rare moment of clarity about this one issue.

And then, shades of Gary Hart - somebody found a photo of my 1984 Halloween costume. Where I dressed like Michael Jackson, down to the parachute pants (thank you dorkiness), the permed wig (thank you dorkiness), the face paint (yeah) and can of flaming Sterno on my head.

I'm sorry. But in '84, that was a hilarious costume.

In '87, out of context, cropped so you couldn't see the clothes or the Sterno, so it looked like I was performing in a minstrel show…it was not. I was Ted Danson before Ted Danson wasn't cool.

And a few people at the **Wisconsin State Journal** (the morning daily in Madison) were (in some ways, deservedly) dying to take me down a few pegs. So an editor commissioned John to come up with an editorial cartoon, eviscerating me in front of their 10 or 15 readers.

Luckily for me, John never really figured out how to draw my enormous TV head. Even luckier, most people in Madison didn't give a damn and a half about student politics.

Still, it sucked. A lot. And that was our last contact in the 1980s.

Five years later, Star Trek saved our friendship.

John was dorking out in Vegas for a convention of editorial cartoonists. (If you ever find yourself in that situation, and you want to know who's a tourist and who's an editorial cartoonist, look at the pants. The tourists have grease stains on their shorts. The cartoonists have them on their Dockers, and in their hair.)

I was dorking out in Vegas for a comedy festival of some sort. I don't remember much. You can carry drinks on the street in Vegas, so a lot of it is a vague blur that involves neon, explosions and white tigers.

And, like the dorks we were, we both headed over to the Las Vegas Hilton to enjoy the "Star Trek: The Experience" ride. Gambling? Sure, they had that. Women that woul come to your room and give you a massage for $100? Sure. They had that too.

So what did John and I do? Independent of each other? Independent of our significar others?

We each chose to go into virtual battle, on a faux *USS Enterprise*, and then enjoy lovely beverage in "Quark's Bar," where you can pay $15 for a one-shot foo-foo drink i the 24th century.

We literally slammed into each other in the hallway and there, under the watchful eye c a guy making $8 an hour to be a Klingon, John apologized. Deeply. Apparently, it ha been eating at him for years and years and years.

Me? I had forgotten about the cartoon a week after it had appeared...

Of course, I didn't tell him that. I made up some story about a botched suicide attempt and then stuck him with the tab for two drinks and nachos.

But we stayed in touch. We still do.

And I realized: When we stopped being dorks, everything got dramatic and not fur When we went back to being dorks, we became friends again.

Time passes.

It's amazing how fast it flies once you get out of college, and how unimportant the dramas of your young 20's seem, out of context: like a bad Halloween costume, or comic strip for a campus paper, or a column.

These are the dramas that John writes about – from the point of view of someone wh has lived them, but is far enough removed from them that he can comment on ther lovingly and humorously.

John is who John is – and Dork Tower is a testament to that. I am amazed at hi success, his humanity, and his heart.

Me? I've gone from writing bitter little columns in newspapers to writing cartoons. I'n blessed, I'm fortunate, I have a wife who loves every geeky molecule of me, and I got ou of the '90s with my liver intact.

John, I think is a testament to the fact that you can nerd your way down your own path Dork your way through life, and still find happiness, success...and someone who accept: you for the comic-book-reading, cartoon-drawing, cartoon-writing, computer-game-playin dink that you are.

So to you, reading this, I say: Don't lose track of your inner dork. Don't fear your early adult dramas. Even if the nerd deep down in your heart balls up in a fetal position an hides for a few years because they cancelled "Stargate SG-1," hold on to him.

He's not just some aspect of your personality.

He's your heart.

Now if you'll excuse me... I'm off to see "The Incredibles" for the fourth time thi weekend.

Steve Marmel
Hollywood, CA
November 7th, 2004

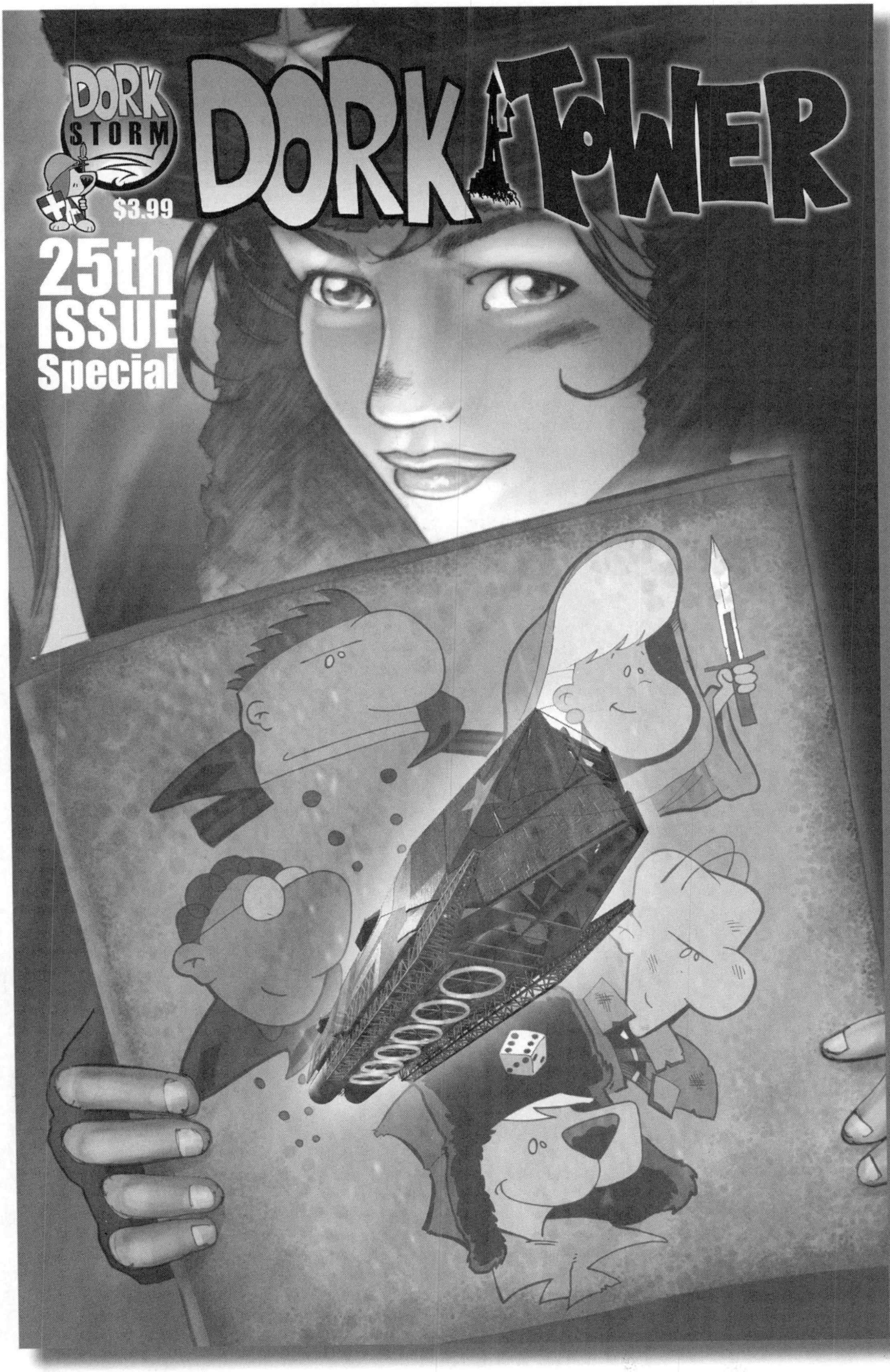
DORK STORM
DORK TOWER
$3.99
25th ISSUE Special

I have a new philosophy. I'm only going to dread one day at a time.
- *Charlie Brown*

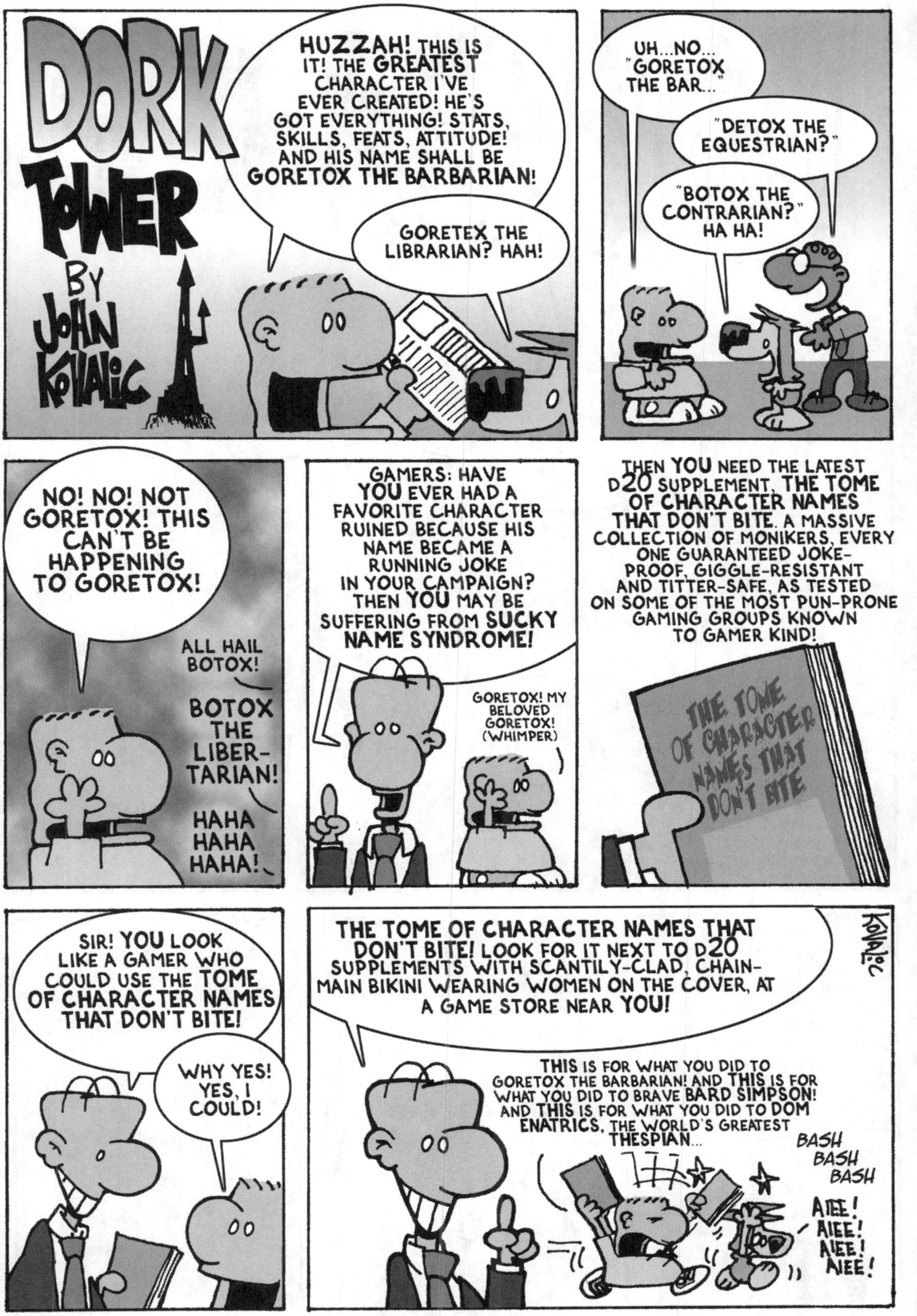
DORK TOWER
BY JOHN KOVALIC
HUZZAH! THIS IS IT! THE GREATEST CHARACTER I'VE EVER CREATED! HE'S GOT EVERYTHING! STATS, SKILLS, FEATS, ATTITUDE! AND HIS NAME SHALL BE GORETOX THE BARBARIAN!
GORETEX THE LIBRARIAN? HAH!
UH...NO... "GORETOX THE BAR..."
"DETOX THE EQUESTRIAN?"
"BOTOX THE CONTRARIAN?" HA HA!
NO! NO! NOT GORETOX! THIS CAN'T BE HAPPENING TO GORETOX!
ALL HAIL BOTOX!
BOTOX THE LIBER-TARIAN!
HAHA HAHA HAHA!
GAMERS: HAVE YOU EVER HAD A FAVORITE CHARACTER RUINED BECAUSE HIS NAME BECAME A RUNNING JOKE IN YOUR CAMPAIGN? THEN YOU MAY BE SUFFERING FROM SUCKY NAME SYNDROME!
GORETOX! MY BELOVED GORETOX! (WHIMPER)
THEN YOU NEED THE LATEST D20 SUPPLEMENT, THE TOME OF CHARACTER NAMES THAT DON'T BITE. A MASSIVE COLLECTION OF MONIKERS, EVERY ONE GUARANTEED JOKE-PROOF, GIGGLE-RESISTANT AND TITTER-SAFE, AS TESTED ON SOME OF THE MOST PUN-PRONE GAMING GROUPS KNOWN TO GAMER KIND!
THE TOME OF CHARACTER NAMES THAT DON'T BITE
SIR! YOU LOOK LIKE A GAMER WHO COULD USE THE TOME OF CHARACTER NAMES THAT DON'T BITE!
WHY YES! YES, I COULD!
THE TOME OF CHARACTER NAMES THAT DON'T BITE! LOOK FOR IT NEXT TO D20 SUPPLEMENTS WITH SCANTILY-CLAD, CHAIN-MAIN BIKINI WEARING WOMEN ON THE COVER, AT A GAME STORE NEAR YOU!
KOVALIC
THIS IS FOR WHAT YOU DID TO GORETOX THE BARBARIAN! AND THIS IS FOR WHAT YOU DID TO BRAVE BARD SIMPSON! AND THIS IS FOR WHAT YOU DID TO DOM ENATRICS, THE WORLD'S GREATEST THESPIAN...
BASH
BASH
BASH
AIEE! AIEE! AIEE! AIEE!

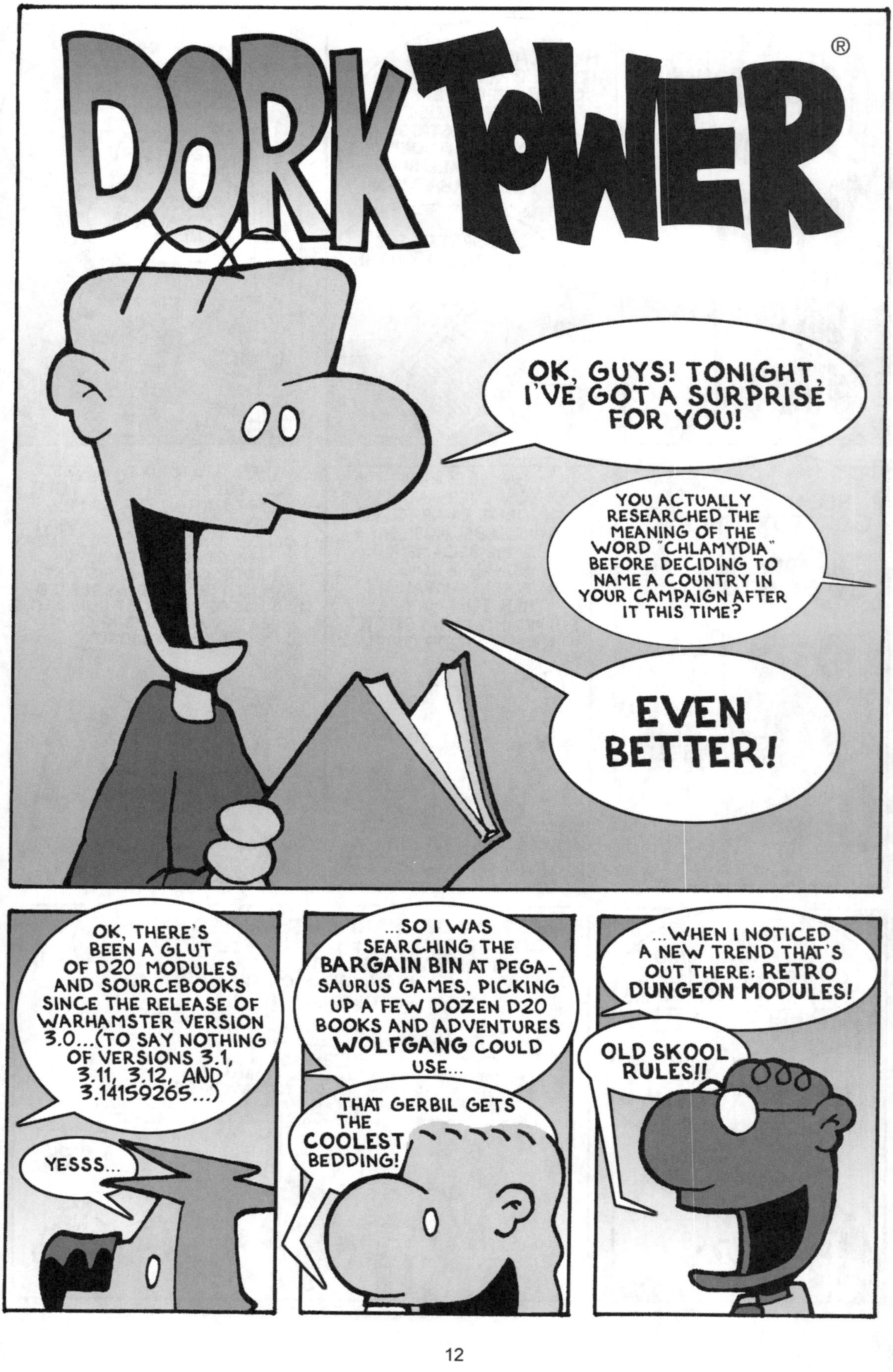
DORK TOWER®
OK, GUYS! TONIGHT, I'VE GOT A SURPRISE FOR YOU!
YOU ACTUALLY RESEARCHED THE MEANING OF THE WORD "CHLAMYDIA" BEFORE DECIDING TO NAME A COUNTRY IN YOUR CAMPAIGN AFTER IT THIS TIME?
EVEN BETTER!
OK, THERE'S BEEN A GLUT OF D20 MODULES AND SOURCEBOOKS SINCE THE RELEASE OF WARHAMSTER VERSION 3.0...(TO SAY NOTHING OF VERSIONS 3.1, 3.11, 3.12, AND 3.14159265...)
YESSS...
...SO I WAS SEARCHING THE BARGAIN BIN AT PEGA-SAURUS GAMES, PICKING UP A FEW DOZEN D20 BOOKS AND ADVENTURES WOLFGANG COULD USE...
THAT GERBIL GETS THE COOLEST BEDDING!
...WHEN I NOTICED A NEW TREND THAT'S OUT THERE: RETRO DUNGEON MODULES!
OLD SKOOL RULES!!

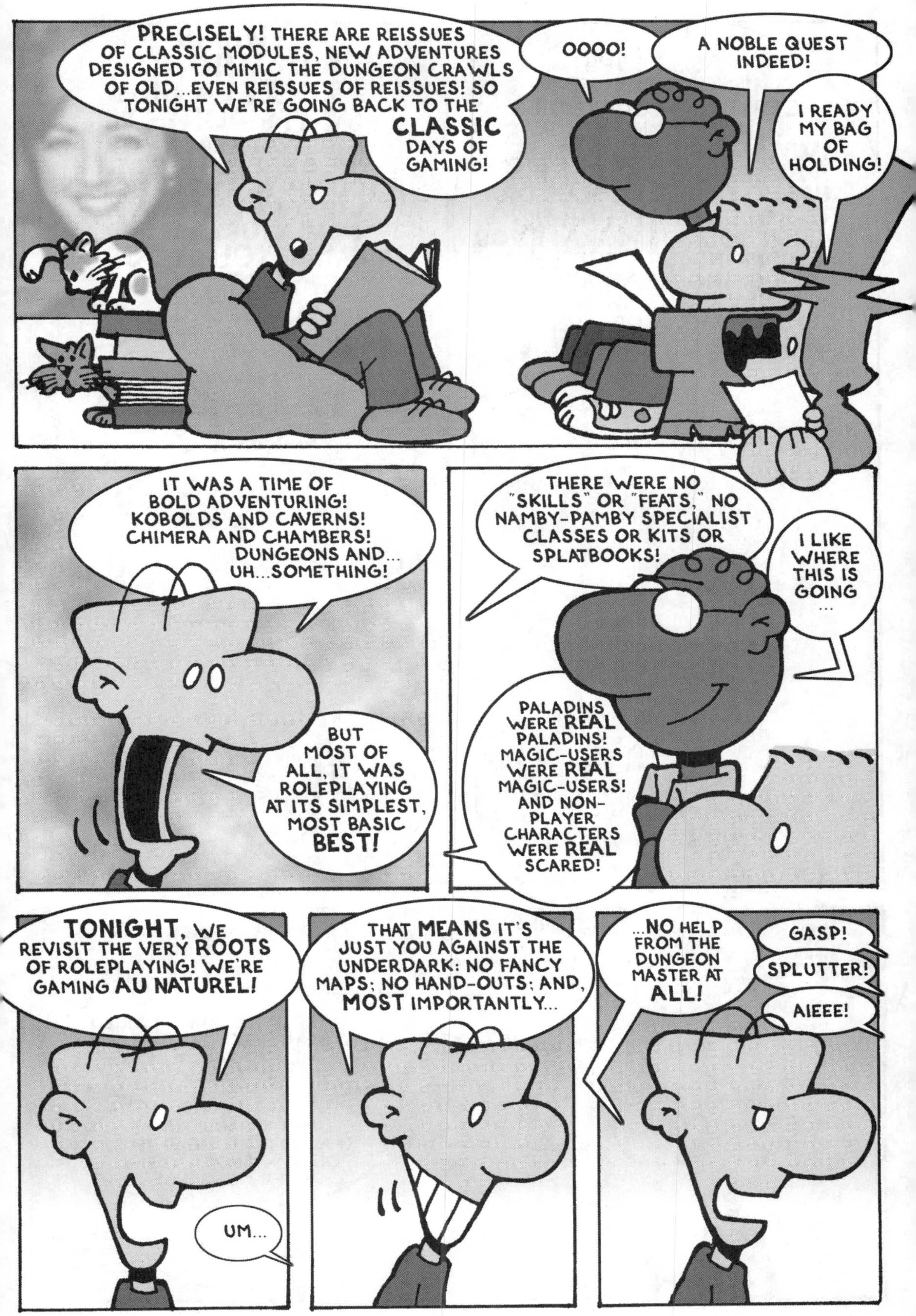
PRECISELY! THERE ARE REISSUES OF CLASSIC MODULES, NEW ADVENTURES DESIGNED TO MIMIC THE DUNGEON CRAWLS OF OLD...EVEN REISSUES OF REISSUES! SO TONIGHT WE'RE GOING BACK TO THE CLASSIC DAYS OF GAMING!
OOOO!
A NOBLE QUEST INDEED!
I READY MY BAG OF HOLDING!
IT WAS A TIME OF BOLD ADVENTURING! KOBOLDS AND CAVERNS! CHIMERA AND CHAMBERS! DUNGEONS AND... UH...SOMETHING!
BUT MOST OF ALL, IT WAS ROLEPLAYING AT ITS SIMPLEST, MOST BASIC BEST!
THERE WERE NO "SKILLS" OR "FEATS," NO NAMBY-PAMBY SPECIALIST CLASSES OR KITS OR SPLATBOOKS!
I LIKE WHERE THIS IS GOING ...
PALADINS WERE REAL PALADINS! MAGIC-USERS WERE REAL MAGIC-USERS! AND NON-PLAYER CHARACTERS WERE REAL SCARED!
TONIGHT, WE REVISIT THE VERY ROOTS OF ROLEPLAYING! WE'RE GAMING AU NATUREL!
UM...
THAT MEANS IT'S JUST YOU AGAINST THE UNDERDARK: NO FANCY MAPS; NO HAND-OUTS; AND, MOST IMPORTANTLY...
...NO HELP FROM THE DUNGEON MASTER AT ALL!
GASP!
SPLUTTER!
AIEEE!

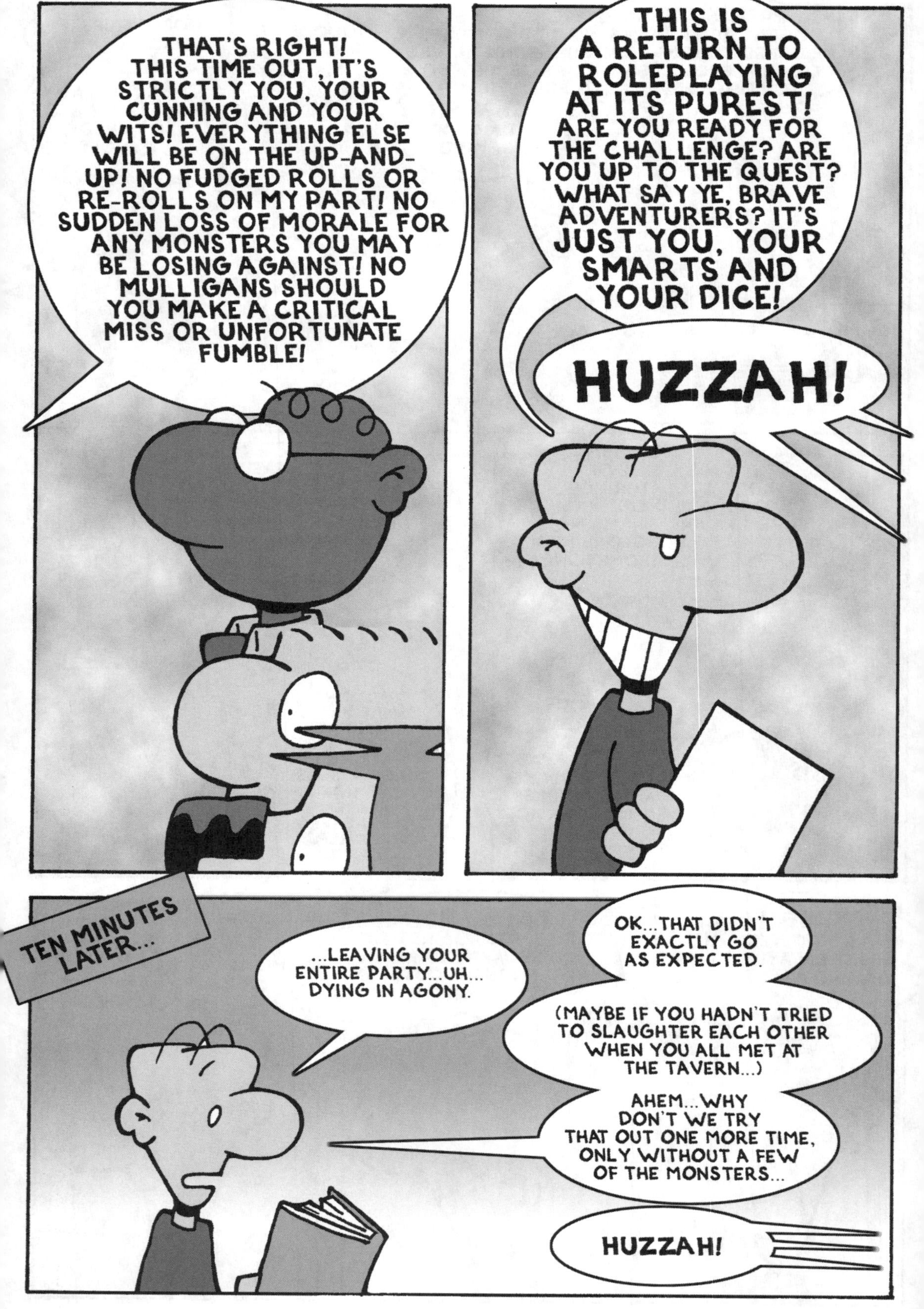
THAT'S RIGHT! THIS TIME OUT, IT'S STRICTLY YOU, YOUR CUNNING AND YOUR WITS! EVERYTHING ELSE WILL BE ON THE UP-AND-UP! NO FUDGED ROLLS OR RE-ROLLS ON MY PART! NO SUDDEN LOSS OF MORALE FOR ANY MONSTERS YOU MAY BE LOSING AGAINST! NO MULLIGANS SHOULD YOU MAKE A CRITICAL MISS OR UNFORTUNATE FUMBLE!
THIS IS A RETURN TO ROLEPLAYING AT ITS PUREST! ARE YOU READY FOR THE CHALLENGE? ARE YOU UP TO THE QUEST? WHAT SAY YE, BRAVE ADVENTURERS? IT'S JUST YOU, YOUR SMARTS AND YOUR DICE!
HUZZAH!
TEN MINUTES LATER...
...LEAVING YOUR ENTIRE PARTY...UH... DYING IN AGONY.
OK...THAT DIDN'T EXACTLY GO AS EXPECTED.
(MAYBE IF YOU HADN'T TRIED TO SLAUGHTER EACH OTHER WHEN YOU ALL MET AT THE TAVERN...)
AHEM...WHY DON'T WE TRY THAT OUT ONE MORE TIME, ONLY WITHOUT A FEW OF THE MONSTERS...
HUZZAH!

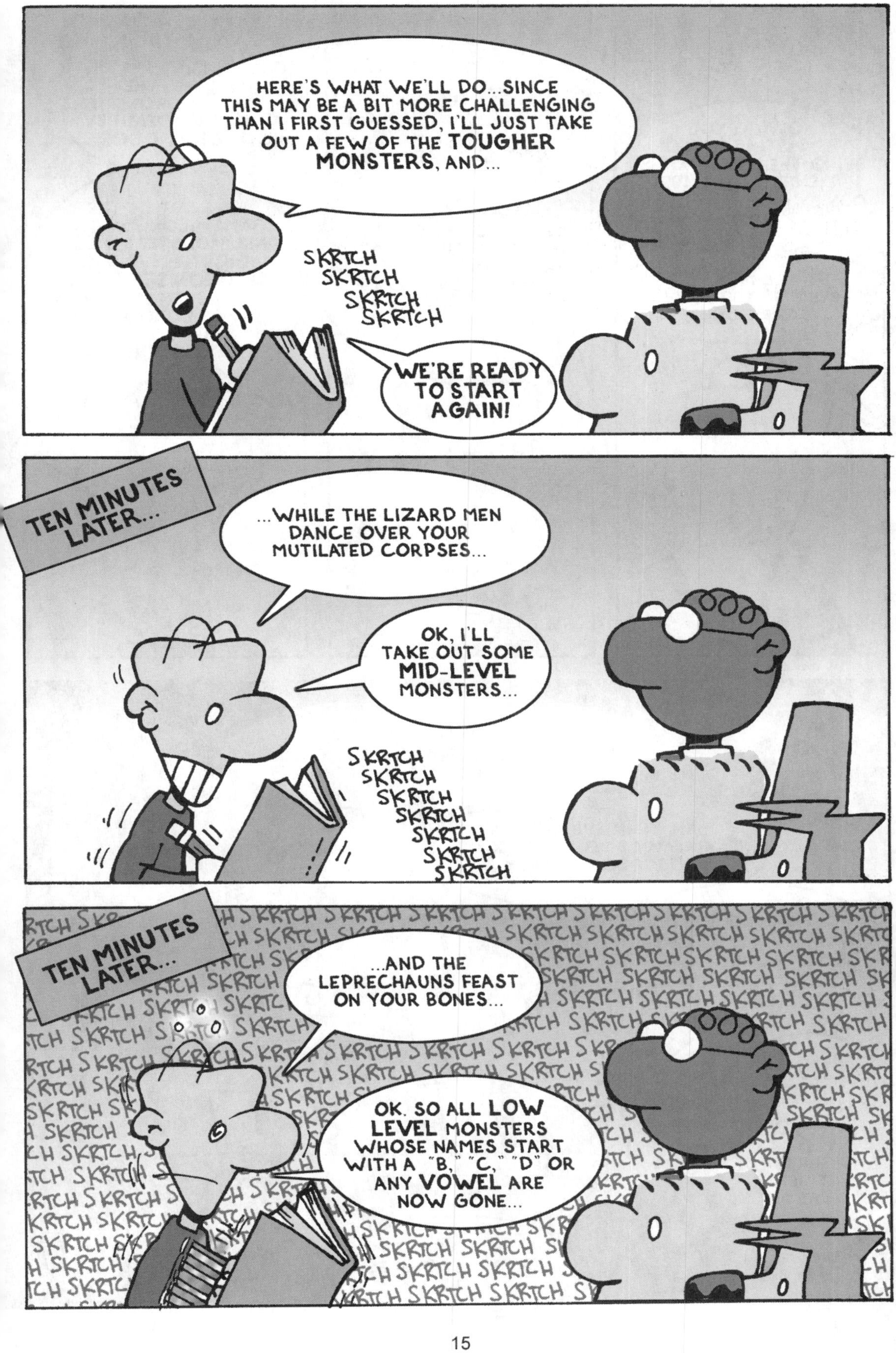
HERE'S WHAT WE'LL DO...SINCE THIS MAY BE A BIT MORE CHALLENGING THAN I FIRST GUESSED, I'LL JUST TAKE OUT A FEW OF THE TOUGHER MONSTERS, AND...
SKRTCH SKRTCH SKRTCH SKRTCH
WE'RE READY TO START AGAIN!
TEN MINUTES LATER...
...WHILE THE LIZARD MEN DANCE OVER YOUR MUTILATED CORPSES...
OK, I'LL TAKE OUT SOME MID-LEVEL MONSTERS...
SKRTCH SKRTCH SKRTCH SKRTCH SKRTCH SKRTCH SKRTCH
TEN MINUTES LATER...
...AND THE LEPRECHAUNS FEAST ON YOUR BONES...
OK. SO ALL LOW LEVEL MONSTERS WHOSE NAMES START WITH A "B," "C," "D" OR ANY VOWEL ARE NOW GONE...

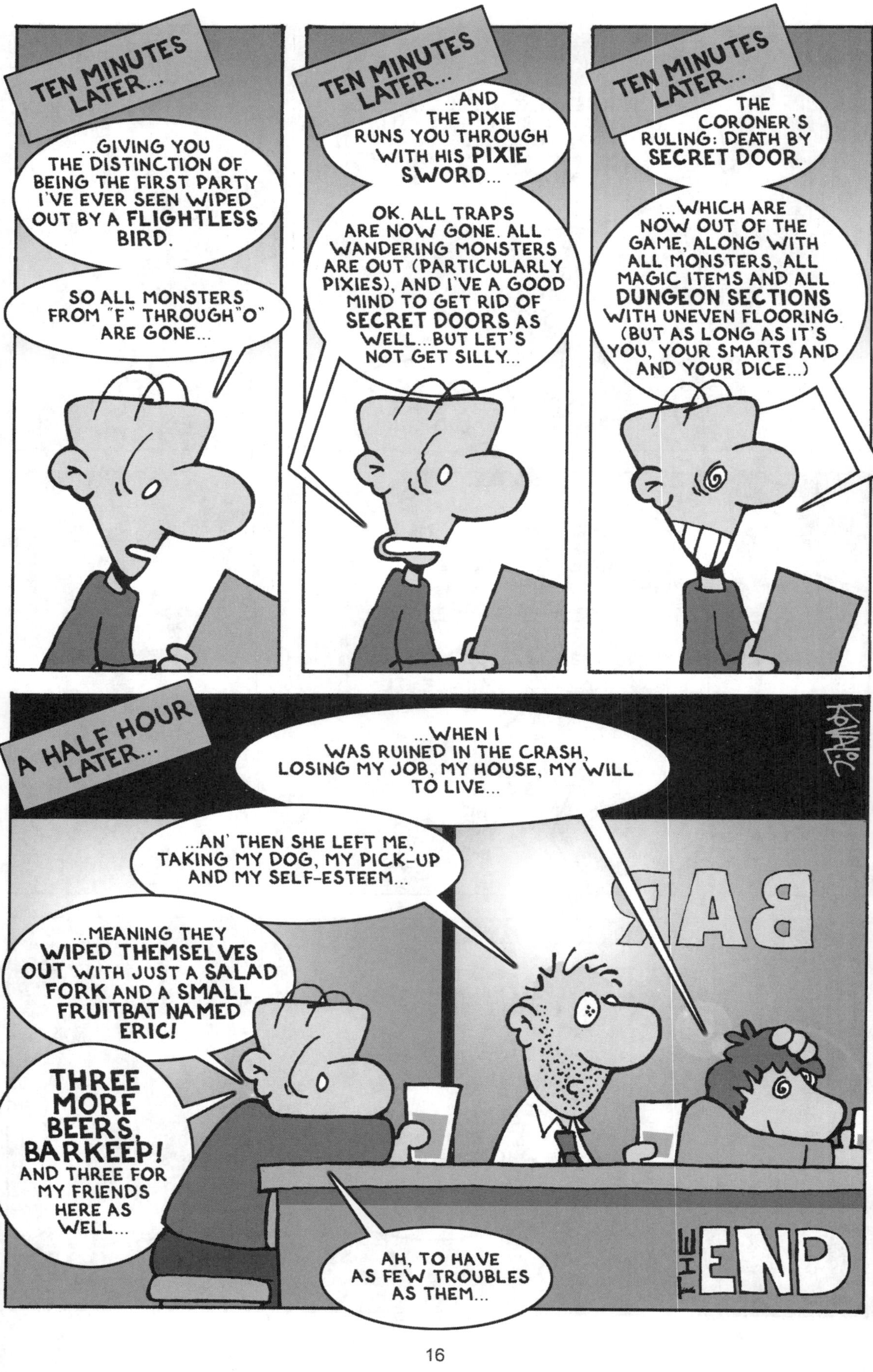
TEN MINUTES LATER...
...GIVING YOU THE DISTINCTION OF BEING THE FIRST PARTY I'VE EVER SEEN WIPED OUT BY A FLIGHTLESS BIRD.
SO ALL MONSTERS FROM "F" THROUGH "O" ARE GONE...
TEN MINUTES LATER...
...AND THE PIXIE RUNS YOU THROUGH WITH HIS PIXIE SWORD...
OK. ALL TRAPS ARE NOW GONE. ALL WANDERING MONSTERS ARE OUT (PARTICULARLY PIXIES), AND I'VE A GOOD MIND TO GET RID OF SECRET DOORS AS WELL...BUT LET'S NOT GET SILLY...
TEN MINUTES LATER...
THE CORONER'S RULING: DEATH BY SECRET DOOR.
...WHICH ARE NOW OUT OF THE GAME, ALONG WITH ALL MONSTERS, ALL MAGIC ITEMS AND ALL DUNGEON SECTIONS WITH UNEVEN FLOORING. (BUT AS LONG AS IT'S YOU, YOUR SMARTS AND AND YOUR DICE...)
A HALF HOUR LATER...
...WHEN I WAS RUINED IN THE CRASH, LOSING MY JOB, MY HOUSE, MY WILL TO LIVE...
...AN' THEN SHE LEFT ME, TAKING MY DOG, MY PICK-UP AND MY SELF-ESTEEM...
...MEANING THEY WIPED THEMSELVES OUT WITH JUST A SALAD FORK AND A SMALL FRUITBAT NAMED ERIC!
THREE MORE BEERS, BARKEEP! AND THREE FOR MY FRIENDS HERE AS WELL...
AH, TO HAVE AS FEW TROUBLES AS THEM...
BAR
THE END

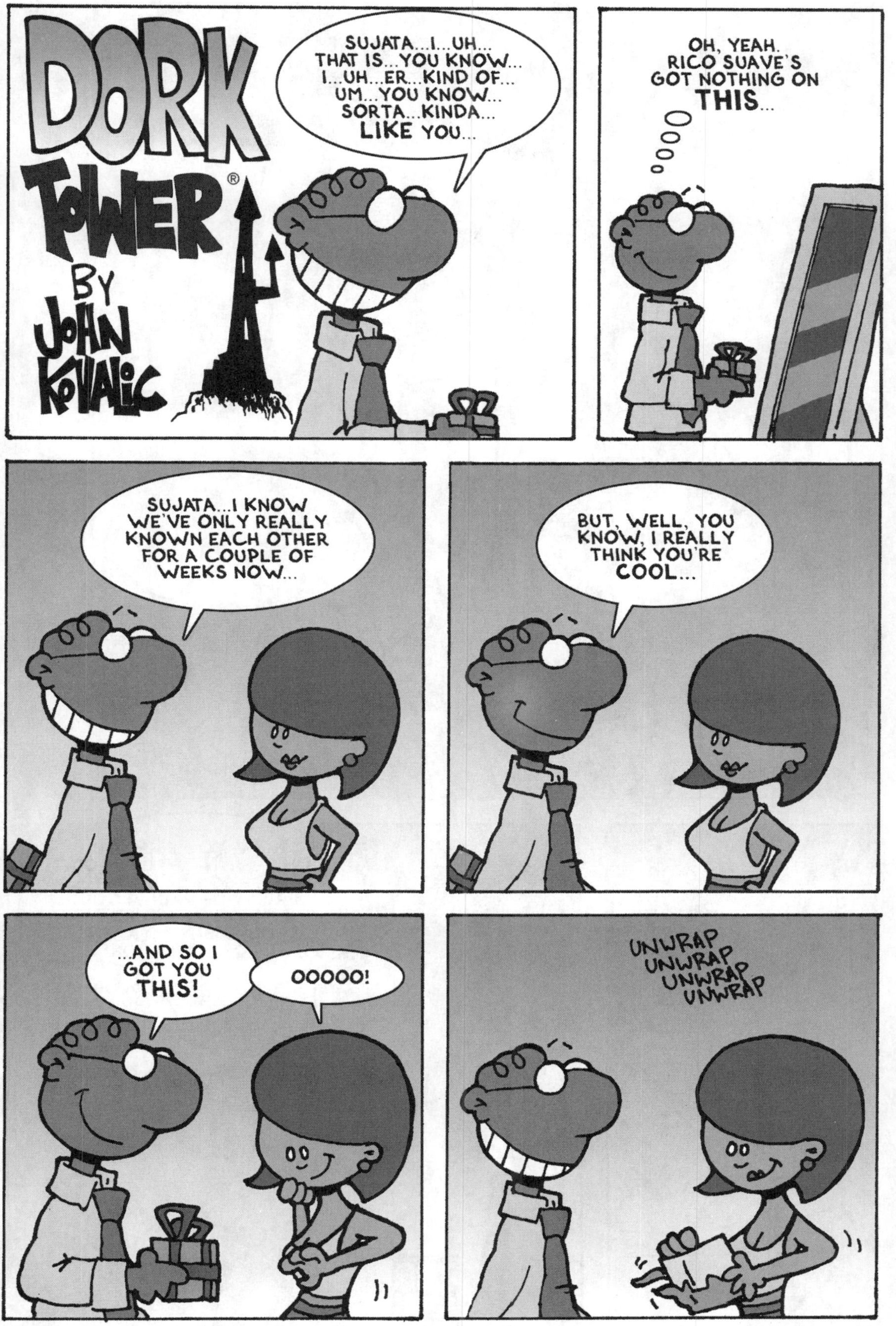
DORK TOWER®
BY JOHN KOVALIC
SUJATA...I...UH... THAT IS...YOU KNOW... I...UH...ER...KIND OF... UM...YOU KNOW... SORTA...KINDA... LIKE YOU...
OH, YEAH. RICO SUAVE'S GOT NOTHING ON THIS...
SUJATA...I KNOW WE'VE ONLY REALLY KNOWN EACH OTHER FOR A COUPLE OF WEEKS NOW...
BUT, WELL, YOU KNOW, I REALLY THINK YOU'RE COOL...
...AND SO I GOT YOU THIS!
OOOOO!
UNWRAP UNWRAP UNWRAP UNWRAP

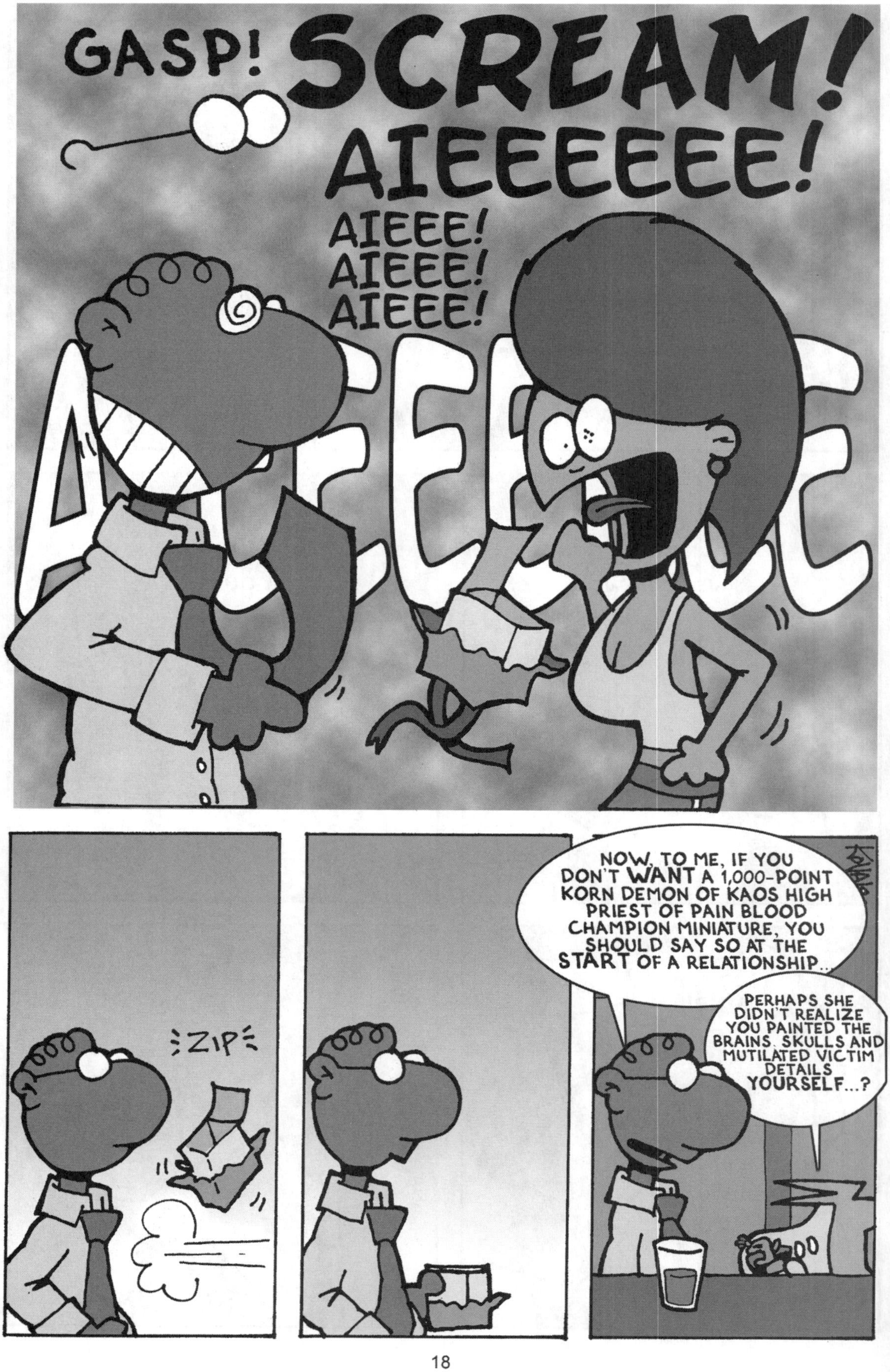
GASP!
SCREAM!
AIEEEEEEE!
AIEEE!
AIEEE!
AIEEE!
ZIP
NOW, TO ME, IF YOU DON'T WANT A 1,000-POINT KORN DEMON OF KAOS HIGH PRIEST OF PAIN BLOOD CHAMPION MINIATURE, YOU SHOULD SAY SO AT THE START OF A RELATIONSHIP...
PERHAPS SHE DIDN'T REALIZE YOU PAINTED THE BRAINS, SKULLS AND MUTILATED VICTIM DETAILS YOURSELF...?

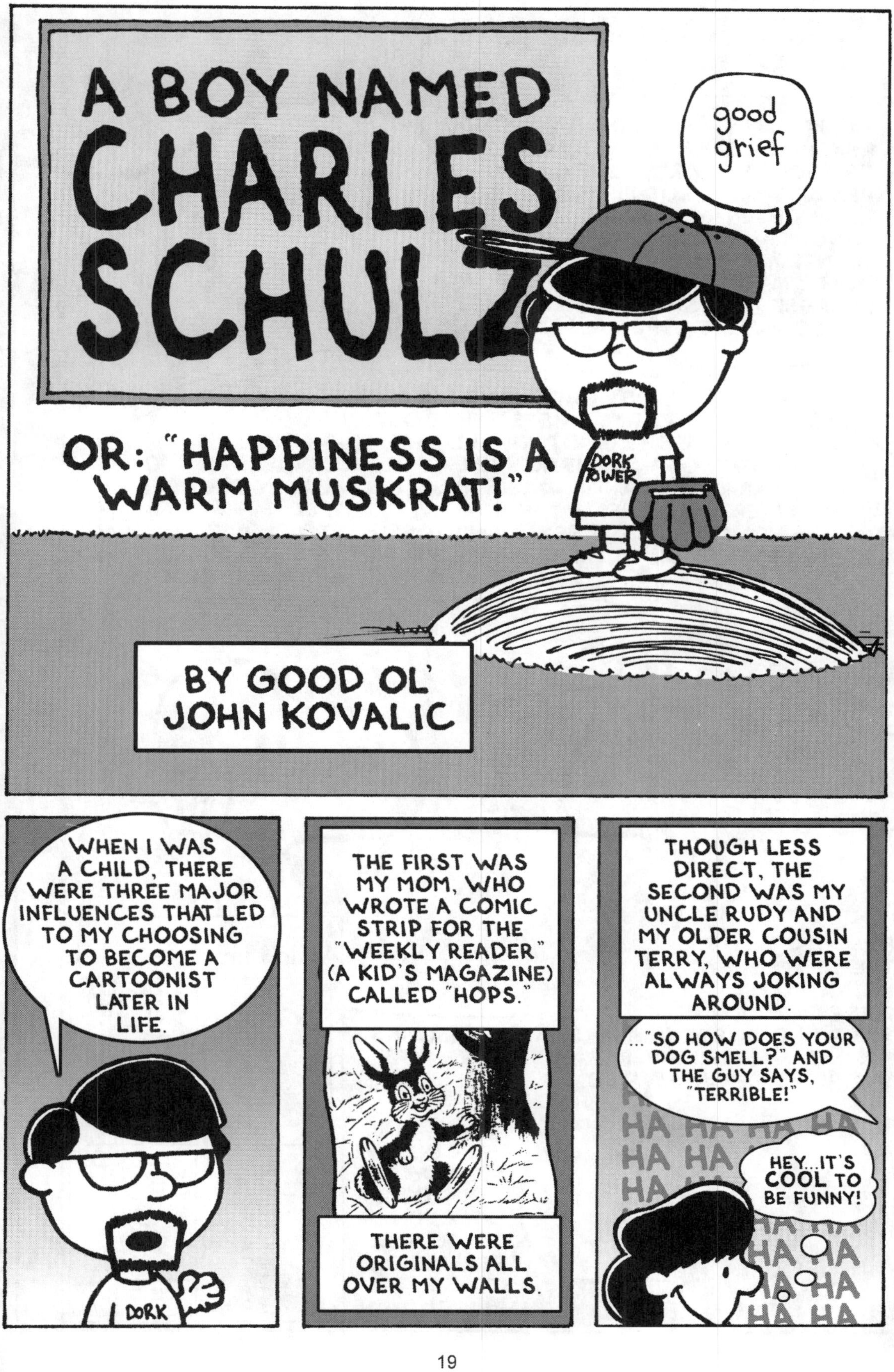
A BOY NAMED CHARLES SCHULZ
good grief
DORK TOWER
OR: "HAPPINESS IS A WARM MUSKRAT!"
BY GOOD OL' JOHN KOVALIC
WHEN I WAS A CHILD, THERE WERE THREE MAJOR INFLUENCES THAT LED TO MY CHOOSING TO BECOME A CARTOONIST LATER IN LIFE.
DORK
THE FIRST WAS MY MOM, WHO WROTE A COMIC STRIP FOR THE "WEEKLY READER" (A KID'S MAGAZINE) CALLED "HOPS."
THERE WERE ORIGINALS ALL OVER MY WALLS.
THOUGH LESS DIRECT, THE SECOND WAS MY UNCLE RUDY AND MY OLDER COUSIN TERRY, WHO WERE ALWAYS JOKING AROUND.
..."SO HOW DOES YOUR DOG SMELL?" AND THE GUY SAYS, "TERRIBLE!"
HA HA HA HA
HEY...IT'S COOL TO BE FUNNY!

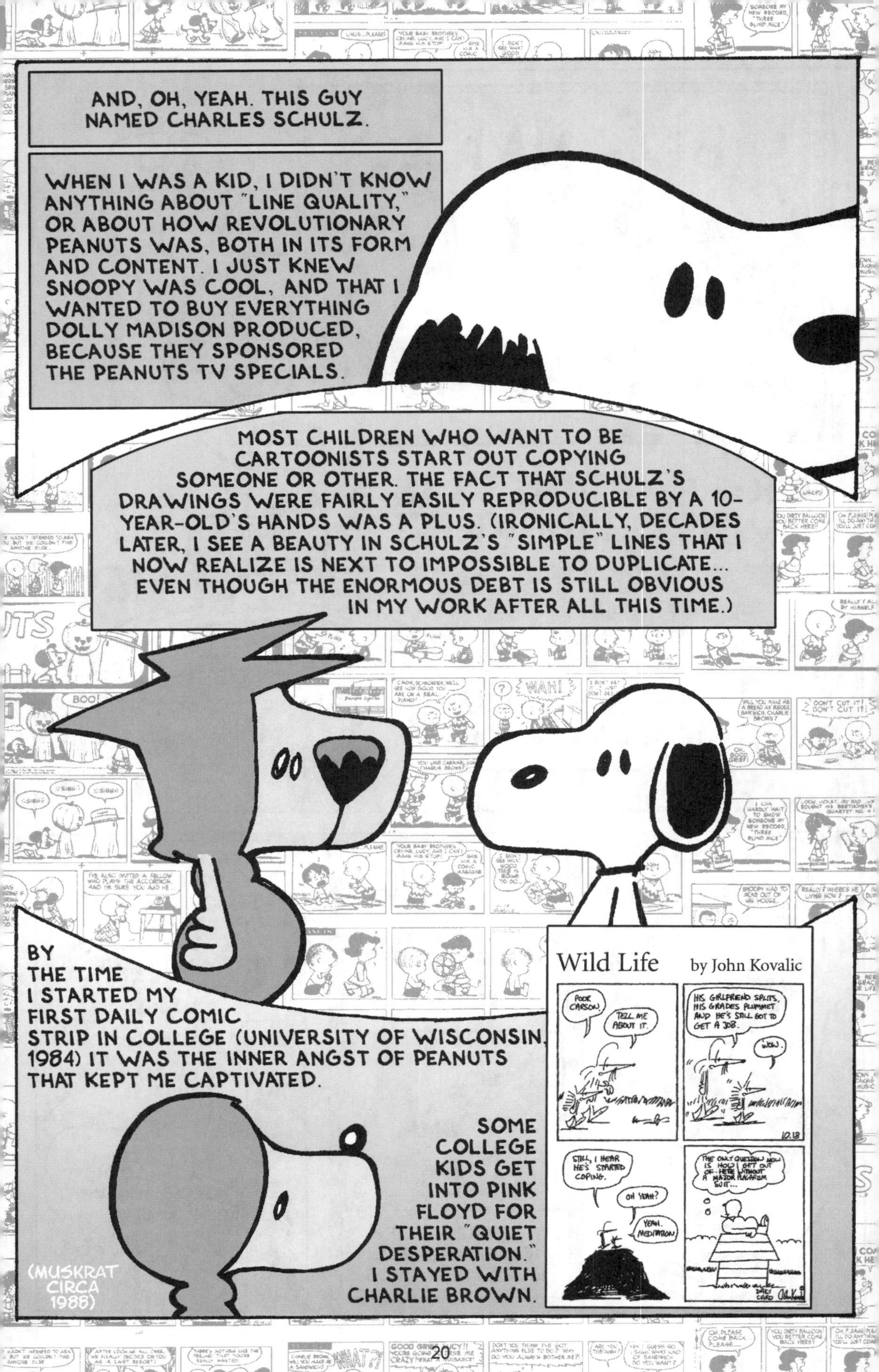
AND, OH, YEAH. THIS GUY NAMED CHARLES SCHULZ.
WHEN I WAS A KID, I DIDN'T KNOW ANYTHING ABOUT "LINE QUALITY," OR ABOUT HOW REVOLUTIONARY PEANUTS WAS, BOTH IN ITS FORM AND CONTENT. I JUST KNEW SNOOPY WAS COOL, AND THAT I WANTED TO BUY EVERYTHING DOLLY MADISON PRODUCED, BECAUSE THEY SPONSORED THE PEANUTS TV SPECIALS.
MOST CHILDREN WHO WANT TO BE CARTOONISTS START OUT COPYING SOMEONE OR OTHER. THE FACT THAT SCHULZ'S DRAWINGS WERE FAIRLY EASILY REPRODUCIBLE BY A 10-YEAR-OLD'S HANDS WAS A PLUS. (IRONICALLY, DECADES LATER, I SEE A BEAUTY IN SCHULZ'S "SIMPLE" LINES THAT I NOW REALIZE IS NEXT TO IMPOSSIBLE TO DUPLICATE... EVEN THOUGH THE ENORMOUS DEBT IS STILL OBVIOUS IN MY WORK AFTER ALL THIS TIME.)
BY THE TIME I STARTED MY FIRST DAILY COMIC STRIP IN COLLEGE (UNIVERSITY OF WISCONSIN, 1984) IT WAS THE INNER ANGST OF PEANUTS THAT KEPT ME CAPTIVATED.
Wild Life by John Kovalic
POOR CARSON.
TELL ME ABOUT IT.
HIS GIRLFREND SPLITS, HIS GRADES PLUMMET AND HE'S STILL GOT TO GET A JOB.
WOW.
10.18
STILL, I HEAR HE'S STARTED COPING.
OH YEAH?
YEAH. MEDITATION.
THE ONLY QUESTION NOW IS HOW I GET OUT OF HERE WITHOUT A MAJOR PLAGARISM SUIT...
DAILY CARD
SOME COLLEGE KIDS GET INTO PINK FLOYD FOR THEIR "QUIET DESPERATION." I STAYED WITH CHARLIE BROWN.
(MUSKRAT CIRCA 1988)

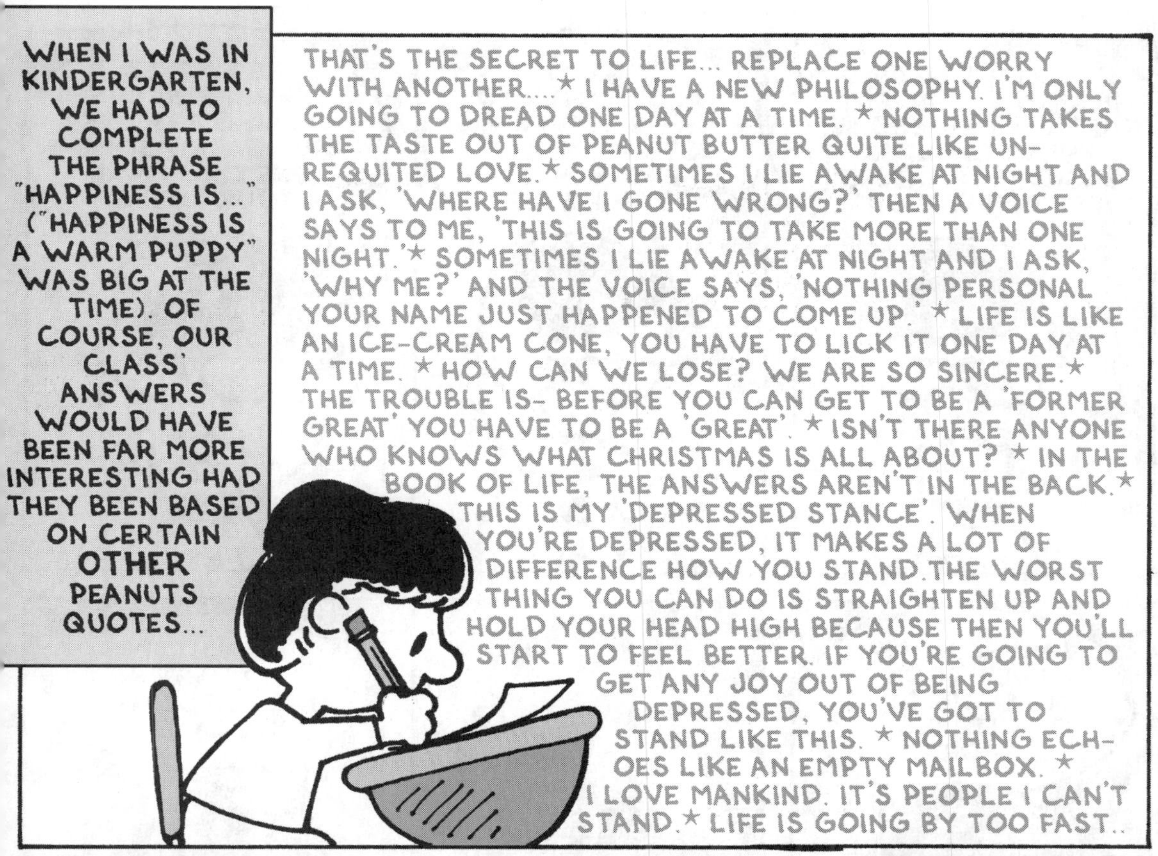
WHEN I WAS IN KINDERGARTEN, WE HAD TO COMPLETE THE PHRASE "HAPPINESS IS..." ("HAPPINESS IS A WARM PUPPY" WAS BIG AT THE TIME). OF COURSE, OUR CLASS' ANSWERS WOULD HAVE BEEN FAR MORE INTERESTING HAD THEY BEEN BASED ON CERTAIN OTHER PEANUTS QUOTES...
THAT'S THE SECRET TO LIFE... REPLACE ONE WORRY WITH ANOTHER....* I HAVE A NEW PHILOSOPHY. I'M ONLY GOING TO DREAD ONE DAY AT A TIME. * NOTHING TAKES THE TASTE OUT OF PEANUT BUTTER QUITE LIKE UN-REQUITED LOVE.* SOMETIMES I LIE AWAKE AT NIGHT AND I ASK, 'WHERE HAVE I GONE WRONG?' THEN A VOICE SAYS TO ME, 'THIS IS GOING TO TAKE MORE THAN ONE NIGHT.'* SOMETIMES I LIE AWAKE AT NIGHT AND I ASK, 'WHY ME?' AND THE VOICE SAYS, 'NOTHING PERSONAL YOUR NAME JUST HAPPENED TO COME UP.' * LIFE IS LIKE AN ICE-CREAM CONE, YOU HAVE TO LICK IT ONE DAY AT A TIME. * HOW CAN WE LOSE? WE ARE SO SINCERE.* THE TROUBLE IS- BEFORE YOU CAN GET TO BE A 'FORMER GREAT' YOU HAVE TO BE A 'GREAT'. * ISN'T THERE ANYONE WHO KNOWS WHAT CHRISTMAS IS ALL ABOUT? * IN THE BOOK OF LIFE, THE ANSWERS AREN'T IN THE BACK.* THIS IS MY 'DEPRESSED STANCE'. WHEN YOU'RE DEPRESSED, IT MAKES A LOT OF DIFFERENCE HOW YOU STAND.THE WORST THING YOU CAN DO IS STRAIGHTEN UP AND HOLD YOUR HEAD HIGH BECAUSE THEN YOU'LL START TO FEEL BETTER. IF YOU'RE GOING TO GET ANY JOY OUT OF BEING DEPRESSED, YOU'VE GOT TO STAND LIKE THIS. * NOTHING ECH-OES LIKE AN EMPTY MAILBOX. * I LOVE MANKIND. IT'S PEOPLE I CAN'T STAND.* LIFE IS GOING BY TOO FAST..

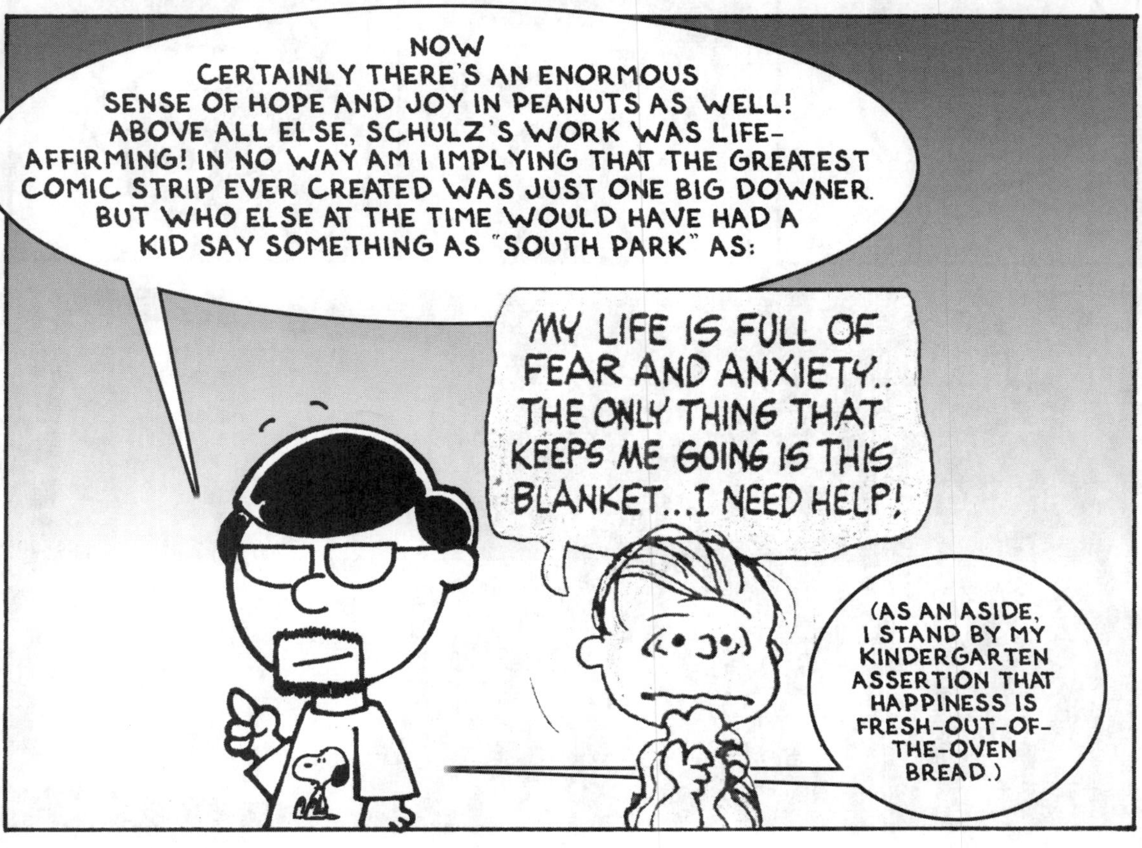
NOW CERTAINLY THERE'S AN ENORMOUS SENSE OF HOPE AND JOY IN PEANUTS AS WELL! ABOVE ALL ELSE, SCHULZ'S WORK WAS LIFE-AFFIRMING! IN NO WAY AM I IMPLYING THAT THE GREATEST COMIC STRIP EVER CREATED WAS JUST ONE BIG DOWNER. BUT WHO ELSE AT THE TIME WOULD HAVE HAD A KID SAY SOMETHING AS "SOUTH PARK" AS:
MY LIFE IS FULL OF FEAR AND ANXIETY.. THE ONLY THING THAT KEEPS ME GOING IS THIS BLANKET...I NEED HELP!
(AS AN ASIDE, I STAND BY MY KINDERGARTEN ASSERTION THAT HAPPINESS IS FRESH-OUT-OF-THE-OVEN BREAD.)

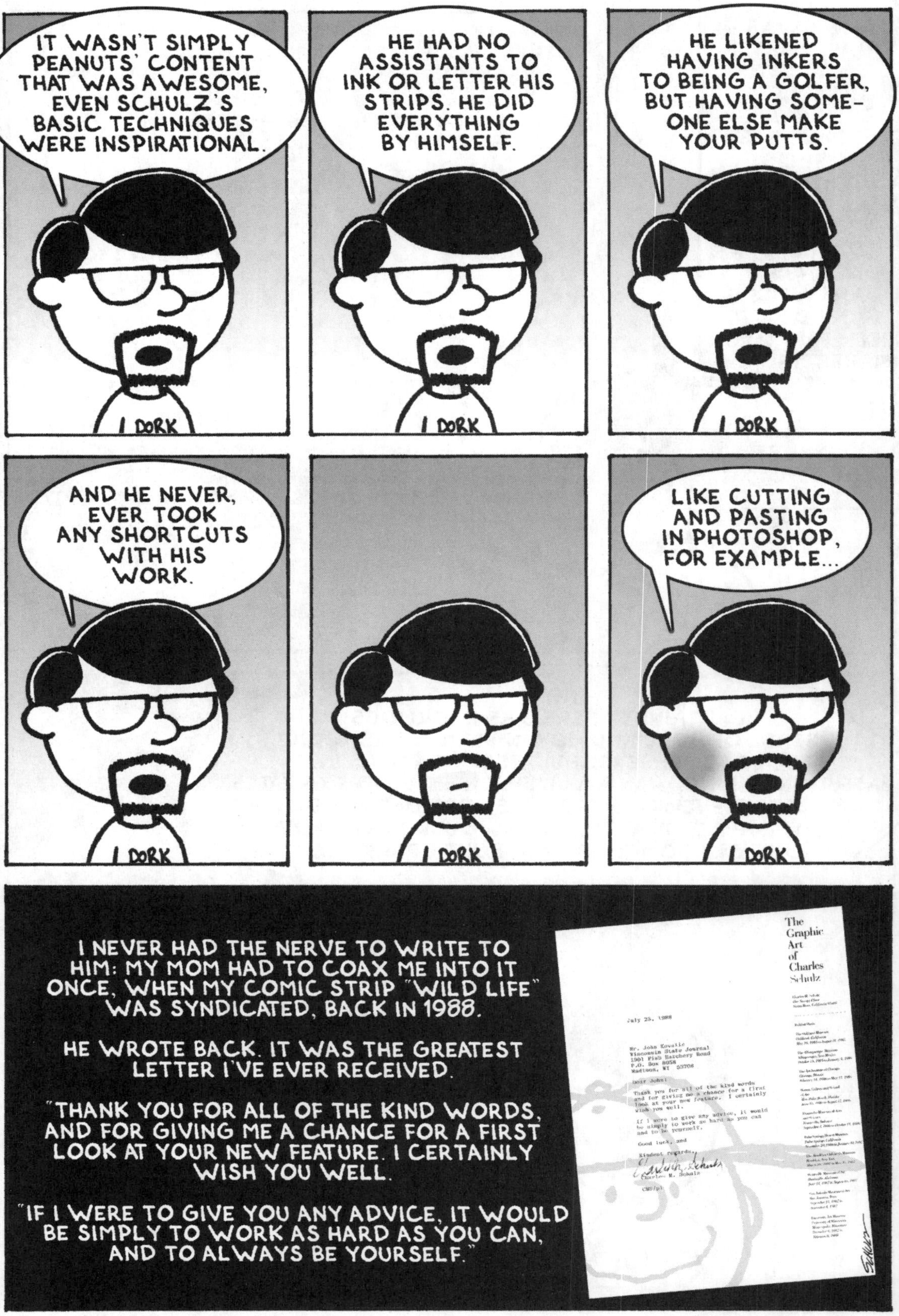
IT WASN'T SIMPLY PEANUTS' CONTENT THAT WAS AWESOME, EVEN SCHULZ'S BASIC TECHNIQUES WERE INSPIRATIONAL.
I DORK
HE HAD NO ASSISTANTS TO INK OR LETTER HIS STRIPS. HE DID EVERYTHING BY HIMSELF.
I DORK
HE LIKENED HAVING INKERS TO BEING A GOLFER, BUT HAVING SOME-ONE ELSE MAKE YOUR PUTTS.
I DORK
AND HE NEVER, EVER TOOK ANY SHORTCUTS WITH HIS WORK.
I DORK
I DORK
LIKE CUTTING AND PASTING IN PHOTOSHOP, FOR EXAMPLE...
I DORK
I NEVER HAD THE NERVE TO WRITE TO HIM: MY MOM HAD TO COAX ME INTO IT ONCE, WHEN MY COMIC STRIP "WILD LIFE" WAS SYNDICATED, BACK IN 1988.
HE WROTE BACK. IT WAS THE GREATEST LETTER I'VE EVER RECEIVED.
"THANK YOU FOR ALL OF THE KIND WORDS, AND FOR GIVING ME A CHANCE FOR A FIRST LOOK AT YOUR NEW FEATURE. I CERTAINLY WISH YOU WELL.
"IF I WERE TO GIVE YOU ANY ADVICE, IT WOULD BE SIMPLY TO WORK AS HARD AS YOU CAN, AND TO ALWAYS BE YOURSELF."
The Graphic Art of Charles Schulz
July 25, 1988
Mr. John Kovalic
Wisconsin State Journal
1901 Fish Hatchery Road
P.O. Box 8058
Madison, WI 53708
Dear John:
Charles M. Schulz
SCHULZ

I DIDN'T JUST HAVE A PROBLEM WRITING LETTERS TO SCHULZ, EITHER. I NEVER MADE THE TREK TO SEE HIM, EVEN THOUGH OTHER CARTOONISTS TOLD ME WHAT A PRINCE HE WAS, ALWAYS GENEROUS WITH HIS TIME AND ADVICE.

BUT I WAS TOO SHY, TOO NERVOUS, DIDN'T WANT TO WASTE HIS TIME...

I MEAN, HOW CHARLIE BROWN IS THAT?

CHARLES SCHULZ WAS 77 WHEN HE SUFFERED A STROKE LATE IN 1999. DOCTORS ALSO FOUND THAT CANCER HAD METASTASIZED TO HIS STOMACH. ACCORDING TO BIOGRAPHER DAVID MICHAELIS, "DOCTORS GOT MOST OF IT, BUT THE STROKE AND THE SURGERY ROBBED SCHULZ OF THE WILL TO GO ON DRAWING. HE COULDN'T SEE CLEARLY, HE COULDN'T READ. HE STRUGGLED TO RECALL THE WORDS HE NEEDED. BUT ALL THAT MIGHT HAVE BEEN TOLERABLE EXCEPT THAT CHEMOTHERAPY HAD BEGUN TO MAKE HIM SICK TO HIS STOMACH, AND THE STATISTICS FOR STAGE-4 COLON CANCER GAVE HIM A 20 PERCENT CHANCE TO LIVE."

THAT DECEMBER SCHULZ ANNOUNCED HIS RETIREMENT. "I NEVER DREAMED THAT THIS WOULD HAPPEN TO ME," HE SAID."I ALWAYS HAD THE FEELING THAT I WOULD STAY WITH THE STRIP UNTIL I WAS IN MY EARLY 80S, OR SOMETHING LIKE THAT. BUT ALL OF SUDDEN...IT'S BEEN TAKEN AWAY FROM ME."

DISTRAUGHT, I FINALLY WORKED UP THE COURAGE TO SEND THIS GREAT, HUMBLE MAN SOME OF MY DOODLINGS, ALONG WITH A HEARTFELT LETTER, LETTING HIM KNOW JUST HOW MUCH HE AND HIS WORK MEANT TO ME.

I THINK MAYBE EVERY SINGLE CARTOONIST IN THE COUNTRY DID LIKEWISE.

ON FEBRUARY 12, 2000, WITH THE RAIN OUTSIDE POURING, CHARLES SCHULZ DIED THE NIGHT BEFORE THE LAST PEANUTS WAS TO RUN. "AS SOON AS HE CEASED TO BE A CARTOONIST, HE CEASED TO BE," WROTE MICHAELIS.

SO LONG, OL' PAL...I'M GONNA MISS YOU...

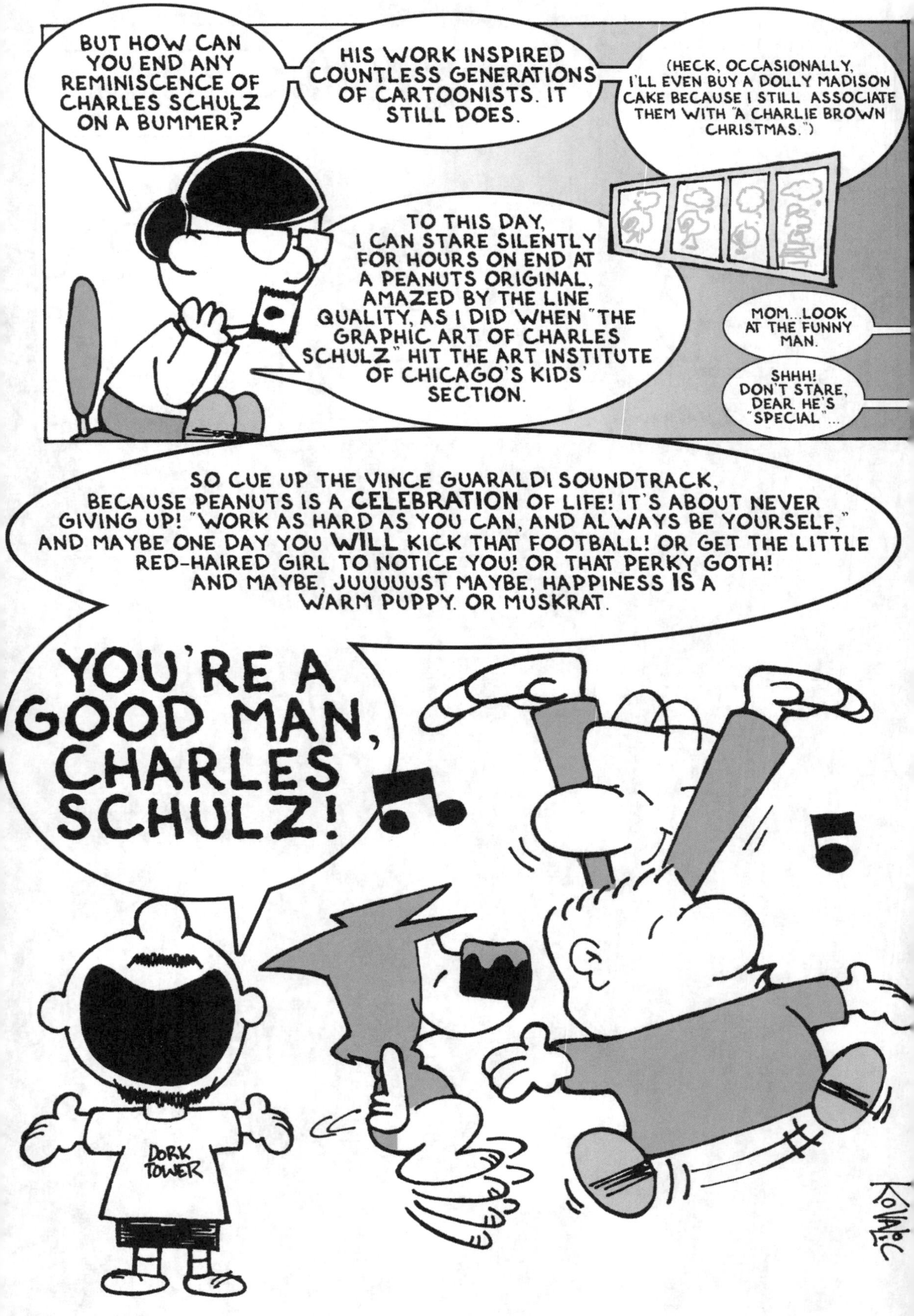
BUT HOW CAN YOU END ANY REMINISCENCE OF CHARLES SCHULZ ON A BUMMER?
HIS WORK INSPIRED COUNTLESS GENERATIONS OF CARTOONISTS. IT STILL DOES.
(HECK, OCCASIONALLY, I'LL EVEN BUY A DOLLY MADISON CAKE BECAUSE I STILL ASSOCIATE THEM WITH "A CHARLIE BROWN CHRISTMAS.")
TO THIS DAY, I CAN STARE SILENTLY FOR HOURS ON END AT A PEANUTS ORIGINAL, AMAZED BY THE LINE QUALITY, AS I DID WHEN "THE GRAPHIC ART OF CHARLES SCHULZ" HIT THE ART INSTITUTE OF CHICAGO'S KIDS' SECTION.
MOM...LOOK AT THE FUNNY MAN.
SHHH! DON'T STARE, DEAR. HE'S "SPECIAL"...
SO CUE UP THE VINCE GUARALDI SOUNDTRACK, BECAUSE PEANUTS IS A CELEBRATION OF LIFE! IT'S ABOUT NEVER GIVING UP! "WORK AS HARD AS YOU CAN, AND ALWAYS BE YOURSELF," AND MAYBE ONE DAY YOU WILL KICK THAT FOOTBALL! OR GET THE LITTLE RED-HAIRED GIRL TO NOTICE YOU! OR THAT PERKY GOTH! AND MAYBE, JUUUUUST MAYBE, HAPPINESS IS A WARM PUPPY. OR MUSKRAT.
YOU'RE A GOOD MAN, CHARLES SCHULZ!
DORK TOWER
KOVALIC

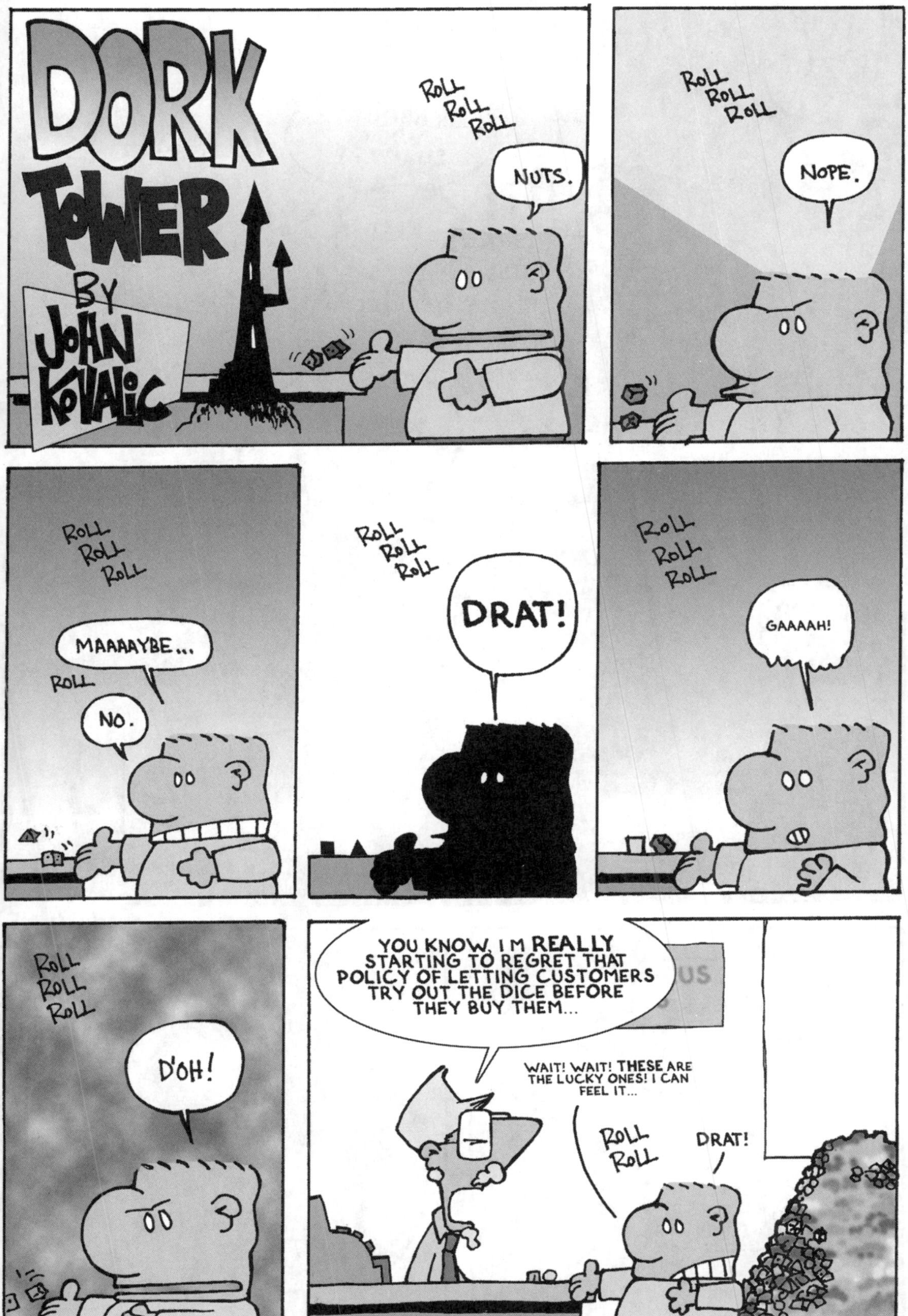
DORK TOWER
BY JOHN KOVALIC
ROLL ROLL ROLL
NUTS.
ROLL ROLL ROLL
NOPE.
ROLL ROLL ROLL
MAAAAYBE...
ROLL
NO.
ROLL ROLL ROLL
DRAT!
ROLL ROLL ROLL
GAAAAH!
ROLL ROLL ROLL
D'OH!
YOU KNOW, I M REALLY STARTING TO REGRET THAT POLICY OF LETTING CUSTOMERS TRY OUT THE DICE BEFORE THEY BUY THEM...
WAIT! WAIT! THESE ARE THE LUCKY ONES! I CAN FEEL IT...
ROLL ROLL
DRAT!

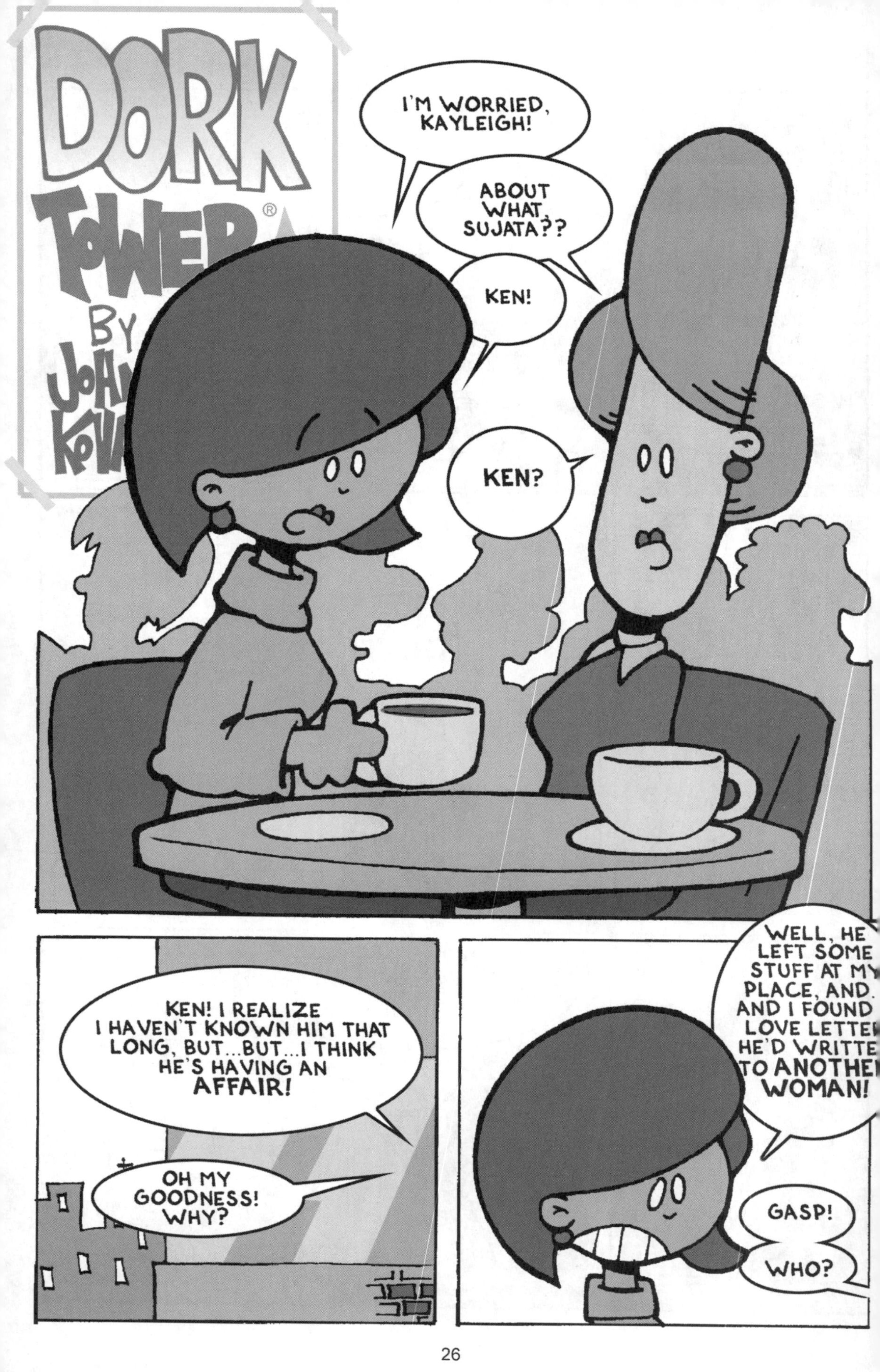
DORK TOWER®
BY JOHN KOV
I'M WORRIED, KAYLEIGH!
ABOUT WHAT, SUJATA??
KEN!
KEN?
KEN! I REALIZE I HAVEN'T KNOWN HIM THAT LONG, BUT...BUT...I THINK HE'S HAVING AN AFFAIR!
OH MY GOODNESS! WHY?
WELL, HE LEFT SOME STUFF AT MY PLACE, AND. AND I FOUND LOVE LETTE HE'D WRITTE TO ANOTHE WOMAN!
GASP!
WHO?

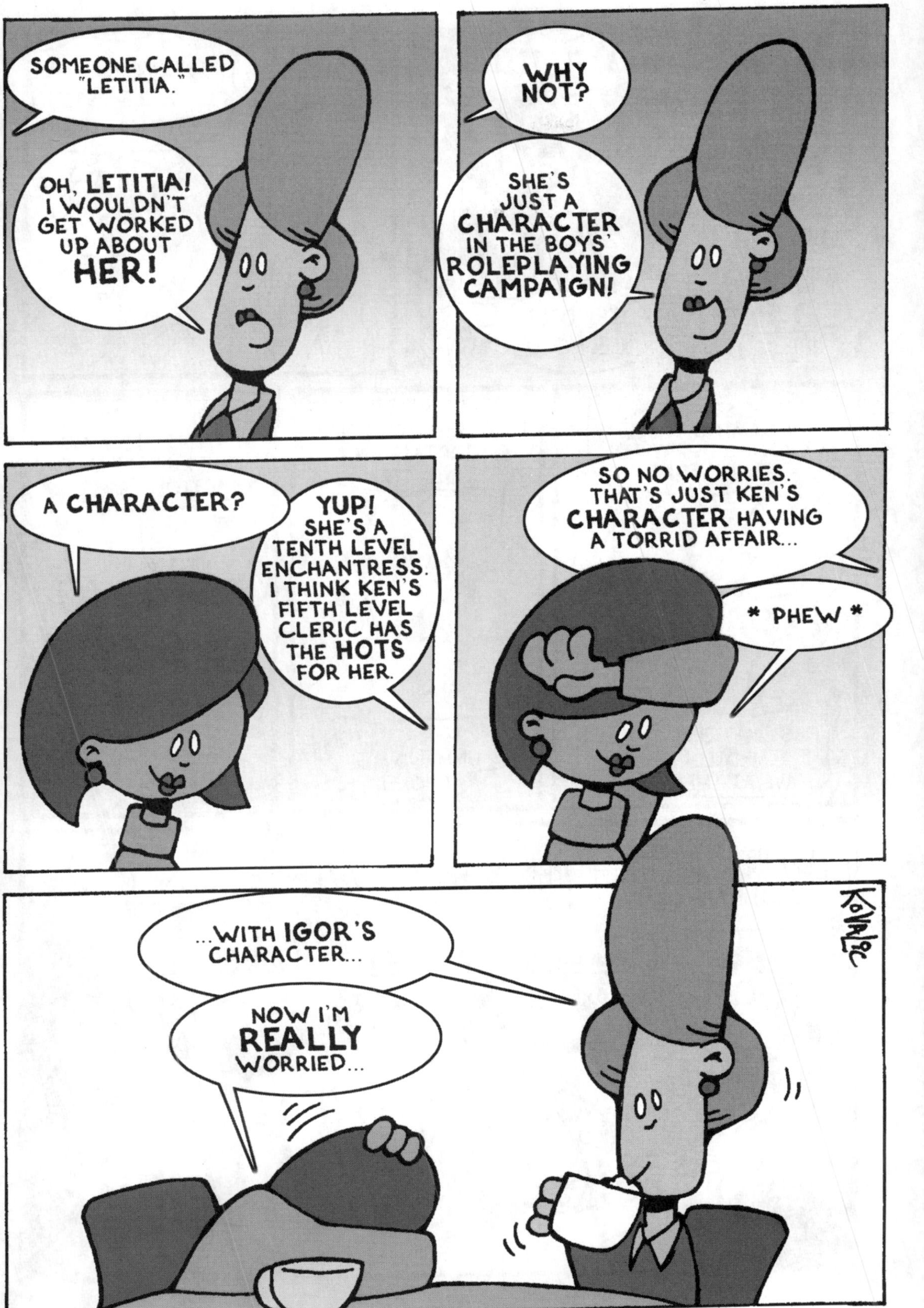

SOMEONE CALLED "LETITIA."
OH, LETITIA! I WOULDN'T GET WORKED UP ABOUT HER!
WHY NOT?
SHE'S JUST A CHARACTER IN THE BOYS' ROLEPLAYING CAMPAIGN!
A CHARACTER?
YUP! SHE'S A TENTH LEVEL ENCHANTRESS. I THINK KEN'S FIFTH LEVEL CLERIC HAS THE HOTS FOR HER.
SO NO WORRIES. THAT'S JUST KEN'S CHARACTER HAVING A TORRID AFFAIR...
* PHEW *
...WITH IGOR'S CHARACTER...
NOW I'M REALLY WORRIED...

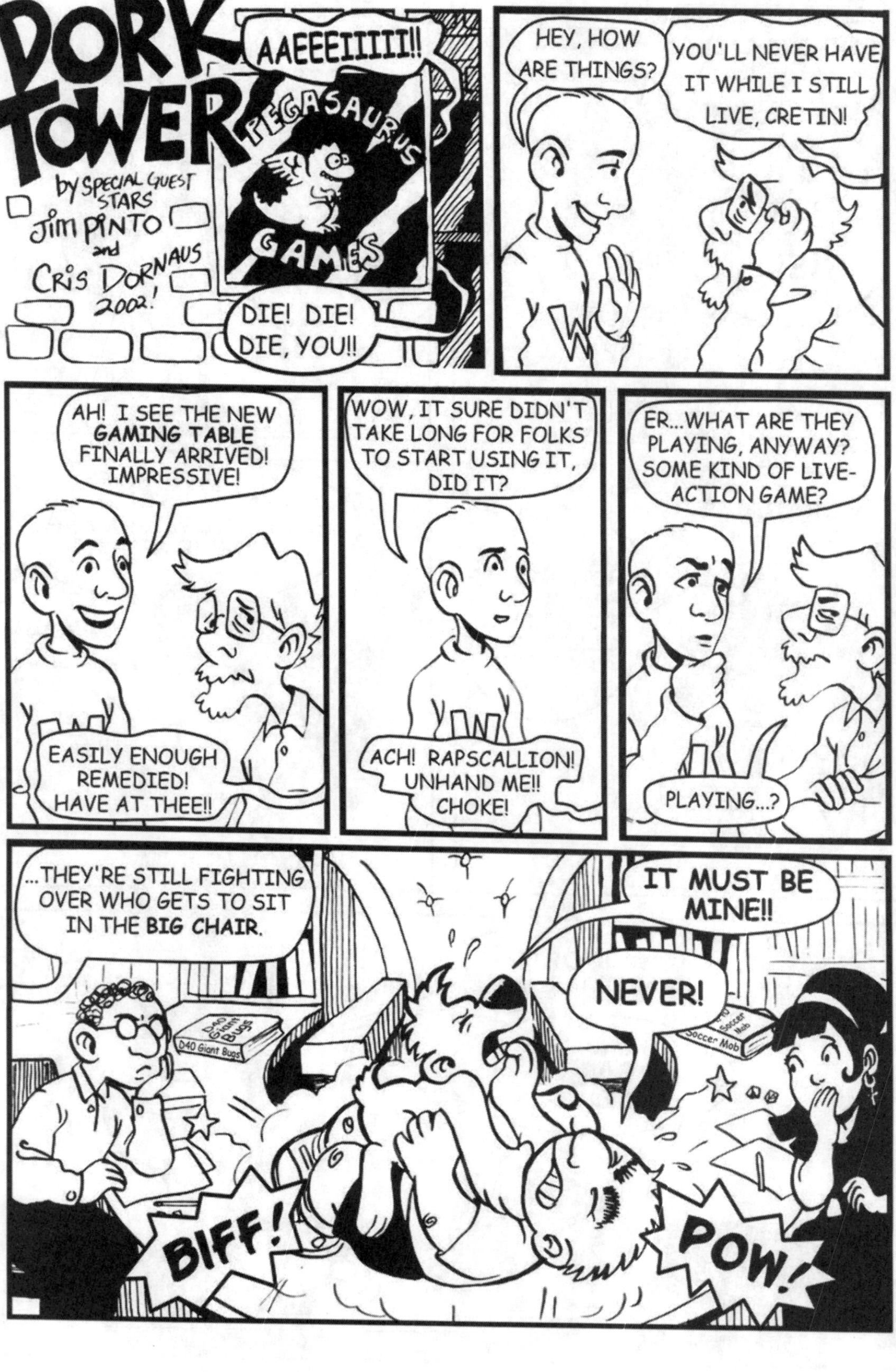
DORK TOWER
by SPECIAL GUEST STARS
Jim Pinto and Cris Dornaus 2002!
AAEEEIIIII!!
PEGASAURUS GAMES
DIE! DIE! DIE, YOU!!
HEY, HOW ARE THINGS?
YOU'LL NEVER HAVE IT WHILE I STILL LIVE, CRETIN!
AH! I SEE THE NEW GAMING TABLE FINALLY ARRIVED! IMPRESSIVE!
EASILY ENOUGH REMEDIED! HAVE AT THEE!!
WOW, IT SURE DIDN'T TAKE LONG FOR FOLKS TO START USING IT, DID IT?
ACH! RAPSCALLION! UNHAND ME!! CHOKE!
ER...WHAT ARE THEY PLAYING, ANYWAY? SOME KIND OF LIVE-ACTION GAME?
PLAYING...?
...THEY'RE STILL FIGHTING OVER WHO GETS TO SIT IN THE BIG CHAIR.
IT MUST BE MINE!!
NEVER!
D40 Giant Bugs
Soccer Mob
BIFF!
POW!

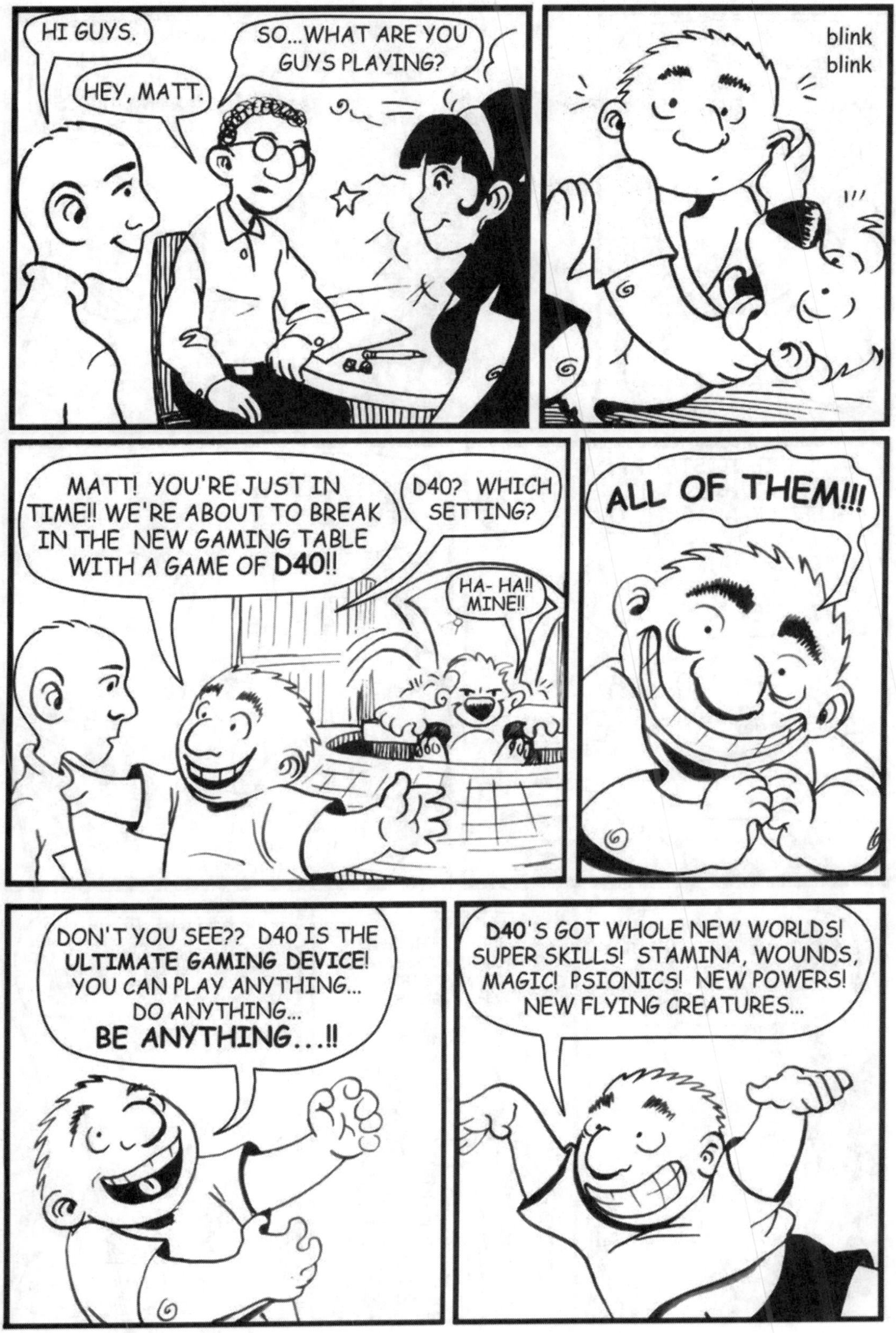
HI GUYS.
HEY, MATT.
SO...WHAT ARE YOU GUYS PLAYING?
blink blink
MATT! YOU'RE JUST IN TIME!! WE'RE ABOUT TO BREAK IN THE NEW GAMING TABLE WITH A GAME OF D40!!
D40? WHICH SETTING?
HA- HA!! MINE!!
ALL OF THEM!!!
DON'T YOU SEE?? D40 IS THE ULTIMATE GAMING DEVICE! YOU CAN PLAY ANYTHING... DO ANYTHING... BE ANYTHING...!!
D40'S GOT WHOLE NEW WORLDS! SUPER SKILLS! STAMINA, WOUNDS, MAGIC! PSIONICS! NEW POWERS! NEW FLYING CREATURES...

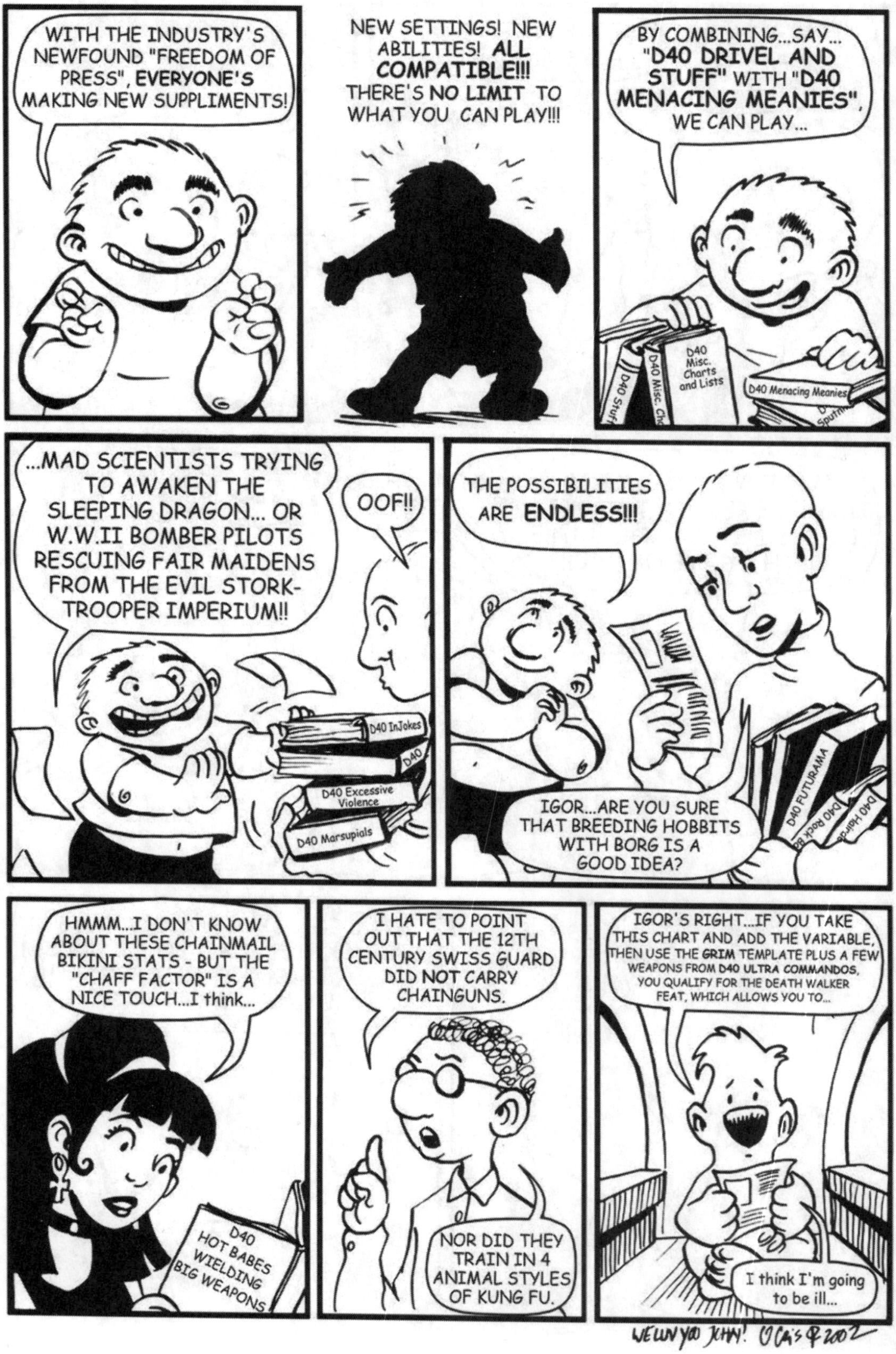
WITH THE INDUSTRY'S NEWFOUND "FREEDOM OF PRESS", EVERYONE'S MAKING NEW SUPPLIMENTS!
NEW SETTINGS! NEW ABILITIES! ALL COMPATIBLE!!! THERE'S NO LIMIT TO WHAT YOU CAN PLAY!!!
BY COMBINING...SAY... "D40 DRIVEL AND STUFF" WITH "D40 MENACING MEANIES", WE CAN PLAY...
D40 Misc. Charts and Lists
D40 Menacing Meanies
...MAD SCIENTISTS TRYING TO AWAKEN THE SLEEPING DRAGON... OR W.W.II BOMBER PILOTS RESCUING FAIR MAIDENS FROM THE EVIL STORK-TROOPER IMPERIUM!!
OOF!!
D40 InJokes
D40 Excessive Violence
D40 Marsupials
THE POSSIBILITIES ARE ENDLESS!!!
IGOR...ARE YOU SURE THAT BREEDING HOBBITS WITH BORG IS A GOOD IDEA?
D40 FUTURAMA
HMMM...I DON'T KNOW ABOUT THESE CHAINMAIL BIKINI STATS - BUT THE "CHAFF FACTOR" IS A NICE TOUCH...I think...
D40 HOT BABES WIELDING BIG WEAPONS
I HATE TO POINT OUT THAT THE 12TH CENTURY SWISS GUARD DID NOT CARRY CHAINGUNS.
NOR DID THEY TRAIN IN 4 ANIMAL STYLES OF KUNG FU.
IGOR'S RIGHT...IF YOU TAKE THIS CHART AND ADD THE VARIABLE, THEN USE THE GRIM TEMPLATE PLUS A FEW WEAPONS FROM D40 ULTRA COMMANDOS, YOU QUALIFY FOR THE DEATH WALKER FEAT, WHICH ALLOWS YOU TO...
I think I'm going to be ill...

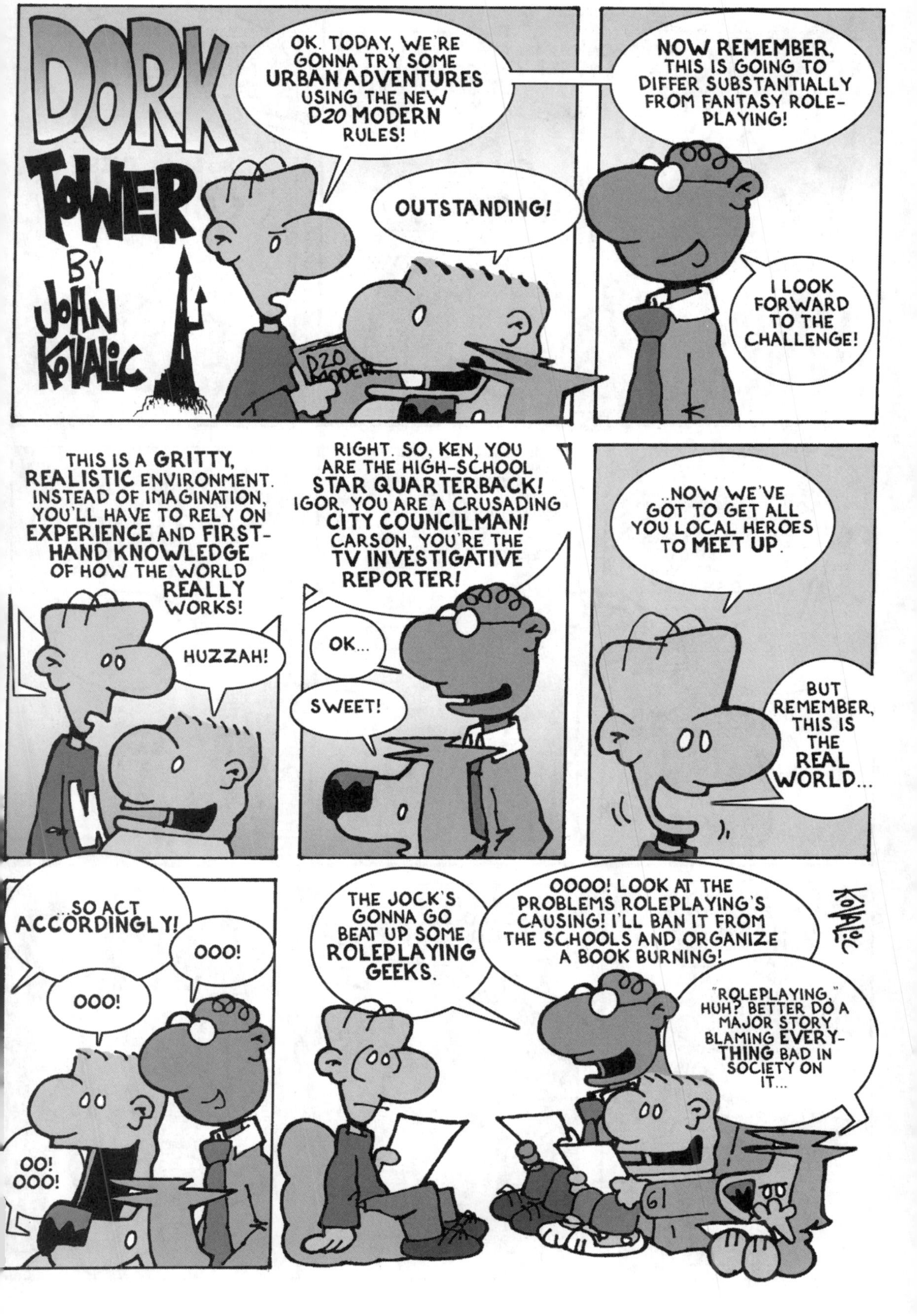
DORK TOWER
BY JOHN KOVALIC
OK. TODAY, WE'RE GONNA TRY SOME URBAN ADVENTURES USING THE NEW D20 MODERN RULES!
OUTSTANDING!
D20 MODERN
NOW REMEMBER, THIS IS GOING TO DIFFER SUBSTANTIALLY FROM FANTASY ROLE-PLAYING!
I LOOK FORWARD TO THE CHALLENGE!
THIS IS A GRITTY, REALISTIC ENVIRONMENT. INSTEAD OF IMAGINATION, YOU'LL HAVE TO RELY ON EXPERIENCE AND FIRST-HAND KNOWLEDGE OF HOW THE WORLD REALLY WORKS!
HUZZAH!
RIGHT. SO, KEN, YOU ARE THE HIGH-SCHOOL STAR QUARTERBACK! IGOR, YOU ARE A CRUSADING CITY COUNCILMAN! CARSON, YOU'RE THE TV INVESTIGATIVE REPORTER!
OK...
SWEET!
..NOW WE'VE GOT TO GET ALL YOU LOCAL HEROES TO MEET UP.
BUT REMEMBER, THIS IS THE REAL WORLD...
...SO ACT ACCORDINGLY!
OOO!
OOO!
OO! OOO!
THE JOCK'S GONNA GO BEAT UP SOME ROLEPLAYING GEEKS.
OOOO! LOOK AT THE PROBLEMS ROLEPLAYING'S CAUSING! I'LL BAN IT FROM THE SCHOOLS AND ORGANIZE A BOOK BURNING!
"ROLEPLAYING," HUH? BETTER DO A MAJOR STORY BLAMING EVERY-THING BAD IN SOCIETY ON IT...
KOVALIC

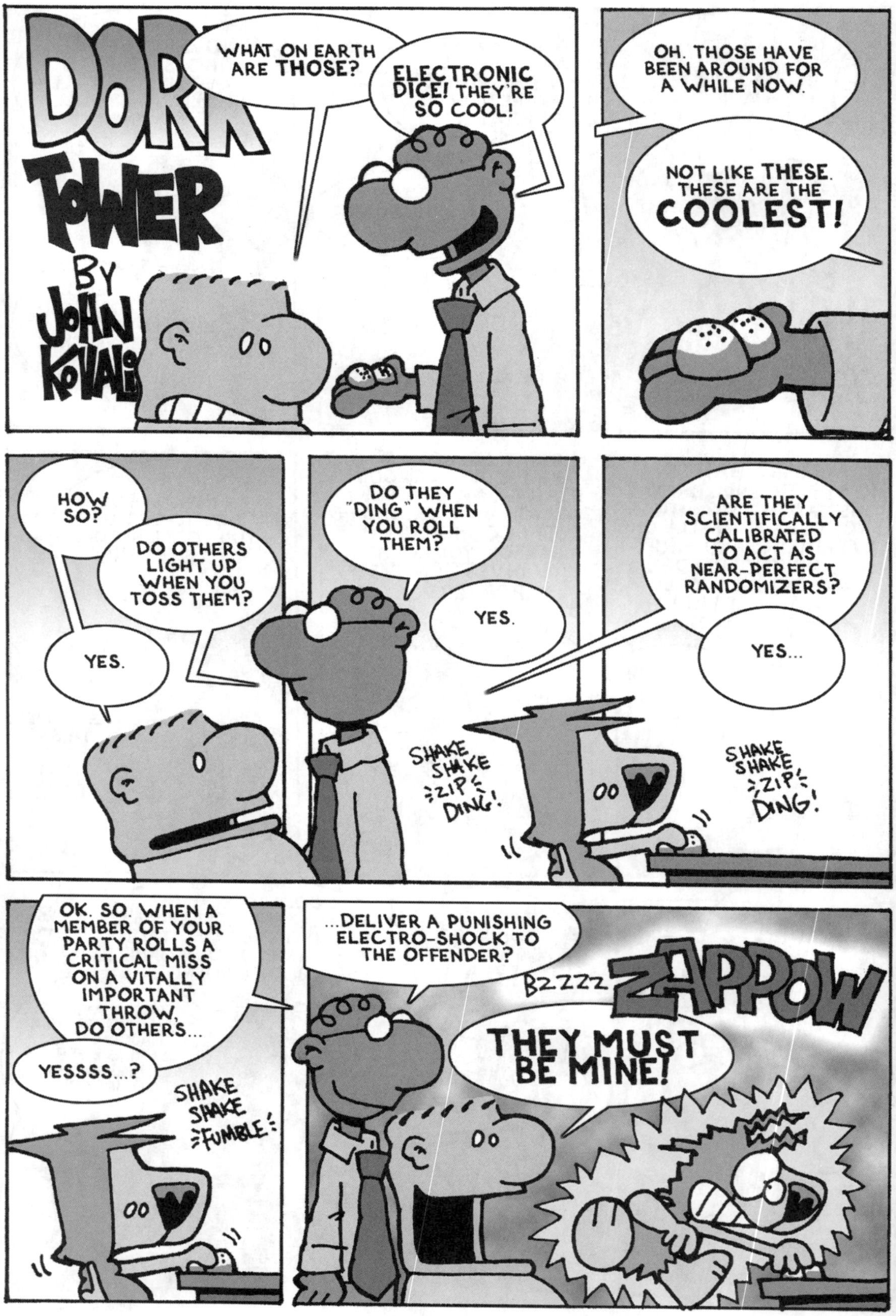
DORK TOWER
BY JOHN KOVALIC
WHAT ON EARTH ARE THOSE?
ELECTRONIC DICE! THEY'RE SO COOL!
OH. THOSE HAVE BEEN AROUND FOR A WHILE NOW.
NOT LIKE THESE. THESE ARE THE COOLEST!
HOW SO?
DO OTHERS LIGHT UP WHEN YOU TOSS THEM?
YES.
DO THEY "DING" WHEN YOU ROLL THEM?
YES.
SHAKE SHAKE ZIP DING!
ARE THEY SCIENTIFICALLY CALIBRATED TO ACT AS NEAR-PERFECT RANDOMIZERS?
YES...
SHAKE SHAKE ZIP DING!
OK. SO. WHEN A MEMBER OF YOUR PARTY ROLLS A CRITICAL MISS ON A VITALLY IMPORTANT THROW, DO OTHERS...
YESSSS...?
SHAKE SHAKE FUMBLE
...DELIVER A PUNISHING ELECTRO-SHOCK TO THE OFFENDER?
BZZZZ ZAPPOW
THEY MUST BE MINE!

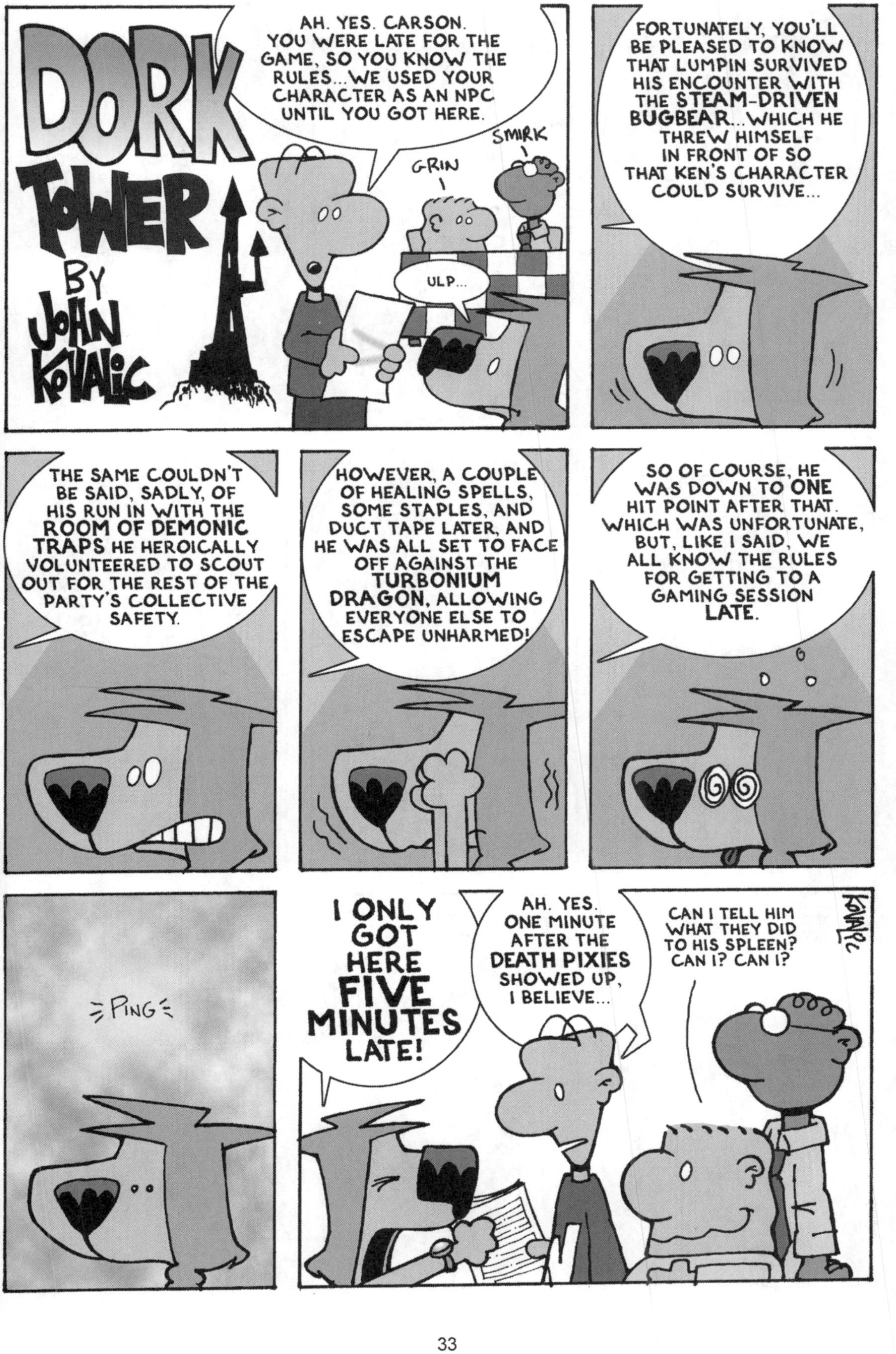
DORK TOWER
BY JOHN KOVALIC
AH. YES. CARSON. YOU WERE LATE FOR THE GAME, SO YOU KNOW THE RULES... WE USED YOUR CHARACTER AS AN NPC UNTIL YOU GOT HERE.
GRIN
SMIRK
ULP...
FORTUNATELY, YOU'LL BE PLEASED TO KNOW THAT LUMPIN SURVIVED HIS ENCOUNTER WITH THE STEAM-DRIVEN BUGBEAR... WHICH HE THREW HIMSELF IN FRONT OF SO THAT KEN'S CHARACTER COULD SURVIVE...
THE SAME COULDN'T BE SAID, SADLY, OF HIS RUN IN WITH THE ROOM OF DEMONIC TRAPS HE HEROICALLY VOLUNTEERED TO SCOUT OUT FOR THE REST OF THE PARTY'S COLLECTIVE SAFETY.
HOWEVER, A COUPLE OF HEALING SPELLS, SOME STAPLES, AND DUCT TAPE LATER, AND HE WAS ALL SET TO FACE OFF AGAINST THE TURBONIUM DRAGON, ALLOWING EVERYONE ELSE TO ESCAPE UNHARMED!
SO OF COURSE, HE WAS DOWN TO ONE HIT POINT AFTER THAT. WHICH WAS UNFORTUNATE, BUT, LIKE I SAID, WE ALL KNOW THE RULES FOR GETTING TO A GAMING SESSION LATE.
PING
I ONLY GOT HERE FIVE MINUTES LATE!
AH. YES. ONE MINUTE AFTER THE DEATH PIXIES SHOWED UP, I BELIEVE...
CAN I TELL HIM WHAT THEY DID TO HIS SPLEEN? CAN I? CAN I?
KOVALIC

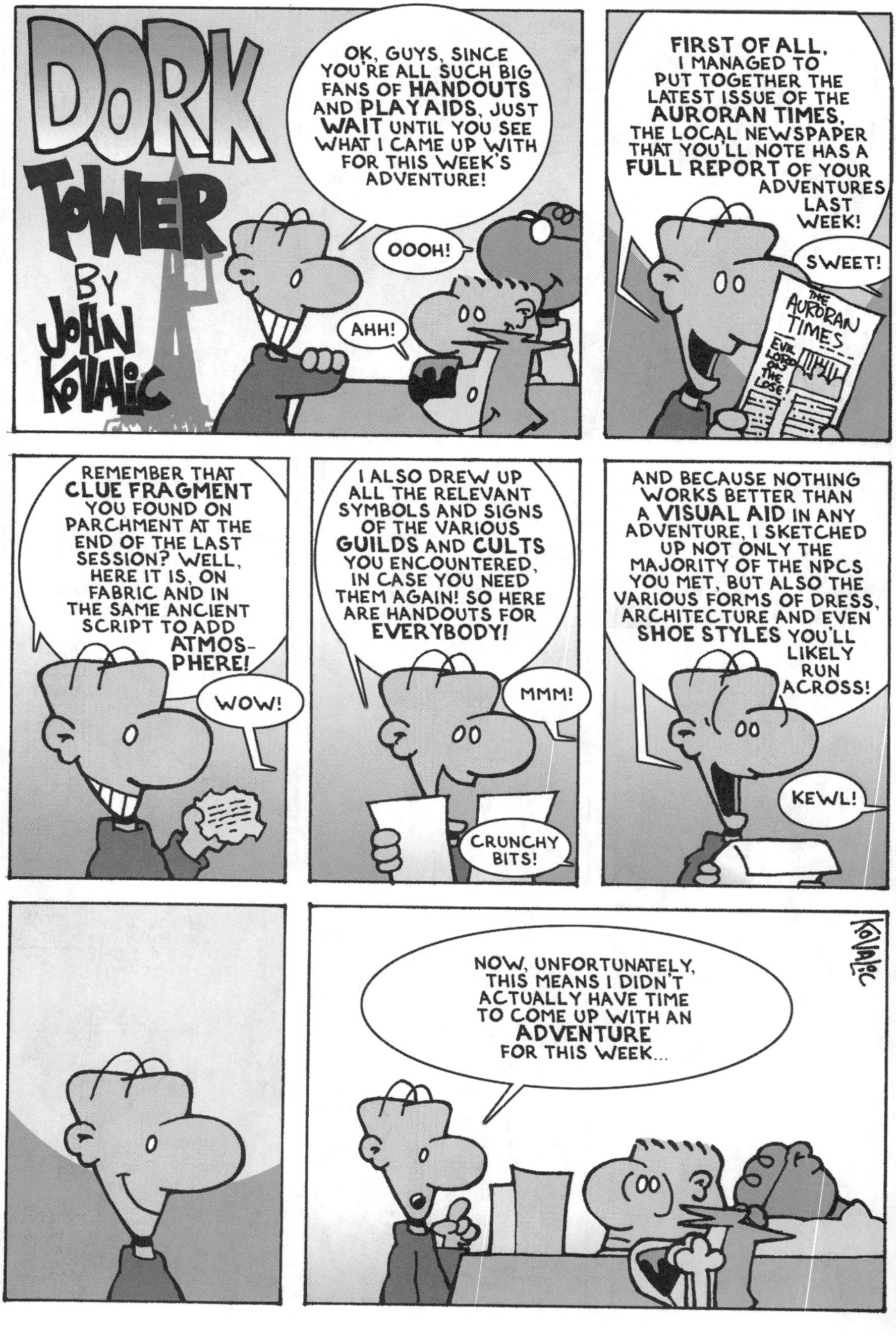

DORK TOWER
BY JOHN KOVALIC
OK, GUYS, SINCE YOU'RE ALL SUCH BIG FANS OF HANDOUTS AND PLAYAIDS, JUST WAIT UNTIL YOU SEE WHAT I CAME UP WITH FOR THIS WEEK'S ADVENTURE!
OOOH!
AHH!
FIRST OF ALL, I MANAGED TO PUT TOGETHER THE LATEST ISSUE OF THE AURORAN TIMES, THE LOCAL NEWSPAPER THAT YOU'LL NOTE HAS A FULL REPORT OF YOUR ADVENTURES LAST WEEK!
SWEET!
THE AURORAN TIMES
EVIL LORD ON THE LOSE
REMEMBER THAT CLUE FRAGMENT YOU FOUND ON PARCHMENT AT THE END OF THE LAST SESSION? WELL, HERE IT IS, ON FABRIC AND IN THE SAME ANCIENT SCRIPT TO ADD ATMOS-PHERE!
WOW!
I ALSO DREW UP ALL THE RELEVANT SYMBOLS AND SIGNS OF THE VARIOUS GUILDS AND CULTS YOU ENCOUNTERED, IN CASE YOU NEED THEM AGAIN! SO HERE ARE HANDOUTS FOR EVERYBODY!
MMM!
CRUNCHY BITS!
AND BECAUSE NOTHING WORKS BETTER THAN A VISUAL AID IN ANY ADVENTURE, I SKETCHED UP NOT ONLY THE MAJORITY OF THE NPCS YOU MET, BUT ALSO THE VARIOUS FORMS OF DRESS, ARCHITECTURE AND EVEN SHOE STYLES YOU'LL LIKELY RUN ACROSS!
KEWL!
KOVALIC
NOW, UNFORTUNATELY, THIS MEANS I DIDN'T ACTUALLY HAVE TIME TO COME UP WITH AN ADVENTURE FOR THIS WEEK...

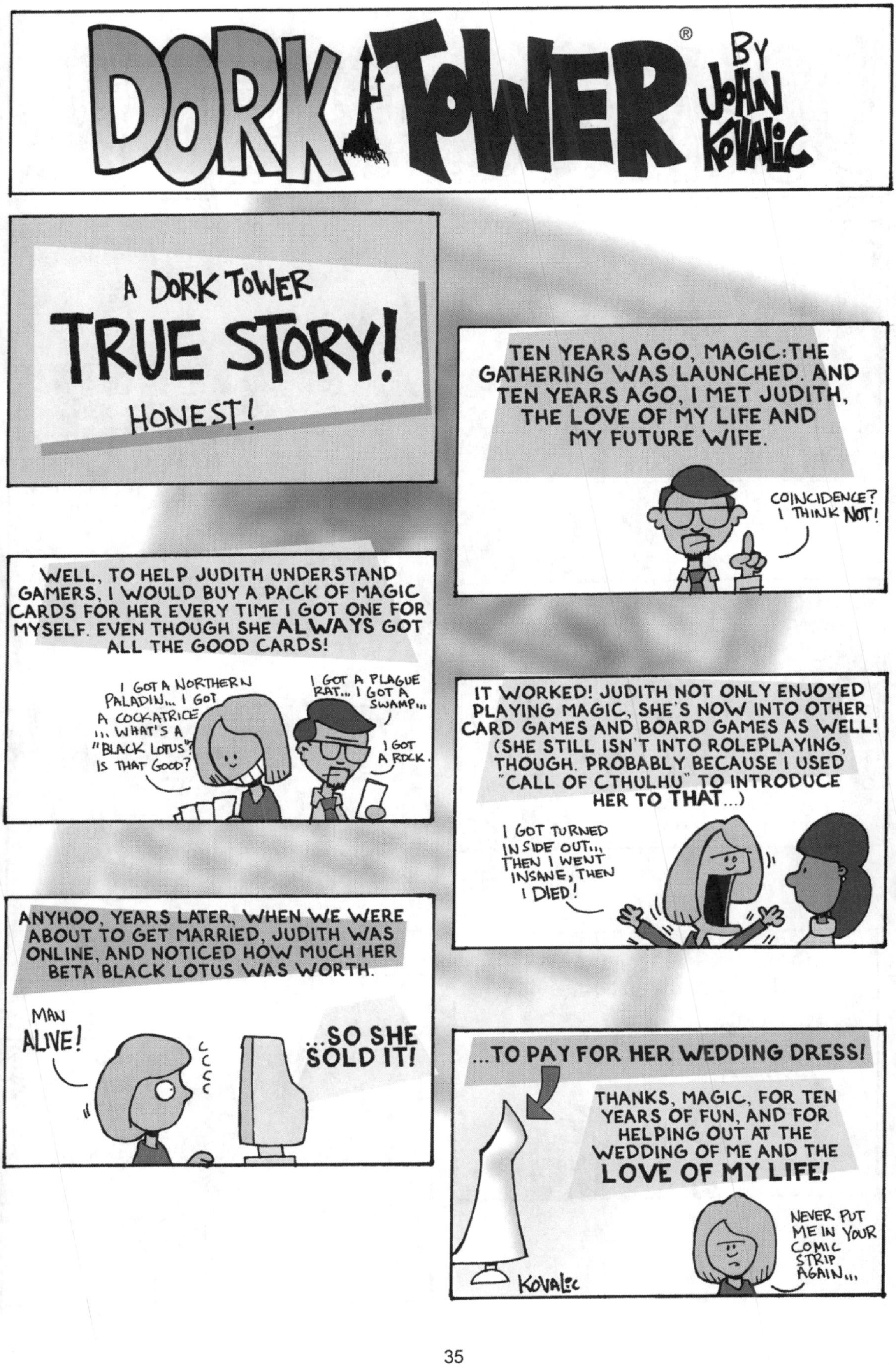
DORK TOWER® BY JOHN KOVALIC
A DORK TOWER TRUE STORY! HONEST!
TEN YEARS AGO, MAGIC: THE GATHERING WAS LAUNCHED. AND TEN YEARS AGO, I MET JUDITH, THE LOVE OF MY LIFE AND MY FUTURE WIFE.
COINCIDENCE? I THINK NOT!
WELL, TO HELP JUDITH UNDERSTAND GAMERS, I WOULD BUY A PACK OF MAGIC CARDS FOR HER EVERY TIME I GOT ONE FOR MYSELF. EVEN THOUGH SHE ALWAYS GOT ALL THE GOOD CARDS!
I GOT A NORTHERN PALADIN... I GOT A COCKATRICE ... WHAT'S A "BLACK LOTUS"? IS THAT GOOD?
I GOT A PLAGUE RAT... I GOT A SWAMP...
I GOT A ROCK.
IT WORKED! JUDITH NOT ONLY ENJOYED PLAYING MAGIC, SHE'S NOW INTO OTHER CARD GAMES AND BOARD GAMES AS WELL! (SHE STILL ISN'T INTO ROLEPLAYING, THOUGH. PROBABLY BECAUSE I USED "CALL OF CTHULHU" TO INTRODUCE HER TO THAT...)
I GOT TURNED INSIDE OUT... THEN I WENT INSANE, THEN I DIED!
ANYHOO, YEARS LATER, WHEN WE WERE ABOUT TO GET MARRIED, JUDITH WAS ONLINE, AND NOTICED HOW MUCH HER BETA BLACK LOTUS WAS WORTH.
MAN ALIVE!
...SO SHE SOLD IT!
...TO PAY FOR HER WEDDING DRESS!
THANKS, MAGIC, FOR TEN YEARS OF FUN, AND FOR HELPING OUT AT THE WEDDING OF ME AND THE LOVE OF MY LIFE!
NEVER PUT ME IN YOUR COMIC STRIP AGAIN...
KOVALIC

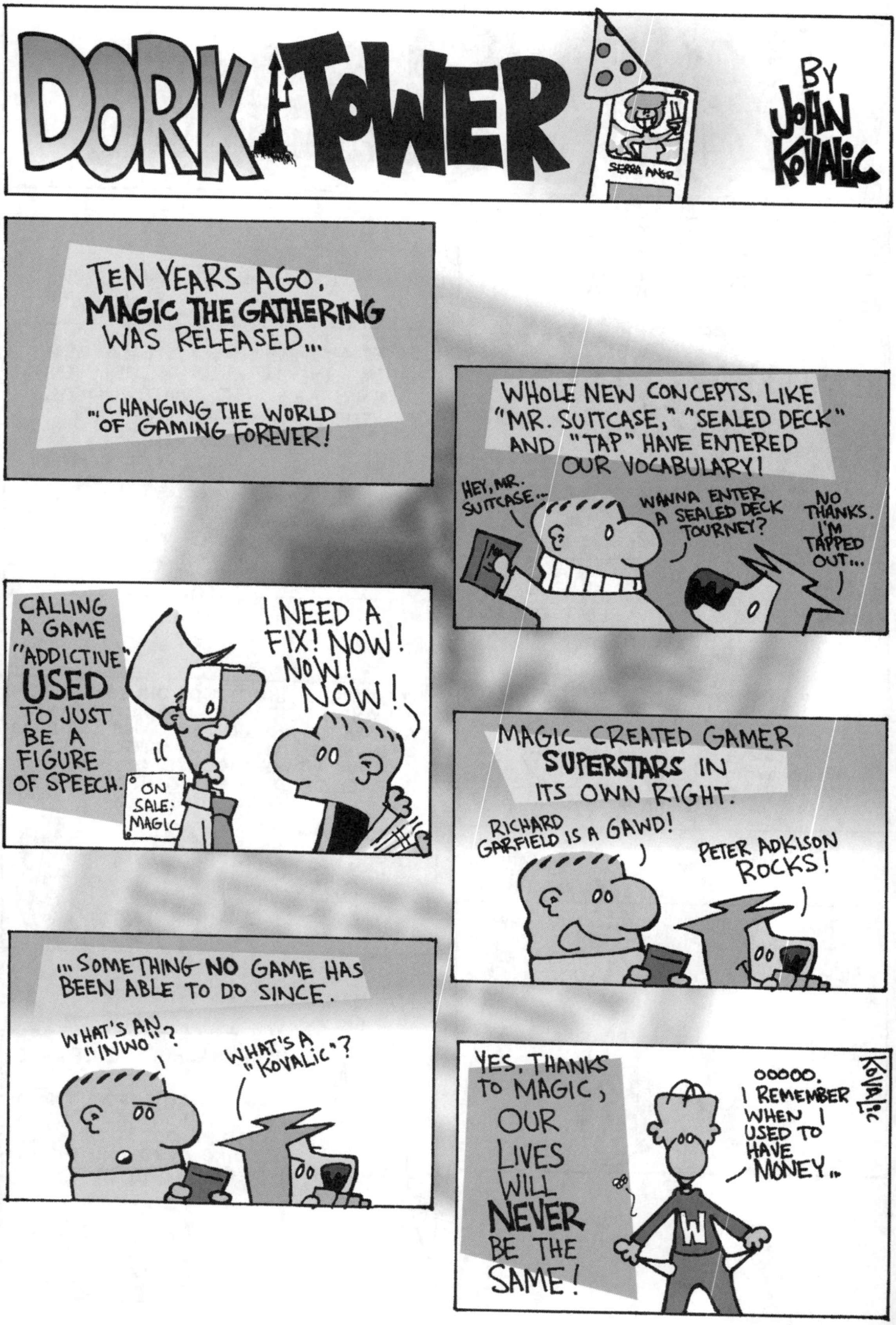
DORK TOWER
BY JOHN KOVALIC
TEN YEARS AGO, MAGIC THE GATHERING WAS RELEASED...
...CHANGING THE WORLD OF GAMING FOREVER!
WHOLE NEW CONCEPTS, LIKE "MR. SUITCASE," "SEALED DECK" AND "TAP" HAVE ENTERED OUR VOCABULARY!
HEY, MR. SUITCASE...
WANNA ENTER A SEALED DECK TOURNEY?
NO THANKS. I'M TAPPED OUT...
CALLING A GAME "ADDICTIVE" USED TO JUST BE A FIGURE OF SPEECH.
I NEED A FIX! NOW! NOW! NOW!
ON SALE: MAGIC
MAGIC CREATED GAMER SUPERSTARS IN ITS OWN RIGHT.
RICHARD GARFIELD IS A GAWD!
PETER ADKISON ROCKS!
...SOMETHING NO GAME HAS BEEN ABLE TO DO SINCE.
WHAT'S AN "INWO"?
WHAT'S A "KOVALIC"?
YES, THANKS TO MAGIC, OUR LIVES WILL NEVER BE THE SAME!
OOOOO. I REMEMBER WHEN I USED TO HAVE MONEY...
KOVALIC

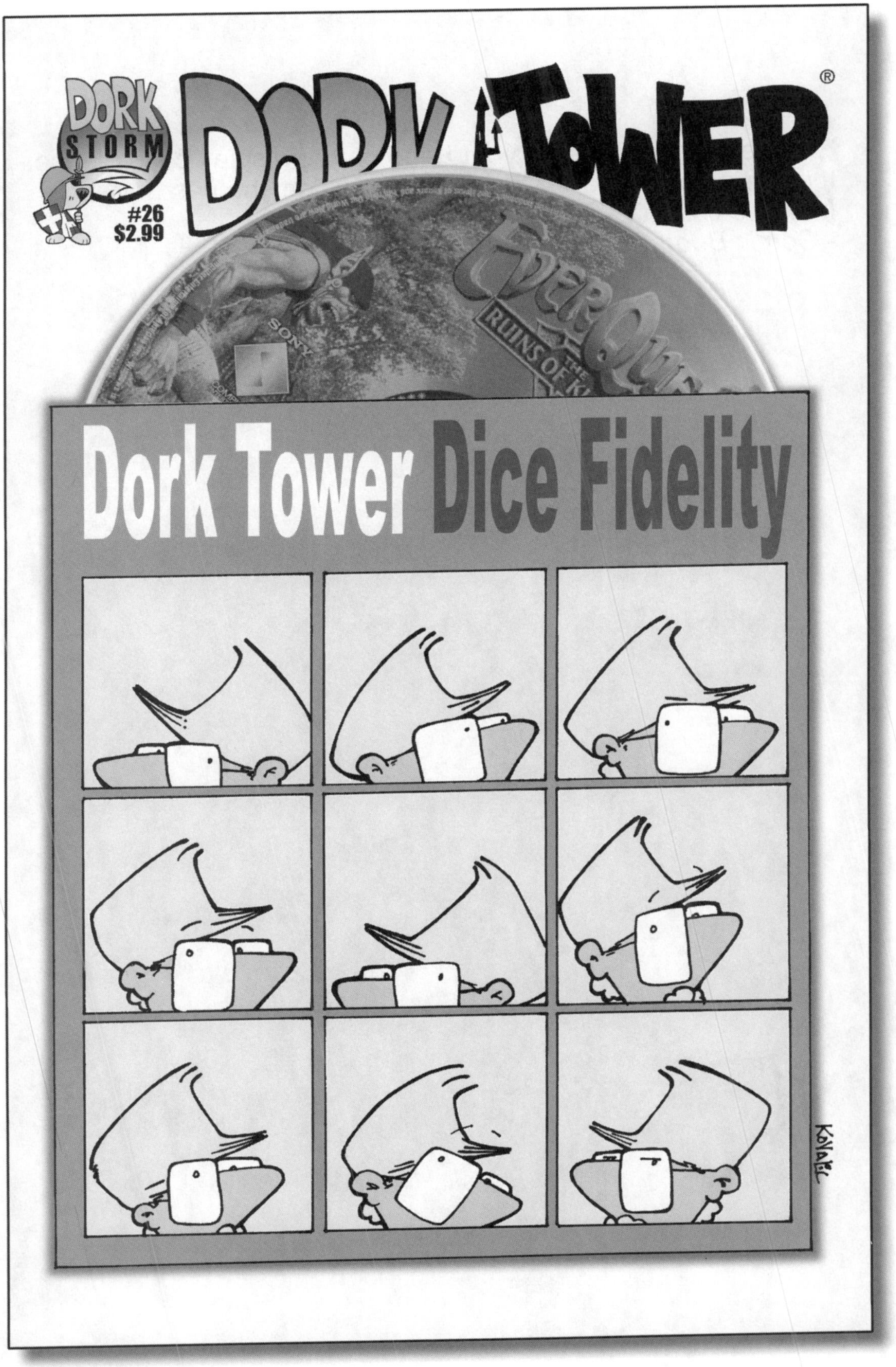
DORK STORM
DORK TOWER ®
#26
$2.99
SONY
Dork Tower Dice Fidelity
KOVALIC

Excuse me. No banging your head on the display case please. It contains a very rare Mary Worth in which she has advised a friend to commit suicide. Thank you.
- *Comic Book Guy*

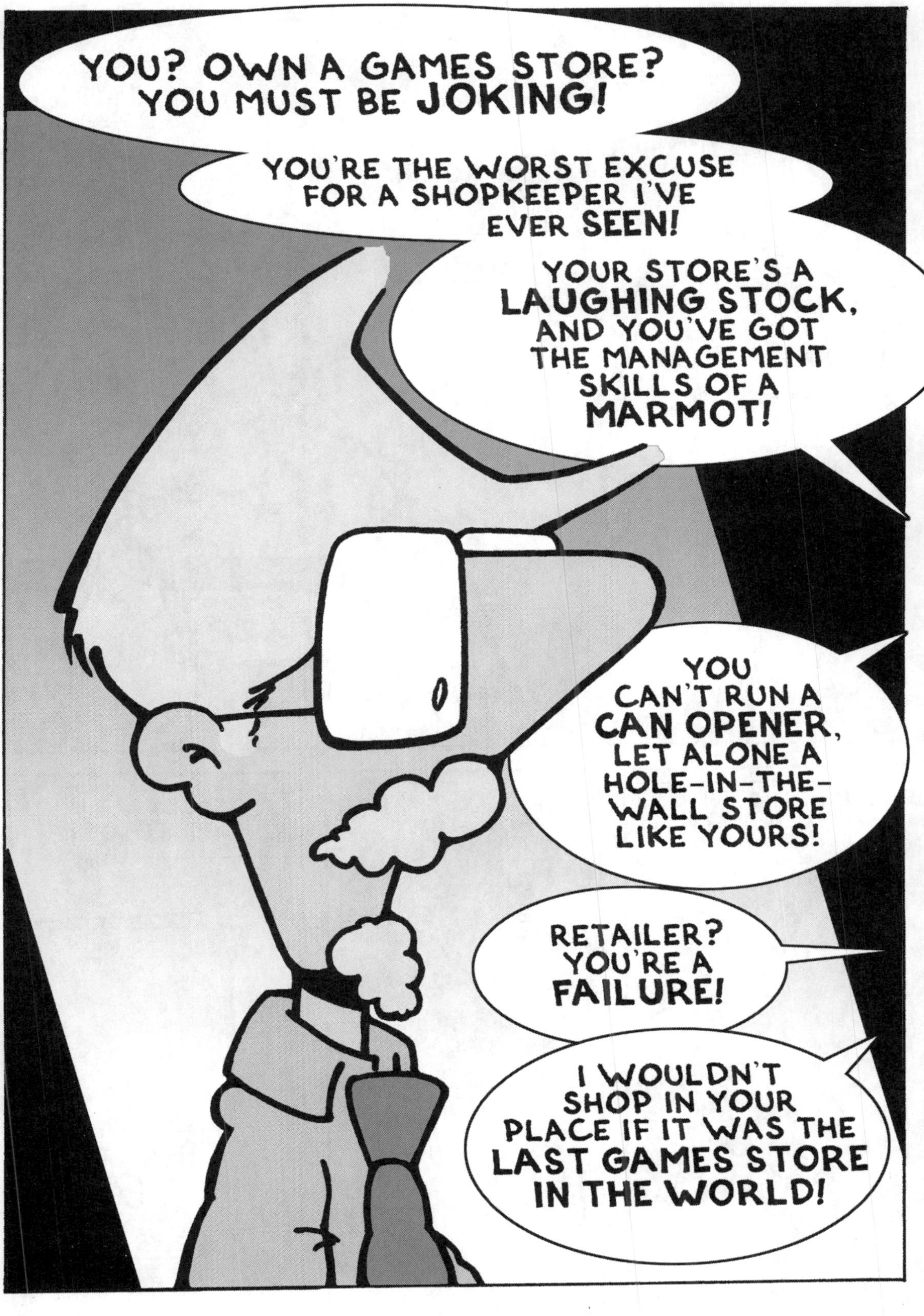
YOU? OWN A GAMES STORE? YOU MUST BE JOKING!
YOU'RE THE WORST EXCUSE FOR A SHOPKEEPER I'VE EVER SEEN!
YOUR STORE'S A LAUGHING STOCK, AND YOU'VE GOT THE MANAGEMENT SKILLS OF A MARMOT!
YOU CAN'T RUN A CAN OPENER, LET ALONE A HOLE-IN-THE-WALL STORE LIKE YOURS!
RETAILER? YOU'RE A FAILURE!
I WOULDN'T SHOP IN YOUR PLACE IF IT WAS THE LAST GAMES STORE IN THE WORLD!

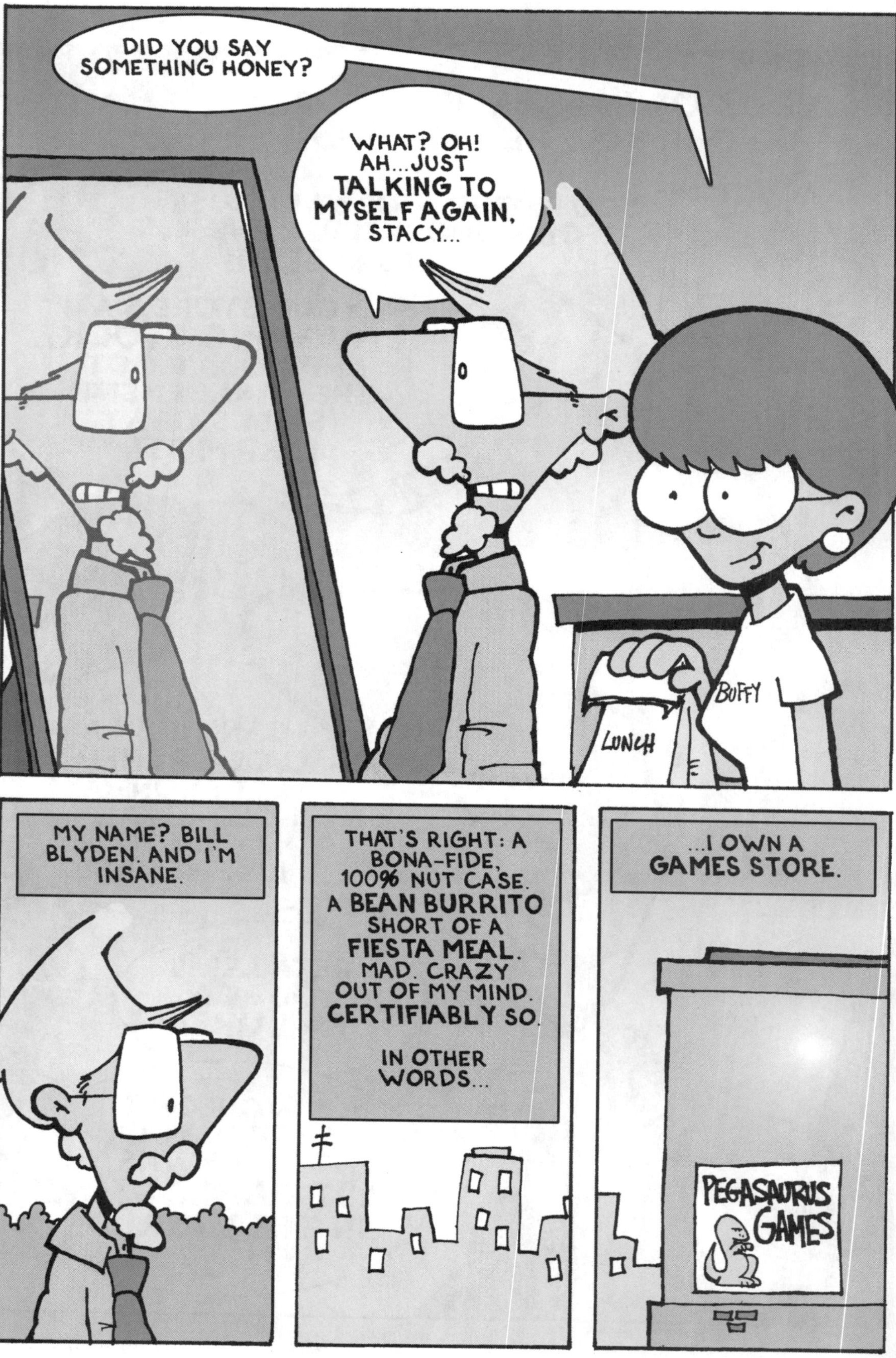

DID YOU SAY SOMETHING HONEY?
WHAT? OH! AH...JUST TALKING TO MYSELF AGAIN, STACY...
BUFFY
LUNCH
MY NAME? BILL BLYDEN. AND I'M INSANE.
THAT'S RIGHT: A BONA-FIDE, 100% NUT CASE. A BEAN BURRITO SHORT OF A FIESTA MEAL. MAD. CRAZY OUT OF MY MIND. CERTIFIABLY SO.
IN OTHER WORDS...
...I OWN A GAMES STORE.
PEGASAURUS GAMES

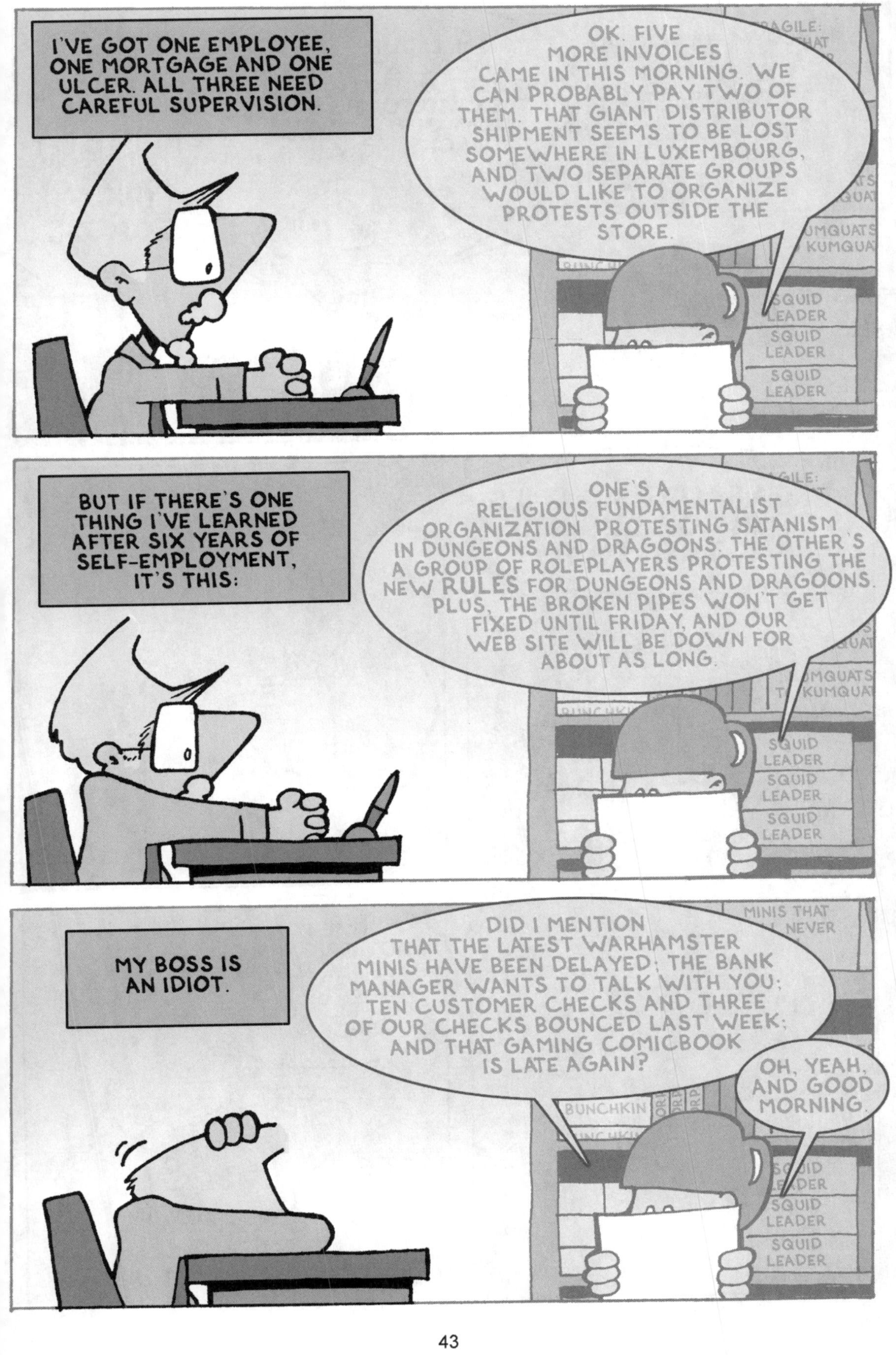
I'VE GOT ONE EMPLOYEE, ONE MORTGAGE AND ONE ULCER. ALL THREE NEED CAREFUL SUPERVISION.
OK. FIVE MORE INVOICES CAME IN THIS MORNING. WE CAN PROBABLY PAY TWO OF THEM. THAT GIANT DISTRIBUTOR SHIPMENT SEEMS TO BE LOST SOMEWHERE IN LUXEMBOURG, AND TWO SEPARATE GROUPS WOULD LIKE TO ORGANIZE PROTESTS OUTSIDE THE STORE.
BUT IF THERE'S ONE THING I'VE LEARNED AFTER SIX YEARS OF SELF-EMPLOYMENT, IT'S THIS:
ONE'S A RELIGIOUS FUNDAMENTALIST ORGANIZATION PROTESTING SATANISM IN DUNGEONS AND DRAGOONS. THE OTHER'S A GROUP OF ROLEPLAYERS PROTESTING THE NEW RULES FOR DUNGEONS AND DRAGOONS. PLUS, THE BROKEN PIPES WON'T GET FIXED UNTIL FRIDAY, AND OUR WEB SITE WILL BE DOWN FOR ABOUT AS LONG.
MY BOSS IS AN IDIOT.
DID I MENTION THAT THE LATEST WARHAMSTER MINIS HAVE BEEN DELAYED; THE BANK MANAGER WANTS TO TALK WITH YOU; TEN CUSTOMER CHECKS AND THREE OF OUR CHECKS BOUNCED LAST WEEK; AND THAT GAMING COMICBOOK IS LATE AGAIN?
OH, YEAH. AND GOOD MORNING.

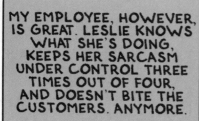

MY EMPLOYEE, HOWEVER, IS GREAT. LESLIE KNOWS WHAT SHE'S DOING, KEEPS HER SARCASM UNDER CONTROL THREE TIMES OUT OF FOUR, AND DOESN'T BITE THE CUSTOMERS. ANYMORE.

WELL, FOR THE MOST PART...

10 AM, LESLIE! TIME TO PAY THE RENT AND KEEP THE CREDITORS OFF OUR BACKS!

TIME TO LET IN THE TEEMING HORDES OF CUSTOMERS, BECAUSE..

...PEGASAURUS GAMES IS OPEN FOR BUSINESS ANOTHER DAY!

SWING!

CR-KET CR-KET

TIME FOR ANOTHER GAME OF "LIST THE TOP FIVE REASONS WHY RETAIL SUCKS"..?

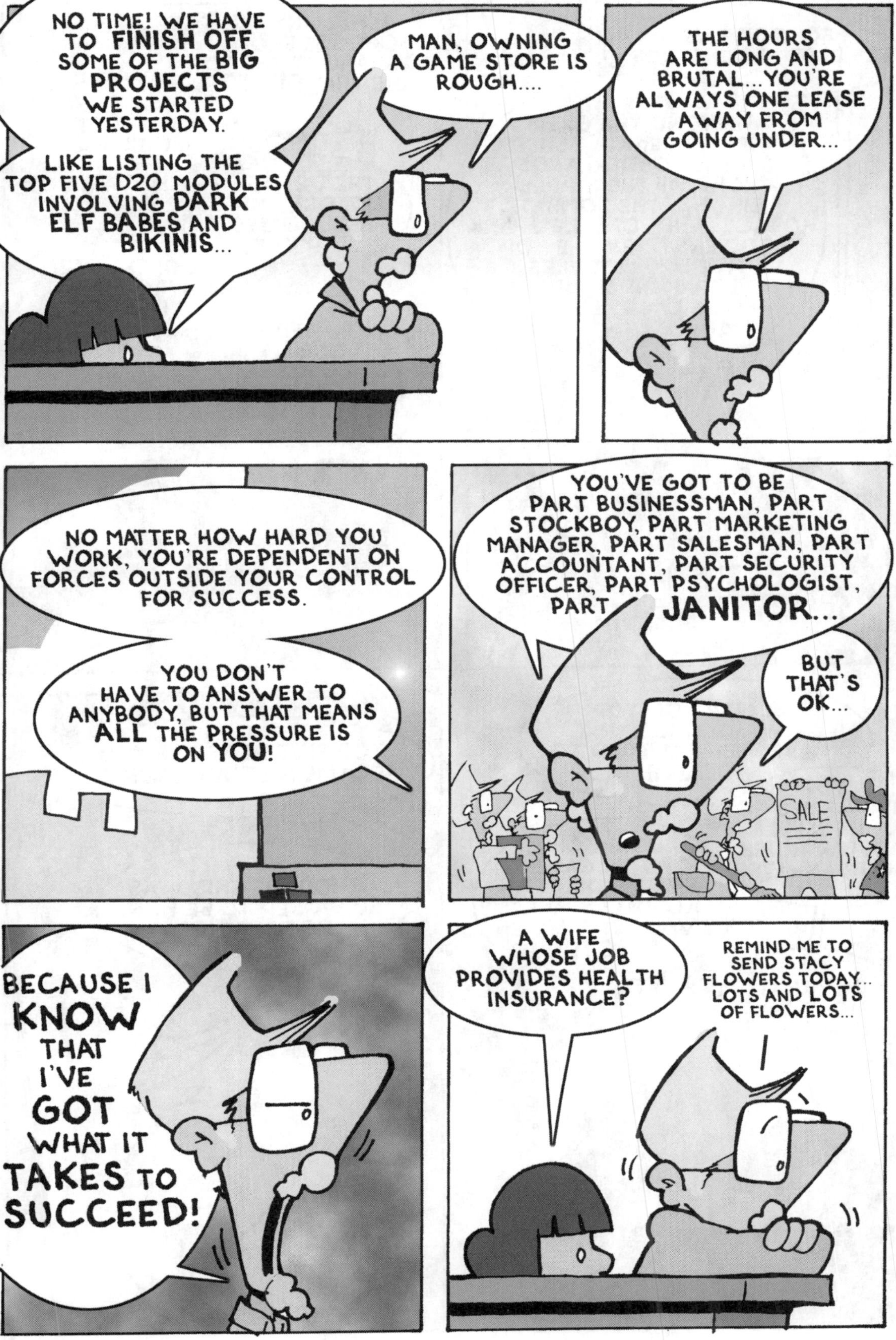
NO TIME! WE HAVE TO FINISH OFF SOME OF THE BIG PROJECTS WE STARTED YESTERDAY.
LIKE LISTING THE TOP FIVE D20 MODULES INVOLVING DARK ELF BABES AND BIKINIS...
MAN, OWNING A GAME STORE IS ROUGH....
THE HOURS ARE LONG AND BRUTAL...YOU'RE ALWAYS ONE LEASE AWAY FROM GOING UNDER...
NO MATTER HOW HARD YOU WORK, YOU'RE DEPENDENT ON FORCES OUTSIDE YOUR CONTROL FOR SUCCESS.
YOU DON'T HAVE TO ANSWER TO ANYBODY, BUT THAT MEANS ALL THE PRESSURE IS ON YOU!
YOU'VE GOT TO BE PART BUSINESSMAN, PART STOCKBOY, PART MARKETING MANAGER, PART SALESMAN, PART ACCOUNTANT, PART SECURITY OFFICER, PART PSYCHOLOGIST, PART JANITOR...
BUT THAT'S OK...
SALE
BECAUSE I KNOW THAT I'VE GOT WHAT IT TAKES TO SUCCEED!
A WIFE WHOSE JOB PROVIDES HEALTH INSURANCE?
REMIND ME TO SEND STACY FLOWERS TODAY... LOTS AND LOTS OF FLOWERS...

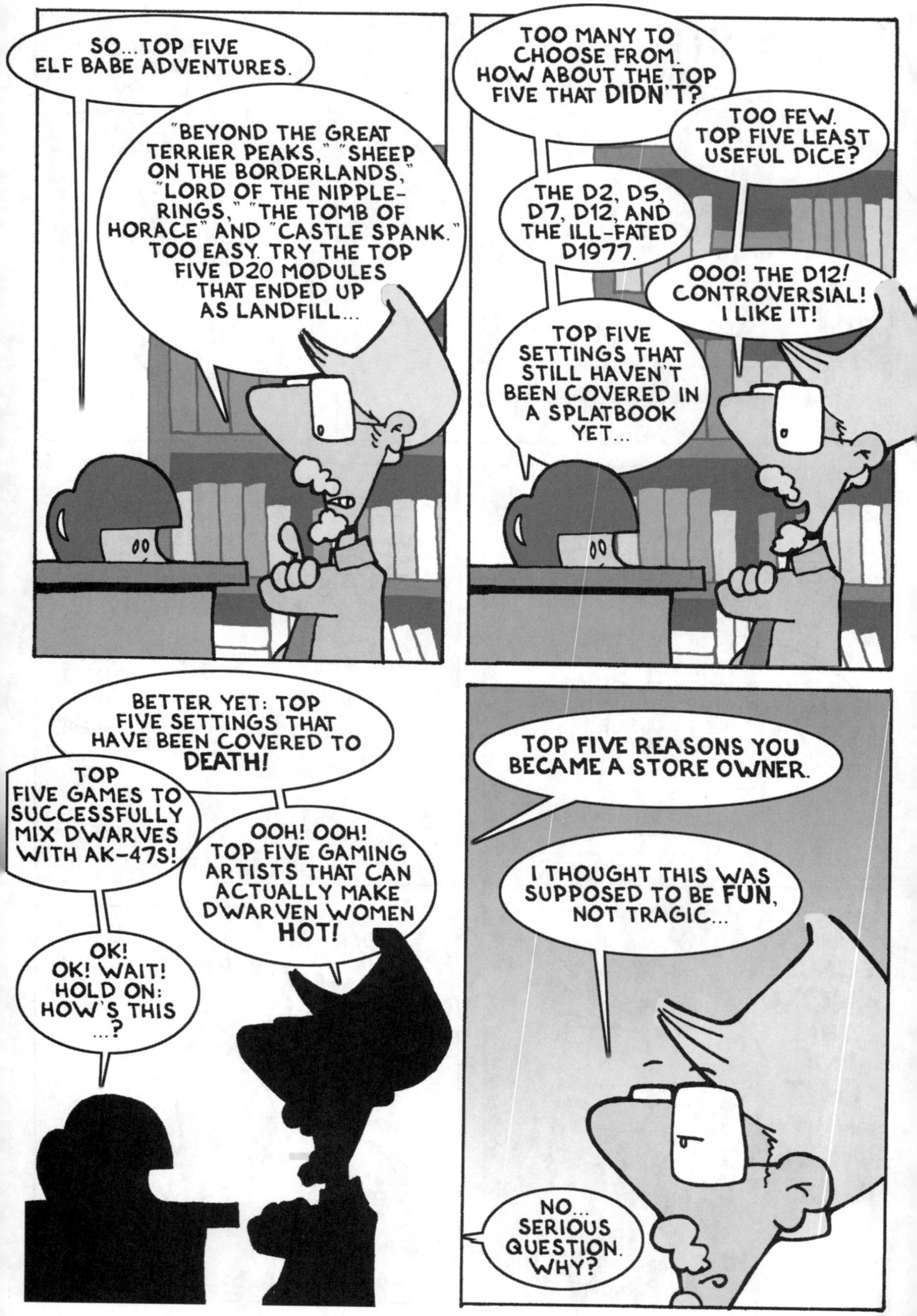
SO...TOP FIVE ELF BABE ADVENTURES.
"BEYOND THE GREAT TERRIER PEAKS," "SHEEP ON THE BORDERLANDS," "LORD OF THE NIPPLE-RINGS," "THE TOMB OF HORACE" AND "CASTLE SPANK." TOO EASY. TRY THE TOP FIVE D20 MODULES THAT ENDED UP AS LANDFILL...
TOO MANY TO CHOOSE FROM. HOW ABOUT THE TOP FIVE THAT DIDN'T?
TOO FEW. TOP FIVE LEAST USEFUL DICE?
THE D2, D5, D7, D12, AND THE ILL-FATED D1977.
OOO! THE D12! CONTROVERSIAL! I LIKE IT!
TOP FIVE SETTINGS THAT STILL HAVEN'T BEEN COVERED IN A SPLATBOOK YET...
BETTER YET: TOP FIVE SETTINGS THAT HAVE BEEN COVERED TO DEATH!
TOP FIVE GAMES TO SUCCESSFULLY MIX DWARVES WITH AK-47S!
OOH! OOH! TOP FIVE GAMING ARTISTS THAT CAN ACTUALLY MAKE DWARVEN WOMEN HOT!
OK! OK! WAIT! HOLD ON: HOW'S THIS ...?
TOP FIVE REASONS YOU BECAME A STORE OWNER.
I THOUGHT THIS WAS SUPPOSED TO BE FUN, NOT TRAGIC...
NO... SERIOUS QUESTION. WHY?

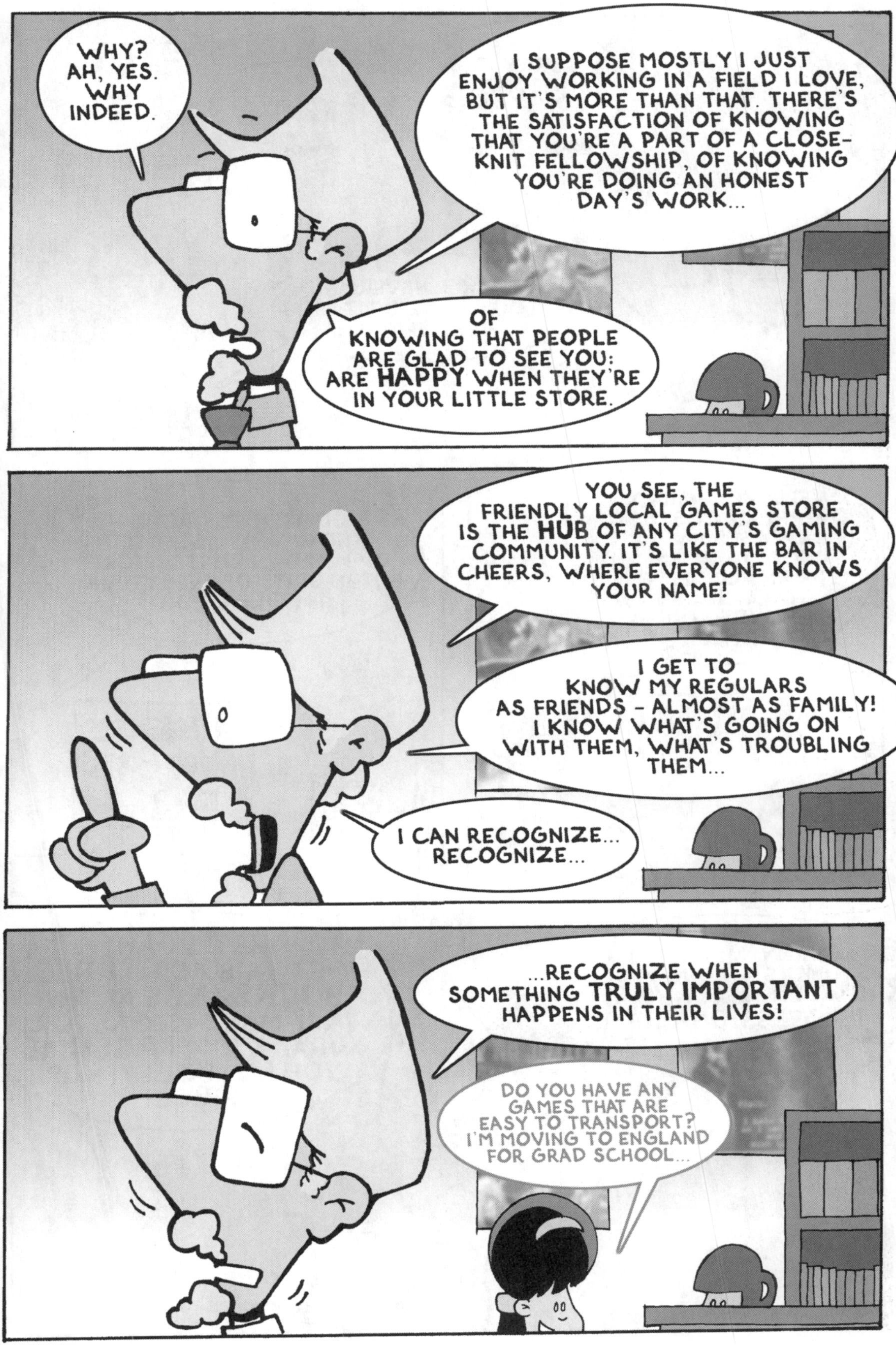
WHY? AH, YES. WHY INDEED.
I SUPPOSE MOSTLY I JUST ENJOY WORKING IN A FIELD I LOVE, BUT IT'S MORE THAN THAT. THERE'S THE SATISFACTION OF KNOWING THAT YOU'RE A PART OF A CLOSE-KNIT FELLOWSHIP, OF KNOWING YOU'RE DOING AN HONEST DAY'S WORK...
OF KNOWING THAT PEOPLE ARE GLAD TO SEE YOU: ARE HAPPY WHEN THEY'RE IN YOUR LITTLE STORE.
YOU SEE, THE FRIENDLY LOCAL GAMES STORE IS THE HUB OF ANY CITY'S GAMING COMMUNITY. IT'S LIKE THE BAR IN CHEERS, WHERE EVERYONE KNOWS YOUR NAME!
I GET TO KNOW MY REGULARS AS FRIENDS - ALMOST AS FAMILY! I KNOW WHAT'S GOING ON WITH THEM, WHAT'S TROUBLING THEM...
I CAN RECOGNIZE... RECOGNIZE...
...RECOGNIZE WHEN SOMETHING TRULY IMPORTANT HAPPENS IN THEIR LIVES!
DO YOU HAVE ANY GAMES THAT ARE EASY TO TRANSPORT? I'M MOVING TO ENGLAND FOR GRAD SCHOOL...

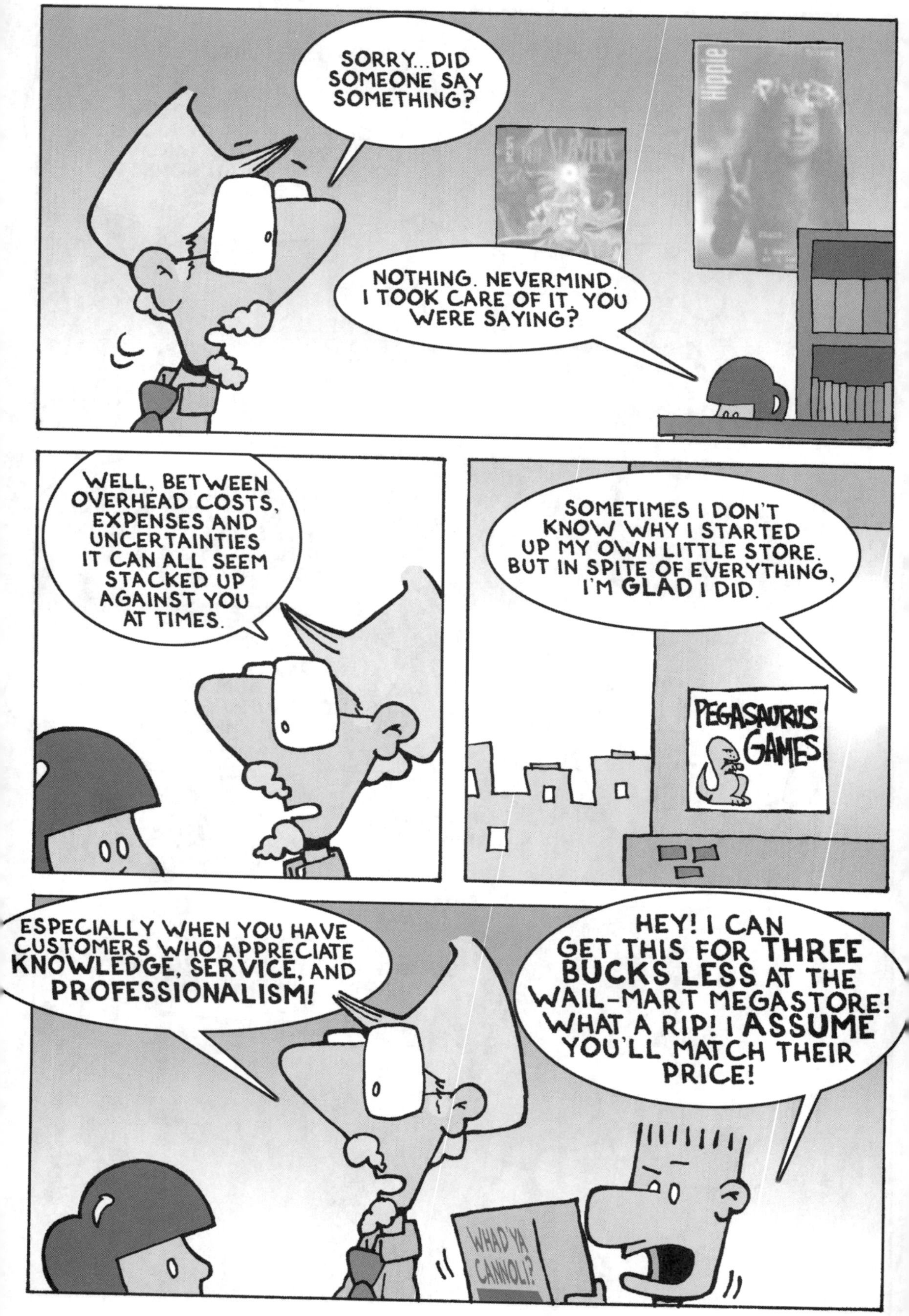
SORRY...DID SOMEONE SAY SOMETHING?
NOTHING. NEVERMIND. I TOOK CARE OF IT. YOU WERE SAYING?
WELL, BETWEEN OVERHEAD COSTS, EXPENSES AND UNCERTAINTIES IT CAN ALL SEEM STACKED UP AGAINST YOU AT TIMES.
SOMETIMES I DON'T KNOW WHY I STARTED UP MY OWN LITTLE STORE. BUT IN SPITE OF EVERYTHING, I'M GLAD I DID.
PEGASAURUS GAMES
ESPECIALLY WHEN YOU HAVE CUSTOMERS WHO APPRECIATE KNOWLEDGE, SERVICE, AND PROFESSIONALISM!
HEY! I CAN GET THIS FOR THREE BUCKS LESS AT THE WAIL-MART MEGASTORE! WHAT A RIP! I ASSUME YOU'LL MATCH THEIR PRICE!
WHAD'YA CANNOLI?

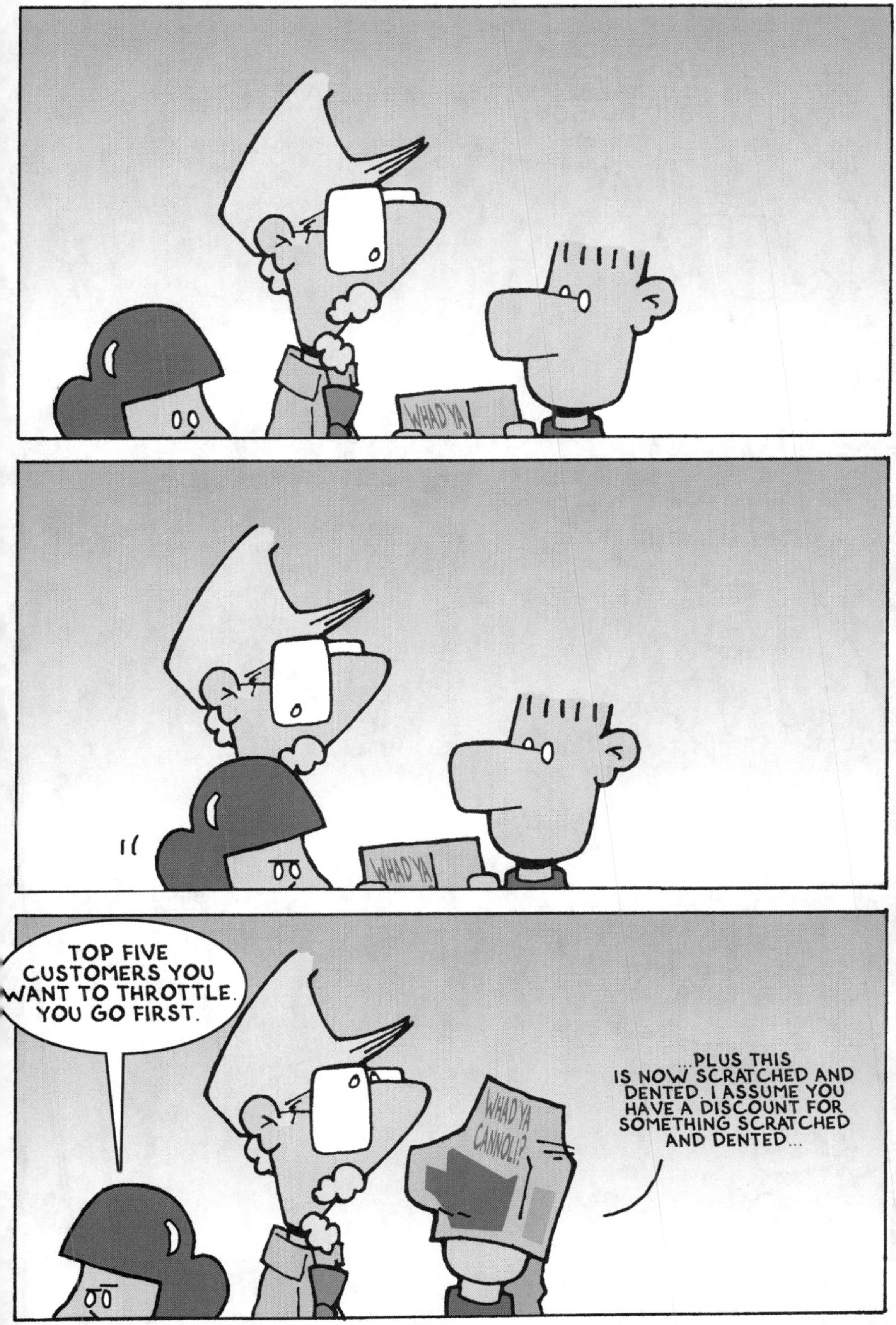
WHAD'YA
WHAD'YA
TOP FIVE CUSTOMERS YOU WANT TO THROTTLE. YOU GO FIRST.
WHAD'YA CANNOLI?
...PLUS THIS IS NOW SCRATCHED AND DENTED. I ASSUME YOU HAVE A DISCOUNT FOR SOMETHING SCRATCHED AND DENTED...

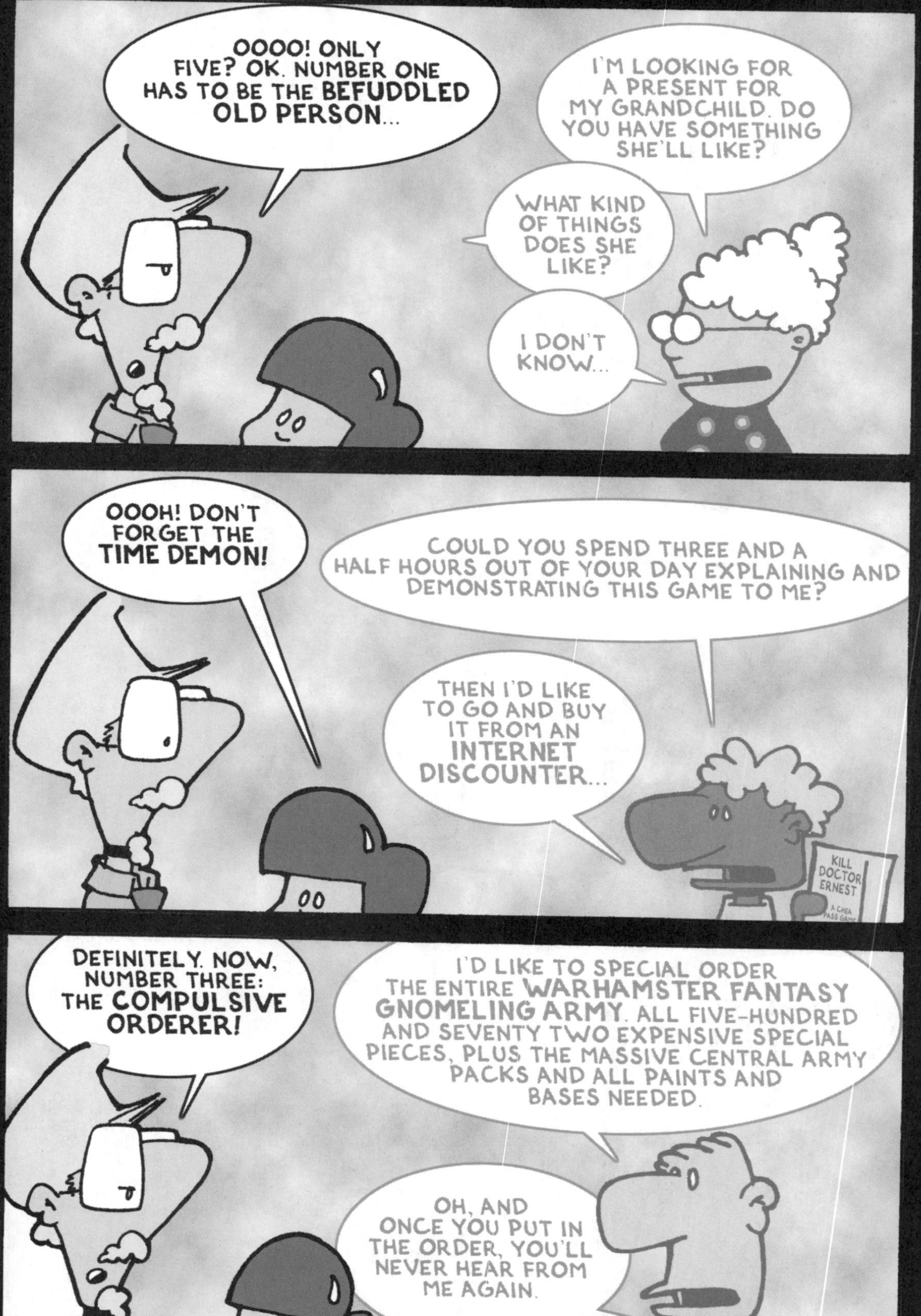
OOOO! ONLY FIVE? OK. NUMBER ONE HAS TO BE THE BEFUDDLED OLD PERSON...
I'M LOOKING FOR A PRESENT FOR MY GRANDCHILD. DO YOU HAVE SOMETHING SHE'LL LIKE?
WHAT KIND OF THINGS DOES SHE LIKE?
I DON'T KNOW...
OOOH! DON'T FORGET THE TIME DEMON!
COULD YOU SPEND THREE AND A HALF HOURS OUT OF YOUR DAY EXPLAINING AND DEMONSTRATING THIS GAME TO ME?
THEN I'D LIKE TO GO AND BUY IT FROM AN INTERNET DISCOUNTER...
KILL DOCTOR ERNEST
DEFINITELY. NOW, NUMBER THREE: THE COMPULSIVE ORDERER!
I'D LIKE TO SPECIAL ORDER THE ENTIRE WARHAMSTER FANTASY GNOMELING ARMY. ALL FIVE-HUNDRED AND SEVENTY TWO EXPENSIVE SPECIAL PIECES, PLUS THE MASSIVE CENTRAL ARMY PACKS AND ALL PAINTS AND BASES NEEDED.
OH, AND ONCE YOU PUT IN THE ORDER, YOU'LL NEVER HEAR FROM ME AGAIN.

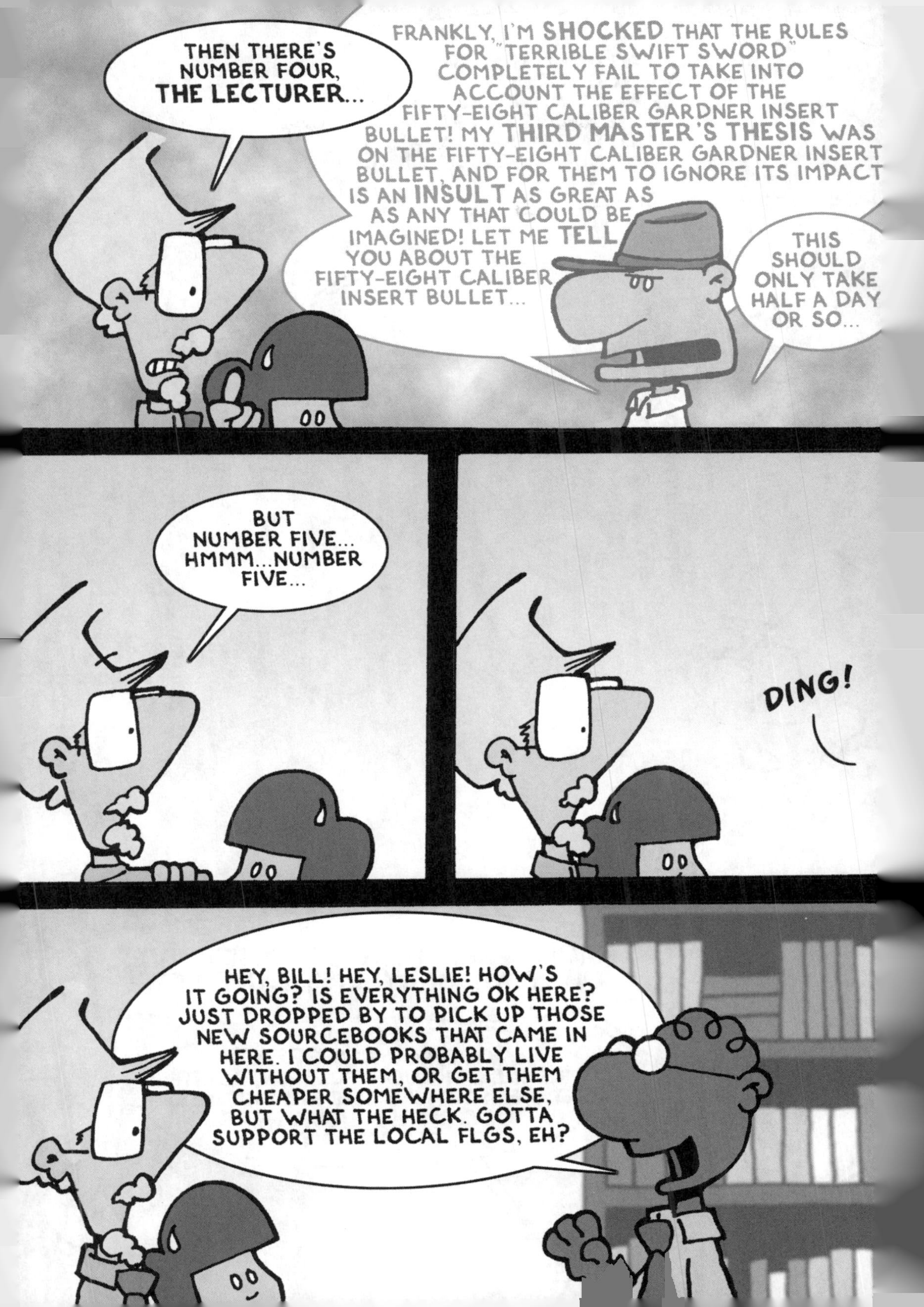
THEN THERE'S NUMBER FOUR, THE LECTURER...
FRANKLY, I'M SHOCKED THAT THE RULES FOR "TERRIBLE SWIFT SWORD" COMPLETELY FAIL TO TAKE INTO ACCOUNT THE EFFECT OF THE FIFTY-EIGHT CALIBER GARDNER INSERT BULLET! MY THIRD MASTER'S THESIS WAS ON THE FIFTY-EIGHT CALIBER GARDNER INSERT BULLET, AND FOR THEM TO IGNORE ITS IMPACT IS AN INSULT AS GREAT AS AS ANY THAT COULD BE IMAGINED! LET ME TELL YOU ABOUT THE FIFTY-EIGHT CALIBER INSERT BULLET...
THIS SHOULD ONLY TAKE HALF A DAY OR SO...
BUT NUMBER FIVE... HMMM...NUMBER FIVE...
DING!
HEY, BILL! HEY, LESLIE! HOW'S IT GOING? IS EVERYTHING OK HERE? JUST DROPPED BY TO PICK UP THOSE NEW SOURCEBOOKS THAT CAME IN HERE. I COULD PROBABLY LIVE WITHOUT THEM, OR GET THEM CHEAPER SOMEWHERE ELSE, BUT WHAT THE HECK. GOTTA SUPPORT THE LOCAL FLGS, EH?

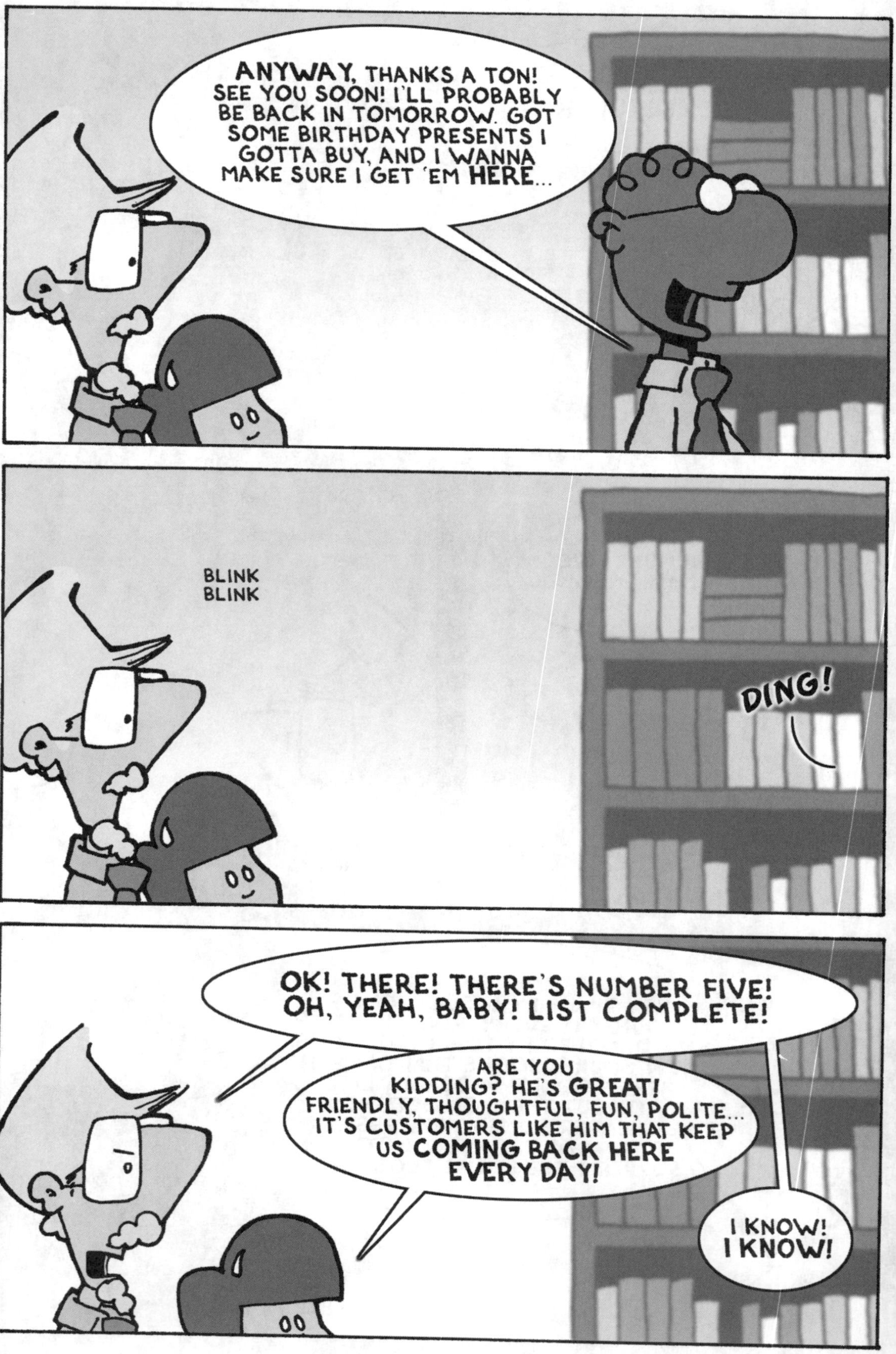
ANYWAY, THANKS A TON! SEE YOU SOON! I'LL PROBABLY BE BACK IN TOMORROW. GOT SOME BIRTHDAY PRESENTS I GOTTA BUY, AND I WANNA MAKE SURE I GET 'EM HERE...
BLINK BLINK
DING!
OK! THERE! THERE'S NUMBER FIVE! OH, YEAH, BABY! LIST COMPLETE!
ARE YOU KIDDING? HE'S GREAT! FRIENDLY, THOUGHTFUL, FUN, POLITE... IT'S CUSTOMERS LIKE HIM THAT KEEP US COMING BACK HERE EVERY DAY!
I KNOW! I KNOW!

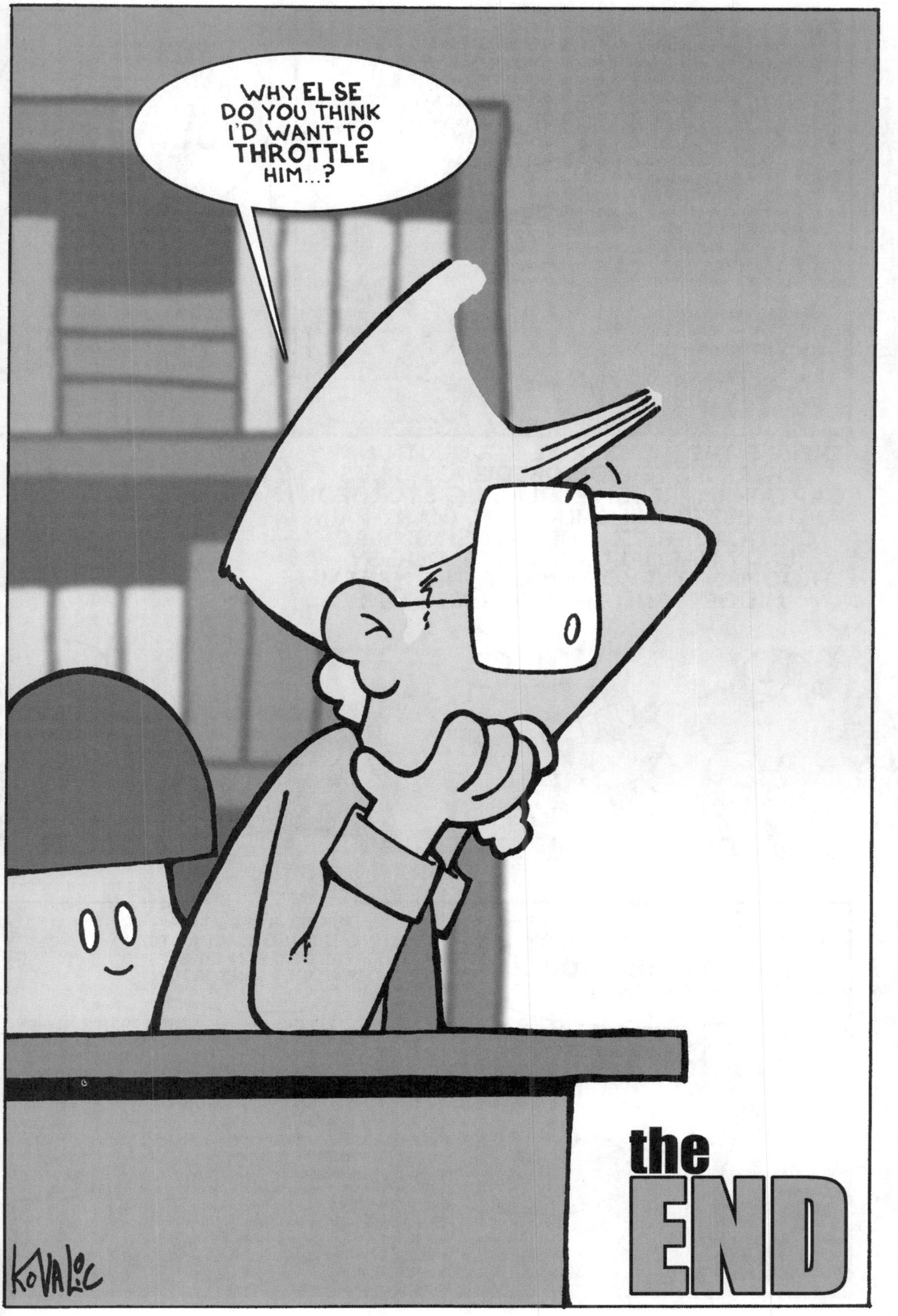
WHY ELSE DO YOU THINK I'D WANT TO THROTTLE HIM...?
the END
KOVALIC

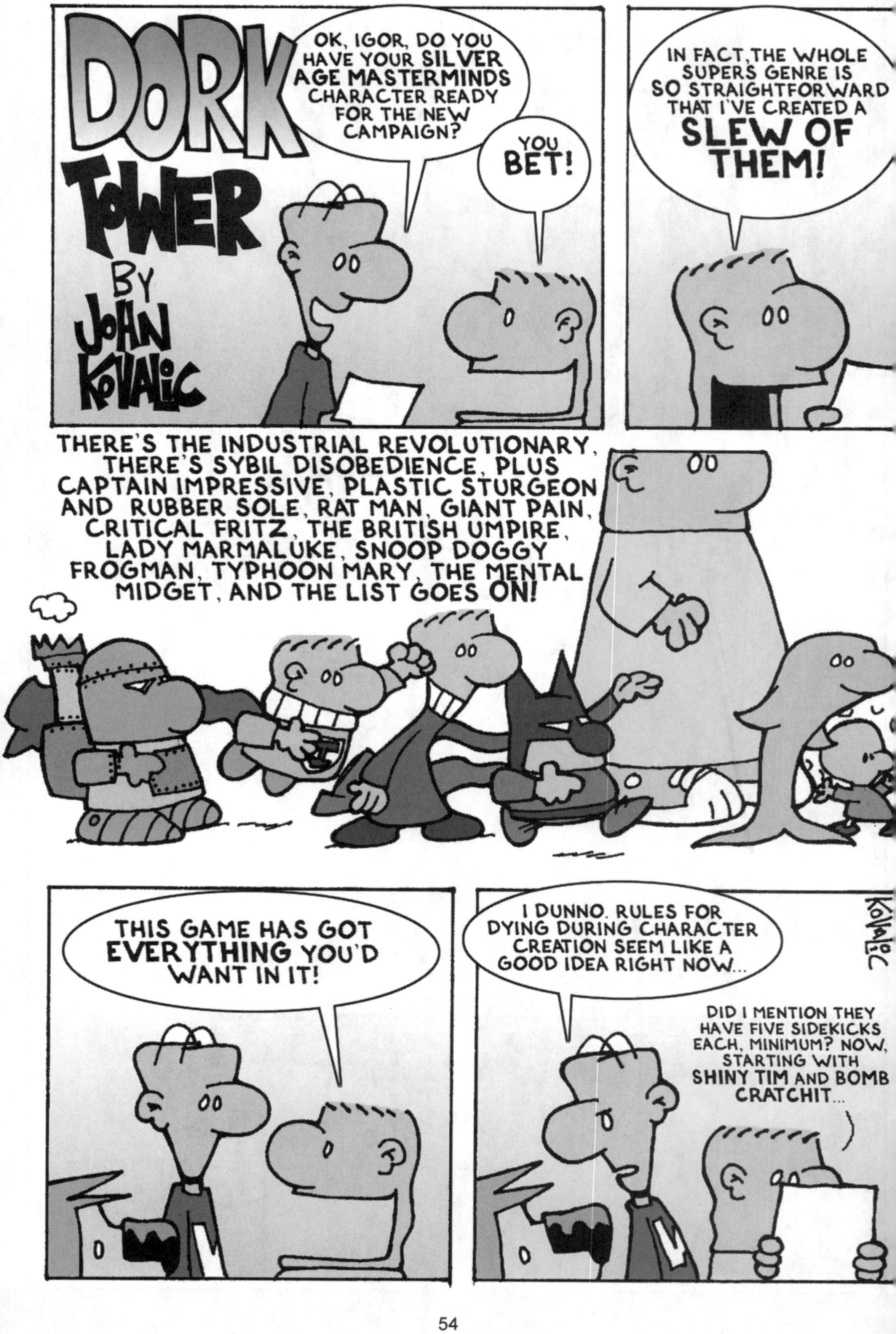
DORK TOWER
BY JOHN KOVALIC
OK, IGOR, DO YOU HAVE YOUR SILVER AGE MASTERMINDS CHARACTER READY FOR THE NEW CAMPAIGN?
YOU BET!
IN FACT, THE WHOLE SUPERS GENRE IS SO STRAIGHTFORWARD THAT I'VE CREATED A SLEW OF THEM!
THERE'S THE INDUSTRIAL REVOLUTIONARY, THERE'S SYBIL DISOBEDIENCE, PLUS CAPTAIN IMPRESSIVE, PLASTIC STURGEON AND RUBBER SOLE, RAT MAN, GIANT PAIN, CRITICAL FRITZ, THE BRITISH UMPIRE, LADY MARMALUKE, SNOOP DOGGY FROGMAN, TYPHOON MARY, THE MENTAL MIDGET, AND THE LIST GOES ON!
THIS GAME HAS GOT EVERYTHING YOU'D WANT IN IT!
I DUNNO. RULES FOR DYING DURING CHARACTER CREATION SEEM LIKE A GOOD IDEA RIGHT NOW...
DID I MENTION THEY HAVE FIVE SIDEKICKS EACH, MINIMUM? NOW, STARTING WITH SHINY TIM AND BOMB CRATCHIT...
KOVALIC

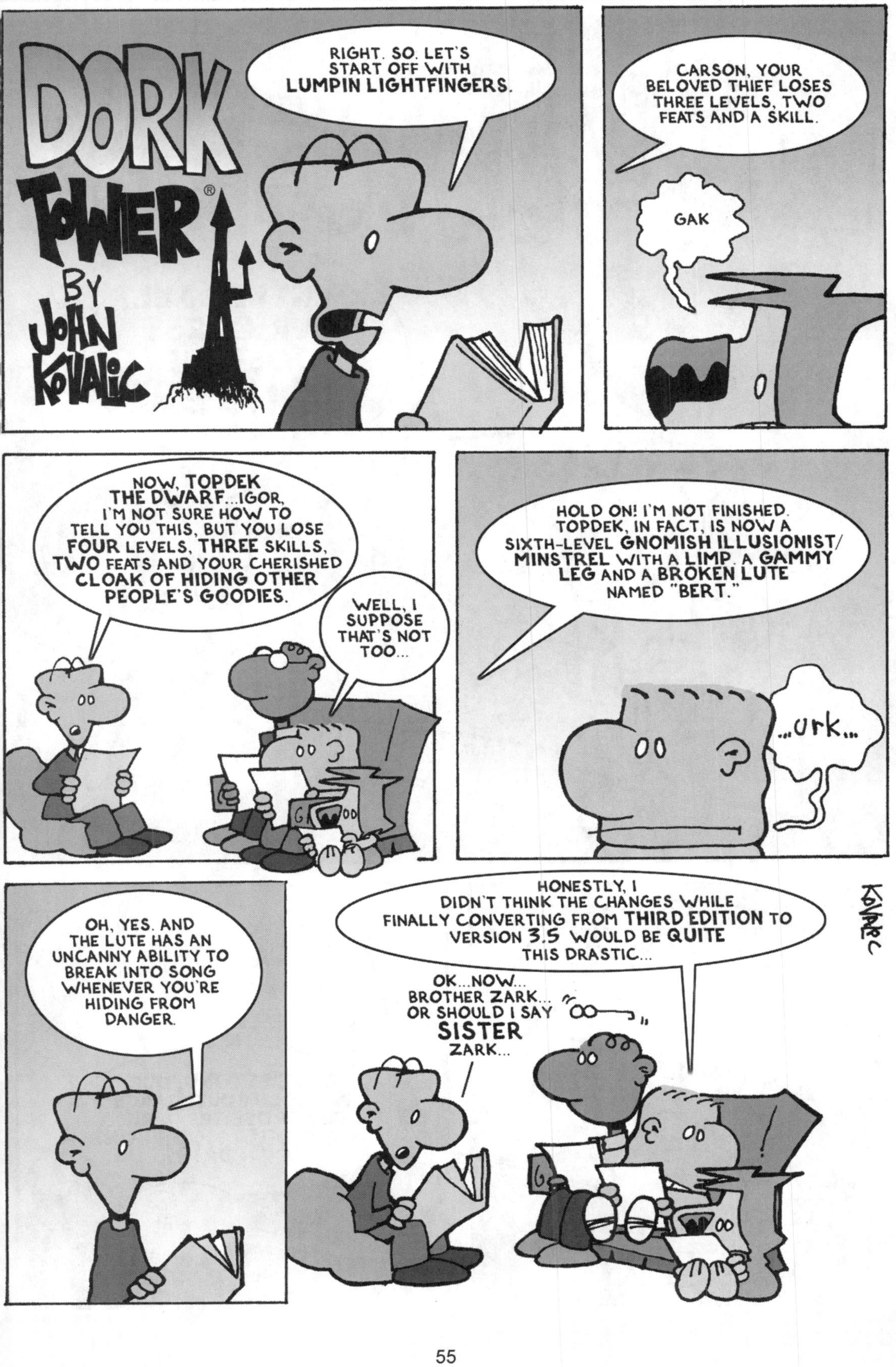
DORK TOWER®
BY JOHN KOVALIC
RIGHT. SO. LET'S START OFF WITH LUMPIN LIGHTFINGERS.
CARSON, YOUR BELOVED THIEF LOSES THREE LEVELS, TWO FEATS AND A SKILL.
GAK
NOW, TOPDEK THE DWARF...IGOR, I'M NOT SURE HOW TO TELL YOU THIS, BUT YOU LOSE FOUR LEVELS, THREE SKILLS, TWO FEATS AND YOUR CHERISHED CLOAK OF HIDING OTHER PEOPLE'S GOODIES.
WELL, I SUPPOSE THAT'S NOT TOO...
HOLD ON! I'M NOT FINISHED. TOPDEK, IN FACT, IS NOW A SIXTH-LEVEL GNOMISH ILLUSIONIST/ MINSTREL WITH A LIMP, A GAMMY LEG AND A BROKEN LUTE NAMED "BERT."
...urk...
OH, YES. AND THE LUTE HAS AN UNCANNY ABILITY TO BREAK INTO SONG WHENEVER YOU'RE HIDING FROM DANGER.
OK...NOW... BROTHER ZARK... OR SHOULD I SAY SISTER ZARK...
HONESTLY, I DIDN'T THINK THE CHANGES WHILE FINALLY CONVERTING FROM THIRD EDITION TO VERSION 3.5 WOULD BE QUITE THIS DRASTIC...
KOVALIC

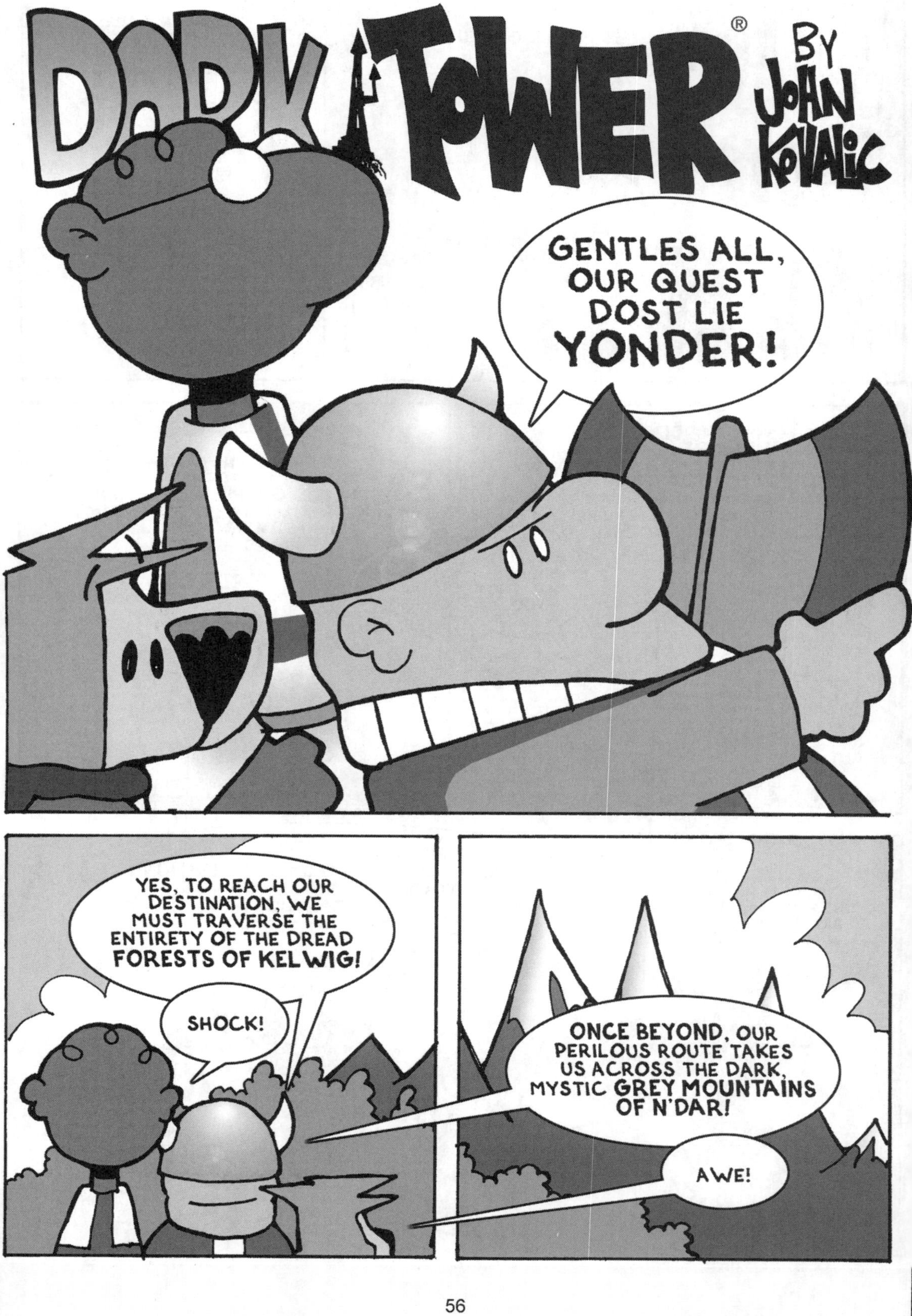
DARK TOWER®
BY JOHN KOVALIC
GENTLES ALL, OUR QUEST DOST LIE YONDER!
YES, TO REACH OUR DESTINATION, WE MUST TRAVERSE THE ENTIRETY OF THE DREAD FORESTS OF KELWIG!
SHOCK!
ONCE BEYOND, OUR PERILOUS ROUTE TAKES US ACROSS THE DARK, MYSTIC GREY MOUNTAINS OF N'DAR!
AWE!

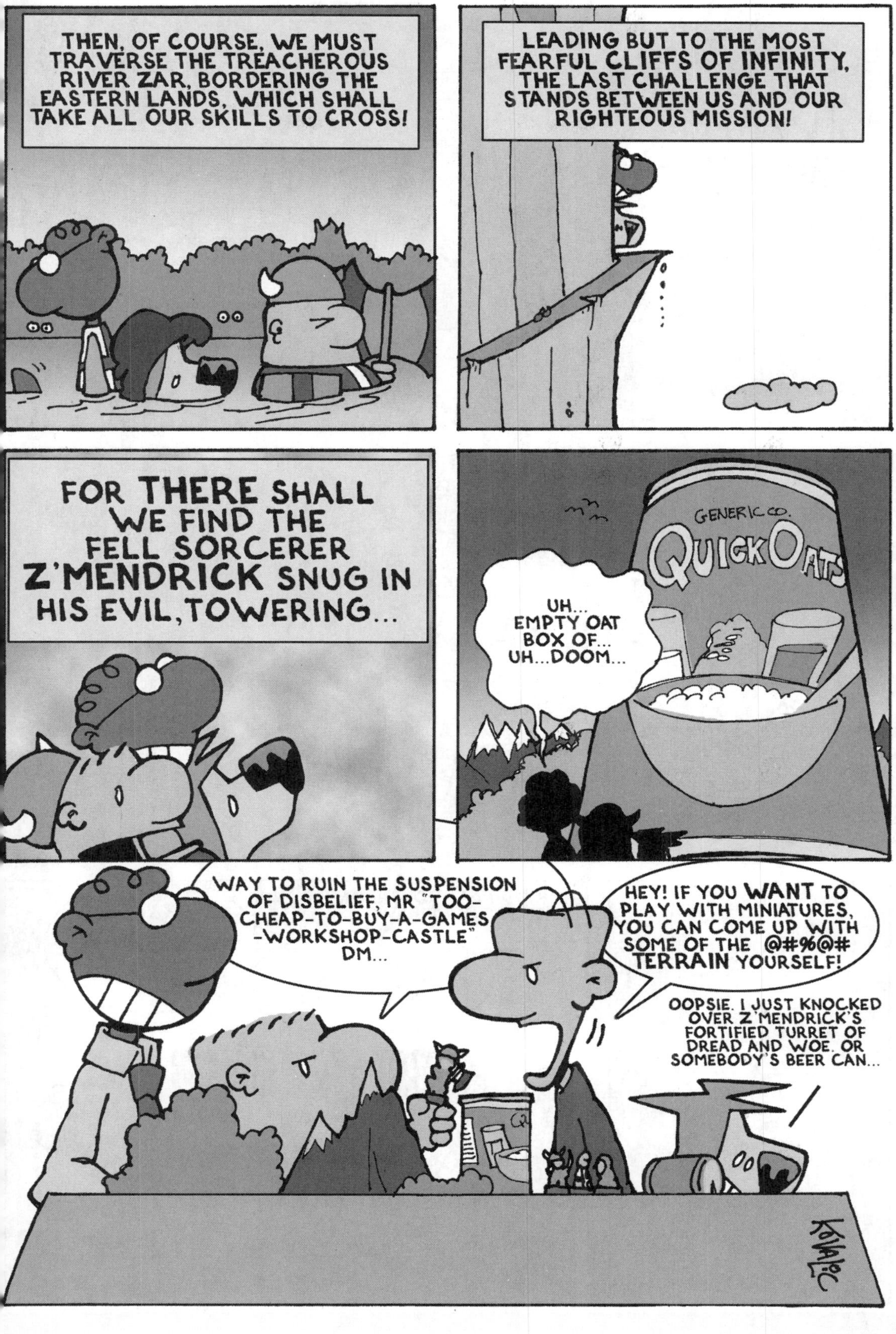
THEN, OF COURSE, WE MUST TRAVERSE THE TREACHEROUS RIVER ZAR, BORDERING THE EASTERN LANDS, WHICH SHALL TAKE ALL OUR SKILLS TO CROSS!
LEADING BUT TO THE MOST FEARFUL CLIFFS OF INFINITY, THE LAST CHALLENGE THAT STANDS BETWEEN US AND OUR RIGHTEOUS MISSION!
FOR THERE SHALL WE FIND THE FELL SORCERER Z'MENDRICK SNUG IN HIS EVIL, TOWERING...
GENERIC CO.
QUICKOATS
UH... EMPTY OAT BOX OF... UH...DOOM...
WAY TO RUIN THE SUSPENSION OF DISBELIEF, MR "TOO-CHEAP-TO-BUY-A-GAMES-WORKSHOP-CASTLE" DM...
HEY! IF YOU WANT TO PLAY WITH MINIATURES, YOU CAN COME UP WITH SOME OF THE @#%@# TERRAIN YOURSELF!
OOPSIE. I JUST KNOCKED OVER Z'MENDRICK'S FORTIFIED TURRET OF DREAD AND WOE. OR SOMEBODY'S BEER CAN...
KOVALIC

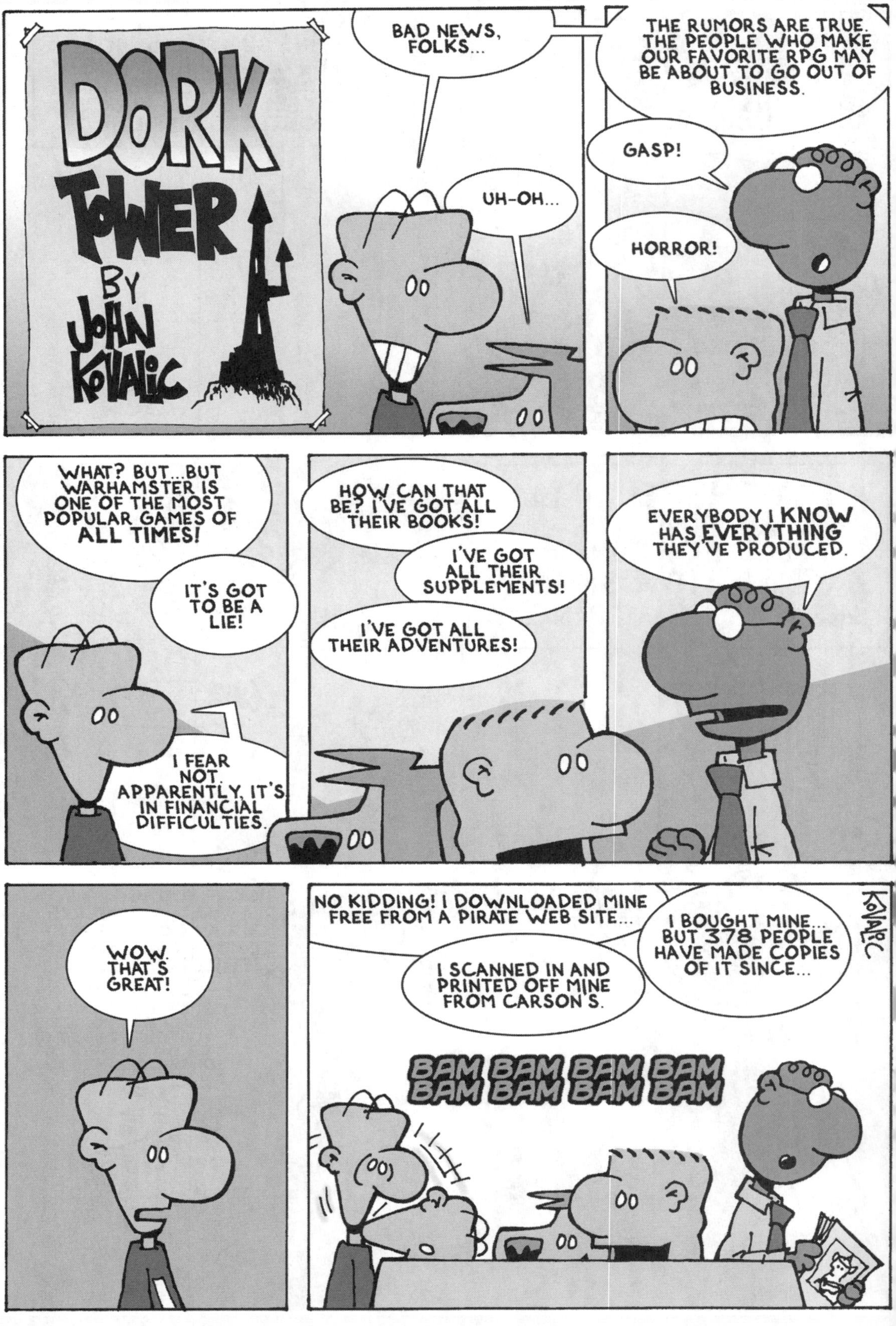
DORK TOWER
BY JOHN KOVALIC
BAD NEWS, FOLKS...
UH-OH...
THE RUMORS ARE TRUE. THE PEOPLE WHO MAKE OUR FAVORITE RPG MAY BE ABOUT TO GO OUT OF BUSINESS.
GASP!
HORROR!
WHAT? BUT...BUT WARHAMSTER IS ONE OF THE MOST POPULAR GAMES OF ALL TIMES!
IT'S GOT TO BE A LIE!
I FEAR NOT. APPARENTLY, IT'S IN FINANCIAL DIFFICULTIES.
HOW CAN THAT BE? I'VE GOT ALL THEIR BOOKS!
I'VE GOT ALL THEIR SUPPLEMENTS!
I'VE GOT ALL THEIR ADVENTURES!
EVERYBODY I KNOW HAS EVERYTHING THEY'VE PRODUCED.
WOW. THAT'S GREAT!
NO KIDDING! I DOWNLOADED MINE FREE FROM A PIRATE WEB SITE...
I SCANNED IN AND PRINTED OFF MINE FROM CARSON'S.
I BOUGHT MINE... BUT 378 PEOPLE HAVE MADE COPIES OF IT SINCE...
KOVALIC
BAM BAM BAM BAM
BAM BAM BAM BAM

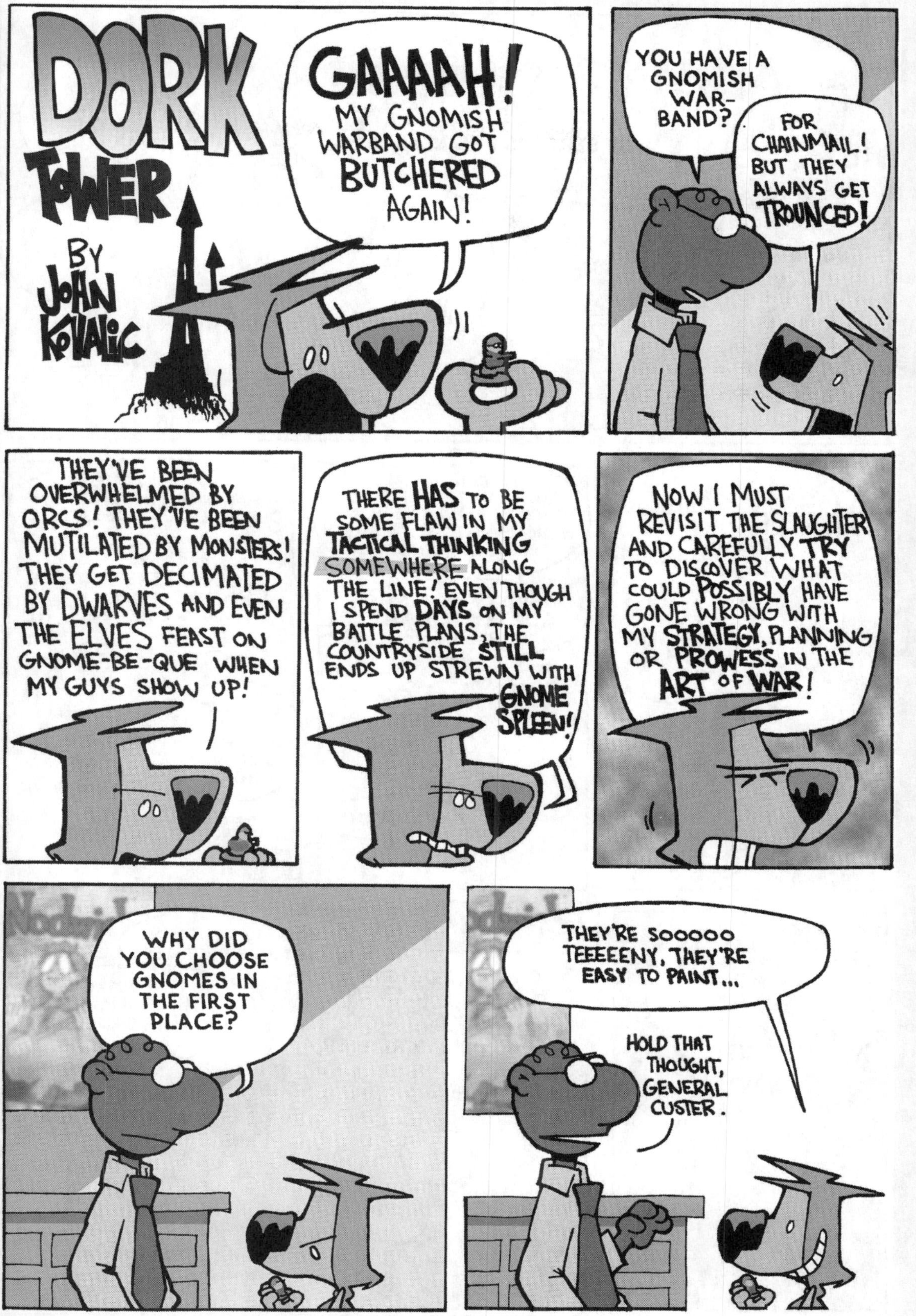
DORK TOWER
BY JOHN KOVALIC
GAAAAH! MY GNOMISH WARBAND GOT BUTCHERED AGAIN!
YOU HAVE A GNOMISH WAR-BAND?
FOR CHAINMAIL! BUT THEY ALWAYS GET TROUNCED!
THEY'VE BEEN OVERWHELMED BY ORCS! THEY'VE BEEN MUTILATED BY MONSTERS! THEY GET DECIMATED BY DWARVES AND EVEN THE ELVES FEAST ON GNOME-BE-QUE WHEN MY GUYS SHOW UP!
THERE HAS TO BE SOME FLAW IN MY TACTICAL THINKING SOMEWHERE ALONG THE LINE! EVEN THOUGH I SPEND DAYS ON MY BATTLE PLANS, THE COUNTRYSIDE STILL ENDS UP STREWN WITH GNOME SPLEEN!
NOW I MUST REVISIT THE SLAUGHTER AND CAREFULLY TRY TO DISCOVER WHAT COULD POSSIBLY HAVE GONE WRONG WITH MY STRATEGY, PLANNING OR PROWESS IN THE ART OF WAR!
WHY DID YOU CHOOSE GNOMES IN THE FIRST PLACE?
THEY'RE SOOOOO TEEEEENY, THEY'RE EASY TO PAINT...
HOLD THAT THOUGHT, GENERAL CUSTER.

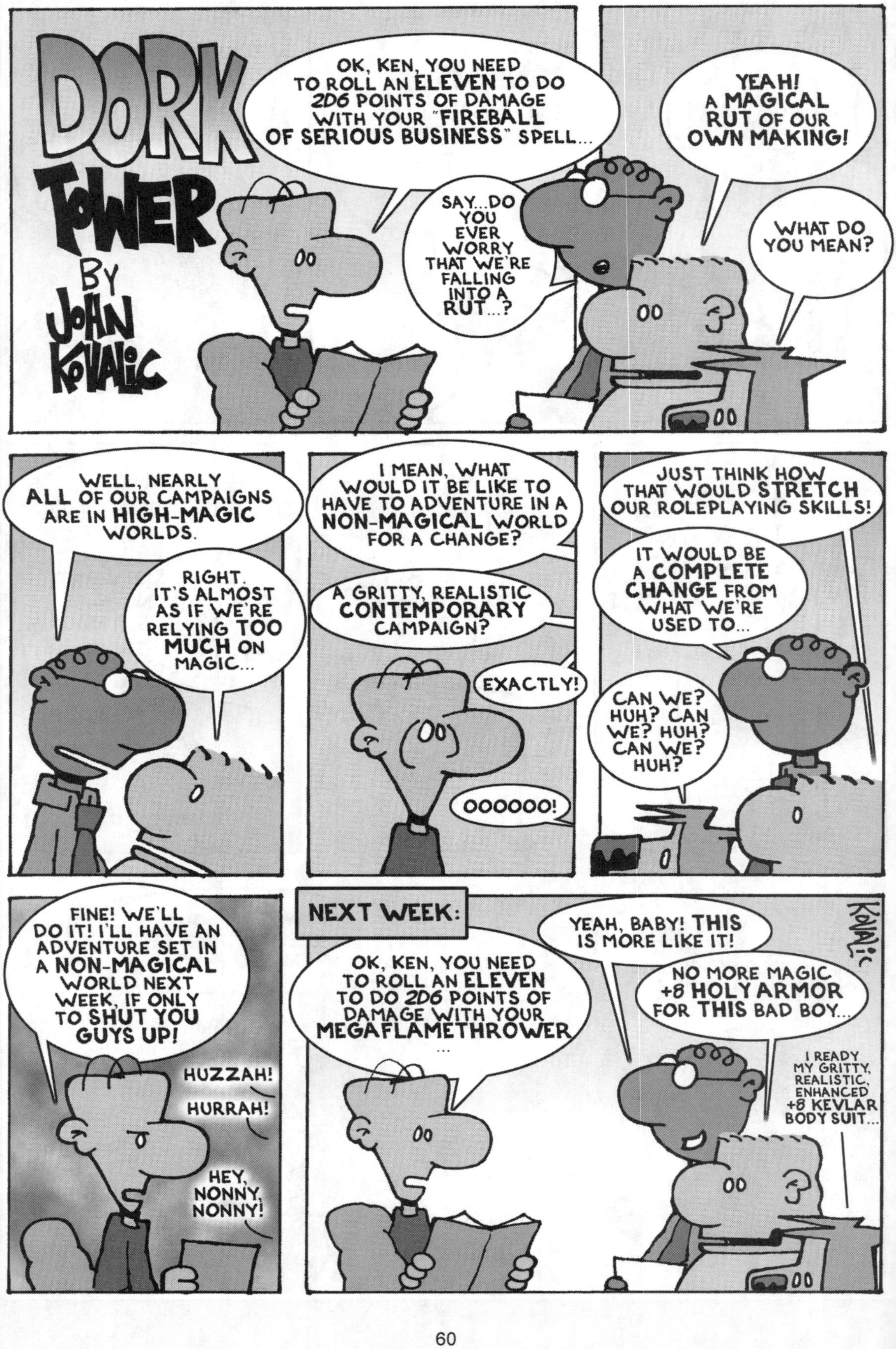
DORK TOWER
BY JOHN KOVALIC
OK, KEN, YOU NEED TO ROLL AN ELEVEN TO DO 2D6 POINTS OF DAMAGE WITH YOUR "FIREBALL OF SERIOUS BUSINESS" SPELL...
SAY...DO YOU EVER WORRY THAT WE'RE FALLING INTO A RUT...?
YEAH! A MAGICAL RUT OF OUR OWN MAKING!
WHAT DO YOU MEAN?
WELL, NEARLY ALL OF OUR CAMPAIGNS ARE IN HIGH-MAGIC WORLDS.
RIGHT. IT'S ALMOST AS IF WE'RE RELYING TOO MUCH ON MAGIC...
I MEAN, WHAT WOULD IT BE LIKE TO HAVE TO ADVENTURE IN A NON-MAGICAL WORLD FOR A CHANGE?
A GRITTY, REALISTIC CONTEMPORARY CAMPAIGN?
EXACTLY!
OOOOOO!
JUST THINK HOW THAT WOULD STRETCH OUR ROLEPLAYING SKILLS!
IT WOULD BE A COMPLETE CHANGE FROM WHAT WE'RE USED TO...
CAN WE? HUH? CAN WE? HUH? CAN WE? HUH?
FINE! WE'LL DO IT! I'LL HAVE AN ADVENTURE SET IN A NON-MAGICAL WORLD NEXT WEEK, IF ONLY TO SHUT YOU GUYS UP!
HUZZAH!
HURRAH!
HEY, NONNY, NONNY!
NEXT WEEK:
OK, KEN, YOU NEED TO ROLL AN ELEVEN TO DO 2D6 POINTS OF DAMAGE WITH YOUR MEGAFLAMETHROWER...
YEAH, BABY! THIS IS MORE LIKE IT!
NO MORE MAGIC +8 HOLY ARMOR FOR THIS BAD BOY...
I READY MY GRITTY, REALISTIC, ENHANCED +8 KEVLAR BODY SUIT...
KOVALIC

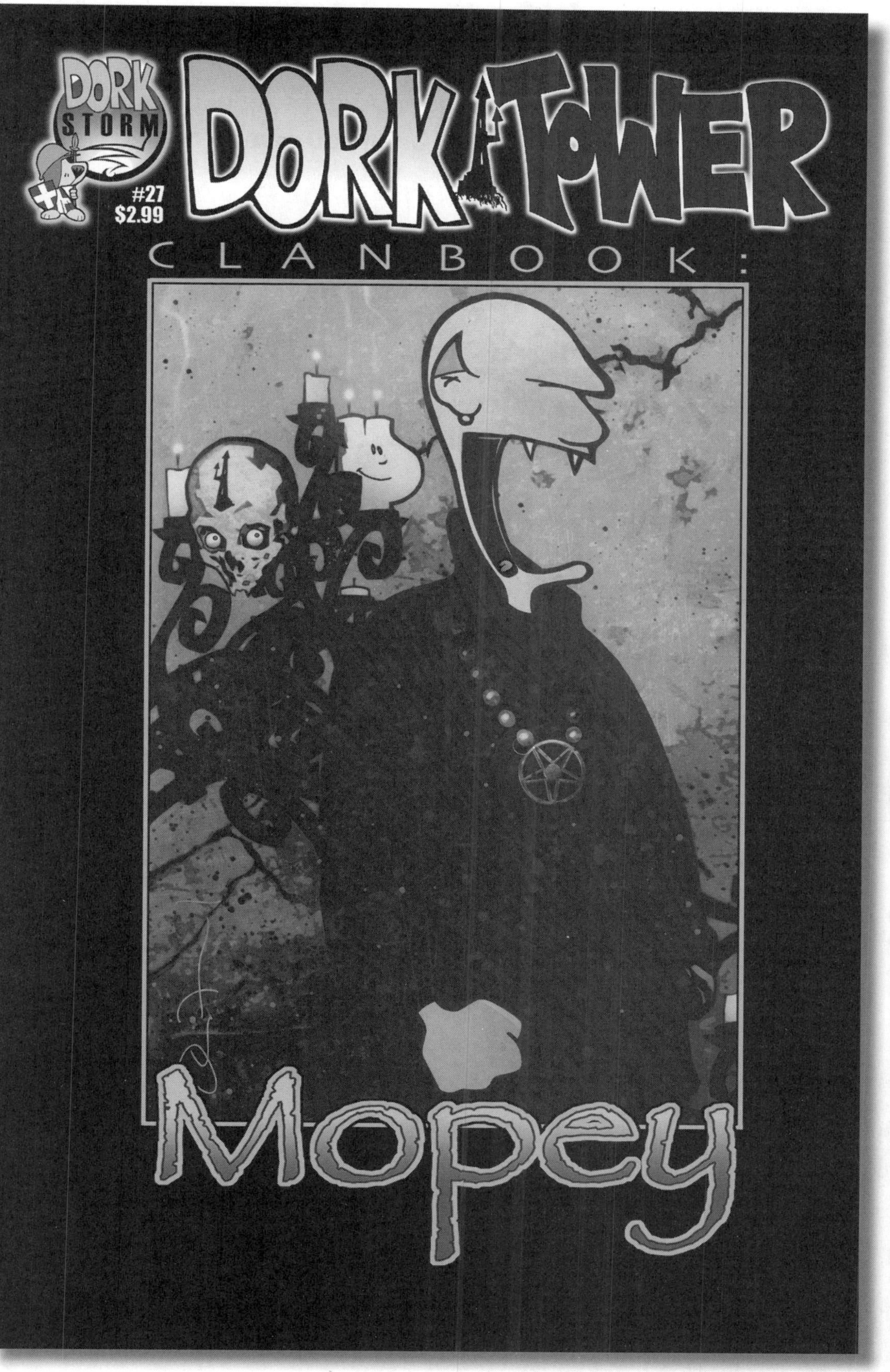
DORK STORM
DORK TOWER
#27
$2.99
CLANBOOK:
Mopey

Xander: You know, it's his trigger. Angel's an okay guy if he's mopey and sad and brooding, but if you give him even one second of pure, real pleasure...
Riley: That sets him off.
Xander: Only in the big ol "kill your friends" kind of way.
- Buffy the Vampire Slayer

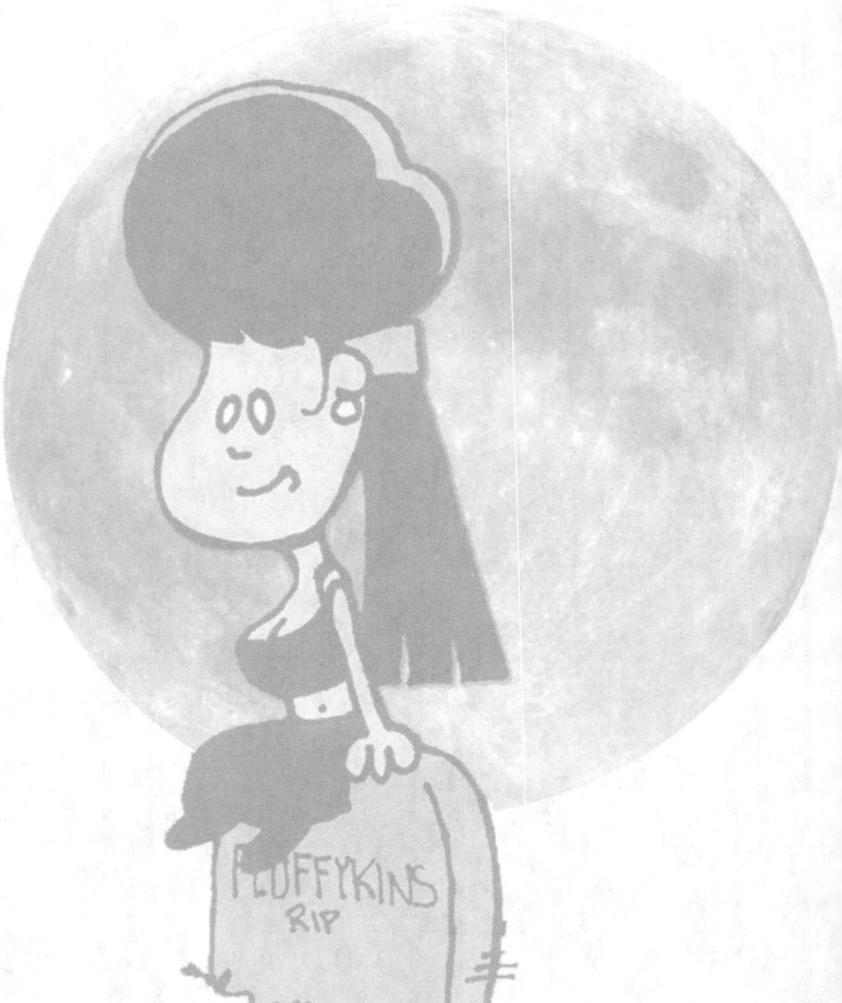
FLUFFYKINS
RIP

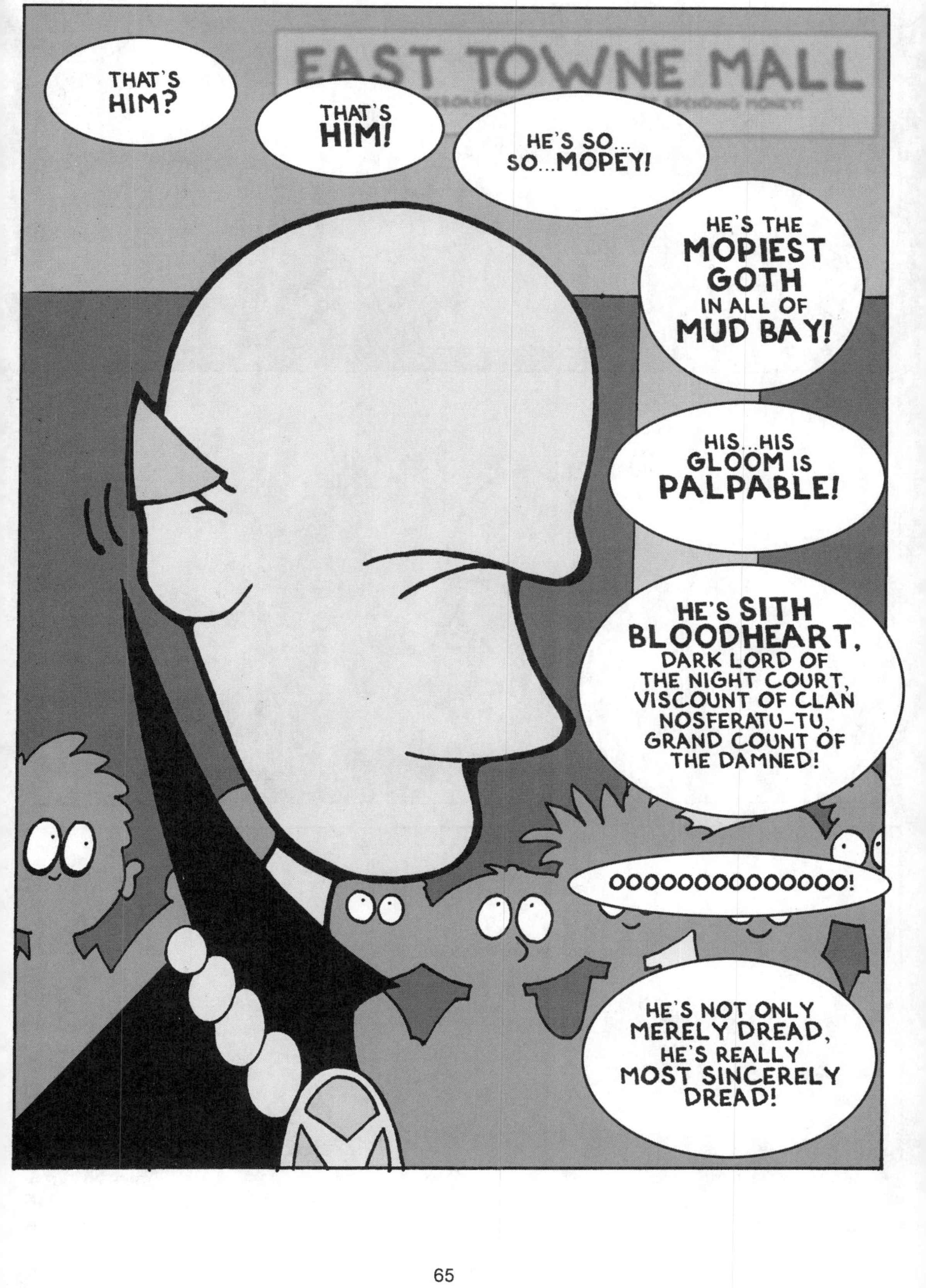
EAST TOWNE MALL
THAT'S HIM?
THAT'S HIM!
HE'S SO... SO...MOPEY!
HE'S THE MOPIEST GOTH IN ALL OF MUD BAY!
HIS...HIS GLOOM IS PALPABLE!
HE'S SITH BLOODHEART, DARK LORD OF THE NIGHT COURT, VISCOUNT OF CLAN NOSFERATU-TU, GRAND COUNT OF THE DAMNED!
OOOOOOOOOOOOOOO!
HE'S NOT ONLY MERELY DREAD, HE'S REALLY MOST SINCERELY DREAD!

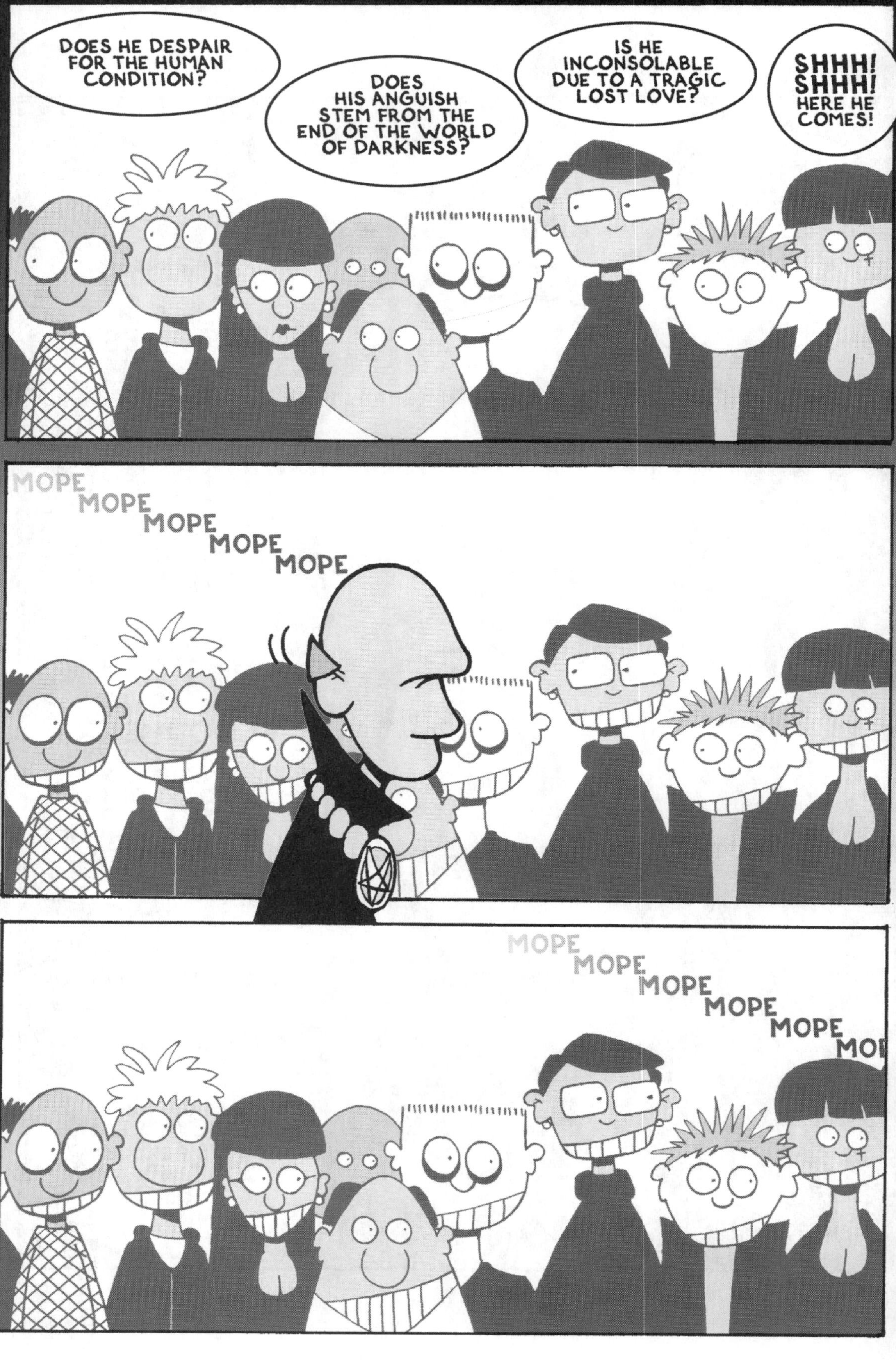
DOES HE DESPAIR FOR THE HUMAN CONDITION?
DOES HIS ANGUISH STEM FROM THE END OF THE WORLD OF DARKNESS?
IS HE INCONSOLABLE DUE TO A TRAGIC LOST LOVE?
SHHH! SHHH! HERE HE COMES!
MOPE MOPE MOPE MOPE MOPE
MOPE MOPE MOPE MOPE MOPE

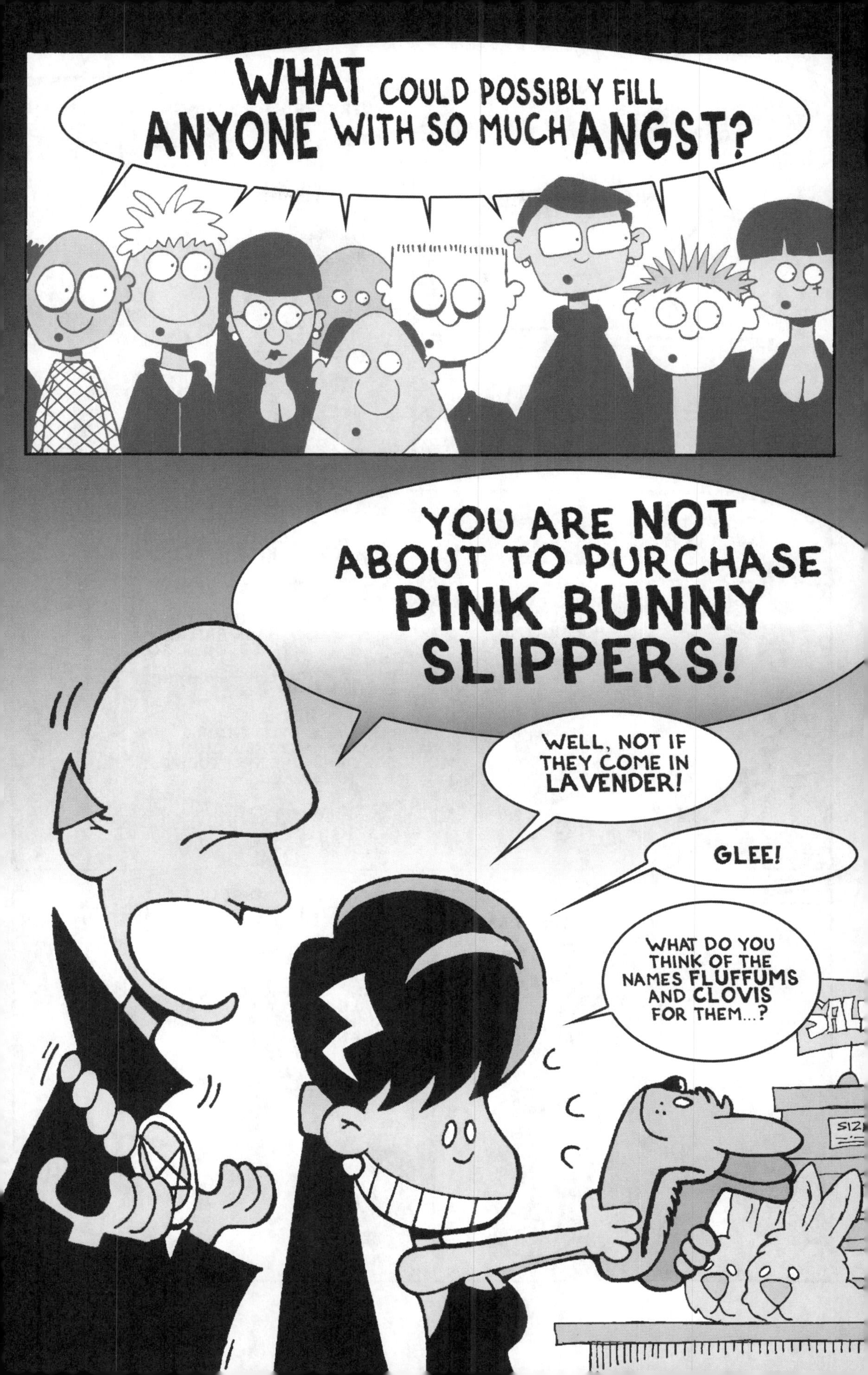
WHAT COULD POSSIBLY FILL ANYONE WITH SO MUCH ANGST?
YOU ARE NOT ABOUT TO PURCHASE PINK BUNNY SLIPPERS!
WELL, NOT IF THEY COME IN LAVENDER!
GLEE!
WHAT DO YOU THINK OF THE NAMES FLUFFUMS AND CLOVIS FOR THEM...?

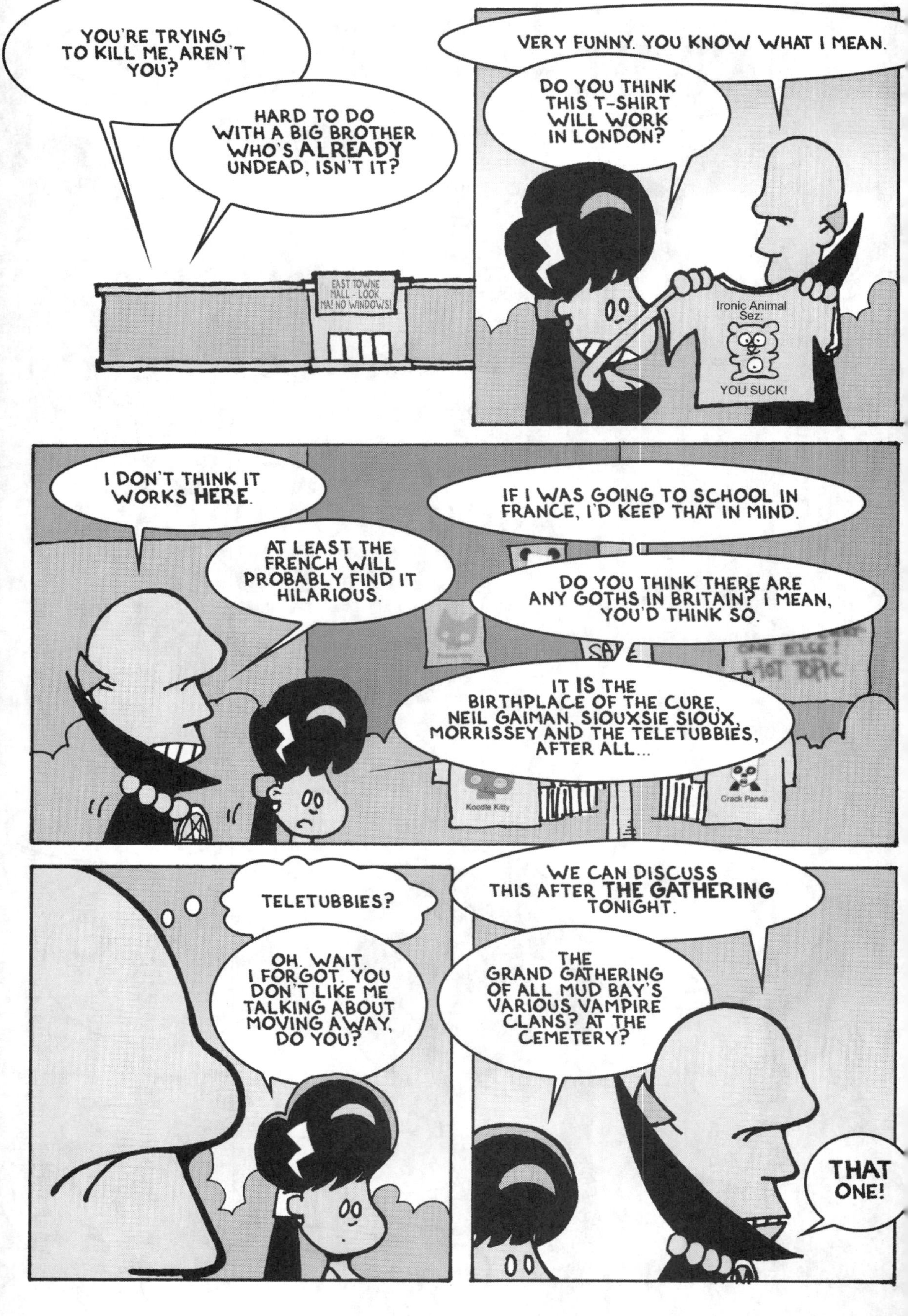
YOU'RE TRYING TO KILL ME, AREN'T YOU?
HARD TO DO WITH A BIG BROTHER WHO'S ALREADY UNDEAD, ISN'T IT?
EAST TOWNE MALL - LOOK, MA! NO WINDOWS!
VERY FUNNY. YOU KNOW WHAT I MEAN.
DO YOU THINK THIS T-SHIRT WILL WORK IN LONDON?
Ironic Animal Sez:
YOU SUCK!
I DON'T THINK IT WORKS HERE.
AT LEAST THE FRENCH WILL PROBABLY FIND IT HILARIOUS.
IF I WAS GOING TO SCHOOL IN FRANCE, I'D KEEP THAT IN MIND.
DO YOU THINK THERE ARE ANY GOTHS IN BRITAIN? I MEAN, YOU'D THINK SO.
IT IS THE BIRTHPLACE OF THE CURE, NEIL GAIMAN, SIOUXSIE SIOUX, MORRISSEY AND THE TELETUBBIES, AFTER ALL...
Koodle Kitty
Crack Panda
TELETUBBIES?
OH. WAIT. I FORGOT. YOU DON'T LIKE ME TALKING ABOUT MOVING AWAY, DO YOU?
WE CAN DISCUSS THIS AFTER THE GATHERING TONIGHT.
THE GRAND GATHERING OF ALL MUD BAY'S VARIOUS VAMPIRE CLANS? AT THE CEMETERY?
THAT ONE!

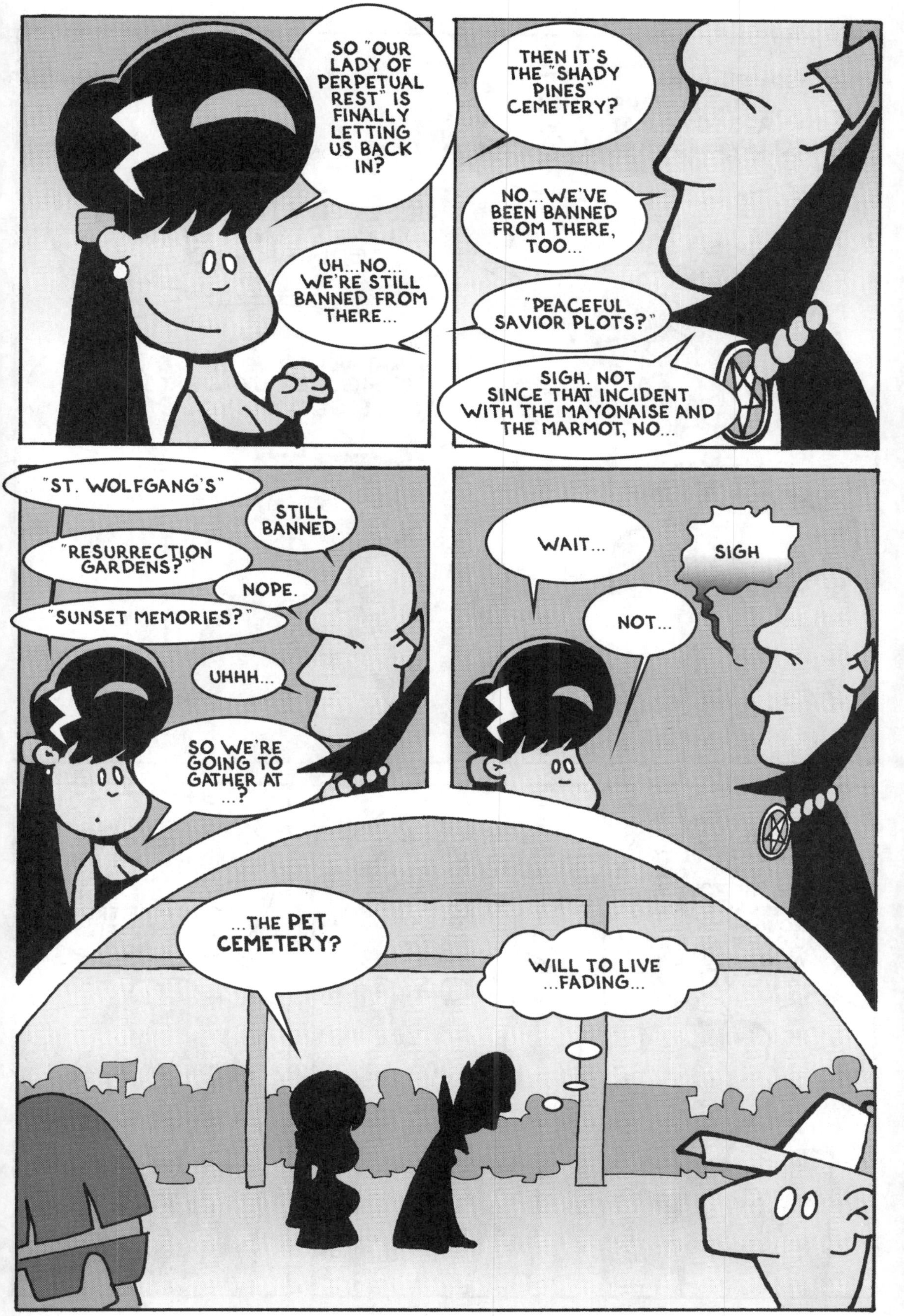
SO "OUR LADY OF PERPETUAL REST" IS FINALLY LETTING US BACK IN?
UH...NO... WE'RE STILL BANNED FROM THERE...
THEN IT'S THE "SHADY PINES" CEMETERY?
NO...WE'VE BEEN BANNED FROM THERE, TOO...
"PEACEFUL SAVIOR PLOTS?"
SIGH. NOT SINCE THAT INCIDENT WITH THE MAYONAISE AND THE MARMOT, NO...
"ST. WOLFGANG'S"
STILL BANNED.
"RESURRECTION GARDENS?"
NOPE.
"SUNSET MEMORIES?"
UHHH...
SO WE'RE GOING TO GATHER AT ...?
WAIT...
SIGH
NOT...
...THE PET CEMETERY?
WILL TO LIVE ...FADING...

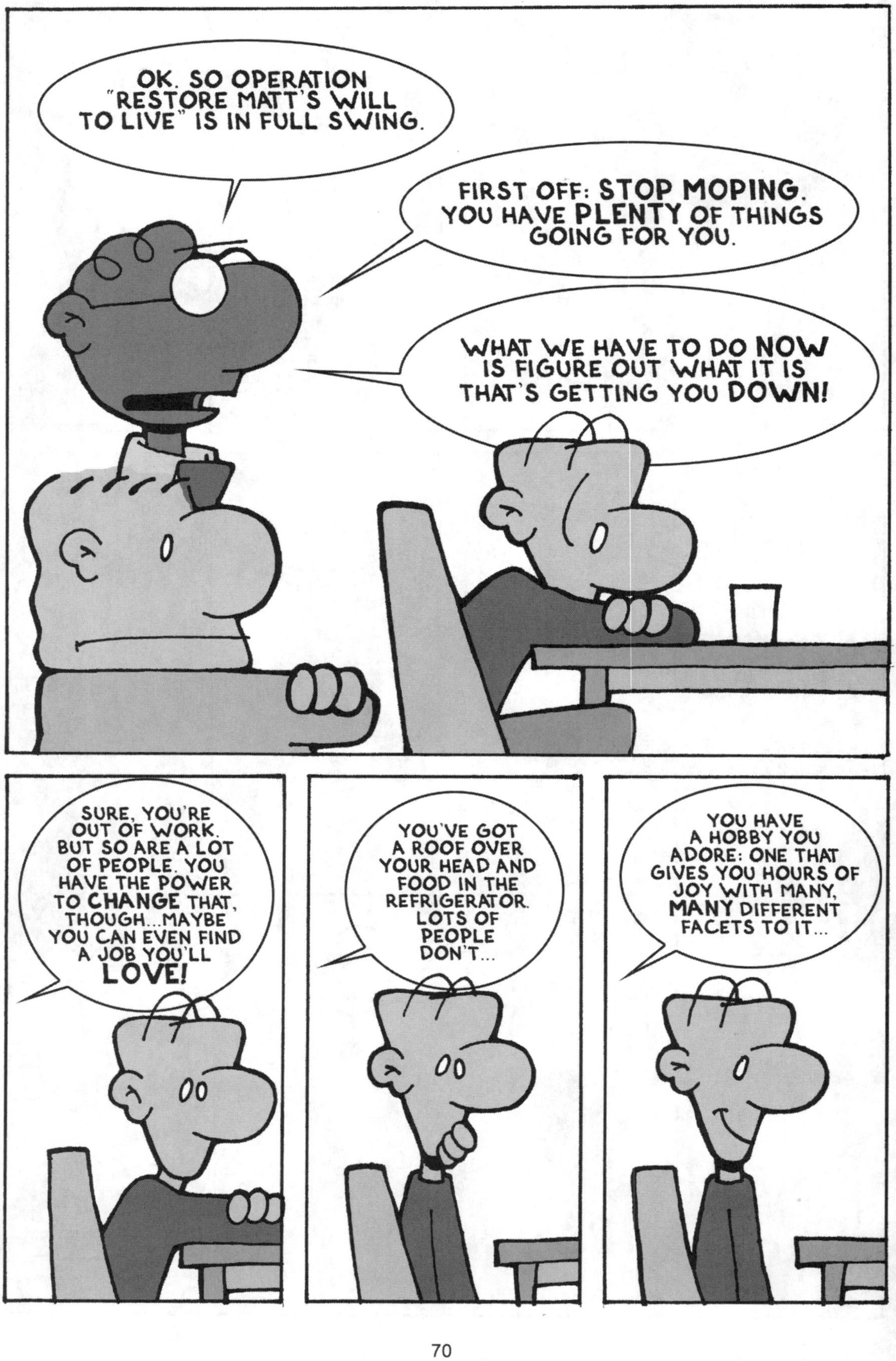
OK. SO OPERATION "RESTORE MATT'S WILL TO LIVE" IS IN FULL SWING.
FIRST OFF: STOP MOPING. YOU HAVE PLENTY OF THINGS GOING FOR YOU.
WHAT WE HAVE TO DO NOW IS FIGURE OUT WHAT IT IS THAT'S GETTING YOU DOWN!
SURE, YOU'RE OUT OF WORK. BUT SO ARE A LOT OF PEOPLE. YOU HAVE THE POWER TO CHANGE THAT, THOUGH...MAYBE YOU CAN EVEN FIND A JOB YOU'LL LOVE!
YOU'VE GOT A ROOF OVER YOUR HEAD AND FOOD IN THE REFRIGERATOR. LOTS OF PEOPLE DON'T...
YOU HAVE A HOBBY YOU ADORE: ONE THAT GIVES YOU HOURS OF JOY WITH MANY, MANY DIFFERENT FACETS TO IT...

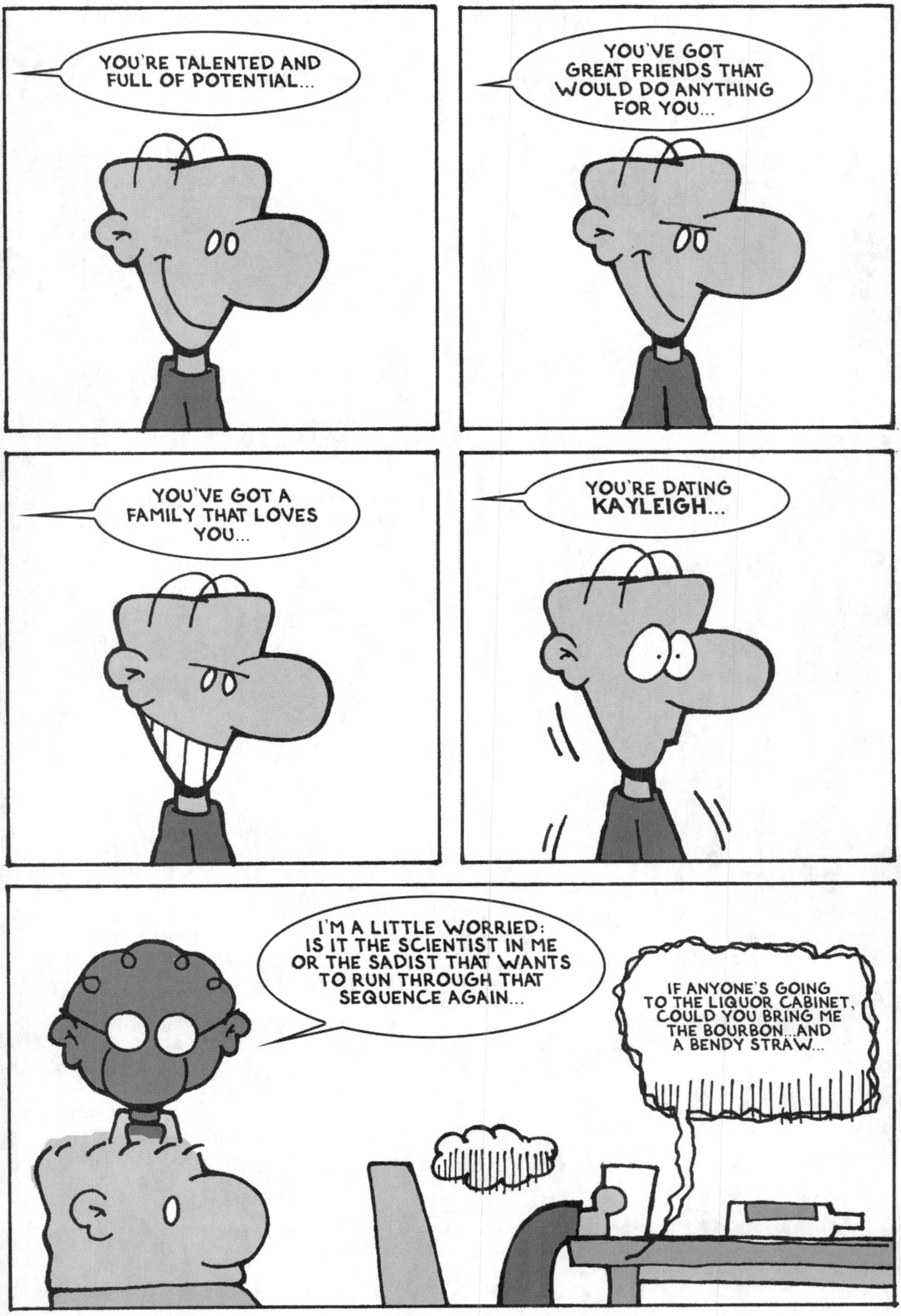
YOU'RE TALENTED AND FULL OF POTENTIAL...
YOU'VE GOT GREAT FRIENDS THAT WOULD DO ANYTHING FOR YOU...
YOU'VE GOT A FAMILY THAT LOVES YOU...
YOU'RE DATING KAYLEIGH...
I'M A LITTLE WORRIED: IS IT THE SCIENTIST IN ME OR THE SADIST THAT WANTS TO RUN THROUGH THAT SEQUENCE AGAIN...
IF ANYONE'S GOING TO THE LIQUOR CABINET, COULD YOU BRING ME THE BOURBON...AND A BENDY STRAW...

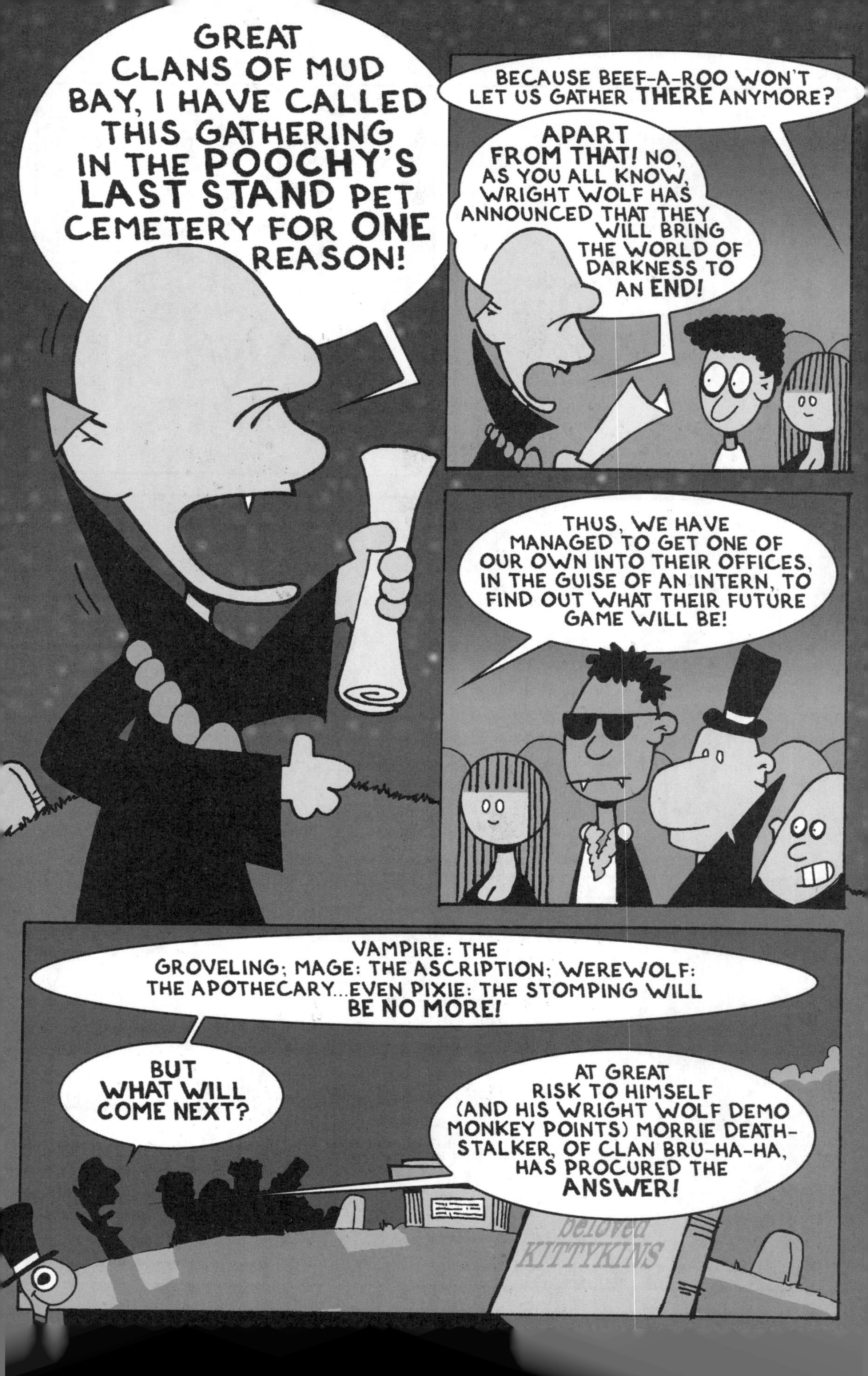
GREAT CLANS OF MUD BAY, I HAVE CALLED THIS GATHERING IN THE POOCHY'S LAST STAND PET CEMETERY FOR ONE REASON!
BECAUSE BEEF-A-ROO WON'T LET US GATHER THERE ANYMORE?
APART FROM THAT! NO, AS YOU ALL KNOW, WRIGHT WOLF HAS ANNOUNCED THAT THEY WILL BRING THE WORLD OF DARKNESS TO AN END!
THUS, WE HAVE MANAGED TO GET ONE OF OUR OWN INTO THEIR OFFICES, IN THE GUISE OF AN INTERN, TO FIND OUT WHAT THEIR FUTURE GAME WILL BE!
VAMPIRE: THE GROVELING; MAGE: THE ASCRIPTION; WEREWOLF: THE APOTHECARY...EVEN PIXIE: THE STOMPING WILL BE NO MORE!
BUT WHAT WILL COME NEXT?
AT GREAT RISK TO HIMSELF (AND HIS WRIGHT WOLF DEMO MONKEY POINTS) MORRIE DEATH-STALKER, OF CLAN BRU-HA-HA, HAS PROCURED THE ANSWER!
beloved KITTYKINS

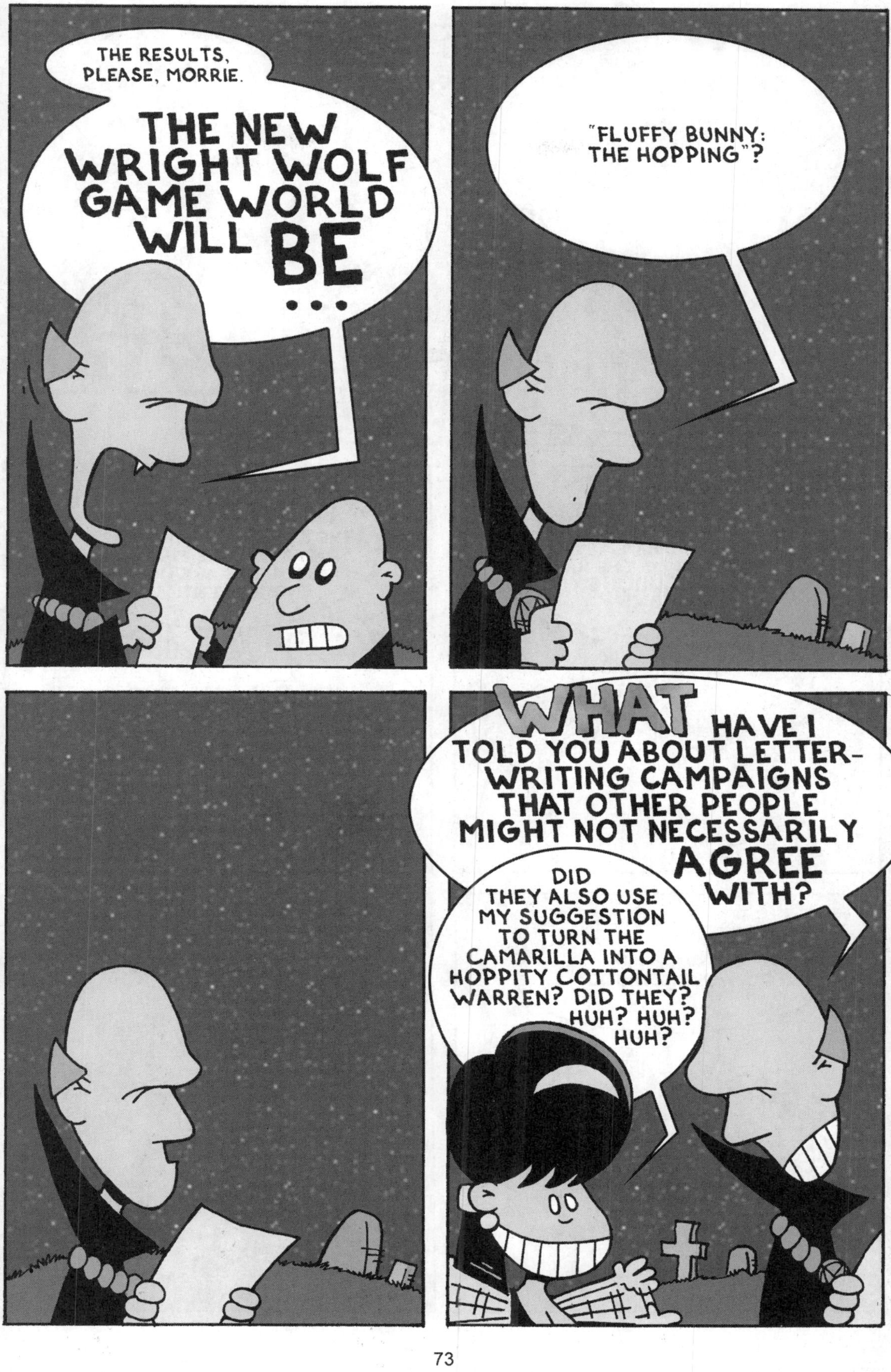
THE RESULTS, PLEASE, MORRIE.
THE NEW WRIGHT WOLF GAME WORLD WILL BE . . .
"FLUFFY BUNNY: THE HOPPING"?
WHAT HAVE I TOLD YOU ABOUT LETTER-WRITING CAMPAIGNS THAT OTHER PEOPLE MIGHT NOT NECESSARILY AGREE WITH?
DID THEY ALSO USE MY SUGGESTION TO TURN THE CAMARILLA INTO A HOPPITY COTTONTAIL WARREN? DID THEY? HUH? HUH? HUH?

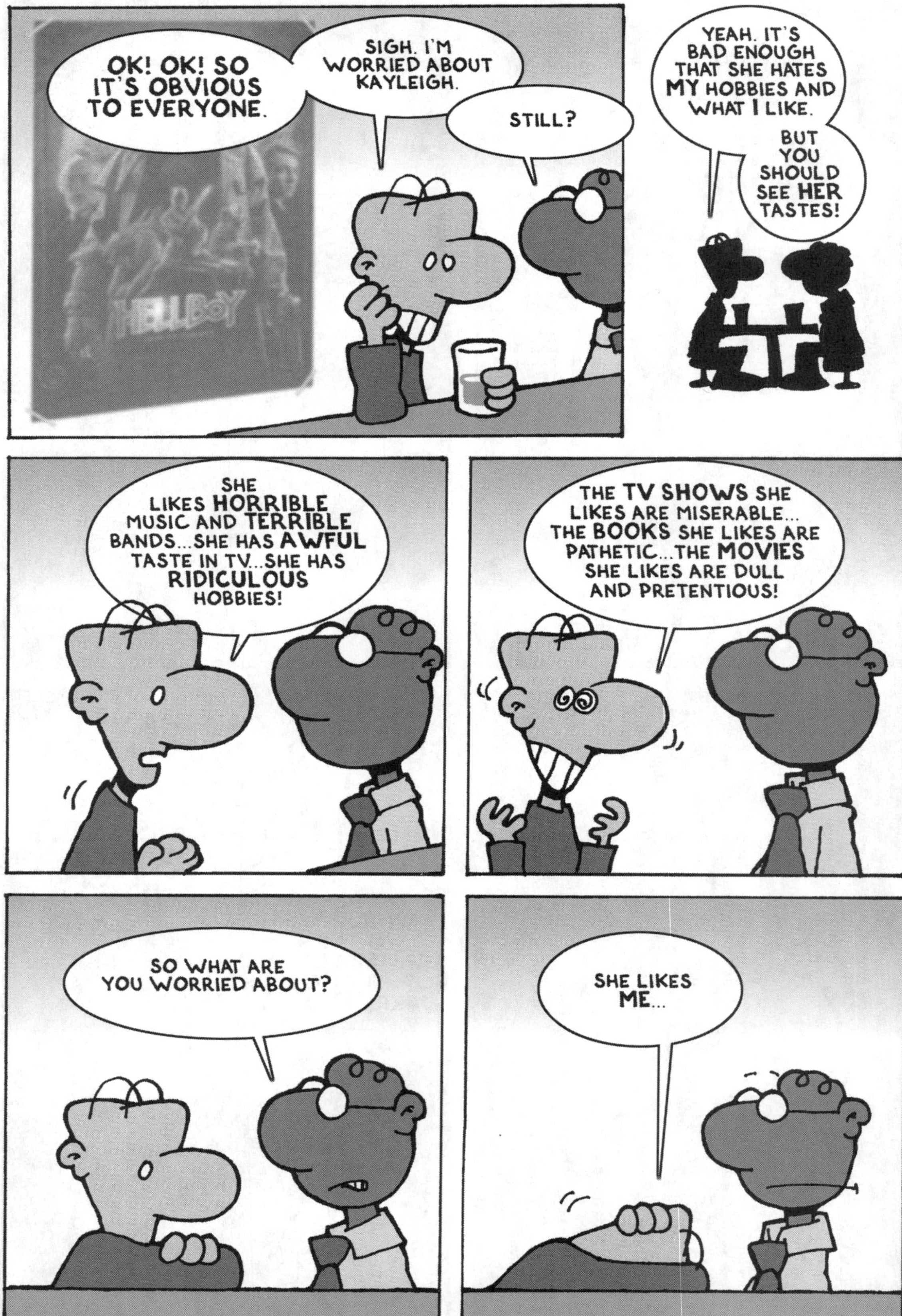
OK! OK! SO IT'S OBVIOUS TO EVERYONE.
SIGH. I'M WORRIED ABOUT KAYLEIGH.
STILL?
YEAH. IT'S BAD ENOUGH THAT SHE HATES MY HOBBIES AND WHAT I LIKE.
BUT YOU SHOULD SEE HER TASTES!
SHE LIKES HORRIBLE MUSIC AND TERRIBLE BANDS...SHE HAS AWFUL TASTE IN TV...SHE HAS RIDICULOUS HOBBIES!
THE TV SHOWS SHE LIKES ARE MISERABLE... THE BOOKS SHE LIKES ARE PATHETIC...THE MOVIES SHE LIKES ARE DULL AND PRETENTIOUS!
SO WHAT ARE YOU WORRIED ABOUT?
SHE LIKES ME...

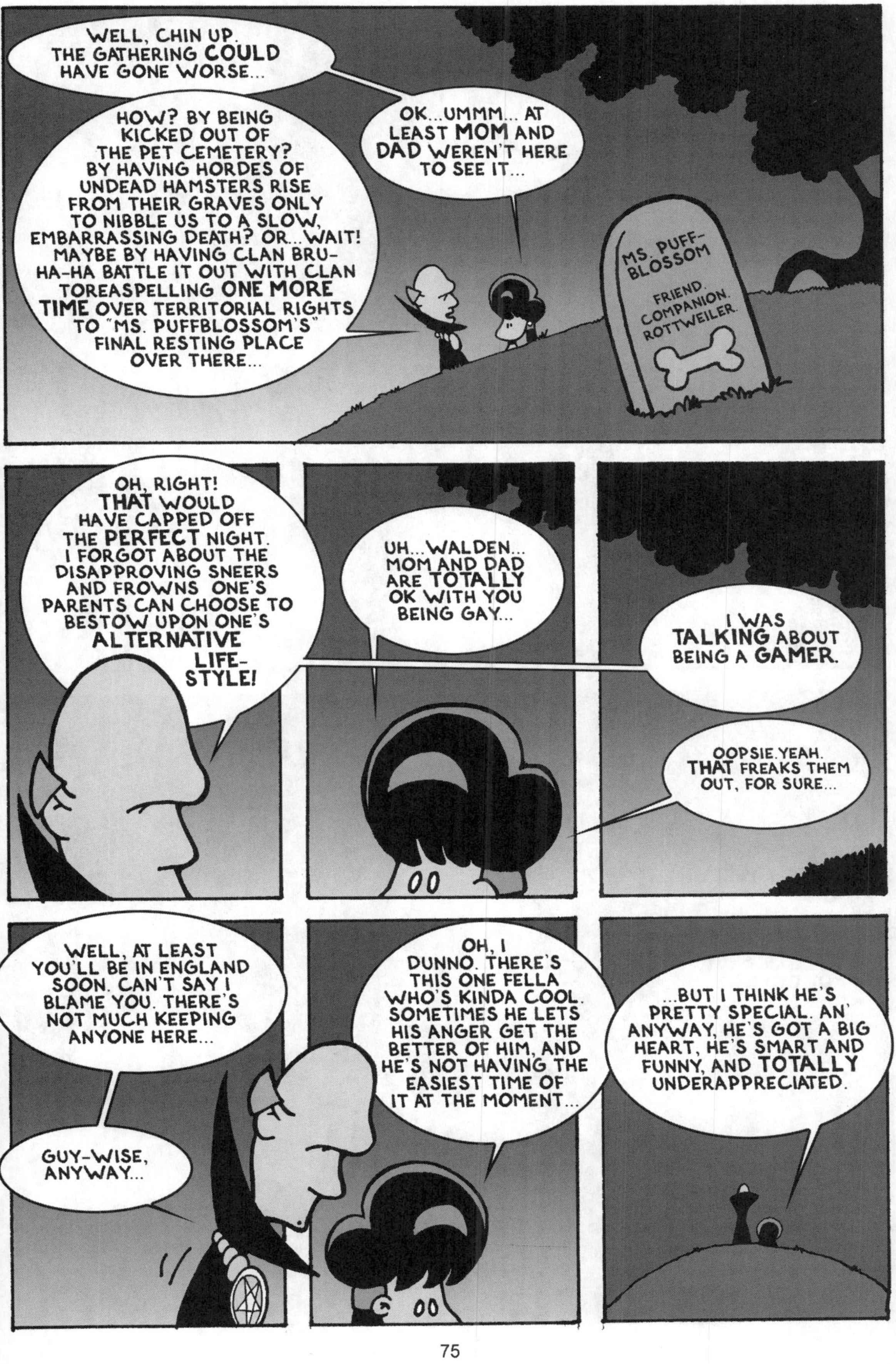
WELL, CHIN UP. THE GATHERING COULD HAVE GONE WORSE...
HOW? BY BEING KICKED OUT OF THE PET CEMETERY? BY HAVING HORDES OF UNDEAD HAMSTERS RISE FROM THEIR GRAVES ONLY TO NIBBLE US TO A SLOW, EMBARRASSING DEATH? OR...WAIT! MAYBE BY HAVING CLAN BRU-HA-HA BATTLE IT OUT WITH CLAN TOREASPELLING ONE MORE TIME OVER TERRITORIAL RIGHTS TO "MS. PUFFBLOSSOM'S" FINAL RESTING PLACE OVER THERE...
OK...UMMM... AT LEAST MOM AND DAD WEREN'T HERE TO SEE IT...
MS. PUFF-BLOSSOM
FRIEND. COMPANION. ROTTWEILER.
OH, RIGHT! THAT WOULD HAVE CAPPED OFF THE PERFECT NIGHT. I FORGOT ABOUT THE DISAPPROVING SNEERS AND FROWNS ONE'S PARENTS CAN CHOOSE TO BESTOW UPON ONE'S ALTERNATIVE LIFE-STYLE!
UH...WALDEN... MOM AND DAD ARE TOTALLY OK WITH YOU BEING GAY...
I WAS TALKING ABOUT BEING A GAMER.
OOPSIE. YEAH. THAT FREAKS THEM OUT, FOR SURE...
WELL, AT LEAST YOU'LL BE IN ENGLAND SOON. CAN'T SAY I BLAME YOU. THERE'S NOT MUCH KEEPING ANYONE HERE...
GUY-WISE, ANYWAY...
OH, I DUNNO. THERE'S THIS ONE FELLA WHO'S KINDA COOL. SOMETIMES HE LETS HIS ANGER GET THE BETTER OF HIM, AND HE'S NOT HAVING THE EASIEST TIME OF IT AT THE MOMENT...
...BUT I THINK HE'S PRETTY SPECIAL. AN' ANYWAY, HE'S GOT A BIG HEART, HE'S SMART AND FUNNY, AND TOTALLY UNDERAPPRECIATED.

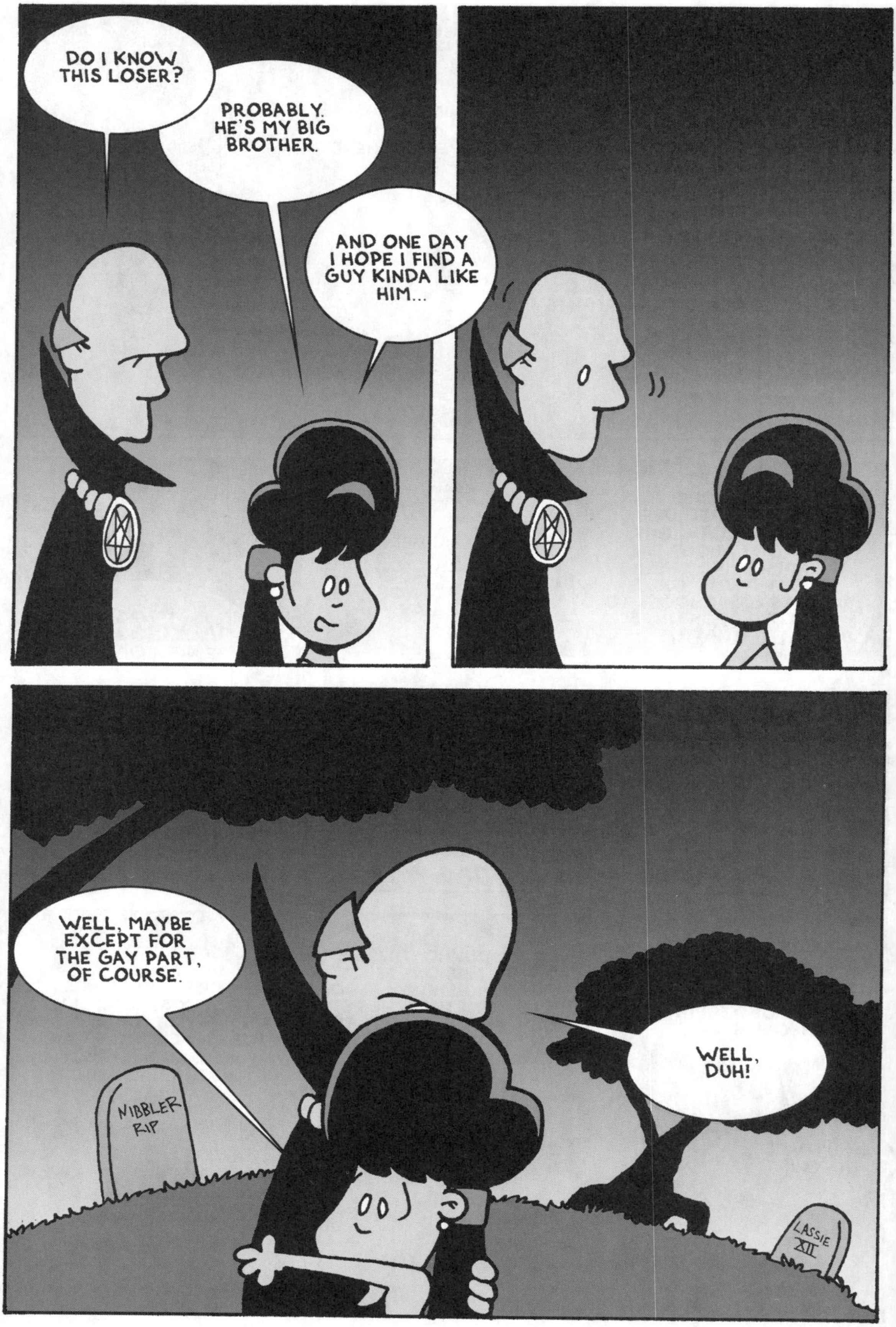
DO I KNOW THIS LOSER?
PROBABLY. HE'S MY BIG BROTHER.
AND ONE DAY I HOPE I FIND A GUY KINDA LIKE HIM...
WELL, MAYBE EXCEPT FOR THE GAY PART, OF COURSE.
WELL, DUH!
NIBBLER RIP
LASSIE XII

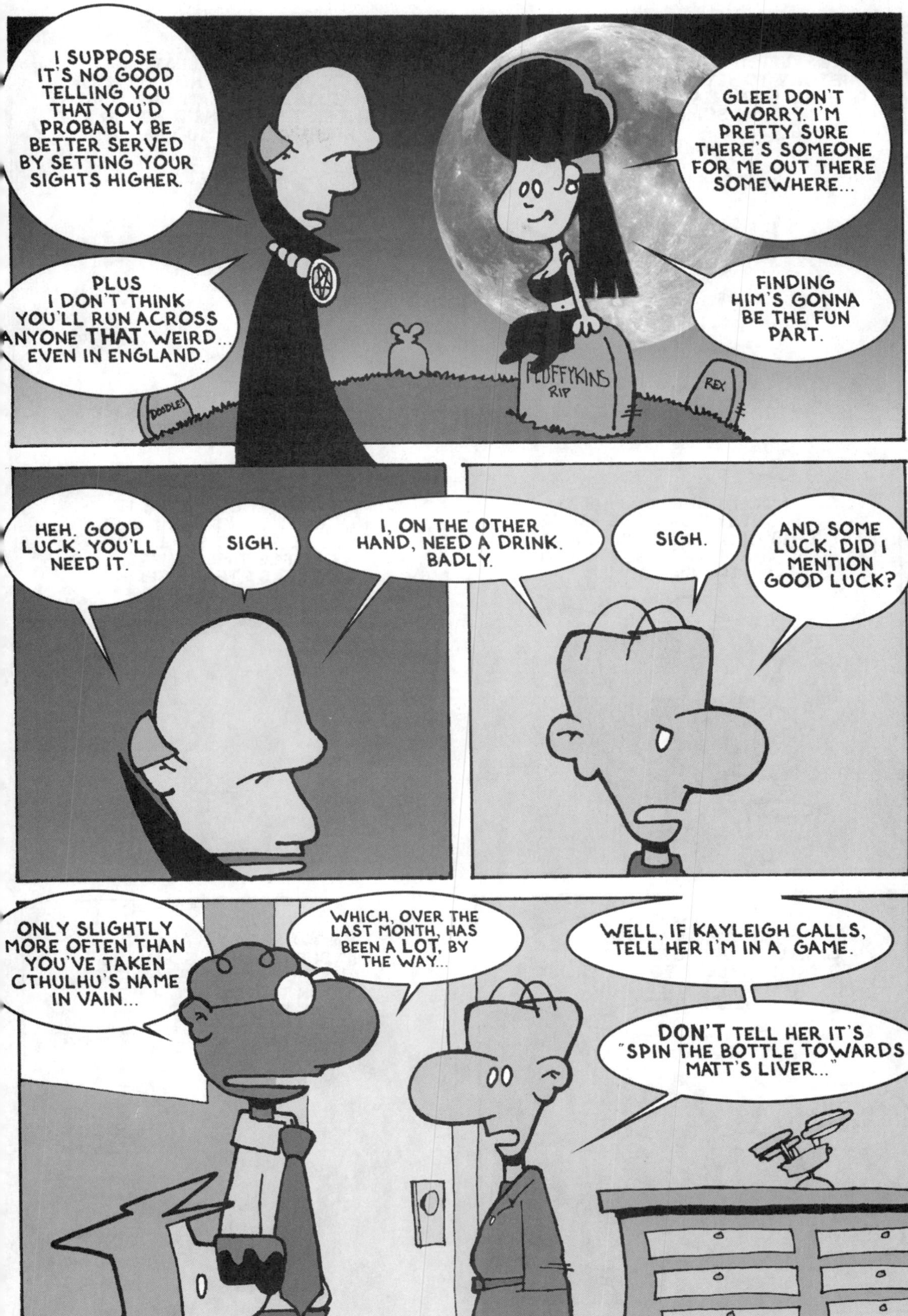
I SUPPOSE IT'S NO GOOD TELLING YOU THAT YOU'D PROBABLY BE BETTER SERVED BY SETTING YOUR SIGHTS HIGHER.
PLUS I DON'T THINK YOU'LL RUN ACROSS ANYONE THAT WEIRD... EVEN IN ENGLAND.
GLEE! DON'T WORRY. I'M PRETTY SURE THERE'S SOMEONE FOR ME OUT THERE SOMEWHERE...
FINDING HIM'S GONNA BE THE FUN PART.
DOODLES
FLUFFYKINS RIP
REX
HEH. GOOD LUCK. YOU'LL NEED IT.
SIGH.
I, ON THE OTHER HAND, NEED A DRINK. BADLY.
SIGH.
AND SOME LUCK. DID I MENTION GOOD LUCK?
ONLY SLIGHTLY MORE OFTEN THAN YOU'VE TAKEN CTHULHU'S NAME IN VAIN...
WHICH, OVER THE LAST MONTH, HAS BEEN A LOT, BY THE WAY...
WELL, IF KAYLEIGH CALLS, TELL HER I'M IN A GAME.
DON'T TELL HER IT'S "SPIN THE BOTTLE TOWARDS MATT'S LIVER..."

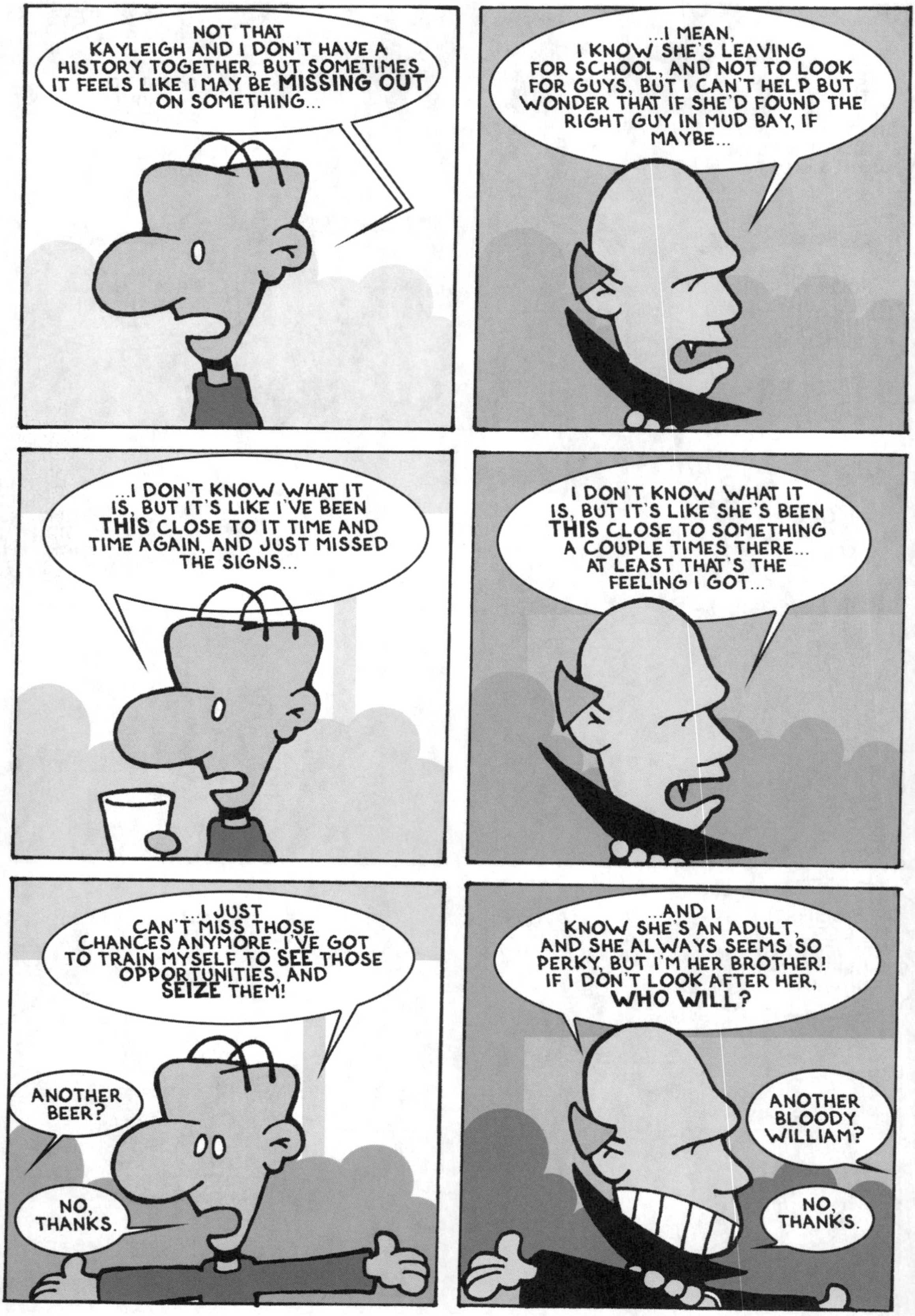
NOT THAT KAYLEIGH AND I DON'T HAVE A HISTORY TOGETHER, BUT SOMETIMES IT FEELS LIKE I MAY BE MISSING OUT ON SOMETHING...
...I MEAN, I KNOW SHE'S LEAVING FOR SCHOOL, AND NOT TO LOOK FOR GUYS, BUT I CAN'T HELP BUT WONDER THAT IF SHE'D FOUND THE RIGHT GUY IN MUD BAY, IF MAYBE...
...I DON'T KNOW WHAT IT IS, BUT IT'S LIKE I'VE BEEN THIS CLOSE TO IT TIME AND TIME AGAIN, AND JUST MISSED THE SIGNS...
I DON'T KNOW WHAT IT IS, BUT IT'S LIKE SHE'S BEEN THIS CLOSE TO SOMETHING A COUPLE TIMES THERE... AT LEAST THAT'S THE FEELING I GOT...
...I JUST CAN'T MISS THOSE CHANCES ANYMORE. I'VE GOT TO TRAIN MYSELF TO SEE THOSE OPPORTUNITIES, AND SEIZE THEM!
ANOTHER BEER?
NO, THANKS.
...AND I KNOW SHE'S AN ADULT, AND SHE ALWAYS SEEMS SO PERKY, BUT I'M HER BROTHER! IF I DON'T LOOK AFTER HER, WHO WILL?
ANOTHER BLOODY WILLIAM?
NO, THANKS.

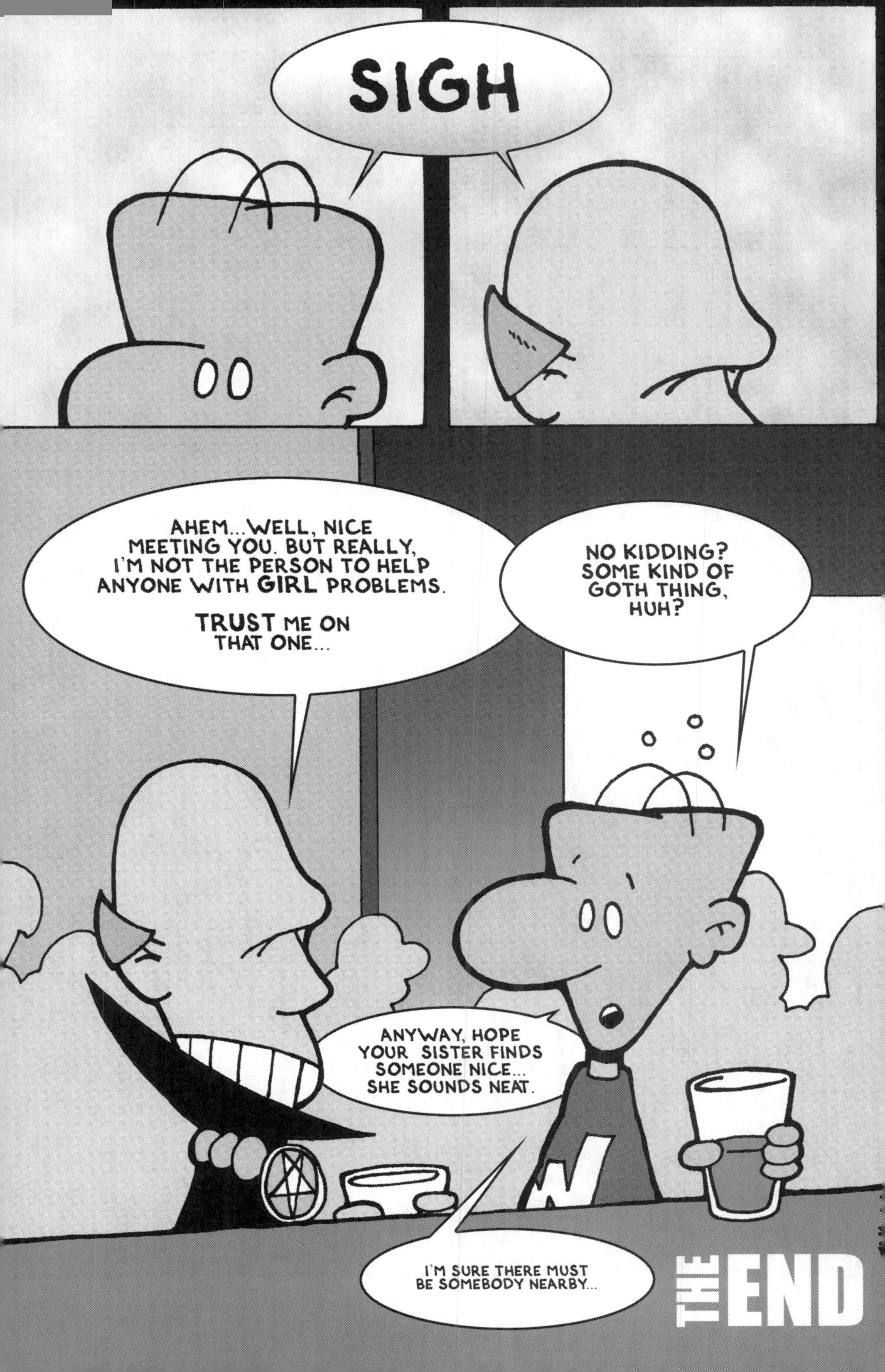
SIGH
AHEM... WELL, NICE MEETING YOU. BUT REALLY, I'M NOT THE PERSON TO HELP ANYONE WITH GIRL PROBLEMS.
TRUST ME ON THAT ONE...
NO KIDDING? SOME KIND OF GOTH THING, HUH?
ANYWAY, HOPE YOUR SISTER FINDS SOMEONE NICE... SHE SOUNDS NEAT.
I'M SURE THERE MUST BE SOMEBODY NEARBY...
THE END

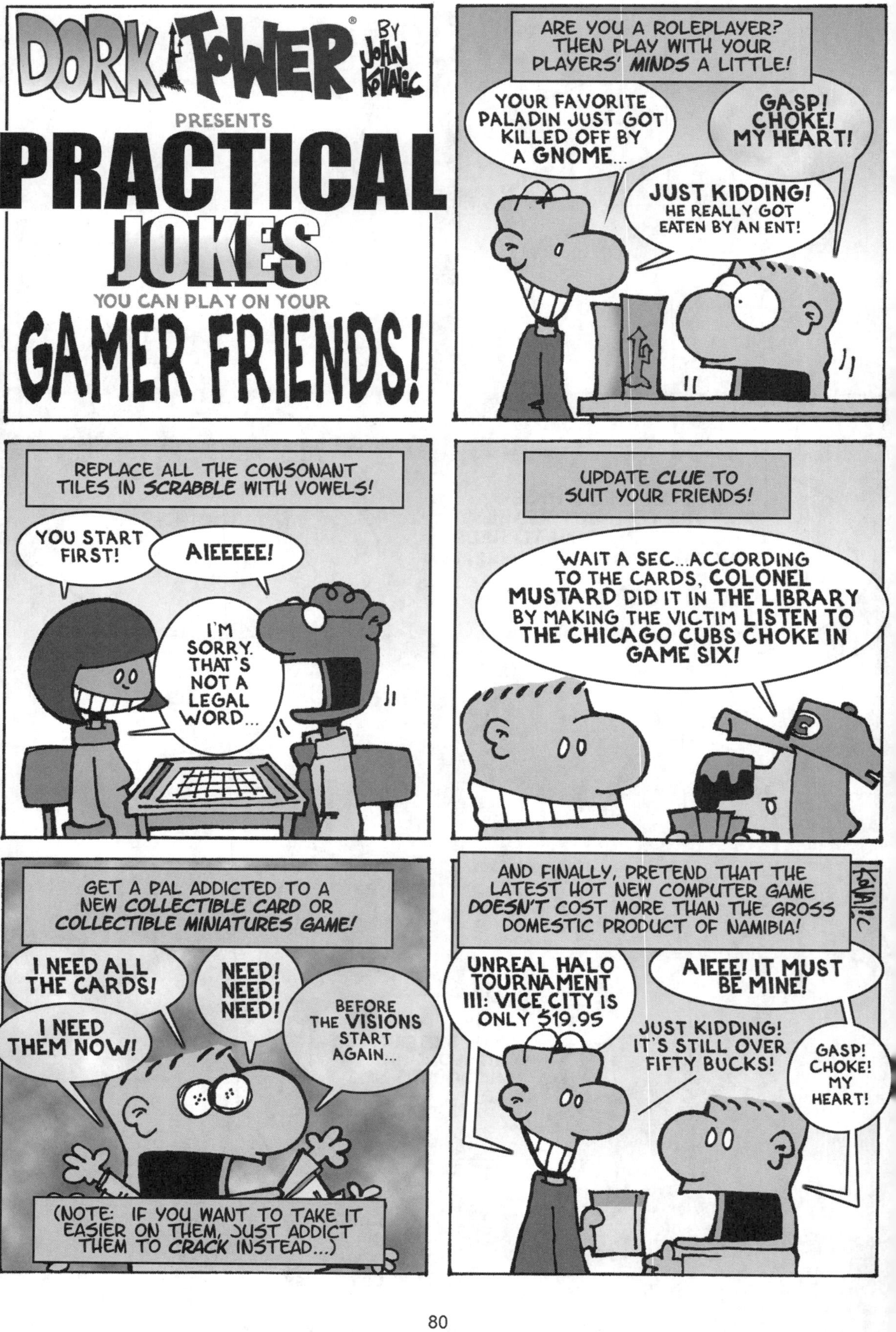

DORK TOWER® BY JOHN KOVALIC
PRESENTS
PRACTICAL JOKES YOU CAN PLAY ON YOUR GAMER FRIENDS!
ARE YOU A ROLEPLAYER? THEN PLAY WITH YOUR PLAYERS' MINDS A LITTLE!
YOUR FAVORITE PALADIN JUST GOT KILLED OFF BY A GNOME...
GASP! CHOKE! MY HEART!
JUST KIDDING! HE REALLY GOT EATEN BY AN ENT!
REPLACE ALL THE CONSONANT TILES IN SCRABBLE WITH VOWELS!
YOU START FIRST!
AIEEEEE!
I'M SORRY. THAT'S NOT A LEGAL WORD...
UPDATE CLUE TO SUIT YOUR FRIENDS!
WAIT A SEC...ACCORDING TO THE CARDS, COLONEL MUSTARD DID IT IN THE LIBRARY BY MAKING THE VICTIM LISTEN TO THE CHICAGO CUBS CHOKE IN GAME SIX!
GET A PAL ADDICTED TO A NEW COLLECTIBLE CARD OR COLLECTIBLE MINIATURES GAME!
I NEED ALL THE CARDS!
NEED! NEED! NEED!
I NEED THEM NOW!
BEFORE THE VISIONS START AGAIN...
(NOTE: IF YOU WANT TO TAKE IT EASIER ON THEM, JUST ADDICT THEM TO CRACK INSTEAD...)
AND FINALLY, PRETEND THAT THE LATEST HOT NEW COMPUTER GAME DOESN'T COST MORE THAN THE GROSS DOMESTIC PRODUCT OF NAMIBIA!
KOVALIC
UNREAL HALO TOURNAMENT III: VICE CITY IS ONLY $19.95
AIEEE! IT MUST BE MINE!
JUST KIDDING! IT'S STILL OVER FIFTY BUCKS!
GASP! CHOKE! MY HEART!

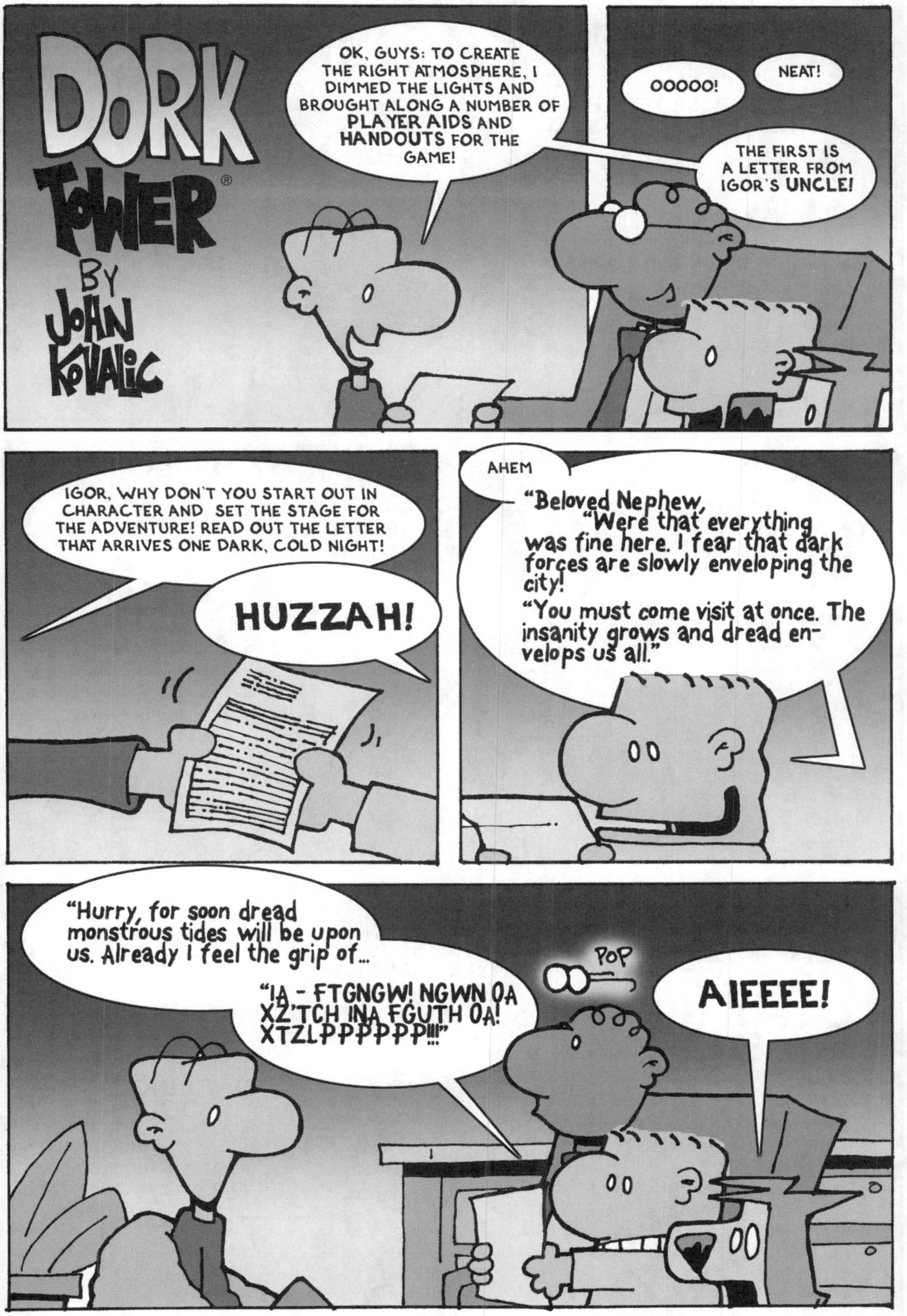
DORK TOWER®
BY JOHN KOVALIC
OK, GUYS: TO CREATE THE RIGHT ATMOSPHERE, I DIMMED THE LIGHTS AND BROUGHT ALONG A NUMBER OF PLAYER AIDS AND HANDOUTS FOR THE GAME!
OOOOO!
NEAT!
THE FIRST IS A LETTER FROM IGOR'S UNCLE!
IGOR, WHY DON'T YOU START OUT IN CHARACTER AND SET THE STAGE FOR THE ADVENTURE! READ OUT THE LETTER THAT ARRIVES ONE DARK, COLD NIGHT!
HUZZAH!
AHEM
"Beloved Nephew, "Were that everything was fine here. I fear that dark forces are slowly enveloping the city!
"You must come visit at once. The insanity grows and dread envelops us all."
"Hurry, for soon dread monstrous tides will be upon us. Already I feel the grip of...
"IA - FTGNGW! NGWN OA XZ'TCH INA FGUTH OA! XTZLPPPPPPP!!!"
POP
AIEEEE!

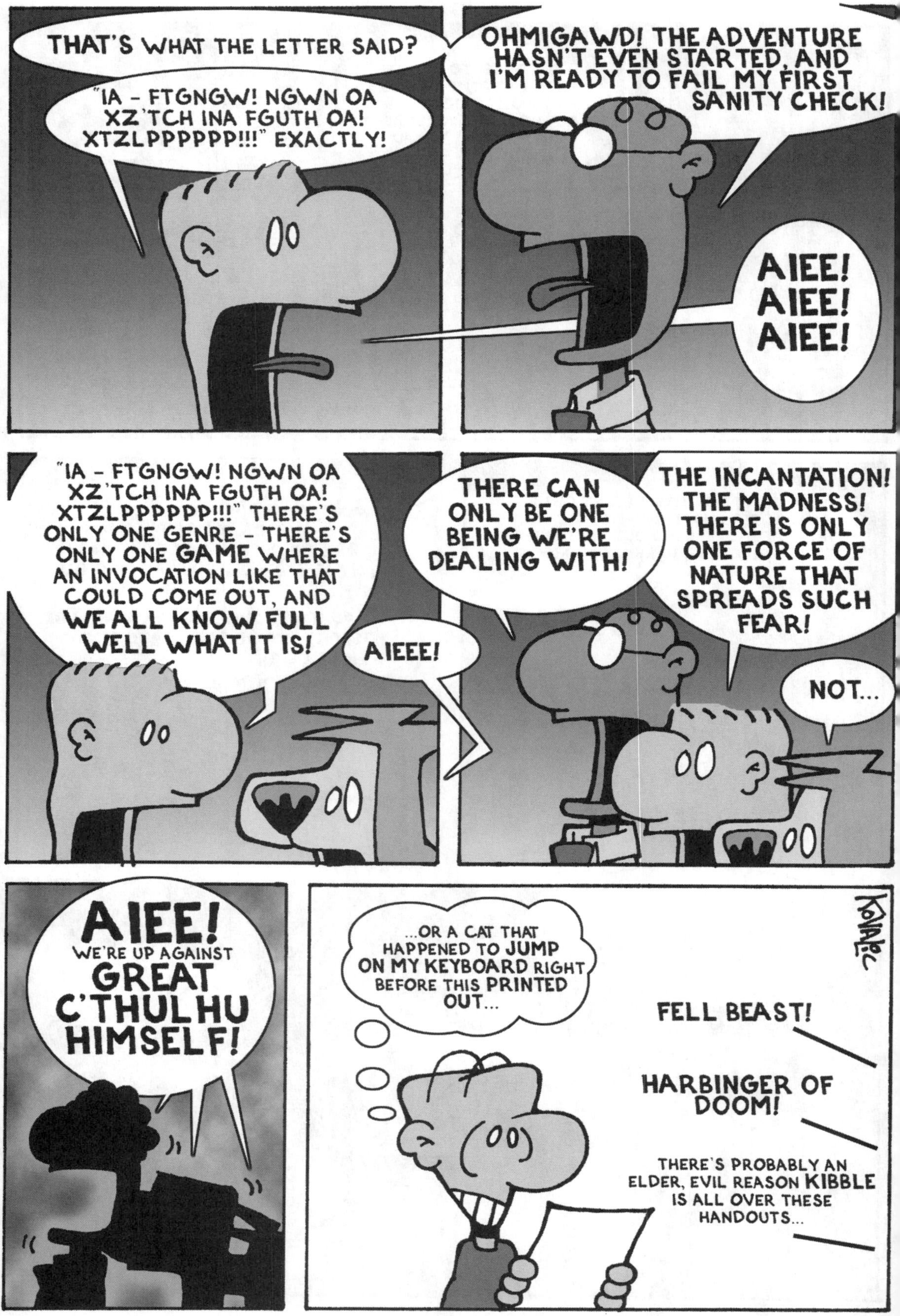

THAT'S WHAT THE LETTER SAID?
"IA - FTGNGW! NGWN OA XZ'TCH INA FGUTH OA! XTZLPPPPPP!!!" EXACTLY!
OHMIGAWD! THE ADVENTURE HASN'T EVEN STARTED, AND I'M READY TO FAIL MY FIRST SANITY CHECK!
AIEE! AIEE! AIEE!
"IA - FTGNGW! NGWN OA XZ'TCH INA FGUTH OA! XTZLPPPPPP!!!" THERE'S ONLY ONE GENRE - THERE'S ONLY ONE GAME WHERE AN INVOCATION LIKE THAT COULD COME OUT, AND WE ALL KNOW FULL WELL WHAT IT IS!
AIEEE!
THERE CAN ONLY BE ONE BEING WE'RE DEALING WITH!
THE INCANTATION! THE MADNESS! THERE IS ONLY ONE FORCE OF NATURE THAT SPREADS SUCH FEAR!
NOT...
AIEE! WE'RE UP AGAINST GREAT C'THULHU HIMSELF!
...OR A CAT THAT HAPPENED TO JUMP ON MY KEYBOARD RIGHT BEFORE THIS PRINTED OUT...
FELL BEAST!
HARBINGER OF DOOM!
THERE'S PROBABLY AN ELDER, EVIL REASON KIBBLE IS ALL OVER THESE HANDOUTS...
KOVALIC

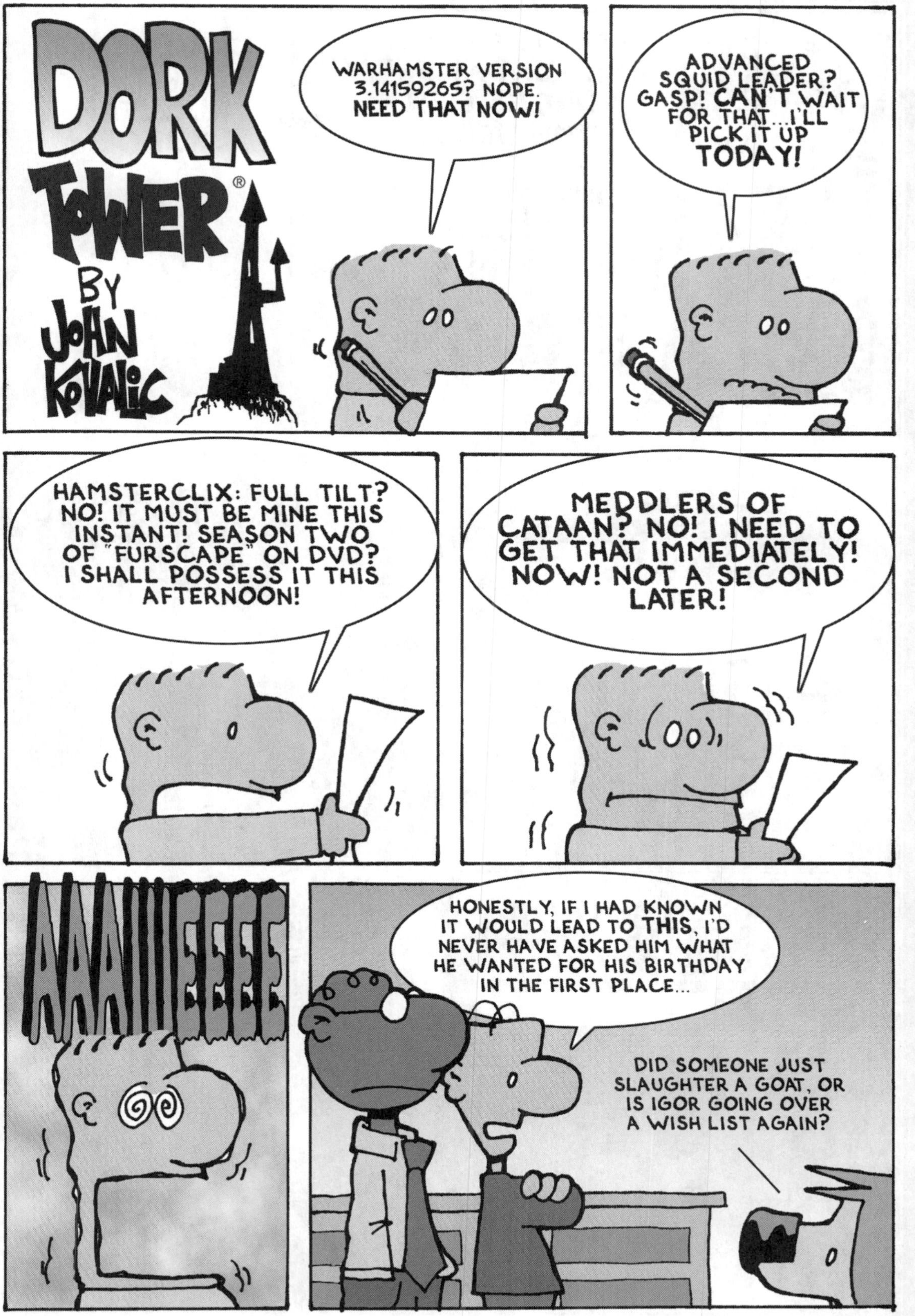
DORK TOWER®
BY JOHN KOVALIC
WARHAMSTER VERSION 3.14159265? NOPE. NEED THAT NOW!
ADVANCED SQUID LEADER? GASP! CAN'T WAIT FOR THAT...I'LL PICK IT UP TODAY!
HAMSTERCLIX: FULL TILT? NO! IT MUST BE MINE THIS INSTANT! SEASON TWO OF "FURSCAPE" ON DVD? I SHALL POSSESS IT THIS AFTERNOON!
MEDDLERS OF CATAAN? NO! I NEED TO GET THAT IMMEDIATELY! NOW! NOT A SECOND LATER!
AAAIIIEEEE
HONESTLY, IF I HAD KNOWN IT WOULD LEAD TO THIS, I'D NEVER HAVE ASKED HIM WHAT HE WANTED FOR HIS BIRTHDAY IN THE FIRST PLACE...
DID SOMEONE JUST SLAUGHTER A GOAT, OR IS IGOR GOING OVER A WISH LIST AGAIN?

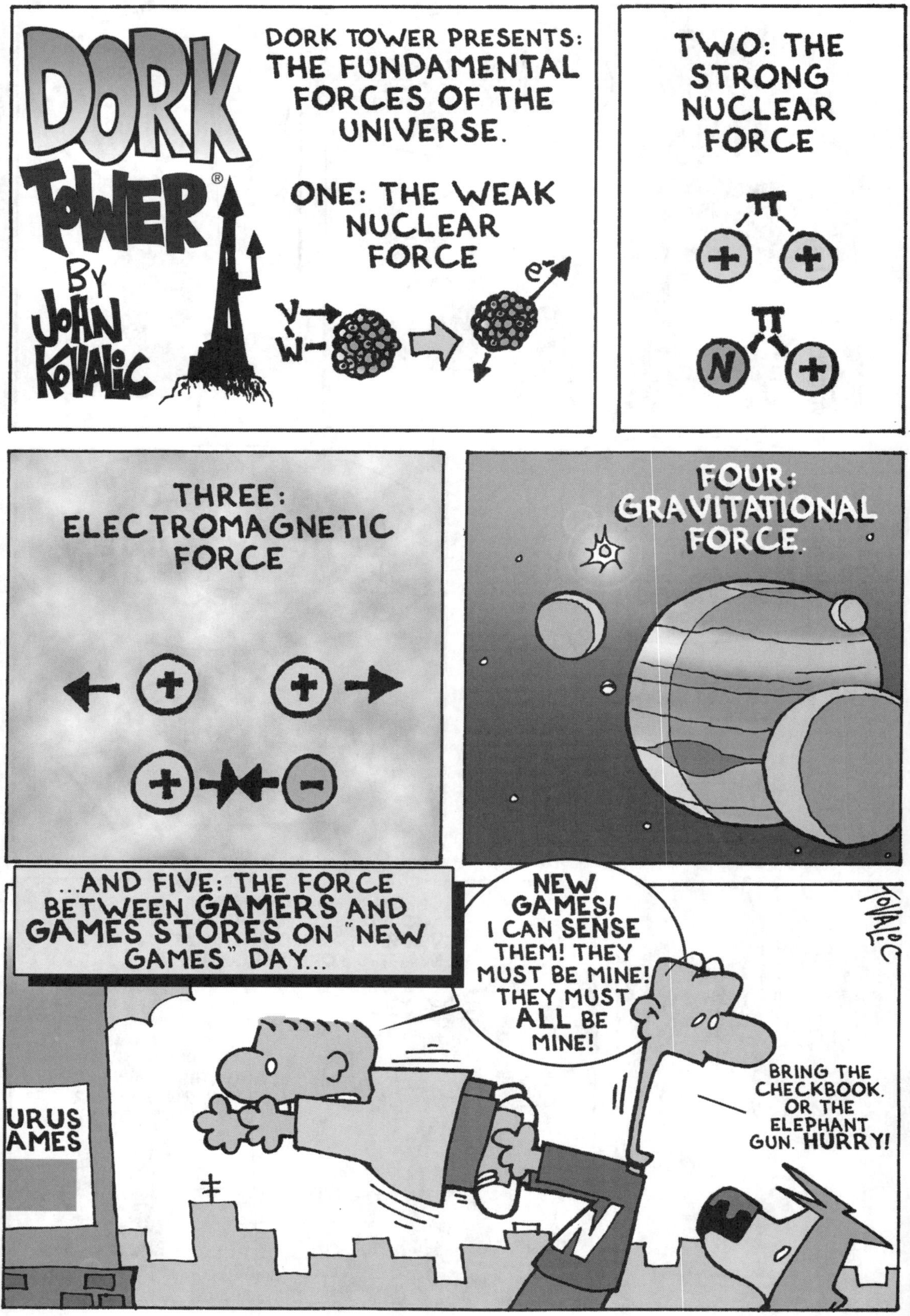
DORK TOWER
BY JOHN KOVALIC
DORK TOWER PRESENTS: THE FUNDAMENTAL FORCES OF THE UNIVERSE.
ONE: THE WEAK NUCLEAR FORCE
TWO: THE STRONG NUCLEAR FORCE
THREE: ELECTROMAGNETIC FORCE
FOUR: GRAVITATIONAL FORCE.
...AND FIVE: THE FORCE BETWEEN GAMERS AND GAMES STORES ON "NEW GAMES" DAY...
NEW GAMES! I CAN SENSE THEM! THEY MUST BE MINE! THEY MUST ALL BE MINE!
BRING THE CHECKBOOK. OR THE ELEPHANT GUN. HURRY!
URUS
AMES
KOVALIC

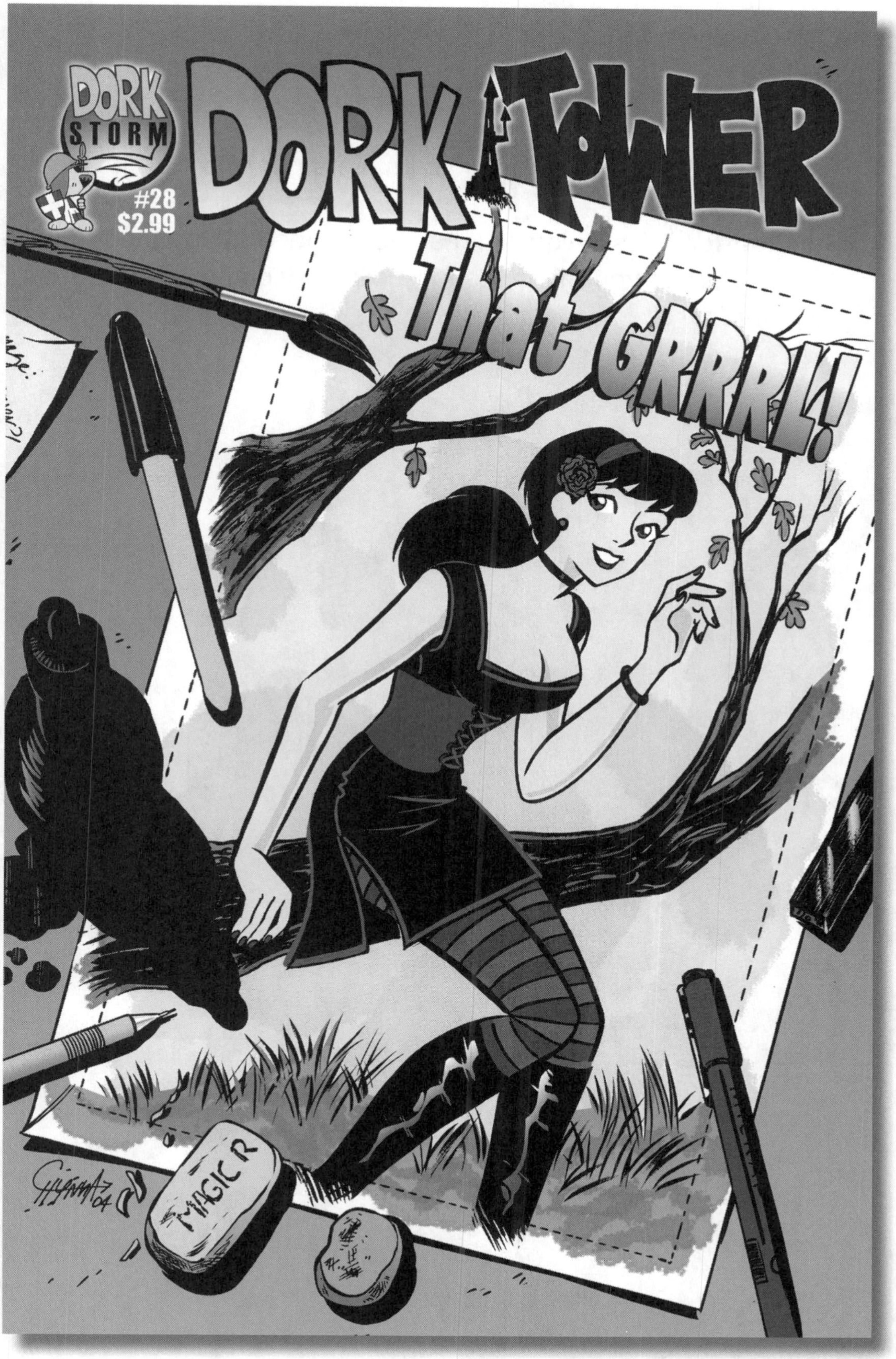
DORK STORM
DORK TOWER
#28
$2.99
That GRRRL!
MAGIC R

Baldrick : Don't worry, Mister B: I have a *cunning plan* to solve the problem.
Blackadder : Yes Baldrick, let us not forget that you tried to solve the problem of your mother's low ceiling by cutting off her head.
- Blackadder III

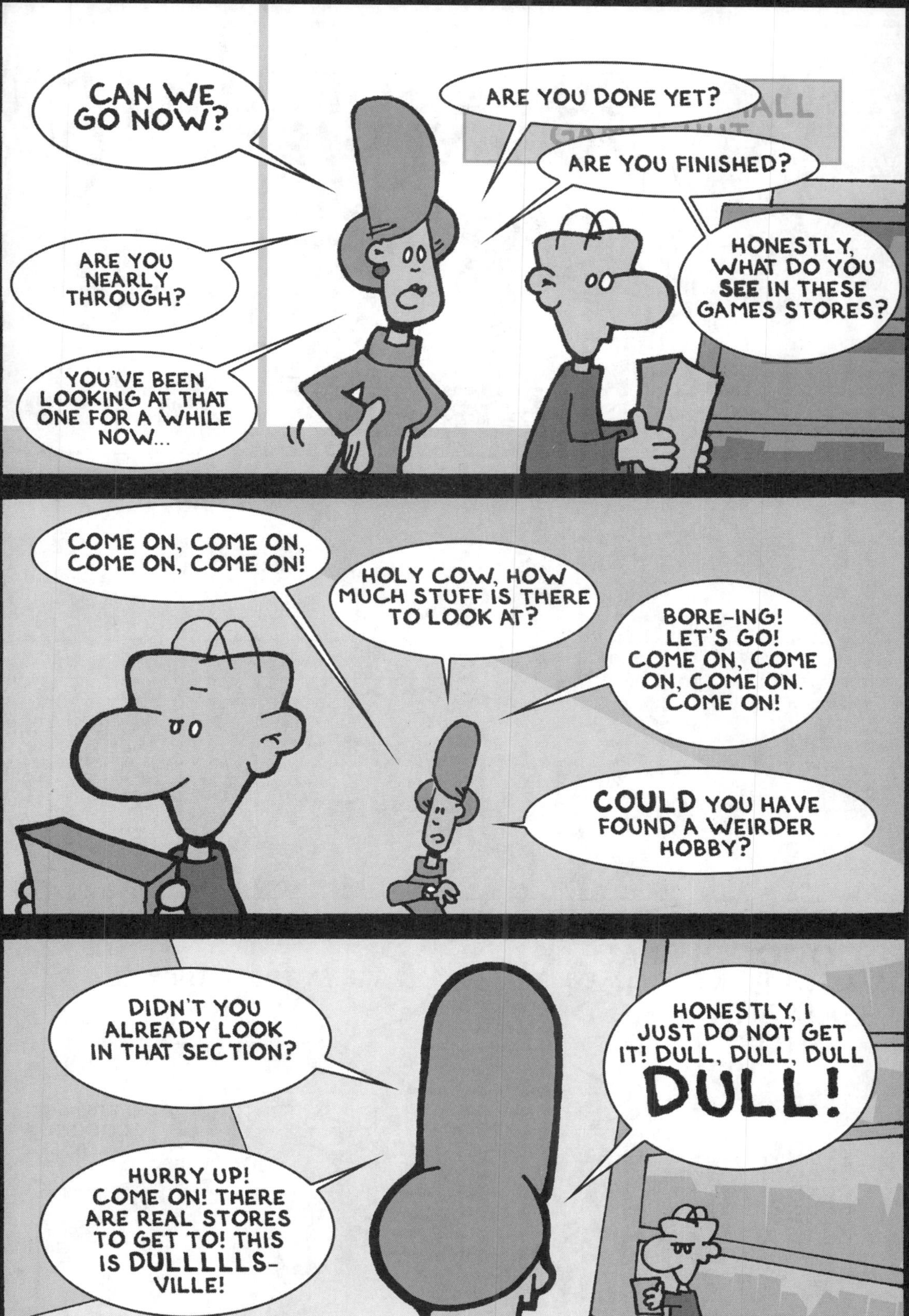
CAN WE GO NOW?
ARE YOU DONE YET?
ARE YOU FINISHED?
ARE YOU NEARLY THROUGH?
YOU'VE BEEN LOOKING AT THAT ONE FOR A WHILE NOW...
HONESTLY, WHAT DO YOU SEE IN THESE GAMES STORES?
COME ON, COME ON, COME ON, COME ON!
HOLY COW, HOW MUCH STUFF IS THERE TO LOOK AT?
BORE-ING! LET'S GO! COME ON, COME ON, COME ON. COME ON!
COULD YOU HAVE FOUND A WEIRDER HOBBY?
DIDN'T YOU ALREADY LOOK IN THAT SECTION?
HONESTLY, I JUST DO NOT GET IT! DULL, DULL, DULL DULL!
HURRY UP! COME ON! THERE ARE REAL STORES TO GET TO! THIS IS DULLLLLS-VILLE!

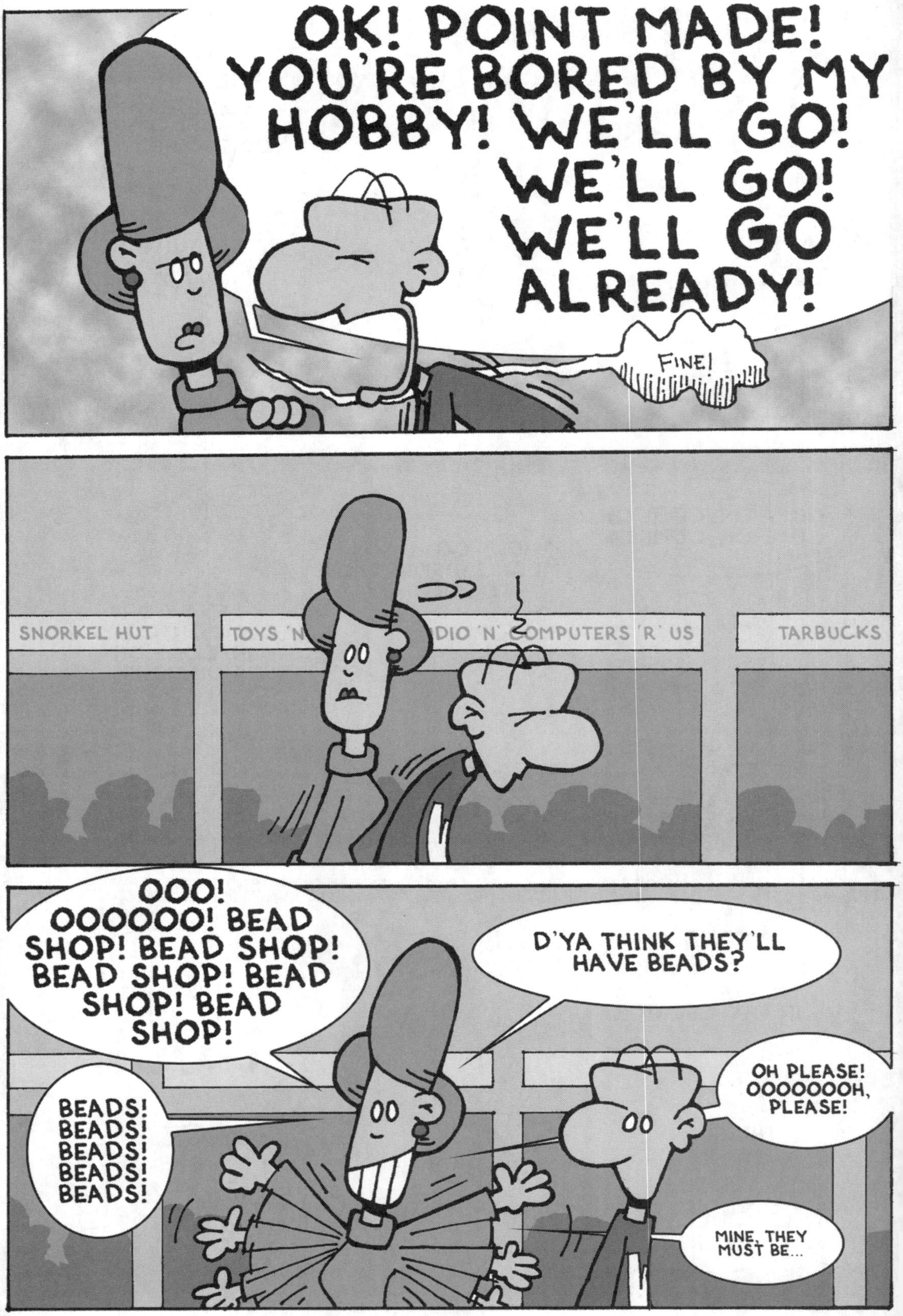
OK! POINT MADE! YOU'RE BORED BY MY HOBBY! WE'LL GO! WE'LL GO! WE'LL GO ALREADY!
FINE!
SNORKEL HUT
TOYS 'N
DIO 'N' COMPUTERS 'R' US
TARBUCKS
OOO! OOOOOO! BEAD SHOP! BEAD SHOP! BEAD SHOP! BEAD SHOP! BEAD SHOP!
D'YA THINK THEY'LL HAVE BEADS?
BEADS! BEADS! BEADS! BEADS! BEADS!
OH PLEASE! OOOOOOOH, PLEASE!
MINE, THEY MUST BE...

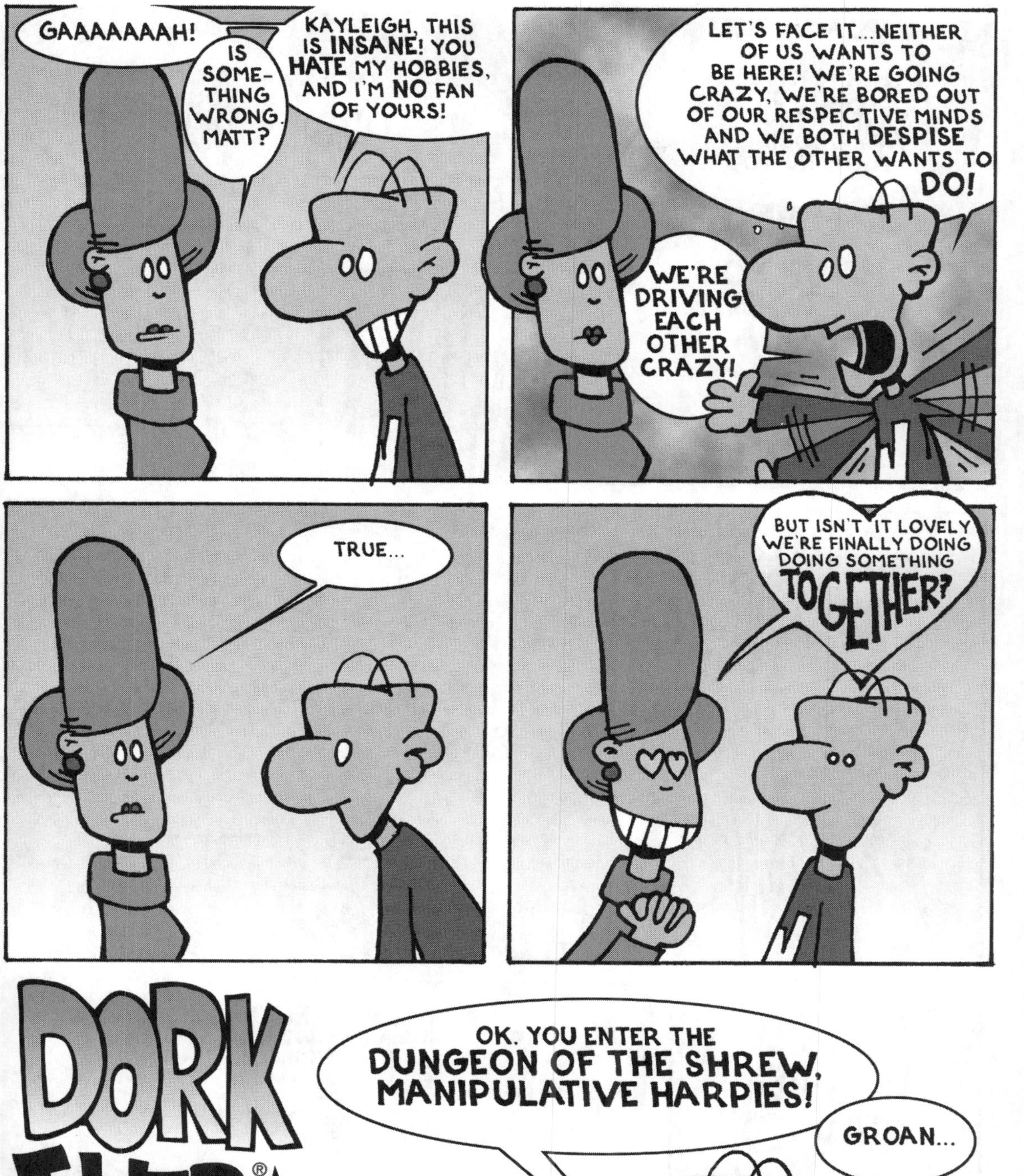
GAAAAAAAH!
IS SOMETHING WRONG, MATT?
KAYLEIGH, THIS IS INSANE! YOU HATE MY HOBBIES, AND I'M NO FAN OF YOURS!
LET'S FACE IT...NEITHER OF US WANTS TO BE HERE! WE'RE GOING CRAZY, WE'RE BORED OUT OF OUR RESPECTIVE MINDS AND WE BOTH DESPISE WHAT THE OTHER WANTS TO DO!
WE'RE DRIVING EACH OTHER CRAZY!
TRUE...
BUT ISN'T IT LOVELY WE'RE FINALLY DOING DOING SOMETHING TOGETHER?

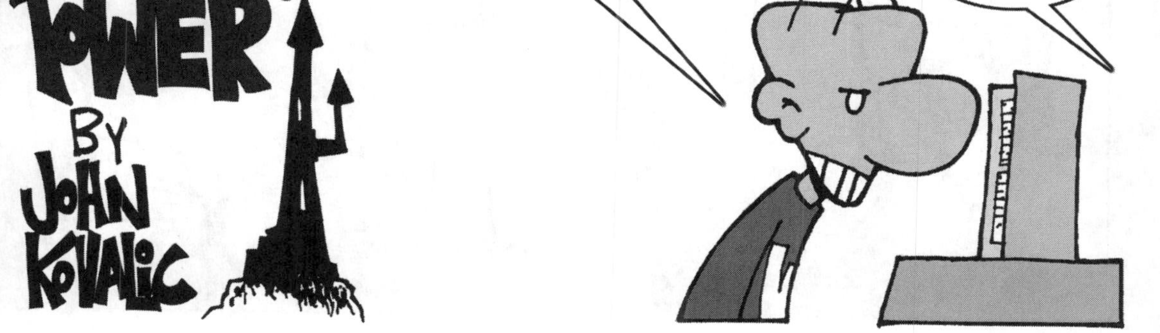
DORK TOWER®
BY JOHN KOVALIC
OK. YOU ENTER THE DUNGEON OF THE SHREW, MANIPULATIVE HARPIES!
GROAN...

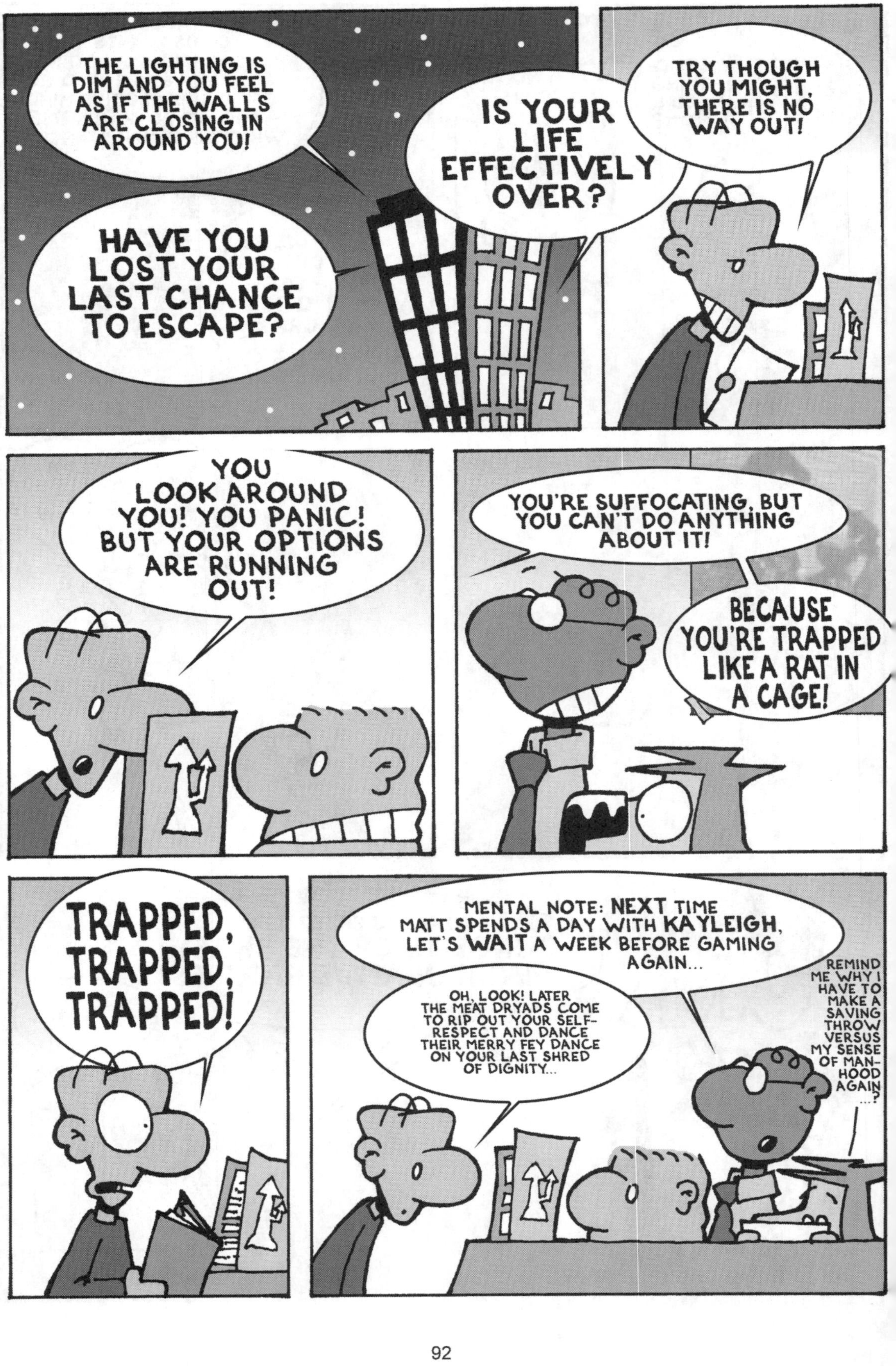
THE LIGHTING IS DIM AND YOU FEEL AS IF THE WALLS ARE CLOSING IN AROUND YOU!
HAVE YOU LOST YOUR LAST CHANCE TO ESCAPE?
IS YOUR LIFE EFFECTIVELY OVER?
TRY THOUGH YOU MIGHT, THERE IS NO WAY OUT!
YOU LOOK AROUND YOU! YOU PANIC! BUT YOUR OPTIONS ARE RUNNING OUT!
YOU'RE SUFFOCATING, BUT YOU CAN'T DO ANYTHING ABOUT IT!
BECAUSE YOU'RE TRAPPED LIKE A RAT IN A CAGE!
TRAPPED, TRAPPED, TRAPPED!
MENTAL NOTE: NEXT TIME MATT SPENDS A DAY WITH KAYLEIGH, LET'S WAIT A WEEK BEFORE GAMING AGAIN...
OH, LOOK! LATER THE MEAT DRYADS COME TO RIP OUT YOUR SELF-RESPECT AND DANCE THEIR MERRY FEY DANCE ON YOUR LAST SHRED OF DIGNITY...
REMIND ME WHY I HAVE TO MAKE A SAVING THROW VERSUS MY SENSE OF MAN-HOOD AGAIN ...?

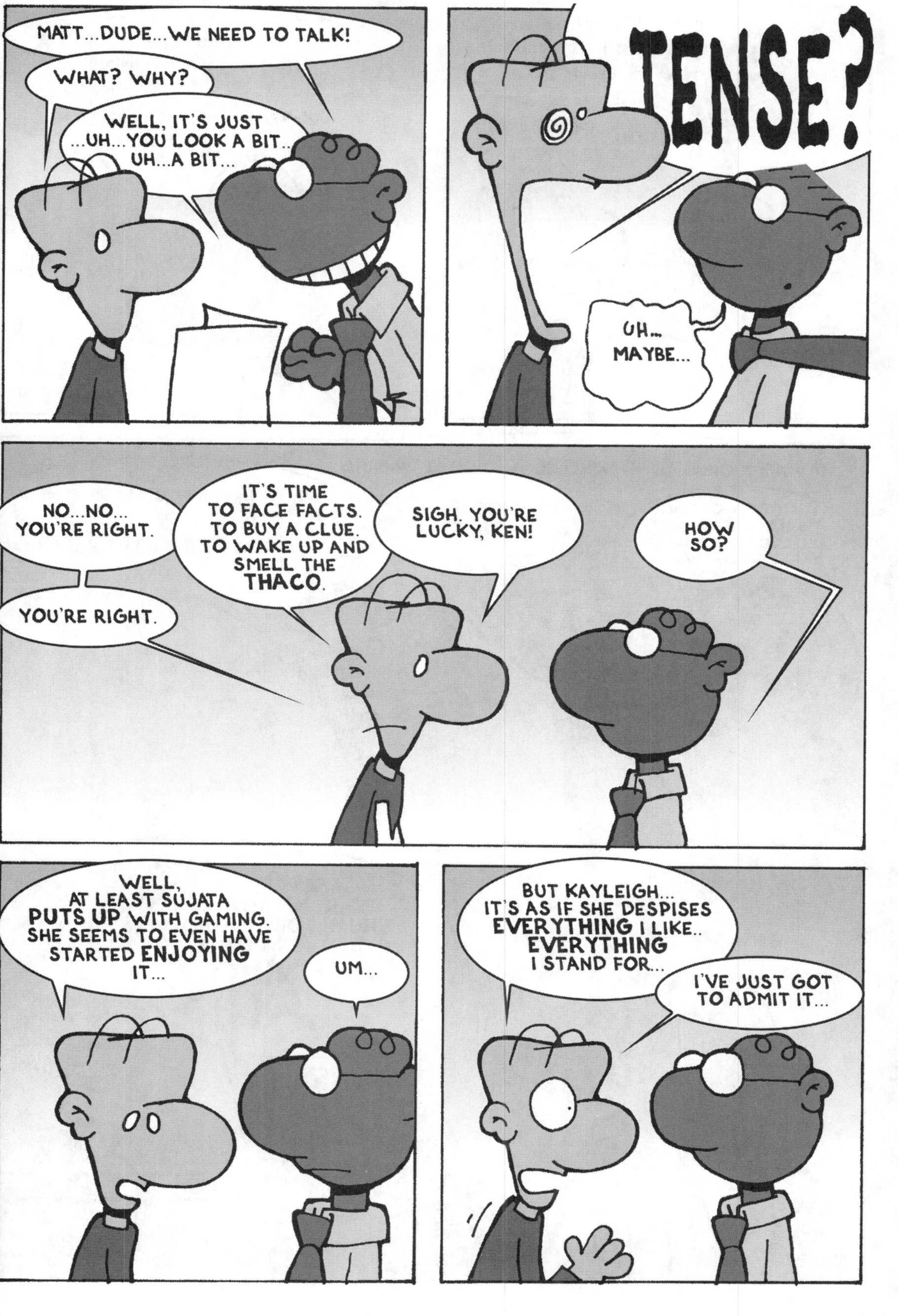

MATT...DUDE...WE NEED TO TALK!
WHAT? WHY?
WELL, IT'S JUST ...UH...YOU LOOK A BIT... UH...A BIT...
TENSE?
UH... MAYBE...
NO...NO... YOU'RE RIGHT.
YOU'RE RIGHT.
IT'S TIME TO FACE FACTS. TO BUY A CLUE. TO WAKE UP AND SMELL THE THACO.
SIGH. YOU'RE LUCKY, KEN!
HOW SO?
WELL, AT LEAST SUJATA PUTS UP WITH GAMING. SHE SEEMS TO EVEN HAVE STARTED ENJOYING IT...
UM...
BUT KAYLEIGH... IT'S AS IF SHE DESPISES EVERYTHING I LIKE.. EVERYTHING I STAND FOR...
I'VE JUST GOT TO ADMIT IT...

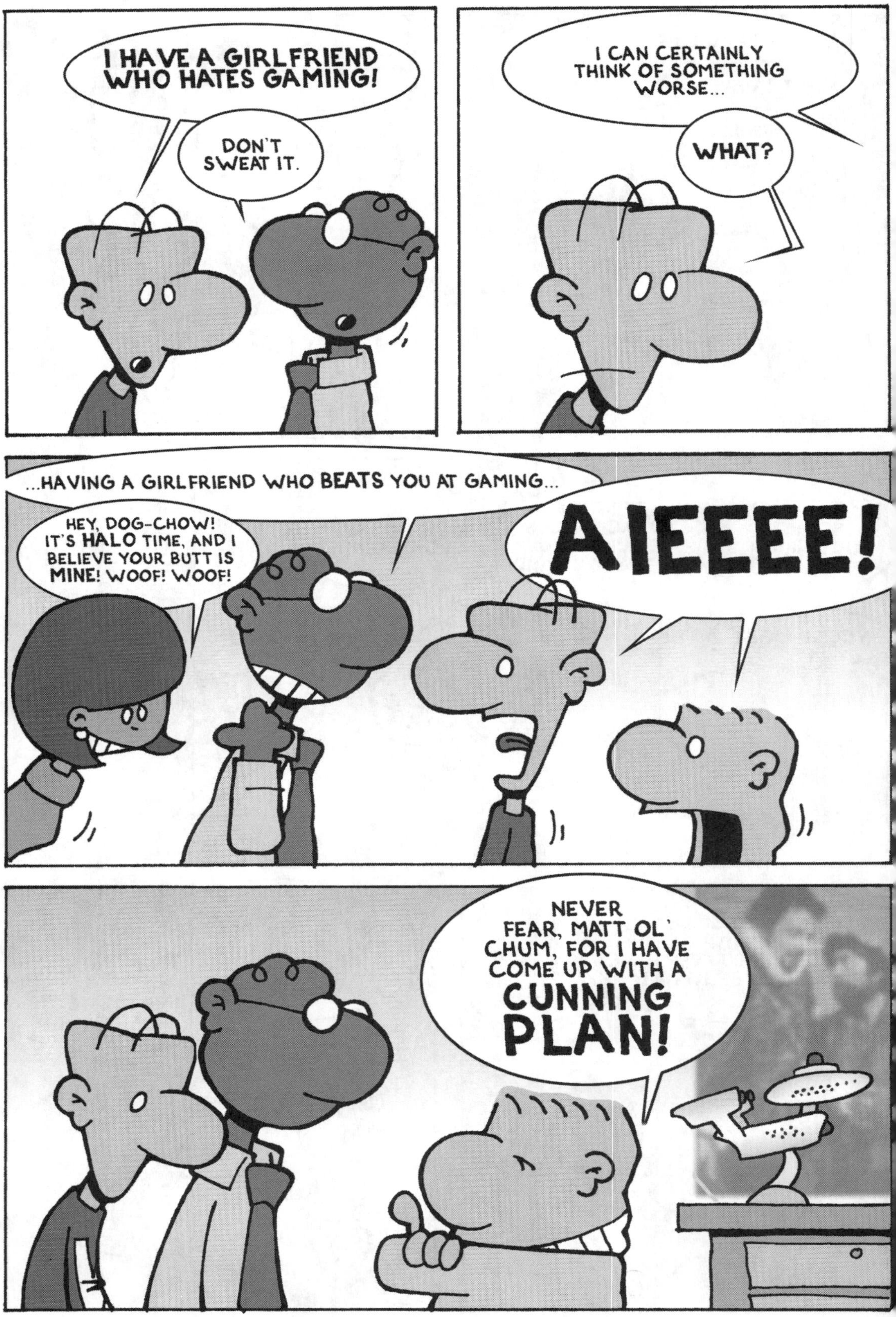
I HAVE A GIRLFRIEND WHO HATES GAMING!
DON'T SWEAT IT.
I CAN CERTAINLY THINK OF SOMETHING WORSE...
WHAT?
...HAVING A GIRLFRIEND WHO BEATS YOU AT GAMING...
HEY, DOG-CHOW! IT'S HALO TIME, AND I BELIEVE YOUR BUTT IS MINE! WOOF! WOOF!
AIEEEE!
NEVER FEAR, MATT OL' CHUM, FOR I HAVE COME UP WITH A CUNNING PLAN!

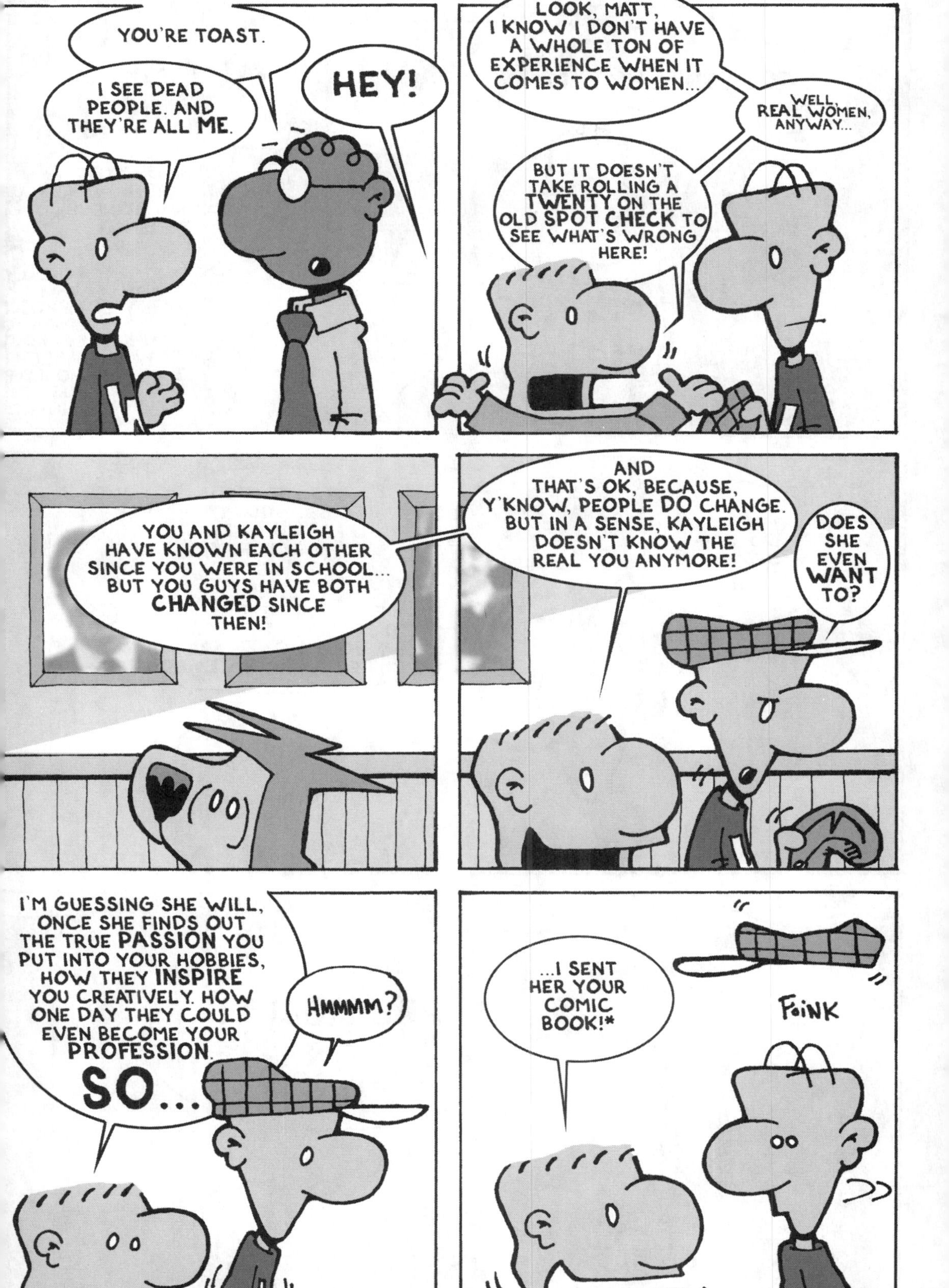
YOU'RE TOAST.
I SEE DEAD PEOPLE. AND THEY'RE ALL ME.
HEY!
LOOK, MATT, I KNOW I DON'T HAVE A WHOLE TON OF EXPERIENCE WHEN IT COMES TO WOMEN...
WELL, REAL WOMEN, ANYWAY...
BUT IT DOESN'T TAKE ROLLING A TWENTY ON THE OLD SPOT CHECK TO SEE WHAT'S WRONG HERE!
YOU AND KAYLEIGH HAVE KNOWN EACH OTHER SINCE YOU WERE IN SCHOOL... BUT YOU GUYS HAVE BOTH CHANGED SINCE THEN!
AND THAT'S OK, BECAUSE, Y'KNOW, PEOPLE DO CHANGE. BUT IN A SENSE, KAYLEIGH DOESN'T KNOW THE REAL YOU ANYMORE!
DOES SHE EVEN WANT TO?
I'M GUESSING SHE WILL, ONCE SHE FINDS OUT THE TRUE PASSION YOU PUT INTO YOUR HOBBIES, HOW THEY INSPIRE YOU CREATIVELY. HOW ONE DAY THEY COULD EVEN BECOME YOUR PROFESSION.
SO...
HMMMM?
...I SENT HER YOUR COMIC BOOK!*
FOINK

* FROM DORK TOWER #12
- JOHN

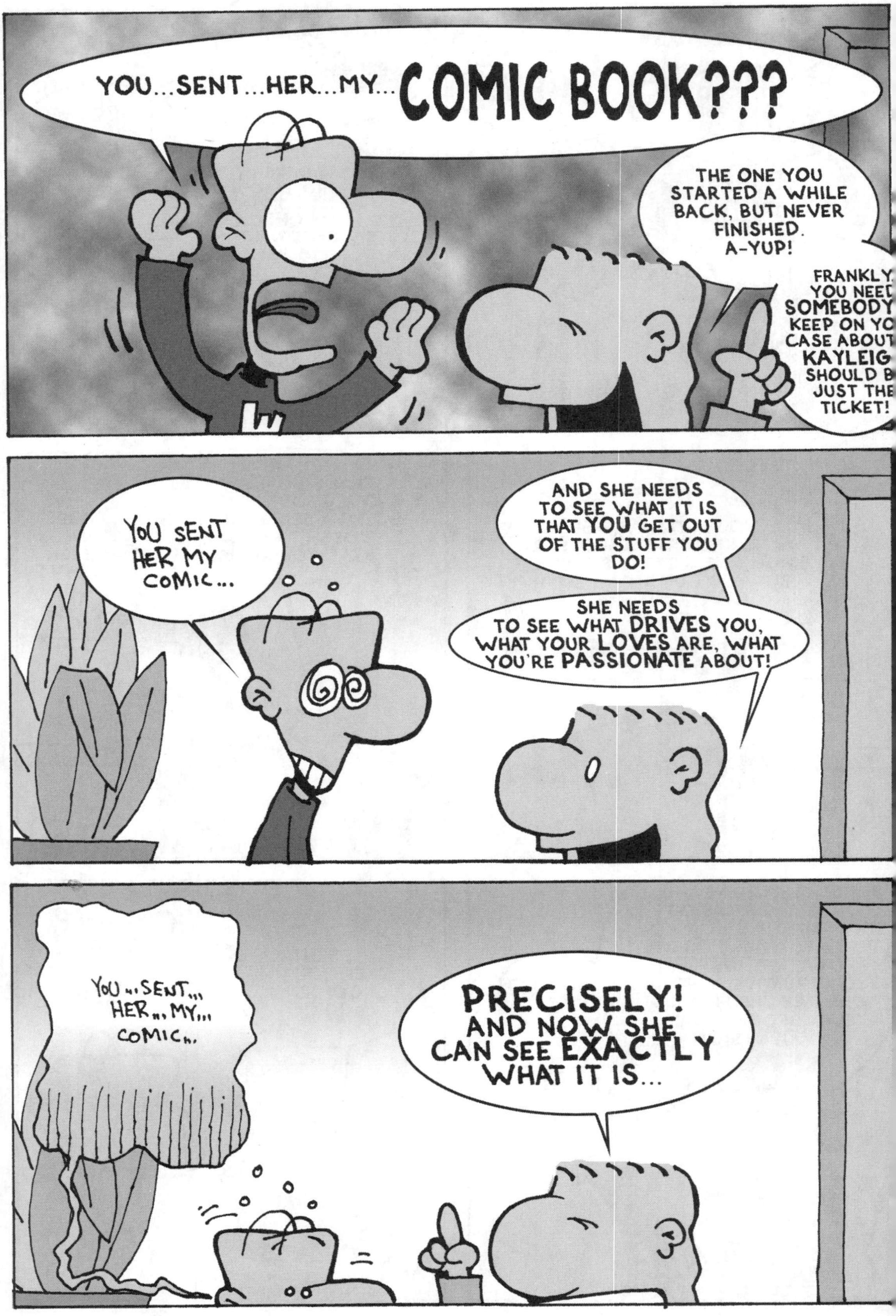
YOU...SENT...HER...MY... COMIC BOOK???
THE ONE YOU STARTED A WHILE BACK, BUT NEVER FINISHED. A-YUP!
FRANKLY, YOU NEED SOMEBODY KEEP ON YO CASE ABOUT KAYLEIG SHOULD B JUST THE TICKET!
YOU SENT HER MY COMIC...
AND SHE NEEDS TO SEE WHAT IT IS THAT YOU GET OUT OF THE STUFF YOU DO!
SHE NEEDS TO SEE WHAT DRIVES YOU, WHAT YOUR LOVES ARE, WHAT YOU'RE PASSIONATE ABOUT!
YOU...SENT... HER... MY... COMIC...
PRECISELY! AND NOW SHE CAN SEE EXACTLY WHAT IT IS...

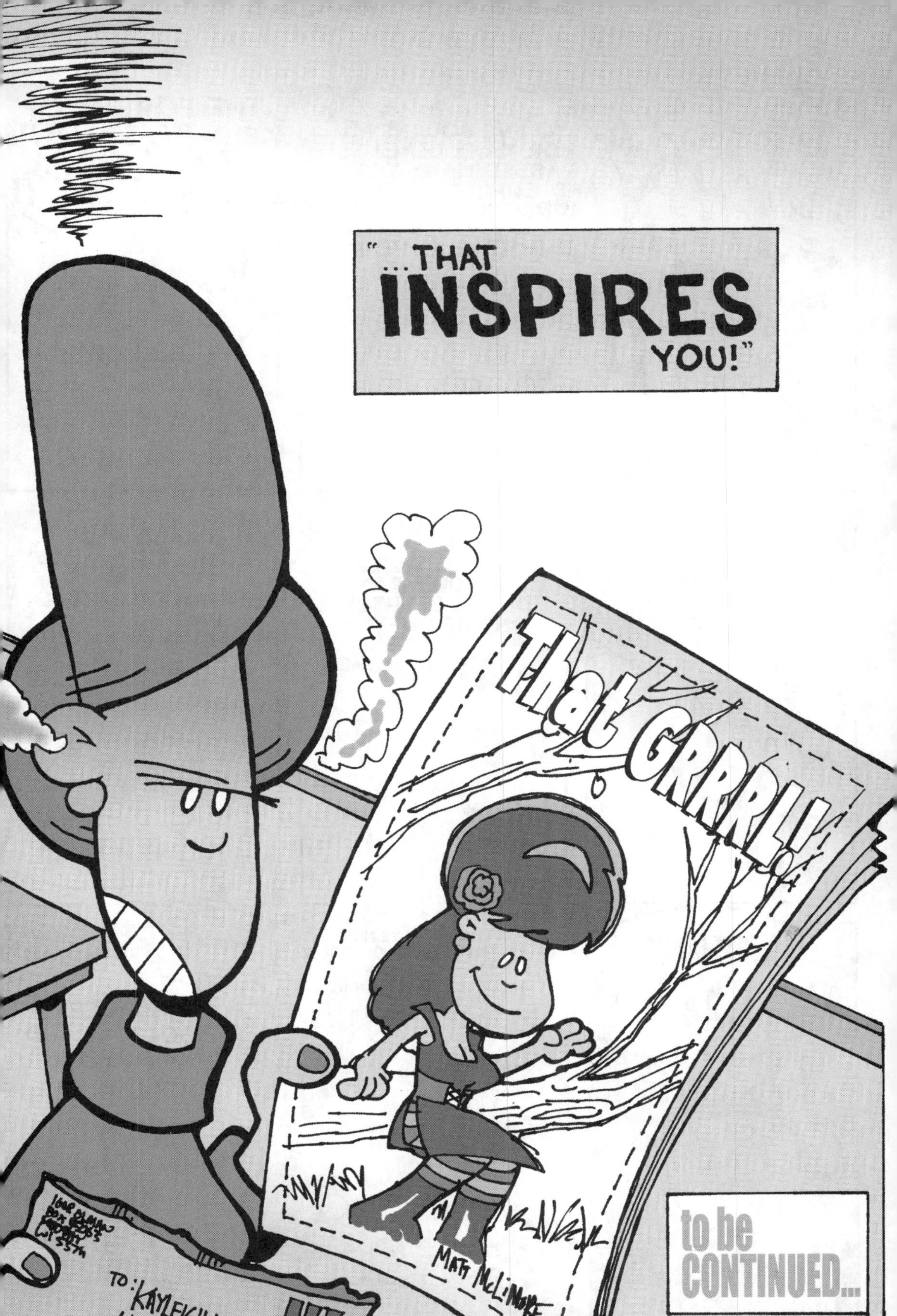
"...THAT INSPIRES YOU!"
That GRRRL!
MATT McLIMORE
to be CONTINUED...

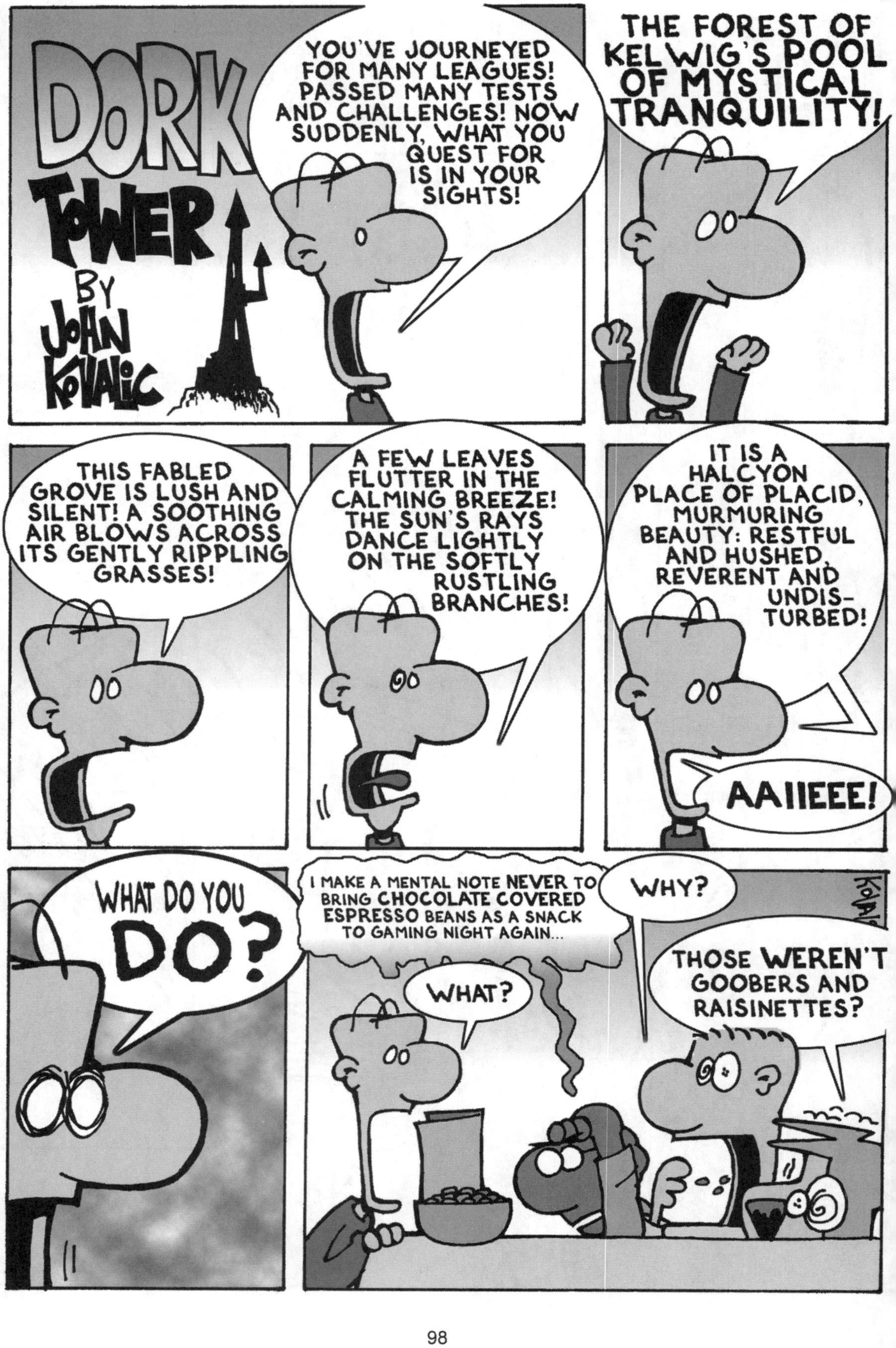
DORK TOWER
BY JOHN KOVALIC
YOU'VE JOURNEYED FOR MANY LEAGUES! PASSED MANY TESTS AND CHALLENGES! NOW SUDDENLY, WHAT YOU QUEST FOR IS IN YOUR SIGHTS!
THE FOREST OF KELWIG'S POOL OF MYSTICAL TRANQUILITY!
THIS FABLED GROVE IS LUSH AND SILENT! A SOOTHING AIR BLOWS ACROSS ITS GENTLY RIPPLING GRASSES!
A FEW LEAVES FLUTTER IN THE CALMING BREEZE! THE SUN'S RAYS DANCE LIGHTLY ON THE SOFTLY RUSTLING BRANCHES!
IT IS A HALCYON PLACE OF PLACID, MURMURING BEAUTY: RESTFUL AND HUSHED, REVERENT AND UNDISTURBED!
AAIIEEE!
WHAT DO YOU DO?
I MAKE A MENTAL NOTE NEVER TO BRING CHOCOLATE COVERED ESPRESSO BEANS AS A SNACK TO GAMING NIGHT AGAIN...
WHY?
WHAT?
THOSE WEREN'T GOOBERS AND RAISINETTES?

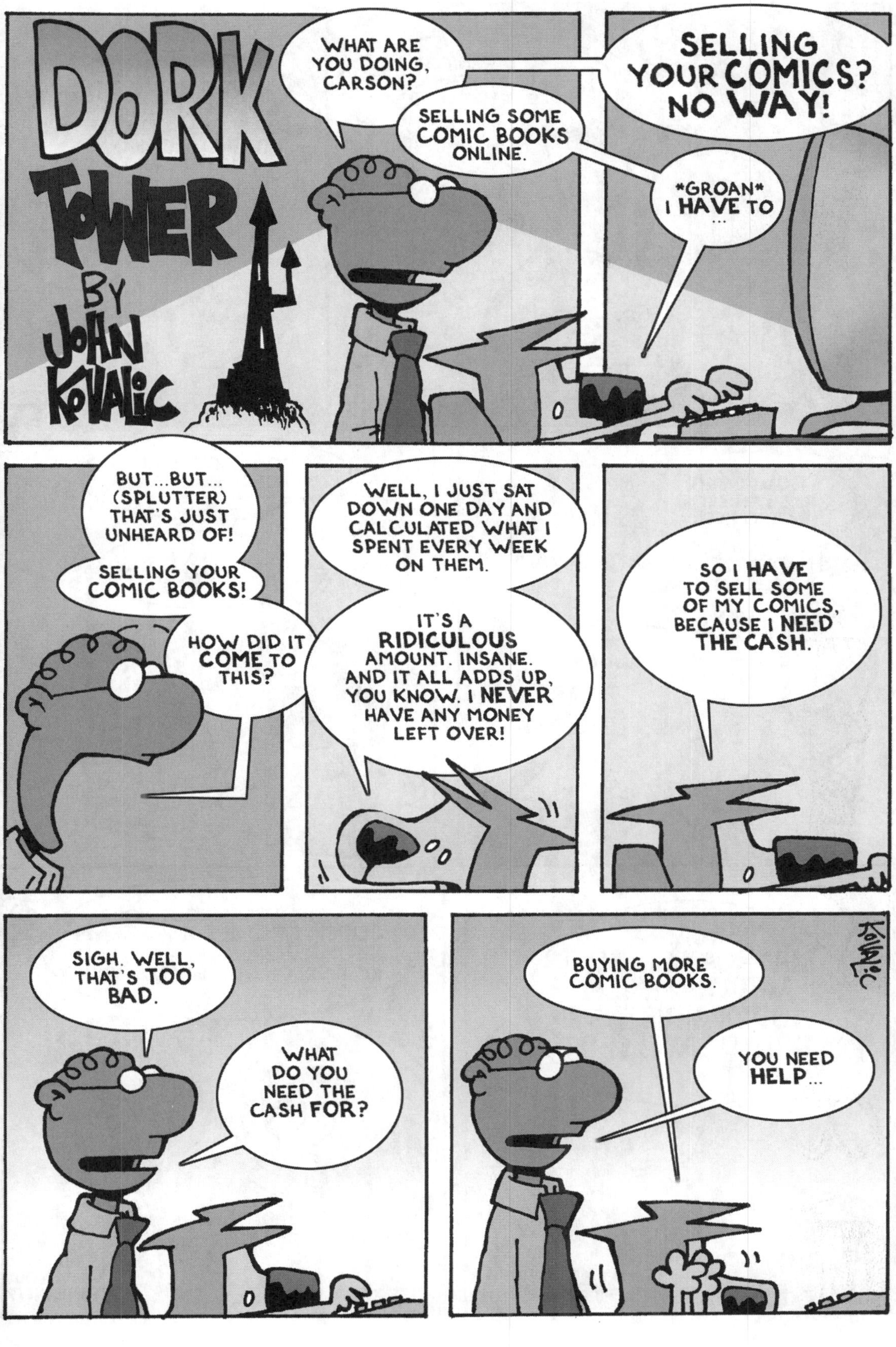
DORK TOWER BY JOHN KOVALIC
WHAT ARE YOU DOING, CARSON?
SELLING SOME COMIC BOOKS ONLINE.
SELLING YOUR COMICS? NO WAY!
GROAN I HAVE TO ...
BUT...BUT... (SPLUTTER) THAT'S JUST UNHEARD OF!
SELLING YOUR COMIC BOOKS!
HOW DID IT COME TO THIS?
WELL, I JUST SAT DOWN ONE DAY AND CALCULATED WHAT I SPENT EVERY WEEK ON THEM.
IT'S A RIDICULOUS AMOUNT. INSANE. AND IT ALL ADDS UP, YOU KNOW. I NEVER HAVE ANY MONEY LEFT OVER!
SO I HAVE TO SELL SOME OF MY COMICS, BECAUSE I NEED THE CASH.
SIGH. WELL, THAT'S TOO BAD.
WHAT DO YOU NEED THE CASH FOR?
BUYING MORE COMIC BOOKS.
YOU NEED HELP...
KOVALIC

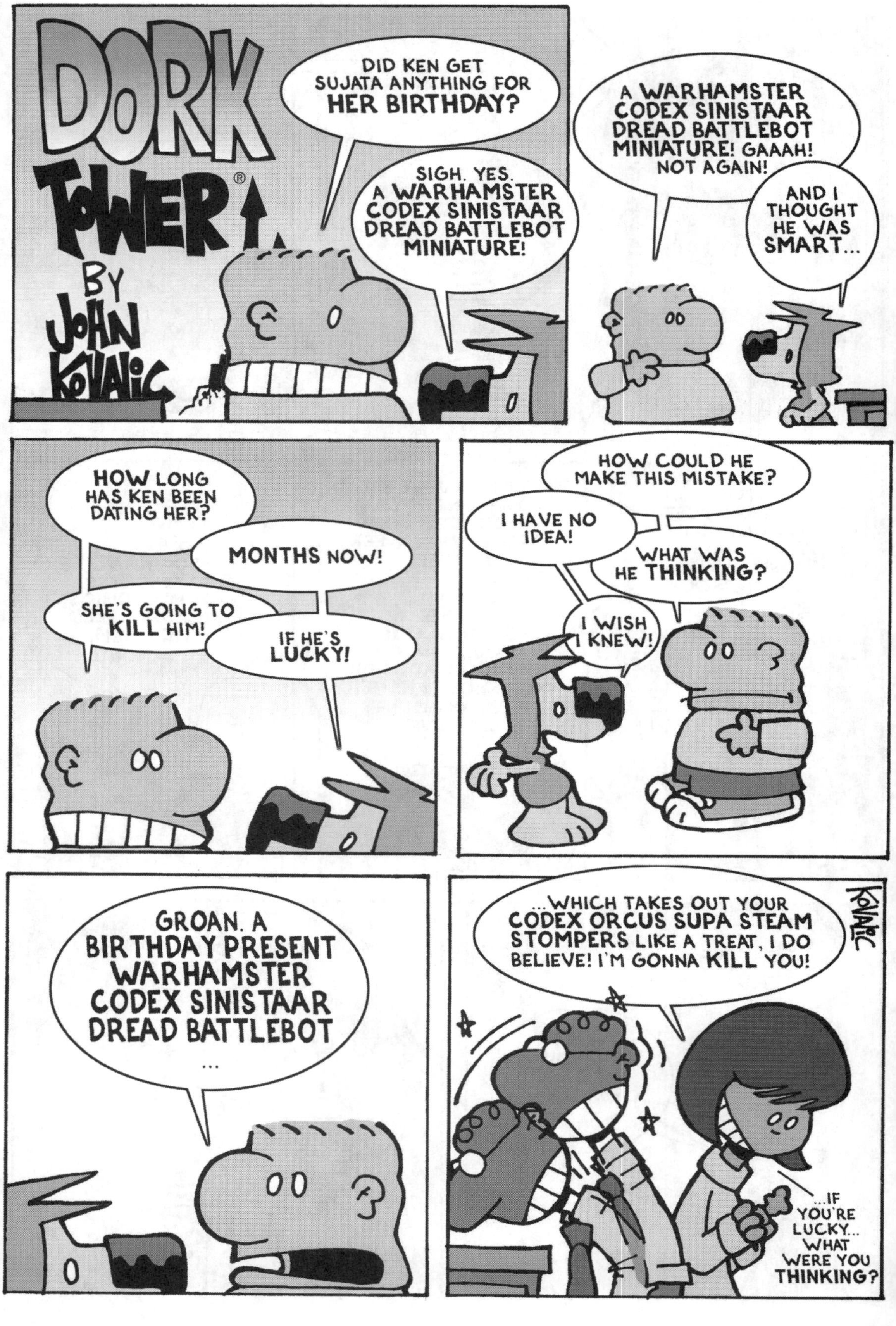
DORK TOWER®
BY JOHN KOVALIC
DID KEN GET SUJATA ANYTHING FOR HER BIRTHDAY?
SIGH. YES. A WARHAMSTER CODEX SINISTAAR DREAD BATTLEBOT MINIATURE!
A WARHAMSTER CODEX SINISTAAR DREAD BATTLEBOT MINIATURE! GAAAH! NOT AGAIN!
AND I THOUGHT HE WAS SMART...
HOW LONG HAS KEN BEEN DATING HER?
MONTHS NOW!
SHE'S GOING TO KILL HIM!
IF HE'S LUCKY!
HOW COULD HE MAKE THIS MISTAKE?
I HAVE NO IDEA!
WHAT WAS HE THINKING?
I WISH I KNEW!
GROAN. A BIRTHDAY PRESENT WARHAMSTER CODEX SINISTAAR DREAD BATTLEBOT ...
KOVALIC
...WHICH TAKES OUT YOUR CODEX ORCUS SUPA STEAM STOMPERS LIKE A TREAT, I DO BELIEVE! I'M GONNA KILL YOU!
...IF YOU'RE LUCKY... WHAT WERE YOU THINKING?

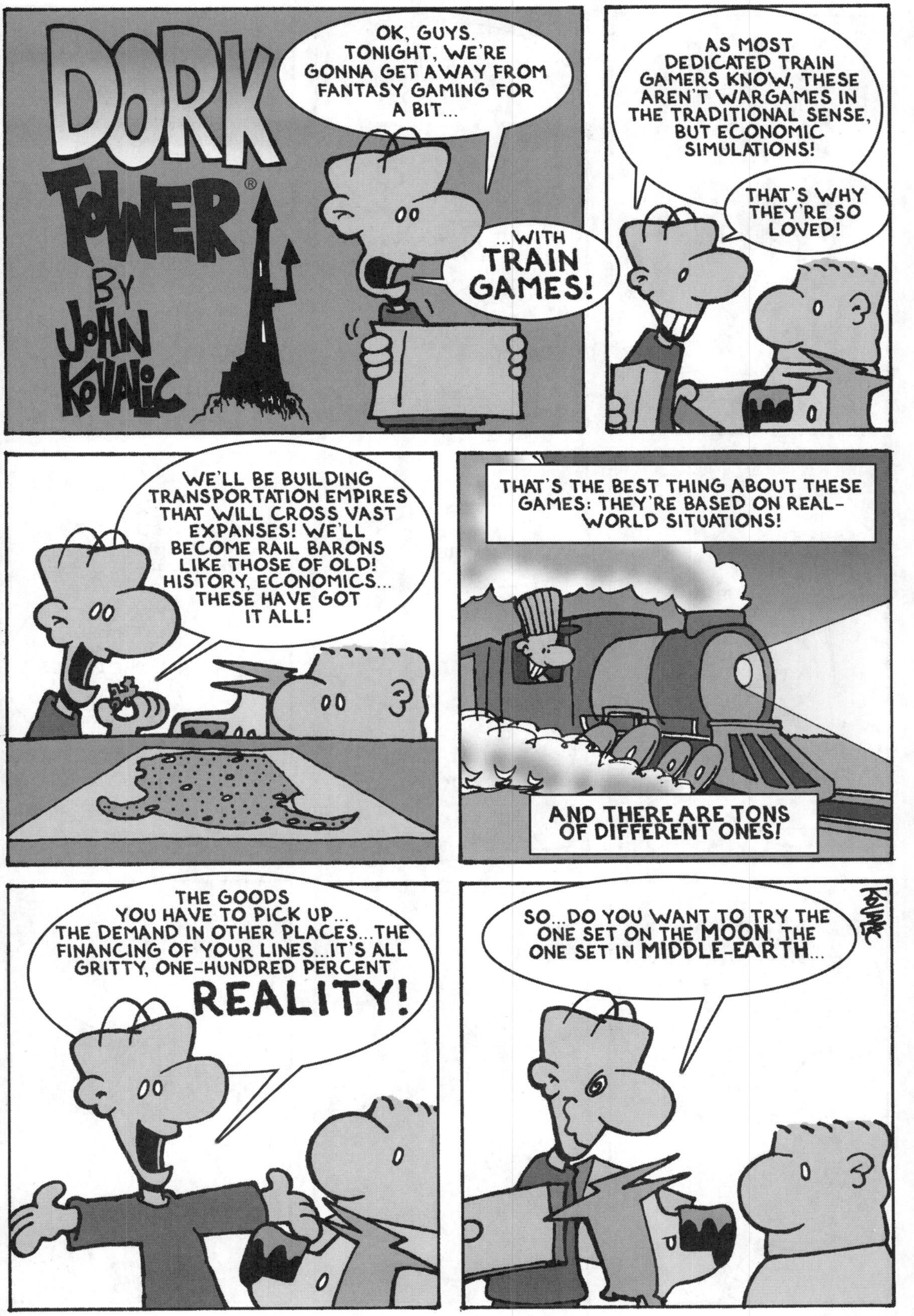
DORK TOWER®
BY JOHN KOVALIC
OK, GUYS. TONIGHT, WE'RE GONNA GET AWAY FROM FANTASY GAMING FOR A BIT...
...WITH TRAIN GAMES!
AS MOST DEDICATED TRAIN GAMERS KNOW, THESE AREN'T WARGAMES IN THE TRADITIONAL SENSE, BUT ECONOMIC SIMULATIONS!
THAT'S WHY THEY'RE SO LOVED!
WE'LL BE BUILDING TRANSPORTATION EMPIRES THAT WILL CROSS VAST EXPANSES! WE'LL BECOME RAIL BARONS LIKE THOSE OF OLD! HISTORY, ECONOMICS... THESE HAVE GOT IT ALL!
THAT'S THE BEST THING ABOUT THESE GAMES: THEY'RE BASED ON REAL-WORLD SITUATIONS!
AND THERE ARE TONS OF DIFFERENT ONES!
THE GOODS YOU HAVE TO PICK UP... THE DEMAND IN OTHER PLACES... THE FINANCING OF YOUR LINES... IT'S ALL GRITTY, ONE-HUNDRED PERCENT REALITY!
SO... DO YOU WANT TO TRY THE ONE SET ON THE MOON, THE ONE SET IN MIDDLE-EARTH...

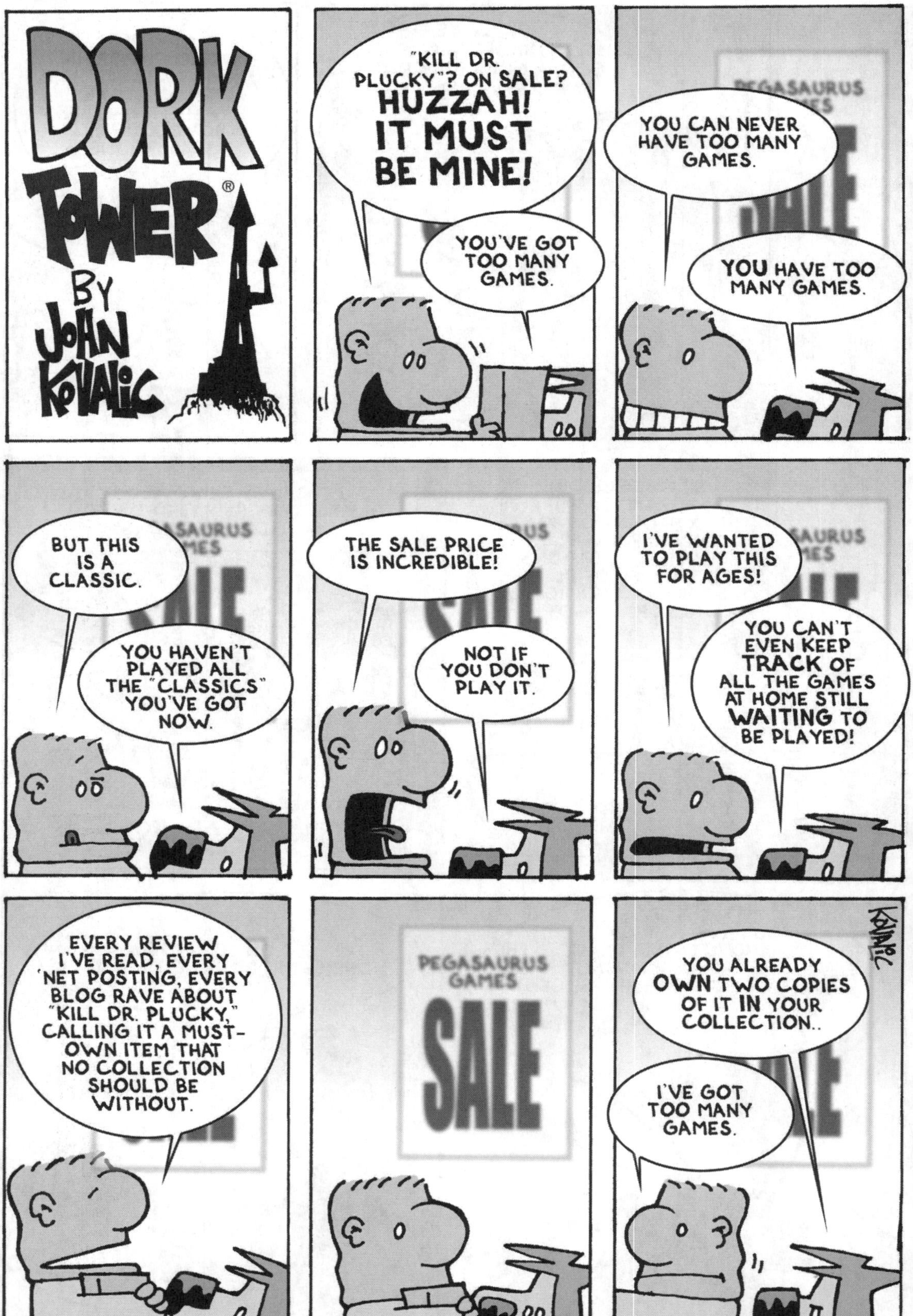
DORK TOWER®
BY JOHN KOVALIC
"KILL DR. PLUCKY"? ON SALE? HUZZAH! IT MUST BE MINE!
YOU'VE GOT TOO MANY GAMES.
PEGASAURUS GAMES
YOU CAN NEVER HAVE TOO MANY GAMES.
YOU HAVE TOO MANY GAMES.
BUT THIS IS A CLASSIC.
YOU HAVEN'T PLAYED ALL THE "CLASSICS" YOU'VE GOT NOW.
THE SALE PRICE IS INCREDIBLE!
NOT IF YOU DON'T PLAY IT.
I'VE WANTED TO PLAY THIS FOR AGES!
YOU CAN'T EVEN KEEP TRACK OF ALL THE GAMES AT HOME STILL WAITING TO BE PLAYED!
EVERY REVIEW I'VE READ, EVERY 'NET POSTING, EVERY BLOG RAVE ABOUT "KILL DR. PLUCKY," CALLING IT A MUST-OWN ITEM THAT NO COLLECTION SHOULD BE WITHOUT.
PEGASAURUS GAMES
SALE
YOU ALREADY OWN TWO COPIES OF IT IN YOUR COLLECTION..
I'VE GOT TOO MANY GAMES.
KOVALIC

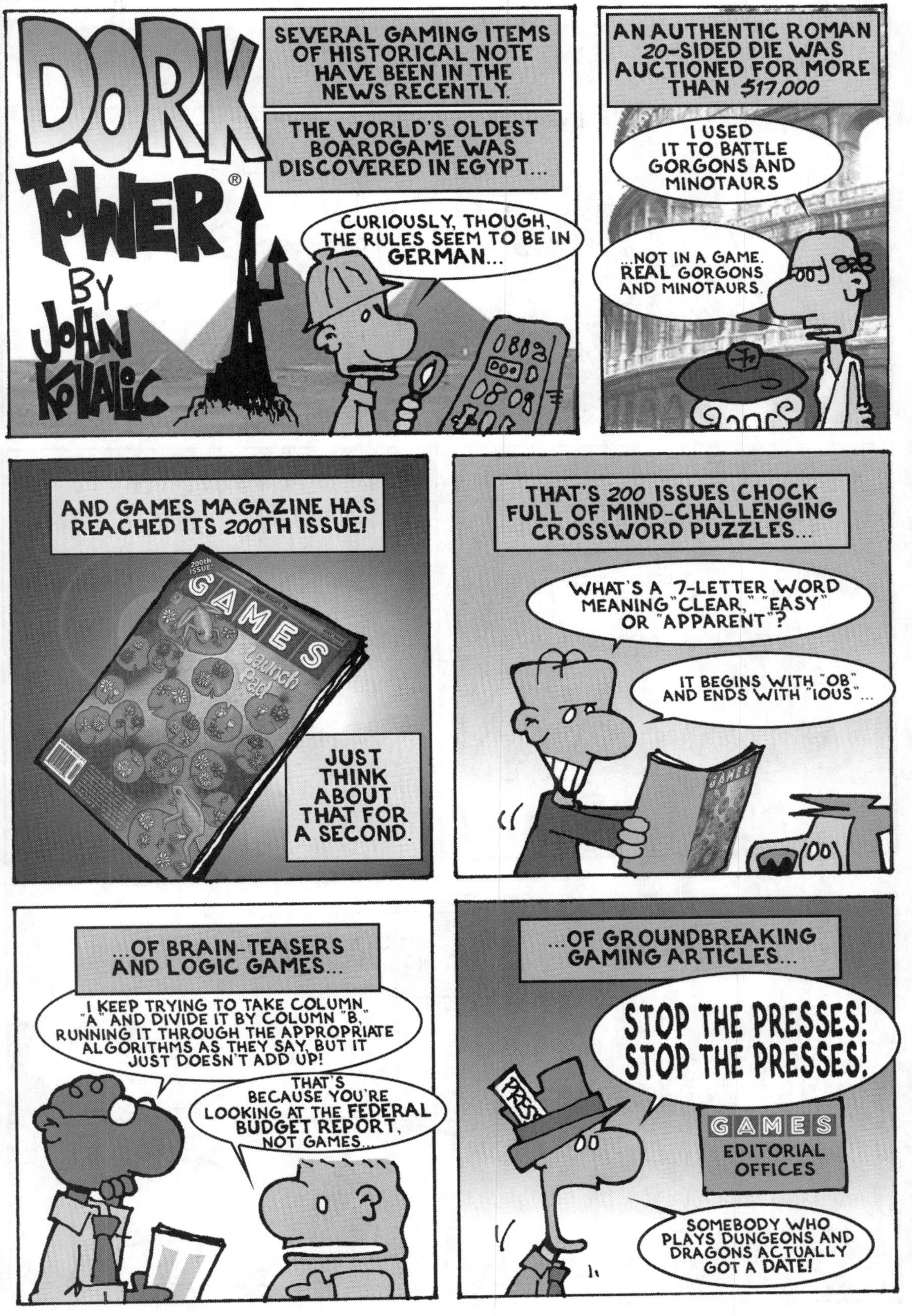
DORK TOWER®
BY JOHN KOVALIC
SEVERAL GAMING ITEMS OF HISTORICAL NOTE HAVE BEEN IN THE NEWS RECENTLY.
THE WORLD'S OLDEST BOARDGAME WAS DISCOVERED IN EGYPT...
CURIOUSLY, THOUGH, THE RULES SEEM TO BE IN GERMAN...
AN AUTHENTIC ROMAN 20-SIDED DIE WAS AUCTIONED FOR MORE THAN $17,000
I USED IT TO BATTLE GORGONS AND MINOTAURS
...NOT IN A GAME. REAL GORGONS AND MINOTAURS.
AND GAMES MAGAZINE HAS REACHED ITS 200TH ISSUE!
200th ISSUE!
GAMES
Launch Pad
JUST THINK ABOUT THAT FOR A SECOND.
THAT'S 200 ISSUES CHOCK FULL OF MIND-CHALLENGING CROSSWORD PUZZLES...
WHAT'S A 7-LETTER WORD MEANING "CLEAR," "EASY" OR "APPARENT"?
IT BEGINS WITH "OB" AND ENDS WITH "IOUS"...
...OF BRAIN-TEASERS AND LOGIC GAMES...
I KEEP TRYING TO TAKE COLUMN "A" AND DIVIDE IT BY COLUMN "B," RUNNING IT THROUGH THE APPROPRIATE ALGORITHMS AS THEY SAY, BUT IT JUST DOESN'T ADD UP!
THAT'S BECAUSE YOU'RE LOOKING AT THE FEDERAL BUDGET REPORT, NOT GAMES...
...OF GROUNDBREAKING GAMING ARTICLES...
STOP THE PRESSES! STOP THE PRESSES!
PRESS
GAMES EDITORIAL OFFICES
SOMEBODY WHO PLAYS DUNGEONS AND DRAGONS ACTUALLY GOT A DATE!

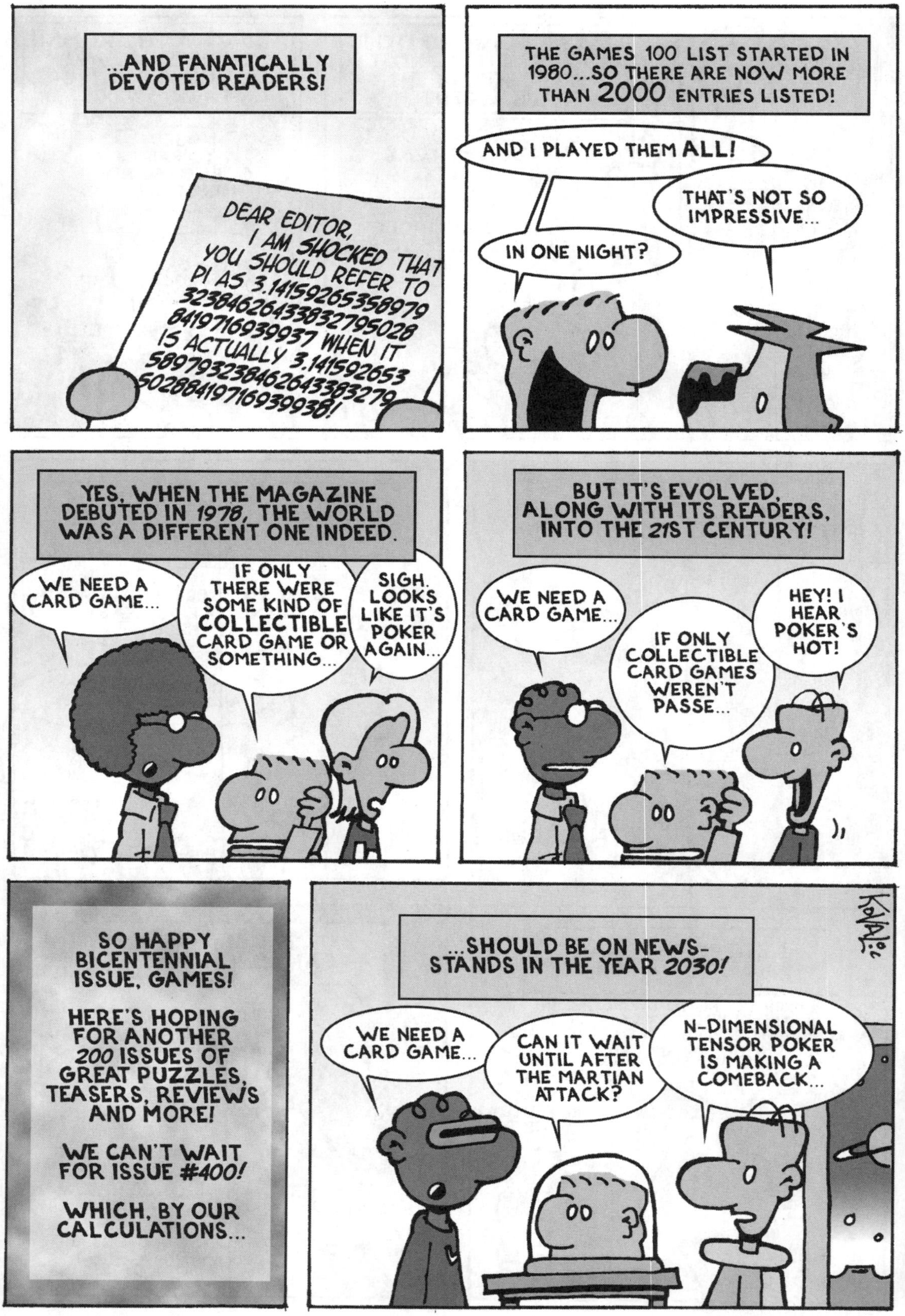

...AND FANATICALLY DEVOTED READERS!
DEAR EDITOR, I AM SHOCKED THAT YOU SHOULD REFER TO PI AS 3.14159265358979 3238462643383279502 8841971693993 7 WHEN IT IS ACTUALLY 3.141592653 58979323846264338327950 288419716939938!
THE GAMES 100 LIST STARTED IN 1980...SO THERE ARE NOW MORE THAN 2000 ENTRIES LISTED!
AND I PLAYED THEM ALL!
THAT'S NOT SO IMPRESSIVE...
IN ONE NIGHT?
YES, WHEN THE MAGAZINE DEBUTED IN 1978, THE WORLD WAS A DIFFERENT ONE INDEED.
WE NEED A CARD GAME...
IF ONLY THERE WERE SOME KIND OF COLLECTIBLE CARD GAME OR SOMETHING...
SIGH. LOOKS LIKE IT'S POKER AGAIN...
BUT IT'S EVOLVED, ALONG WITH ITS READERS, INTO THE 21ST CENTURY!
WE NEED A CARD GAME...
IF ONLY COLLECTIBLE CARD GAMES WEREN'T PASSE...
HEY! I HEAR POKER'S HOT!
SO HAPPY BICENTENNIAL ISSUE, GAMES!
HERE'S HOPING FOR ANOTHER 200 ISSUES OF GREAT PUZZLES, TEASERS, REVIEWS AND MORE!
WE CAN'T WAIT FOR ISSUE #400!
WHICH, BY OUR CALCULATIONS...
...SHOULD BE ON NEWS-STANDS IN THE YEAR 2030!
WE NEED A CARD GAME...
CAN IT WAIT UNTIL AFTER THE MARTIAN ATTACK?
N-DIMENSIONAL TENSOR POKER IS MAKING A COMEBACK...

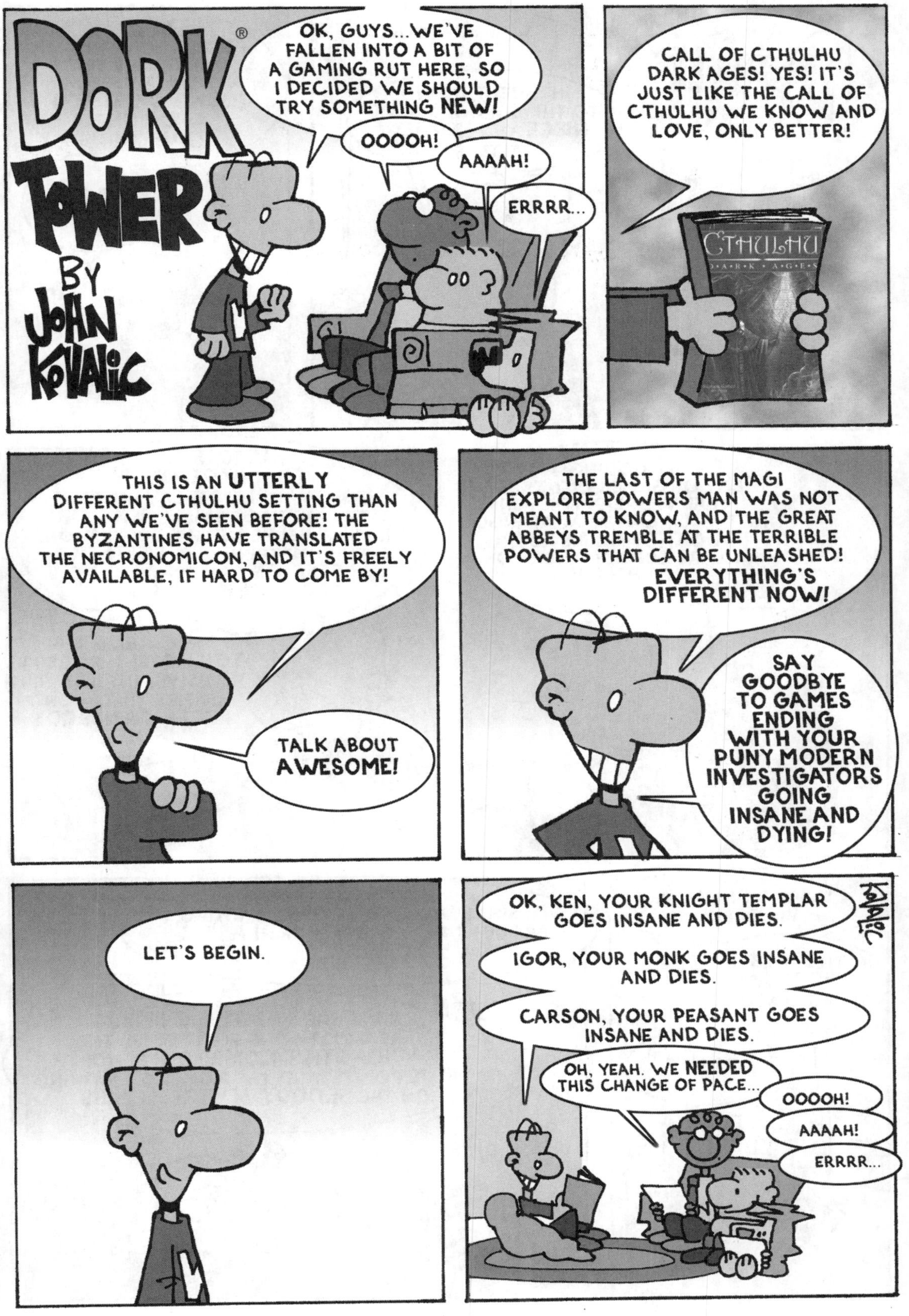
DORK TOWER®
BY JOHN KOVALIC
OK, GUYS... WE'VE FALLEN INTO A BIT OF A GAMING RUT HERE, SO I DECIDED WE SHOULD TRY SOMETHING NEW!
OOOOH!
AAAAH!
ERRRR...
CALL OF CTHULHU DARK AGES! YES! IT'S JUST LIKE THE CALL OF CTHULHU WE KNOW AND LOVE, ONLY BETTER!
CTHULHU
D·A·R·K A·G·E·S
THIS IS AN UTTERLY DIFFERENT CTHULHU SETTING THAN ANY WE'VE SEEN BEFORE! THE BYZANTINES HAVE TRANSLATED THE NECRONOMICON, AND IT'S FREELY AVAILABLE, IF HARD TO COME BY!
TALK ABOUT AWESOME!
THE LAST OF THE MAGI EXPLORE POWERS MAN WAS NOT MEANT TO KNOW, AND THE GREAT ABBEYS TREMBLE AT THE TERRIBLE POWERS THAT CAN BE UNLEASHED! EVERYTHING'S DIFFERENT NOW!
SAY GOODBYE TO GAMES ENDING WITH YOUR PUNY MODERN INVESTIGATORS GOING INSANE AND DYING!
LET'S BEGIN.
OK, KEN, YOUR KNIGHT TEMPLAR GOES INSANE AND DIES.
IGOR, YOUR MONK GOES INSANE AND DIES.
CARSON, YOUR PEASANT GOES INSANE AND DIES.
OH, YEAH. WE NEEDED THIS CHANGE OF PACE...
OOOOH!
AAAAH!
ERRRR...
KOVALIC

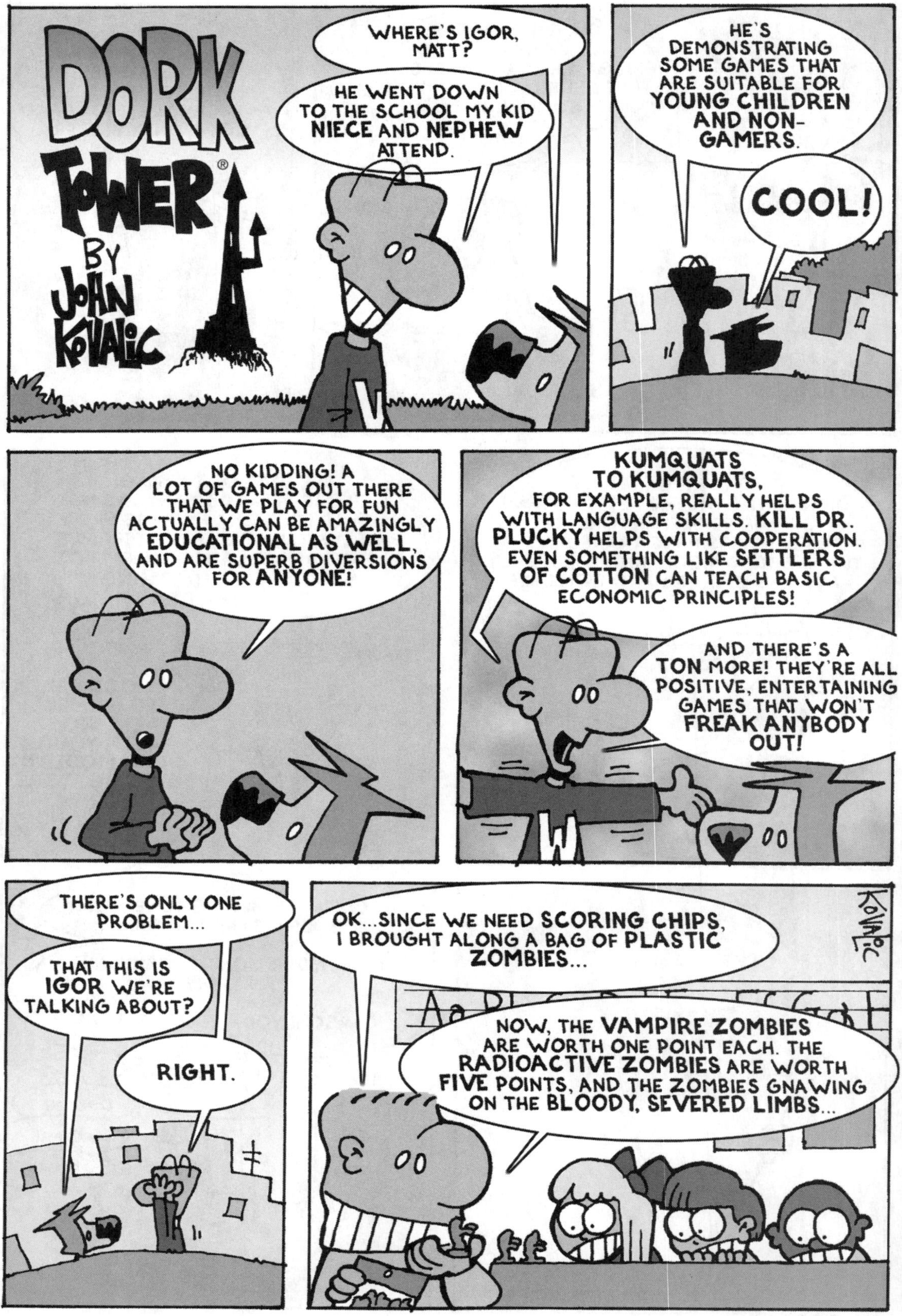

DORK TOWER®
BY JOHN KOVALIC
WHERE'S IGOR, MATT?
HE WENT DOWN TO THE SCHOOL MY KID NIECE AND NEPHEW ATTEND.
HE'S DEMONSTRATING SOME GAMES THAT ARE SUITABLE FOR YOUNG CHILDREN AND NON-GAMERS.
COOL!
NO KIDDING! A LOT OF GAMES OUT THERE THAT WE PLAY FOR FUN ACTUALLY CAN BE AMAZINGLY EDUCATIONAL AS WELL, AND ARE SUPERB DIVERSIONS FOR ANYONE!
KUMQUATS TO KUMQUATS, FOR EXAMPLE, REALLY HELPS WITH LANGUAGE SKILLS. KILL DR. PLUCKY HELPS WITH COOPERATION. EVEN SOMETHING LIKE SETTLERS OF COTTON CAN TEACH BASIC ECONOMIC PRINCIPLES!
AND THERE'S A TON MORE! THEY'RE ALL POSITIVE, ENTERTAINING GAMES THAT WON'T FREAK ANYBODY OUT!
THERE'S ONLY ONE PROBLEM...
THAT THIS IS IGOR WE'RE TALKING ABOUT?
RIGHT.
KOVALIC
OK...SINCE WE NEED SCORING CHIPS, I BROUGHT ALONG A BAG OF PLASTIC ZOMBIES...
NOW, THE VAMPIRE ZOMBIES ARE WORTH ONE POINT EACH. THE RADIOACTIVE ZOMBIES ARE WORTH FIVE POINTS, AND THE ZOMBIES GNAWING ON THE BLOODY, SEVERED LIMBS...

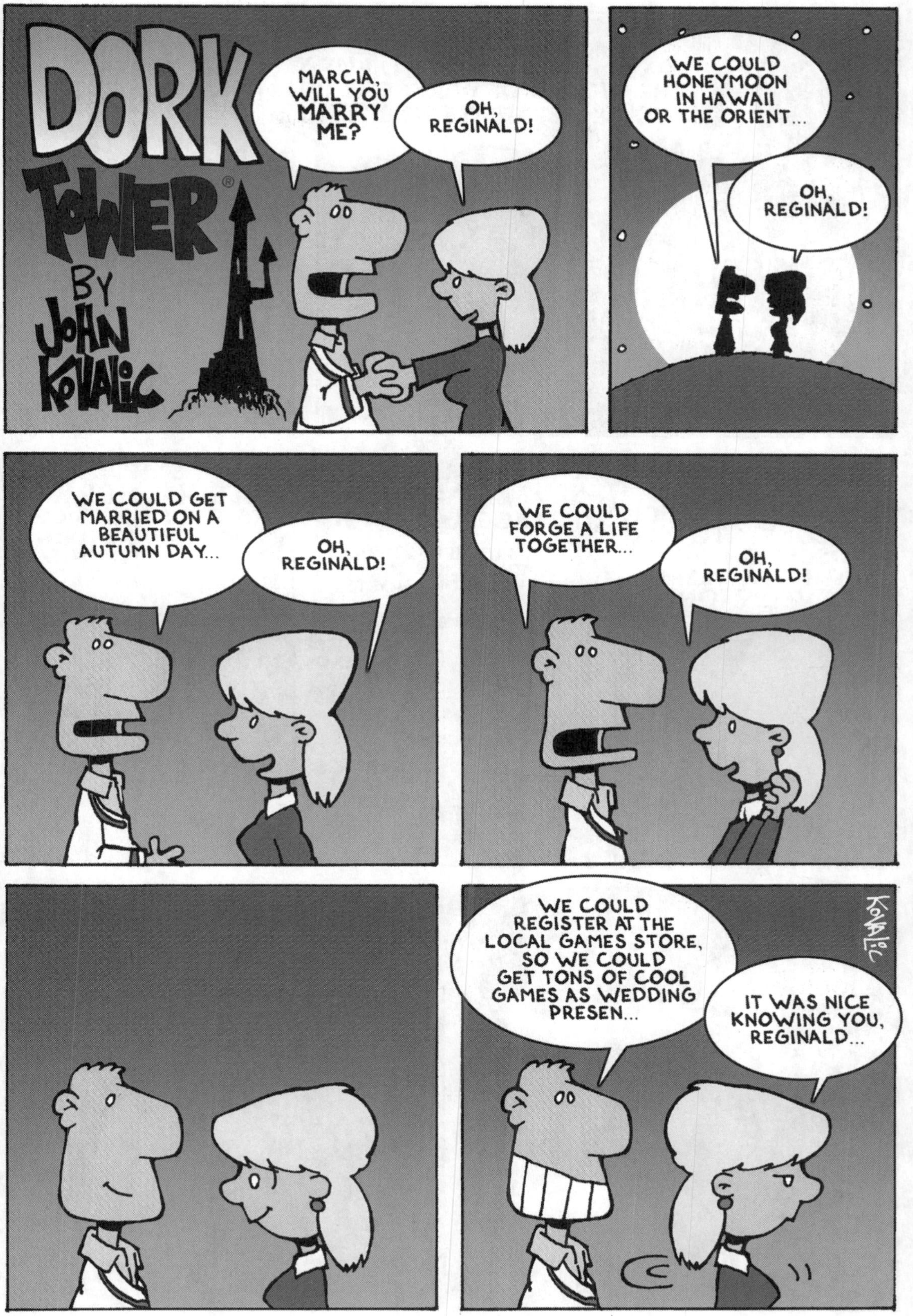
DORK TOWER®
BY JOHN KOVALIC
MARCIA, WILL YOU MARRY ME?
OH, REGINALD!
WE COULD HONEYMOON IN HAWAII OR THE ORIENT...
OH, REGINALD!
WE COULD GET MARRIED ON A BEAUTIFUL AUTUMN DAY...
OH, REGINALD!
WE COULD FORGE A LIFE TOGETHER...
OH, REGINALD!
WE COULD REGISTER AT THE LOCAL GAMES STORE, SO WE COULD GET TONS OF COOL GAMES AS WEDDING PRESEN...
IT WAS NICE KNOWING YOU, REGINALD...
KOVALIC

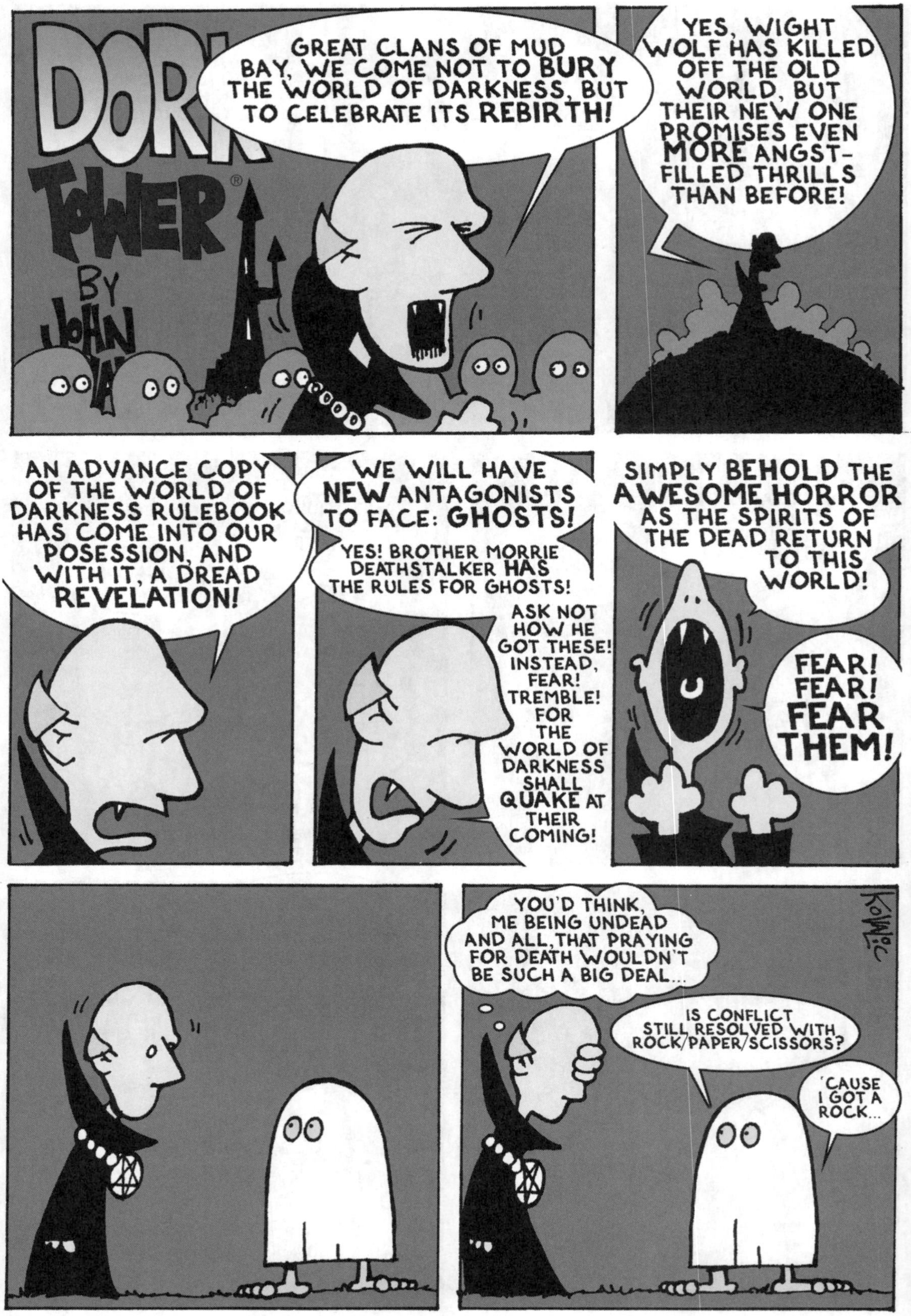
DORK TOWER®
BY JOHN KOVALIC
GREAT CLANS OF MUD BAY, WE COME NOT TO BURY THE WORLD OF DARKNESS, BUT TO CELEBRATE ITS REBIRTH!
YES, WIGHT WOLF HAS KILLED OFF THE OLD WORLD, BUT THEIR NEW ONE PROMISES EVEN MORE ANGST-FILLED THRILLS THAN BEFORE!
AN ADVANCE COPY OF THE WORLD OF DARKNESS RULEBOOK HAS COME INTO OUR POSESSION, AND WITH IT, A DREAD REVELATION!
WE WILL HAVE NEW ANTAGONISTS TO FACE: GHOSTS!
YES! BROTHER MORRIE DEATHSTALKER HAS THE RULES FOR GHOSTS!
ASK NOT HOW HE GOT THESE! INSTEAD, FEAR! TREMBLE! FOR THE WORLD OF DARKNESS SHALL QUAKE AT THEIR COMING!
SIMPLY BEHOLD THE AWESOME HORROR AS THE SPIRITS OF THE DEAD RETURN TO THIS WORLD!
FEAR! FEAR! FEAR THEM!
YOU'D THINK, ME BEING UNDEAD AND ALL, THAT PRAYING FOR DEATH WOULDN'T BE SUCH A BIG DEAL...
IS CONFLICT STILL RESOLVED WITH ROCK/PAPER/SCISSORS?
'CAUSE I GOT A ROCK...
KOVALIC

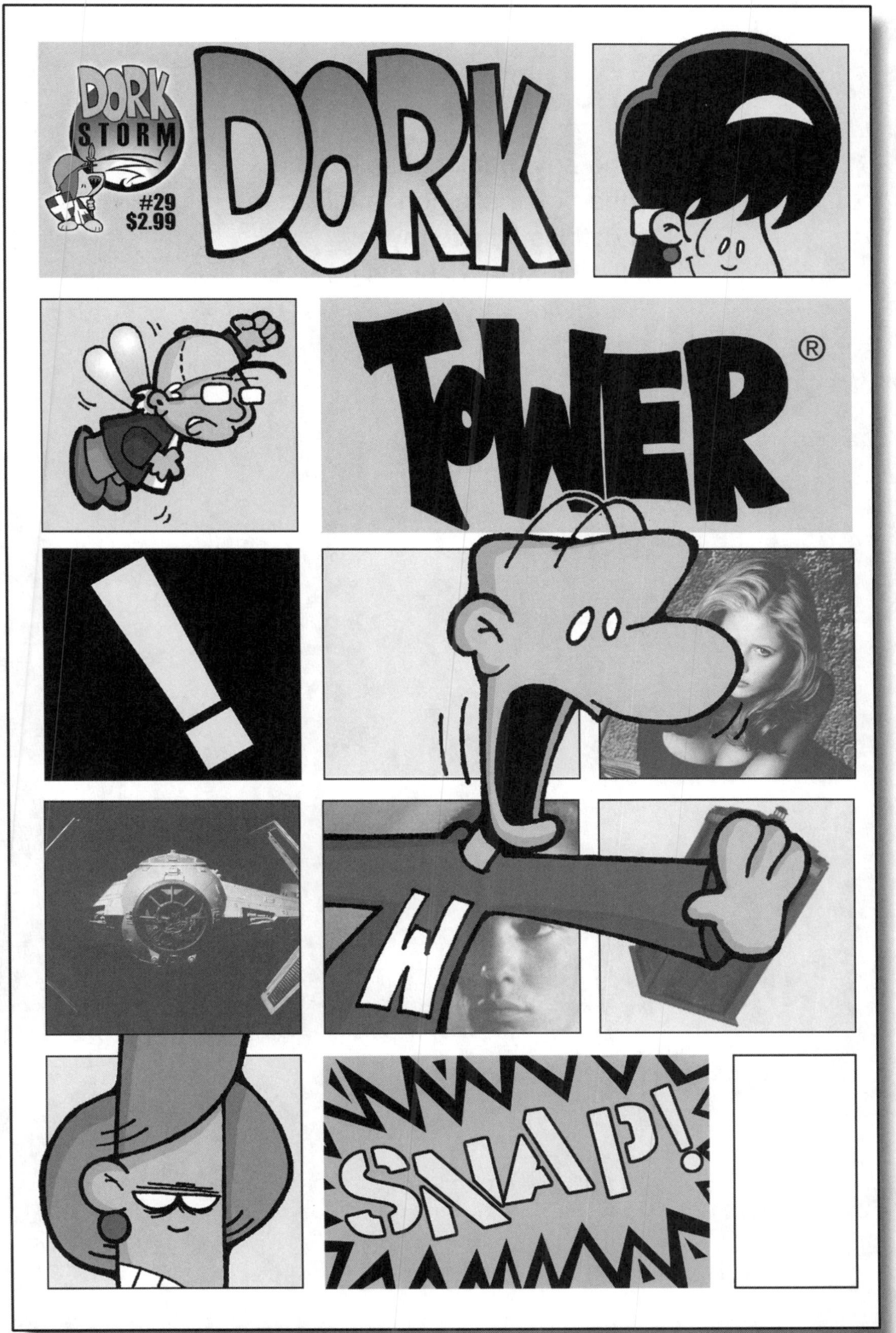

DORK STORM
#29
$2.99
DORK TOWER ®
!
W
SNAP!

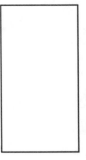

I'm the boy that looks excited,
I'm the boy that's gonna fall apart.
Candyfloss, I lie to myself,
I'm the boy that eats his heart out.
- *"Candyfloss," Wilco*

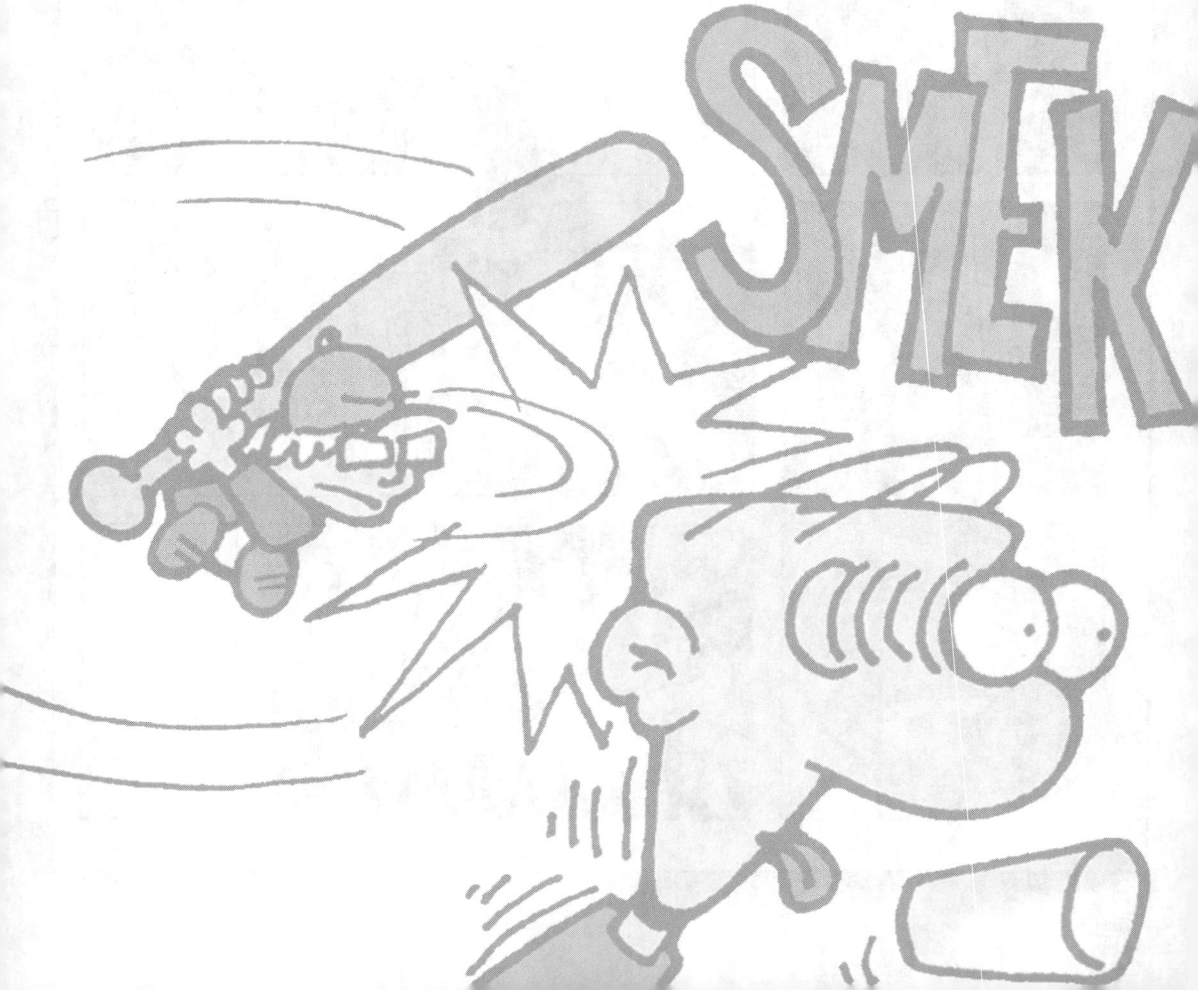
SMEK

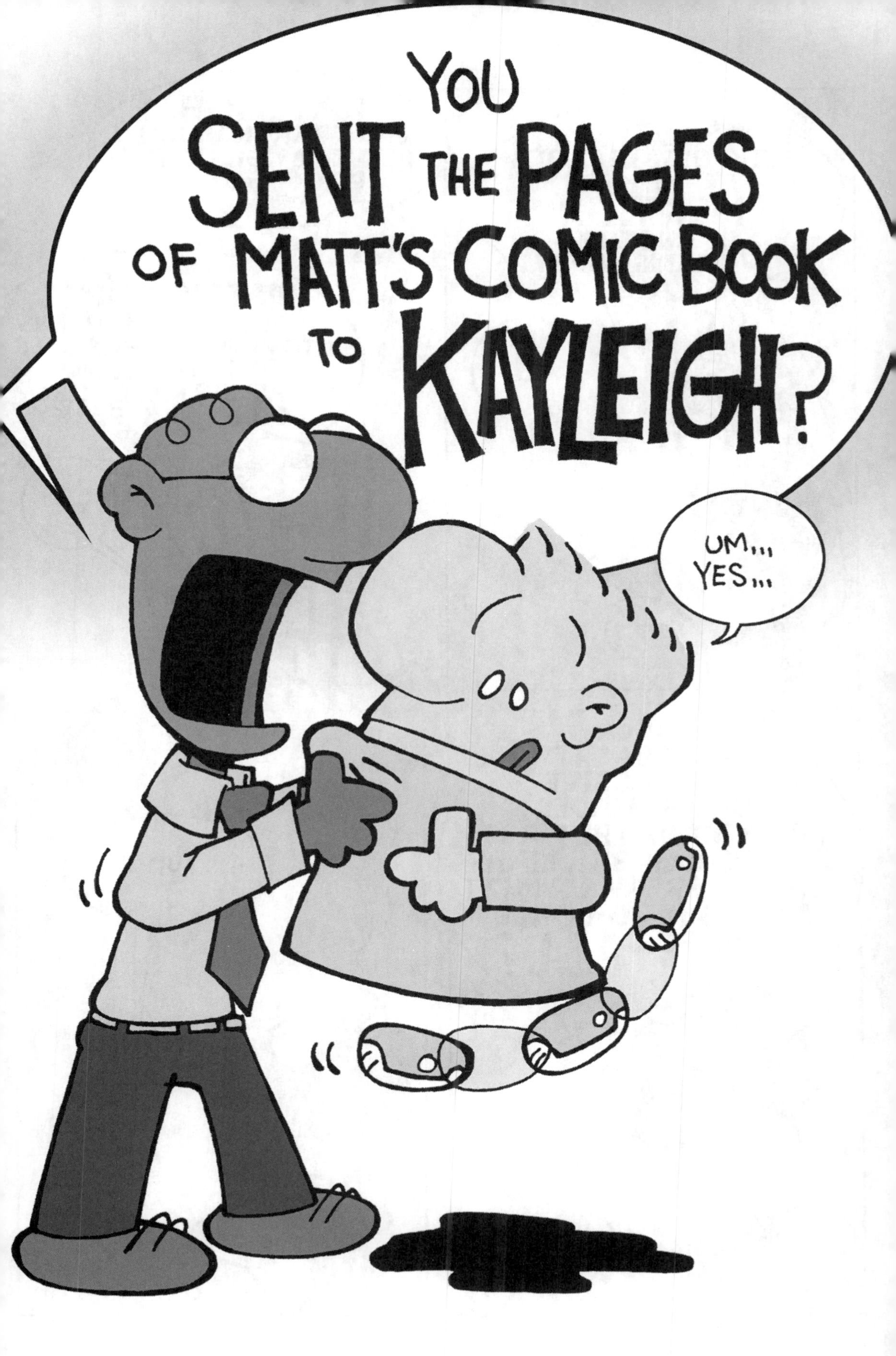
YOU SENT THE PAGES OF MATT'S COMIC BOOK TO KAYLEIGH?
UM... YES...

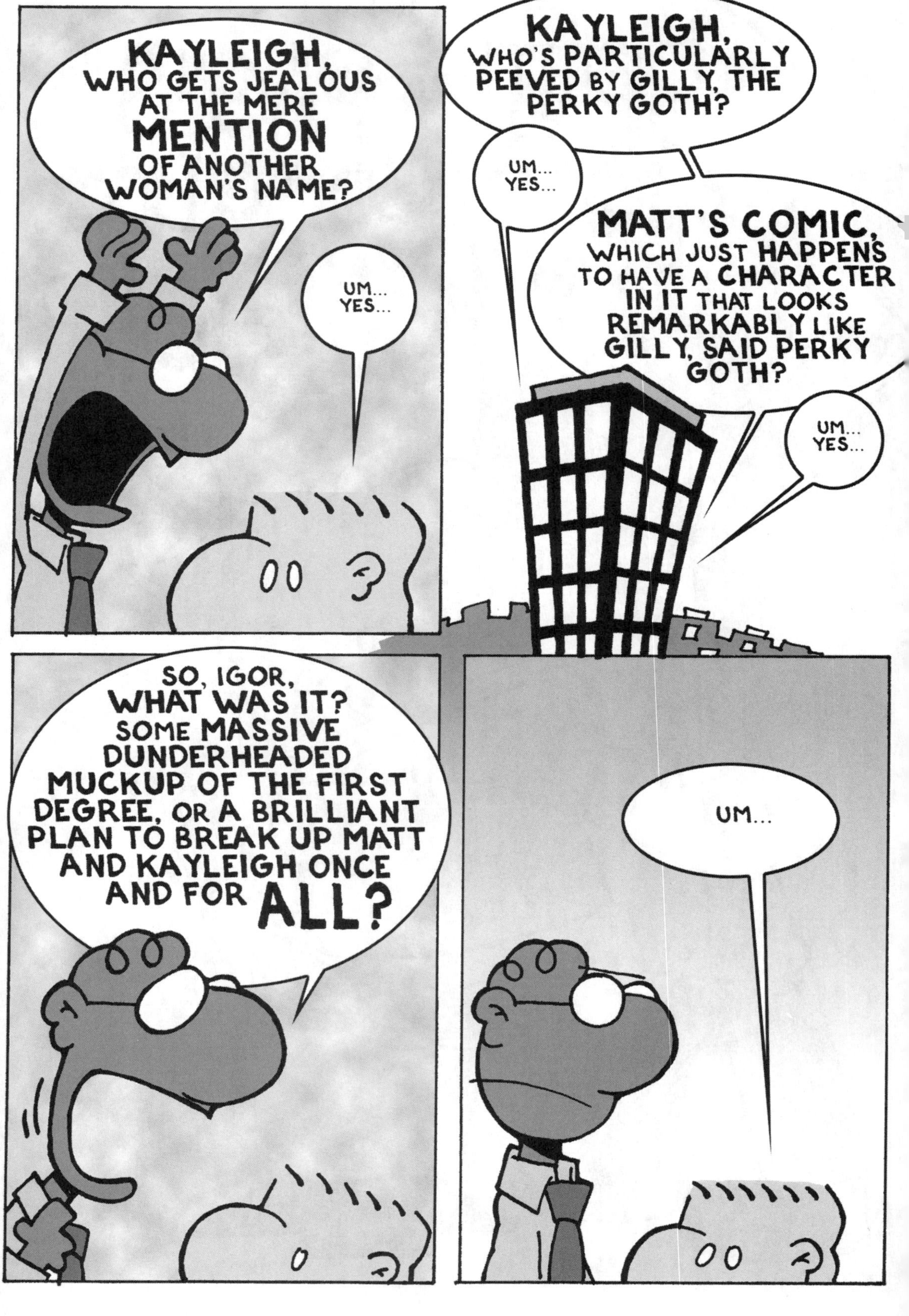

KAYLEIGH, WHO GETS JEALOUS AT THE MERE MENTION OF ANOTHER WOMAN'S NAME?
UM... YES...
KAYLEIGH, WHO'S PARTICULARLY PEEVED BY GILLY, THE PERKY GOTH?
UM... YES...
MATT'S COMIC, WHICH JUST HAPPENS TO HAVE A CHARACTER IN IT THAT LOOKS REMARKABLY LIKE GILLY, SAID PERKY GOTH?
UM... YES...
SO, IGOR, WHAT WAS IT? SOME MASSIVE DUNDERHEADED MUCKUP OF THE FIRST DEGREE, OR A BRILLIANT PLAN TO BREAK UP MATT AND KAYLEIGH ONCE AND FOR ALL?
UM...

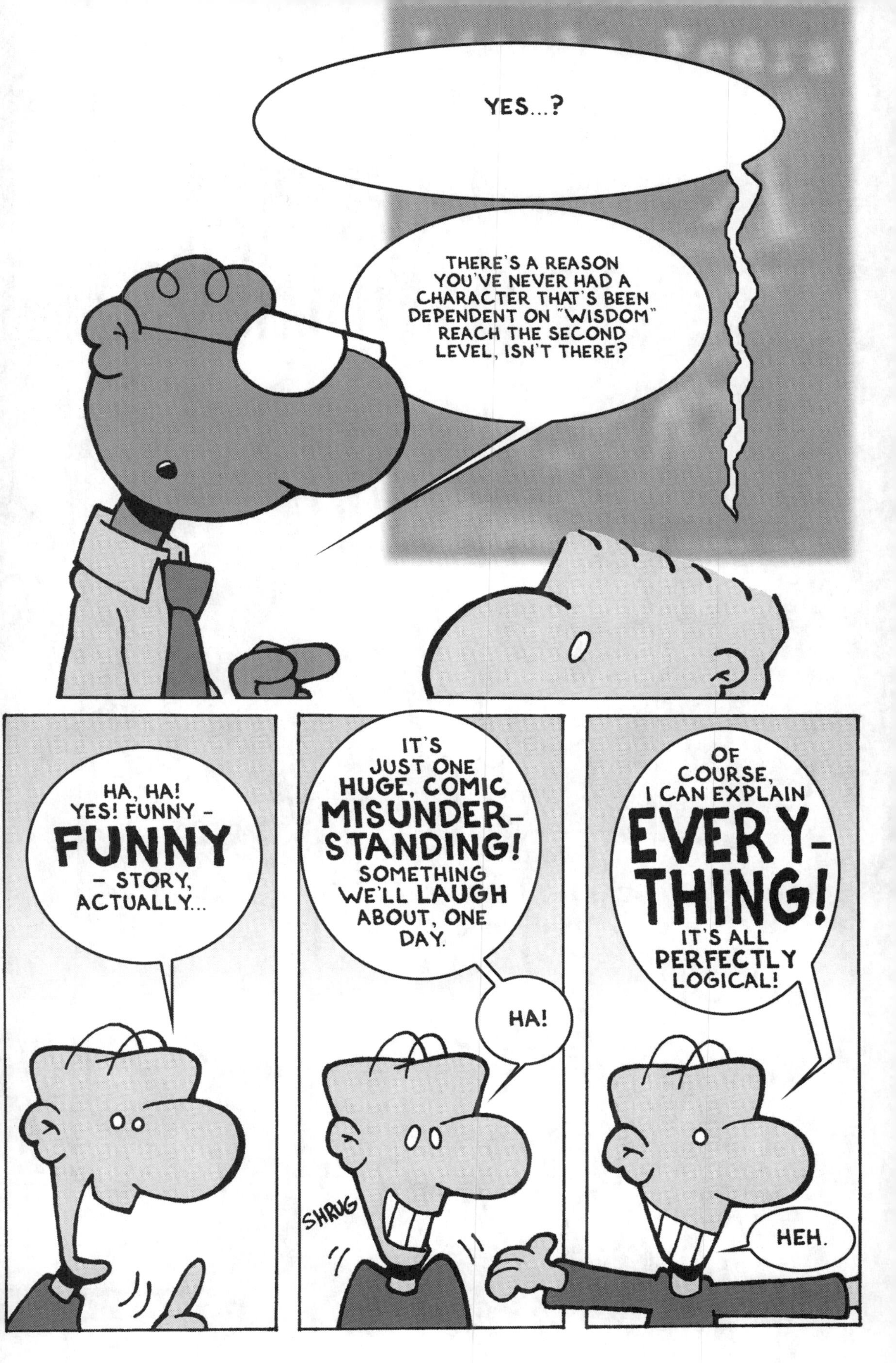
YES...?
THERE'S A REASON YOU'VE NEVER HAD A CHARACTER THAT'S BEEN DEPENDENT ON "WISDOM" REACH THE SECOND LEVEL, ISN'T THERE?
HA, HA! YES! FUNNY - FUNNY - STORY, ACTUALLY...
IT'S JUST ONE HUGE, COMIC MISUNDER-STANDING! SOMETHING WE'LL LAUGH ABOUT, ONE DAY.
HA!
SHRUG
OF COURSE, I CAN EXPLAIN EVERY-THING! IT'S ALL PERFECTLY LOGICAL!
HEH.

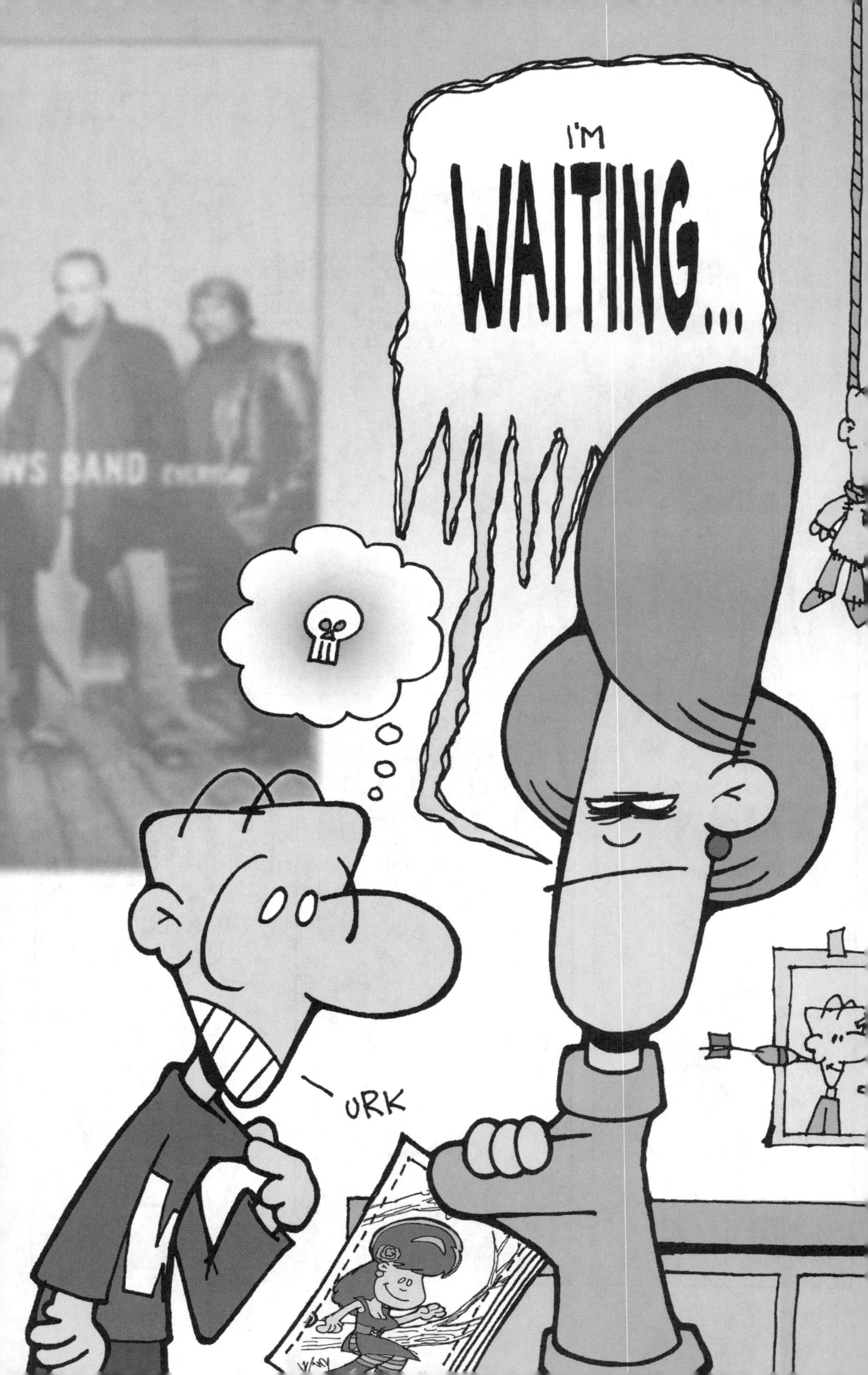
I'M WAITING...
ORK

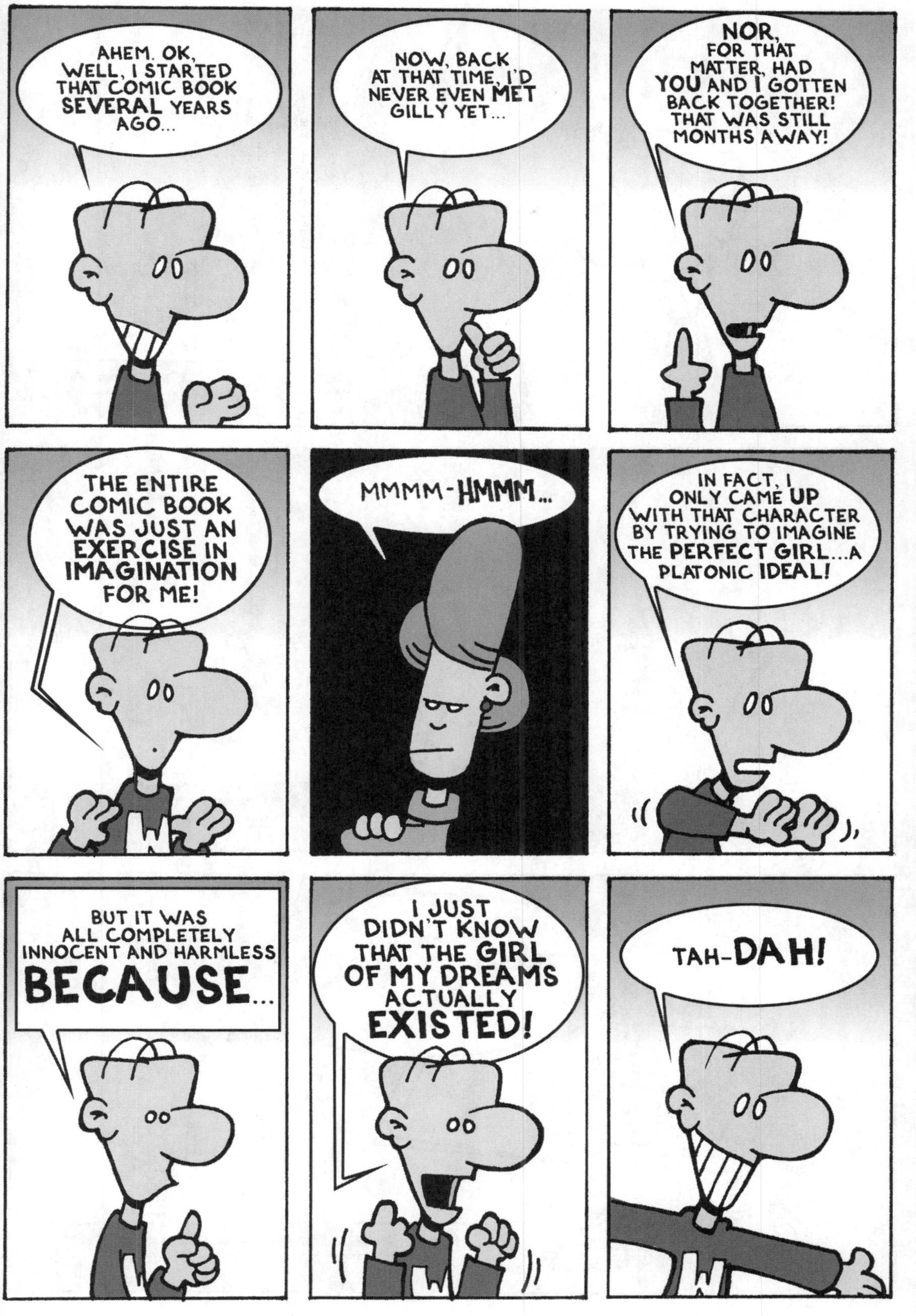
AHEM. OK, WELL, I STARTED THAT COMIC BOOK SEVERAL YEARS AGO...
NOW, BACK AT THAT TIME, I'D NEVER EVEN MET GILLY YET...
NOR, FOR THAT MATTER, HAD YOU AND I GOTTEN BACK TOGETHER! THAT WAS STILL MONTHS AWAY!
THE ENTIRE COMIC BOOK WAS JUST AN EXERCISE IN IMAGINATION FOR ME!
MMMM-HMMM...
IN FACT, I ONLY CAME UP WITH THAT CHARACTER BY TRYING TO IMAGINE THE PERFECT GIRL...A PLATONIC IDEAL!
BUT IT WAS ALL COMPLETELY INNOCENT AND HARMLESS BECAUSE...
I JUST DIDN'T KNOW THAT THE GIRL OF MY DREAMS ACTUALLY EXISTED!
TAH-DAH!

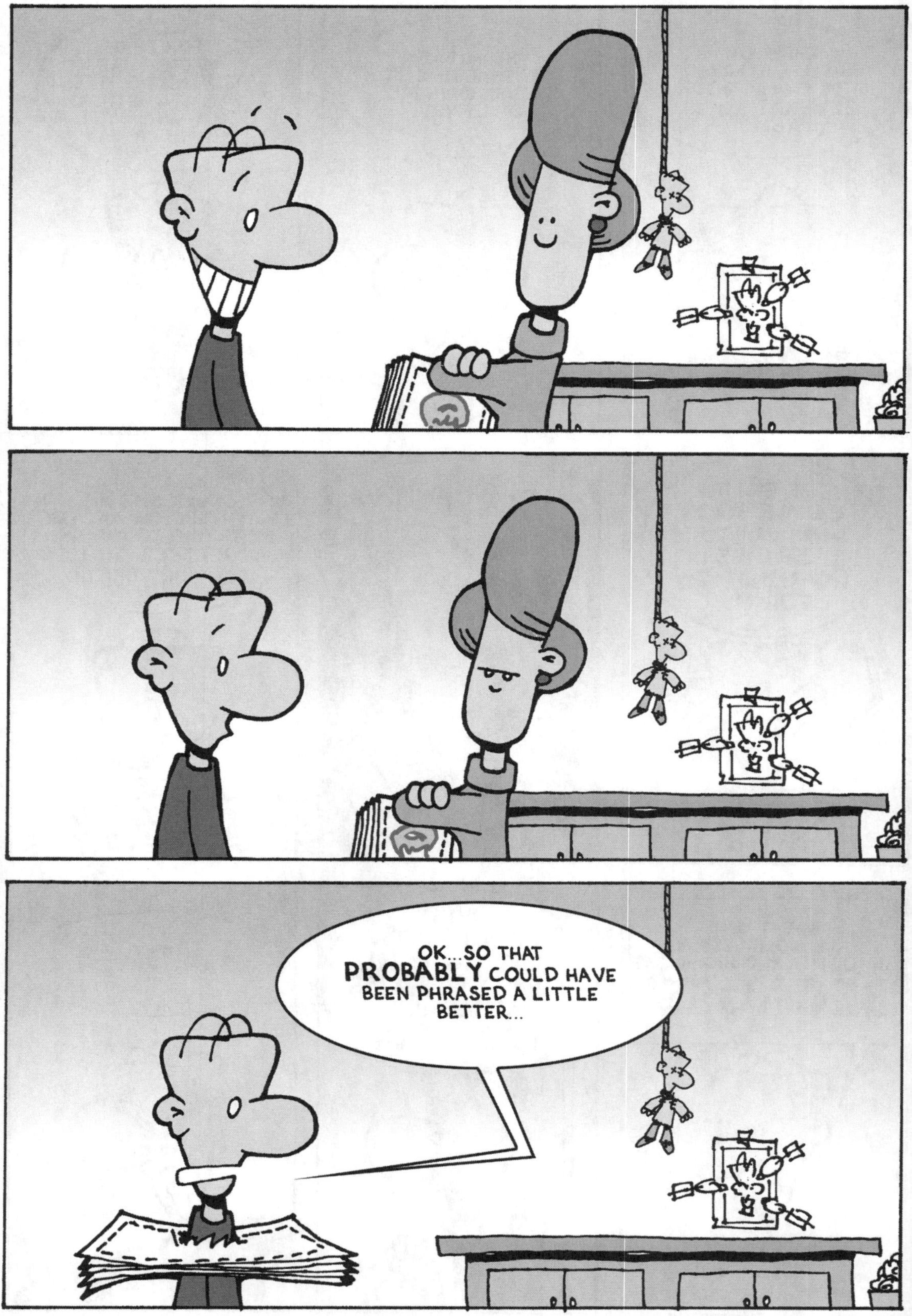
OK...SO THAT PROBABLY COULD HAVE BEEN PHRASED A LITTLE BETTER...

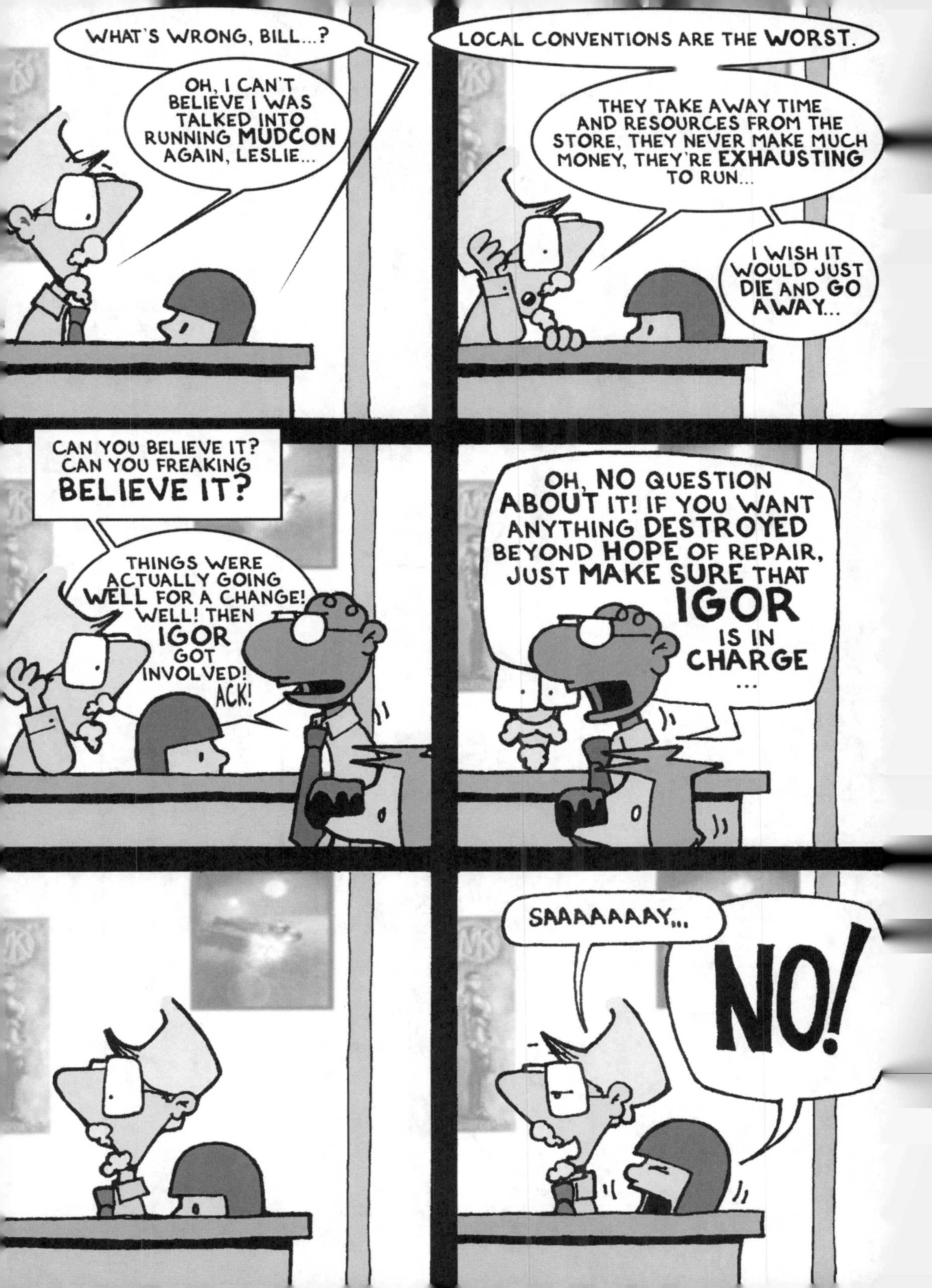
WHAT'S WRONG, BILL...?
OH, I CAN'T BELIEVE I WAS TALKED INTO RUNNING MUDCON AGAIN, LESLIE...
LOCAL CONVENTIONS ARE THE WORST.
THEY TAKE AWAY TIME AND RESOURCES FROM THE STORE, THEY NEVER MAKE MUCH MONEY, THEY'RE EXHAUSTING TO RUN...
I WISH IT WOULD JUST DIE AND GO AWAY...
CAN YOU BELIEVE IT? CAN YOU FREAKING BELIEVE IT?
THINGS WERE ACTUALLY GOING WELL FOR A CHANGE! WELL! THEN IGOR GOT INVOLVED!
ACK!
OH, NO QUESTION ABOUT IT! IF YOU WANT ANYTHING DESTROYED BEYOND HOPE OF REPAIR, JUST MAKE SURE THAT IGOR IS IN CHARGE ...
SAAAAAAAY...
NO!

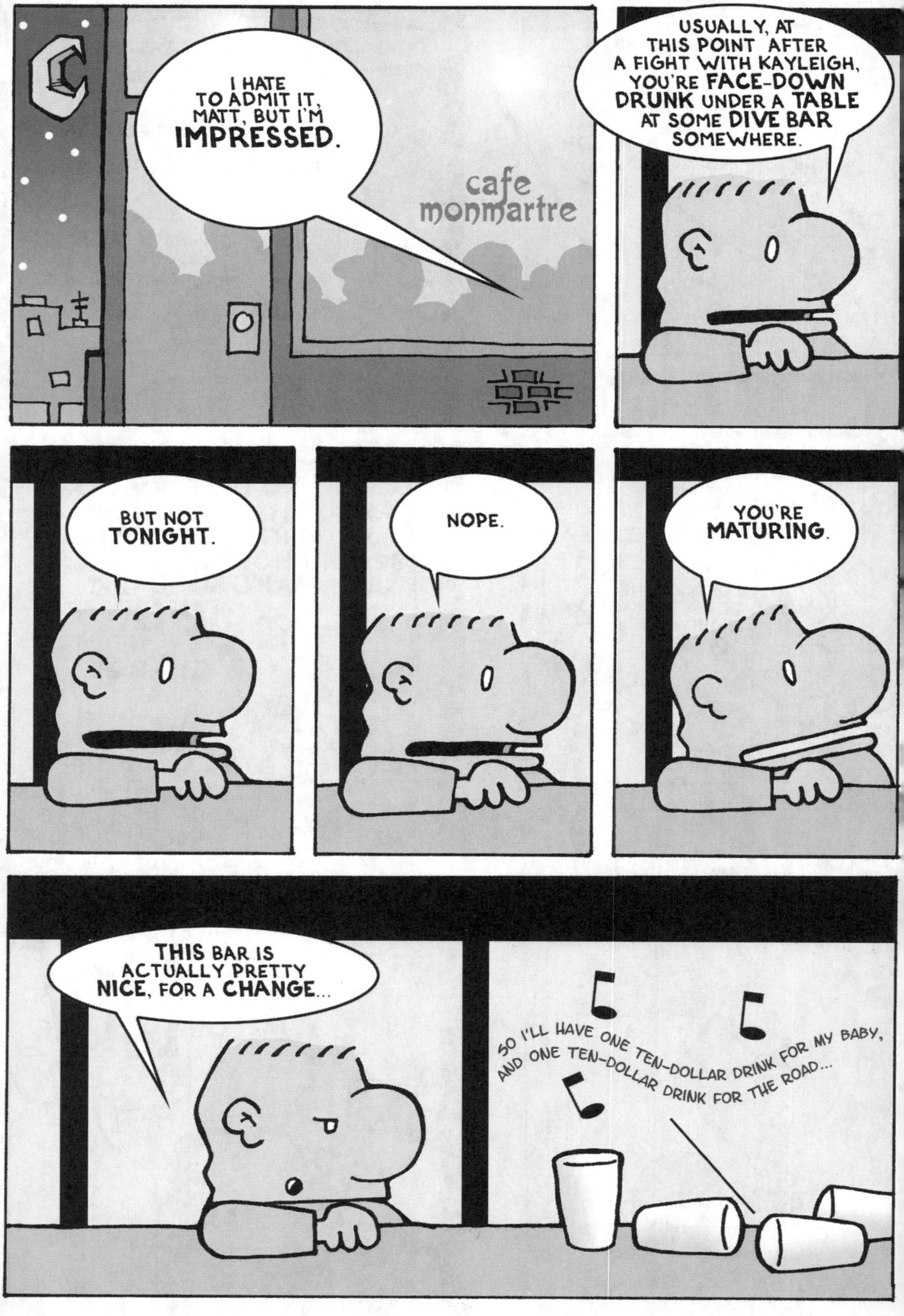
I HATE TO ADMIT IT, MATT, BUT I'M IMPRESSED.
cafe monmartre
USUALLY, AT THIS POINT AFTER A FIGHT WITH KAYLEIGH, YOU'RE FACE-DOWN DRUNK UNDER A TABLE AT SOME DIVE BAR SOMEWHERE.
BUT NOT TONIGHT.
NOPE.
YOU'RE MATURING.
THIS BAR IS ACTUALLY PRETTY NICE, FOR A CHANGE...
SO I'LL HAVE ONE TEN-DOLLAR DRINK FOR MY BABY, AND ONE TEN-DOLLAR DRINK FOR THE ROAD...

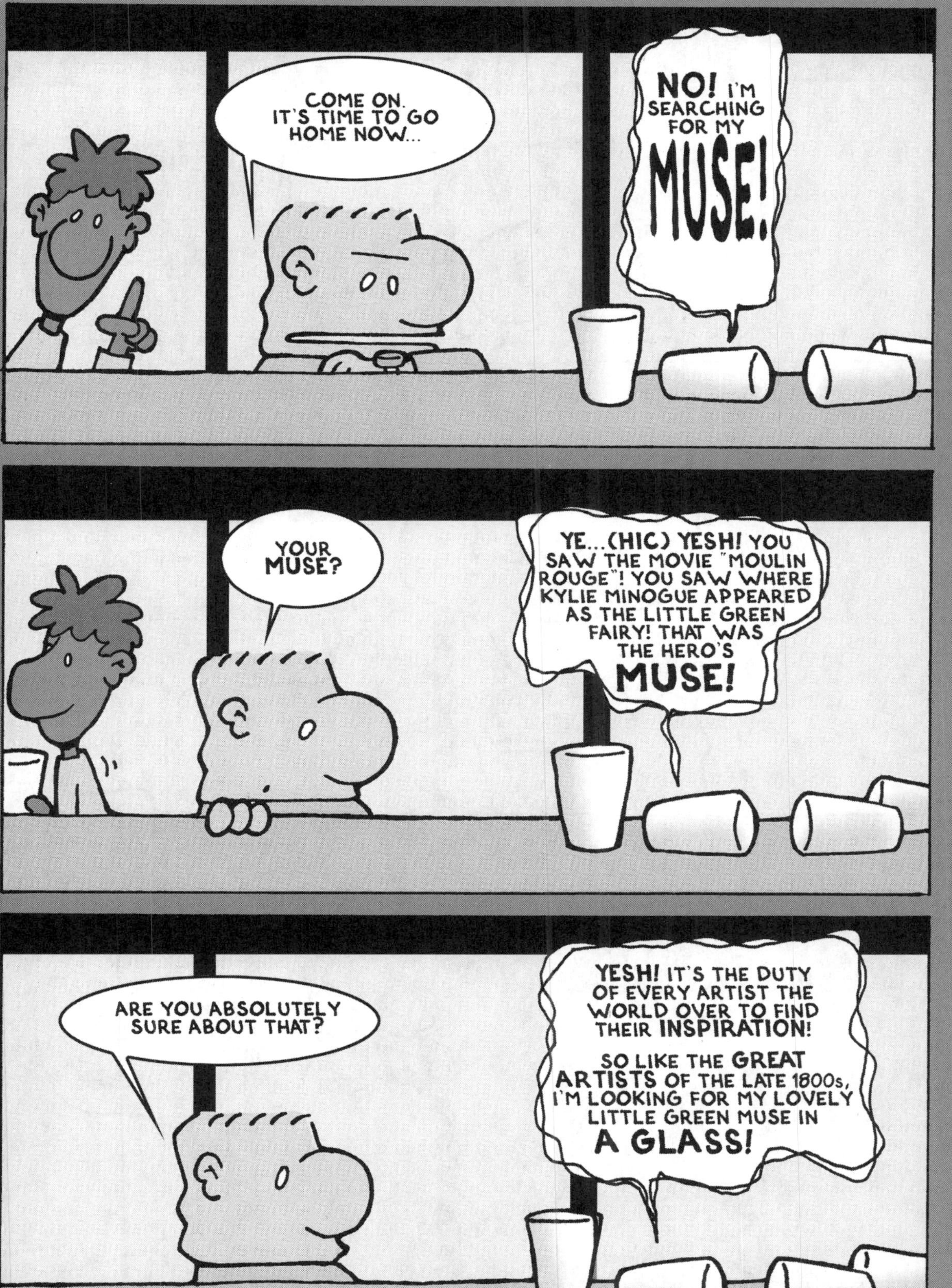
COME ON. IT'S TIME TO GO HOME NOW...
NO! I'M SEARCHING FOR MY MUSE!
YOUR MUSE?
YE...(HIC) YESH! YOU SAW THE MOVIE "MOULIN ROUGE"! YOU SAW WHERE KYLIE MINOGUE APPEARED AS THE LITTLE GREEN FAIRY! THAT WAS THE HERO'S MUSE!
ARE YOU ABSOLUTELY SURE ABOUT THAT?
YESH! IT'S THE DUTY OF EVERY ARTIST THE WORLD OVER TO FIND THEIR INSPIRATION!
SO LIKE THE GREAT ARTISTS OF THE LATE 1800s, I'M LOOKING FOR MY LOVELY LITTLE GREEN MUSE IN A GLASS!

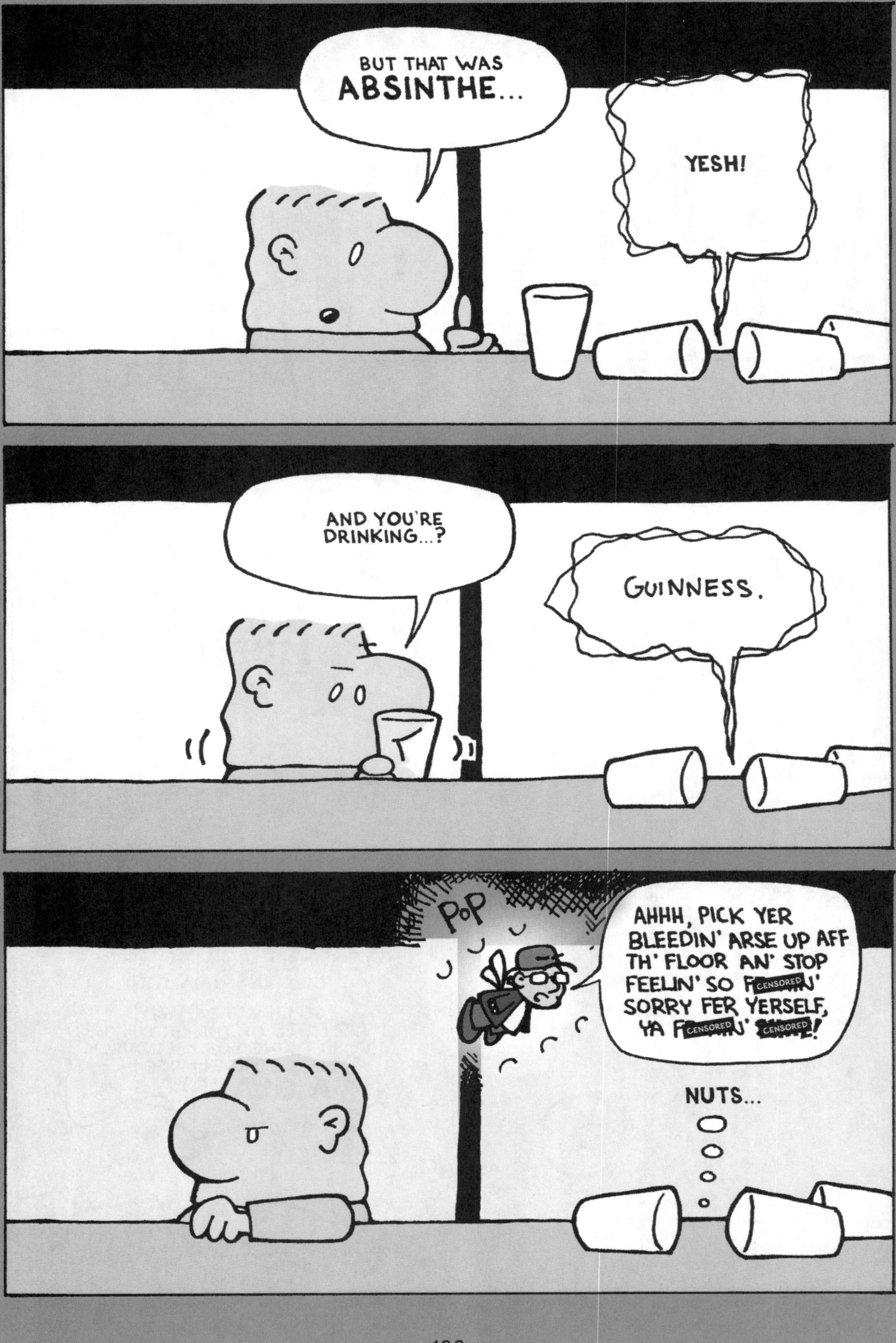
BUT THAT WAS ABSINTHE...
YESH!
AND YOU'RE DRINKING...?
GUINNESS.
POP
AHHH, PICK YER BLEEDIN' ARSE UP AFF TH' FLOOR AN' STOP FEELIN' SO F CENSORED ' SORRY FER YERSELF, YA F CENSORED ' CENSORED !
NUTS...

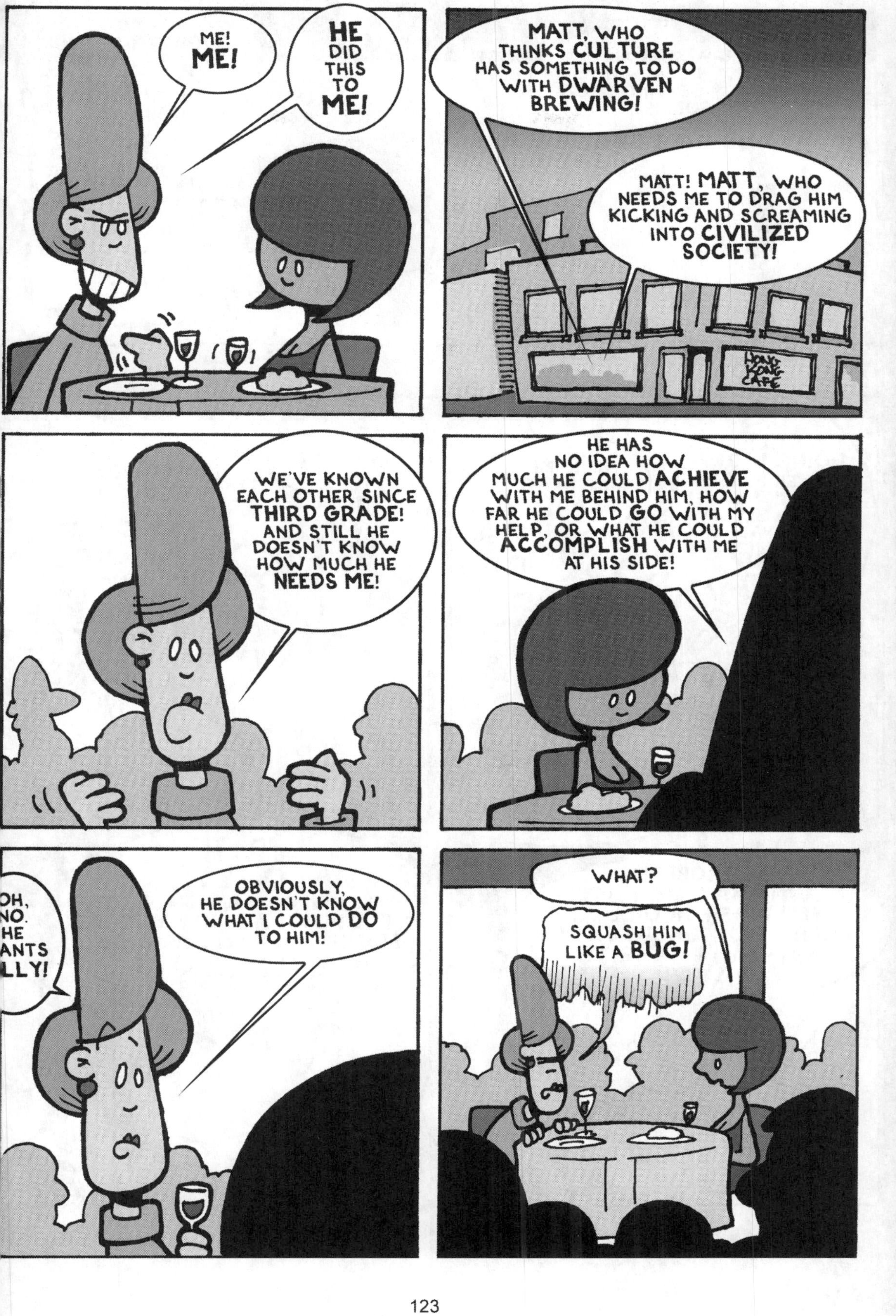
ME! ME!
HE DID THIS TO ME!
MATT, WHO THINKS CULTURE HAS SOMETHING TO DO WITH DWARVEN BREWING!
MATT! MATT, WHO NEEDS ME TO DRAG HIM KICKING AND SCREAMING INTO CIVILIZED SOCIETY!
HONG KONG CAFE
WE'VE KNOWN EACH OTHER SINCE THIRD GRADE! AND STILL HE DOESN'T KNOW HOW MUCH HE NEEDS ME!
HE HAS NO IDEA HOW MUCH HE COULD ACHIEVE WITH ME BEHIND HIM, HOW FAR HE COULD GO WITH MY HELP, OR WHAT HE COULD ACCOMPLISH WITH ME AT HIS SIDE!
OBVIOUSLY, HE DOESN'T KNOW WHAT I COULD DO TO HIM!
WHAT?
SQUASH HIM LIKE A BUG!

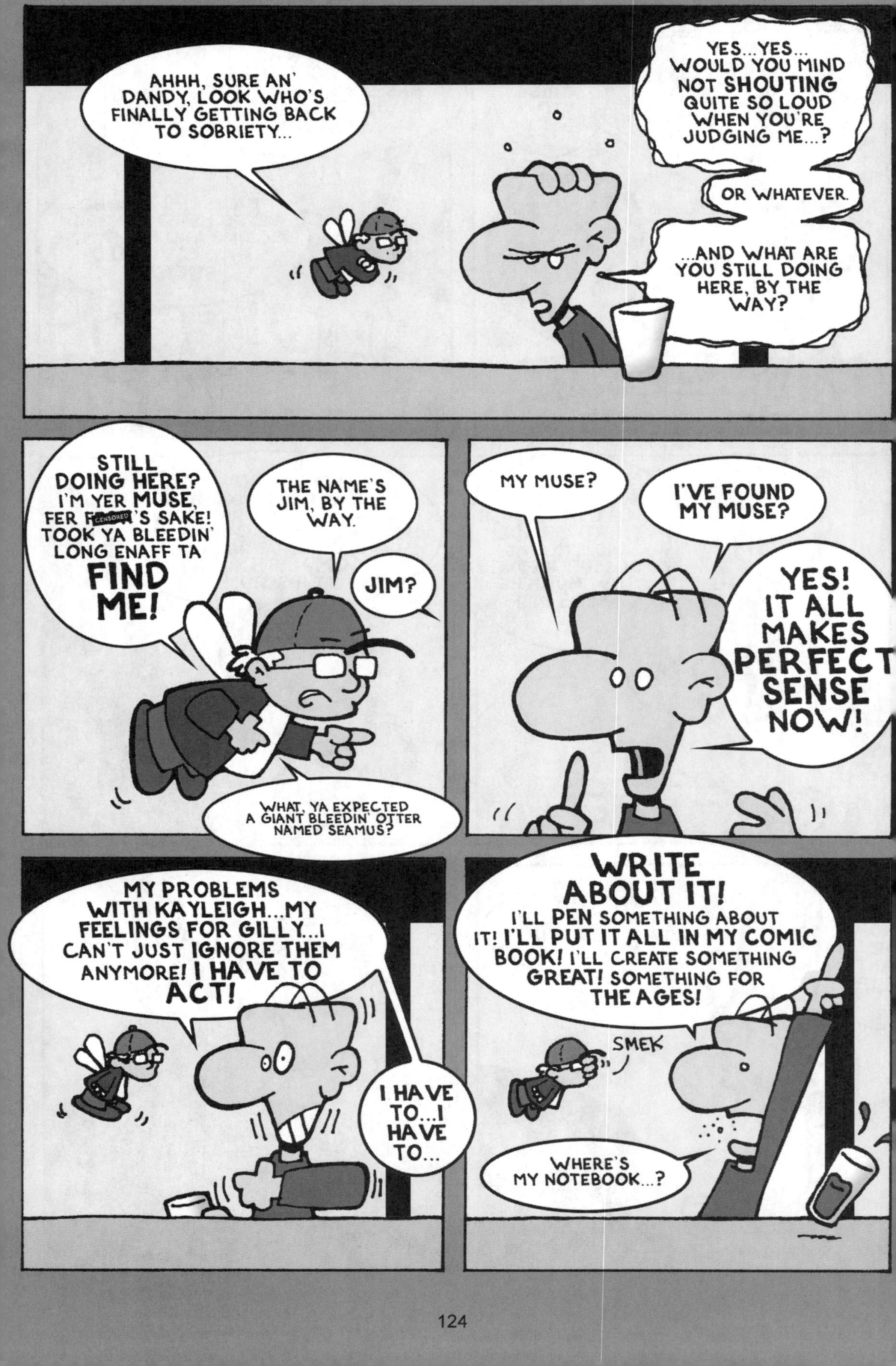
AHHH, SURE AN' DANDY, LOOK WHO'S FINALLY GETTING BACK TO SOBRIETY...
YES...YES... WOULD YOU MIND NOT SHOUTING QUITE SO LOUD WHEN YOU'RE JUDGING ME...?
OR WHATEVER.
...AND WHAT ARE YOU STILL DOING HERE, BY THE WAY?
STILL DOING HERE? I'M YER MUSE, FER F[redacted]'S SAKE! TOOK YA BLEEDIN' LONG ENAFF TA FIND ME!
THE NAME'S JIM, BY THE WAY.
JIM?
WHAT, YA EXPECTED A GIANT BLEEDIN' OTTER NAMED SEAMUS?
MY MUSE?
I'VE FOUND MY MUSE?
YES! IT ALL MAKES PERFECT SENSE NOW!
MY PROBLEMS WITH KAYLEIGH...MY FEELINGS FOR GILLY...I CAN'T JUST IGNORE THEM ANYMORE! I HAVE TO ACT!
I HAVE TO...I HAVE TO...
WRITE ABOUT IT! I'LL PEN SOMETHING ABOUT IT! I'LL PUT IT ALL IN MY COMIC BOOK! I'LL CREATE SOMETHING GREAT! SOMETHING FOR THE AGES!
SMEK
WHERE'S MY NOTEBOOK...?

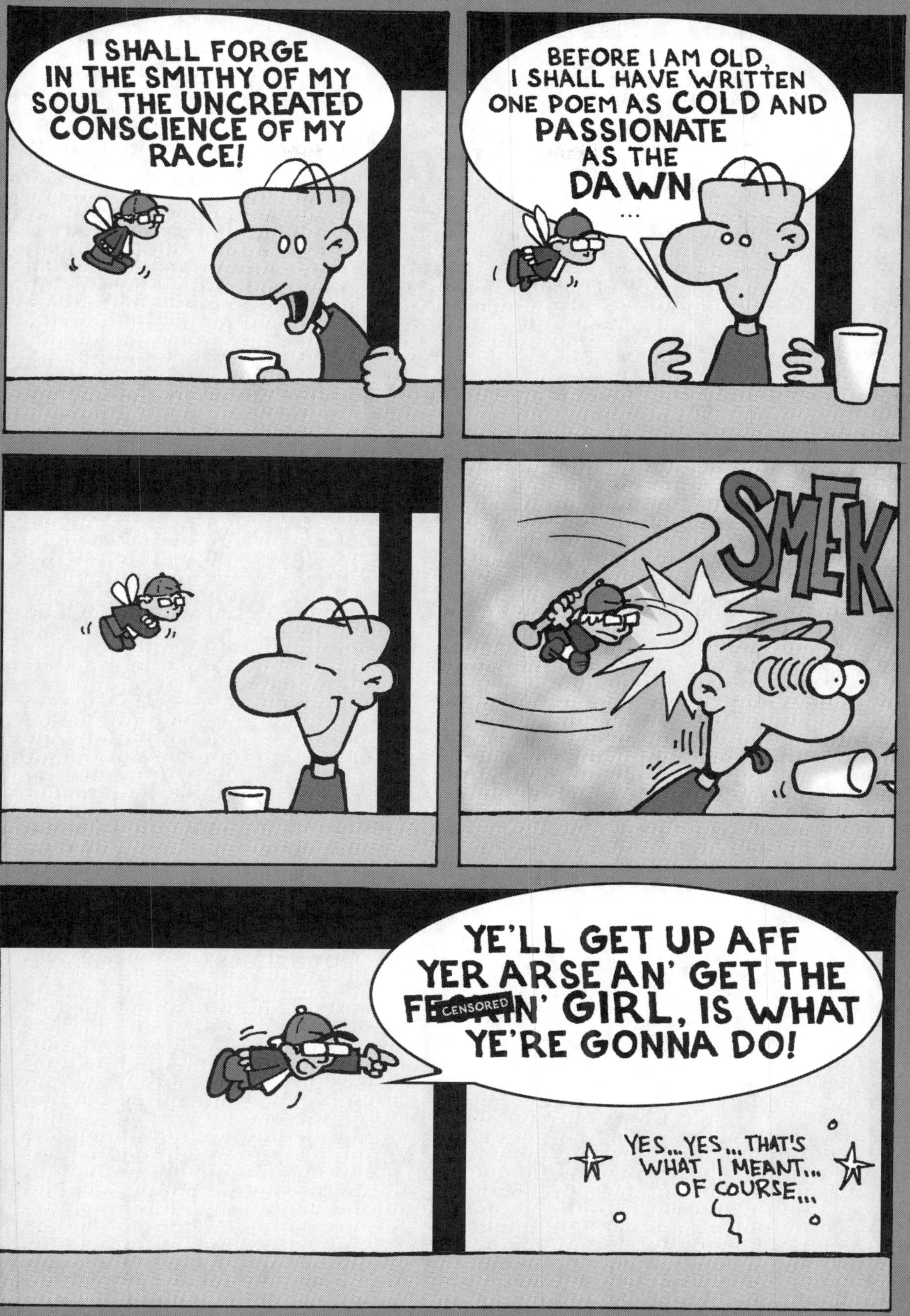
I SHALL FORGE IN THE SMITHY OF MY SOUL THE UNCREATED CONSCIENCE OF MY RACE!
BEFORE I AM OLD, I SHALL HAVE WRITTEN ONE POEM AS COLD AND PASSIONATE AS THE DAWN ...
SMEK
YE'LL GET UP AFF YER ARSE AN' GET THE FE CENSORED IN' GIRL, IS WHAT YE'RE GONNA DO!
YES... YES... THAT'S WHAT I MEANT... OF COURSE...

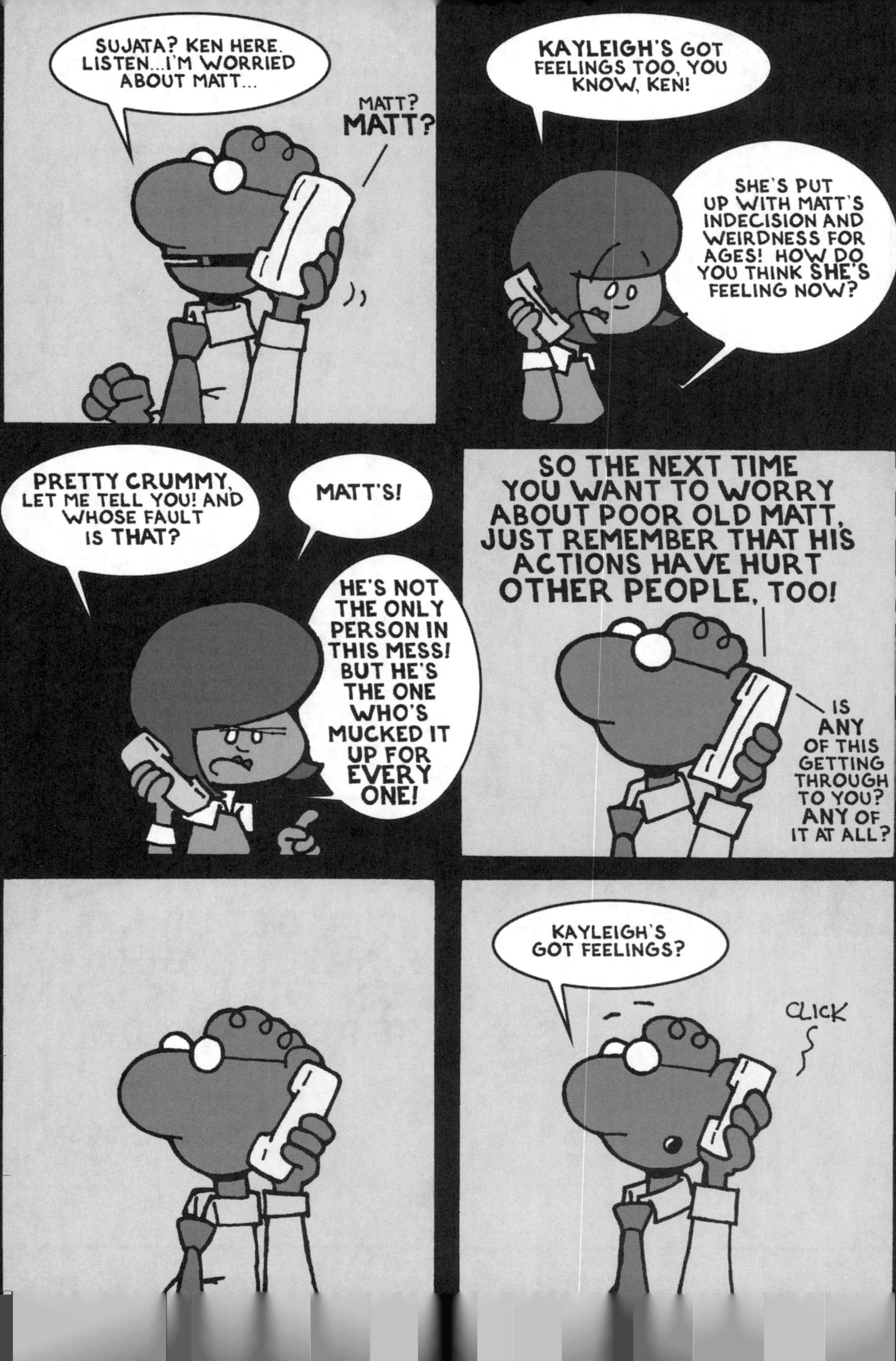
SUJATA? KEN HERE. LISTEN...I'M WORRIED ABOUT MATT...
MATT? MATT?
KAYLEIGH'S GOT FEELINGS TOO, YOU KNOW, KEN!
SHE'S PUT UP WITH MATT'S INDECISION AND WEIRDNESS FOR AGES! HOW DO YOU THINK SHE'S FEELING NOW?
PRETTY CRUMMY, LET ME TELL YOU! AND WHOSE FAULT IS THAT?
MATT'S!
HE'S NOT THE ONLY PERSON IN THIS MESS! BUT HE'S THE ONE WHO'S MUCKED IT UP FOR EVERY ONE!
SO THE NEXT TIME YOU WANT TO WORRY ABOUT POOR OLD MATT, JUST REMEMBER THAT HIS ACTIONS HAVE HURT OTHER PEOPLE, TOO!
IS ANY OF THIS GETTING THROUGH TO YOU? ANY OF IT AT ALL?
KAYLEIGH'S GOT FEELINGS?
CLICK

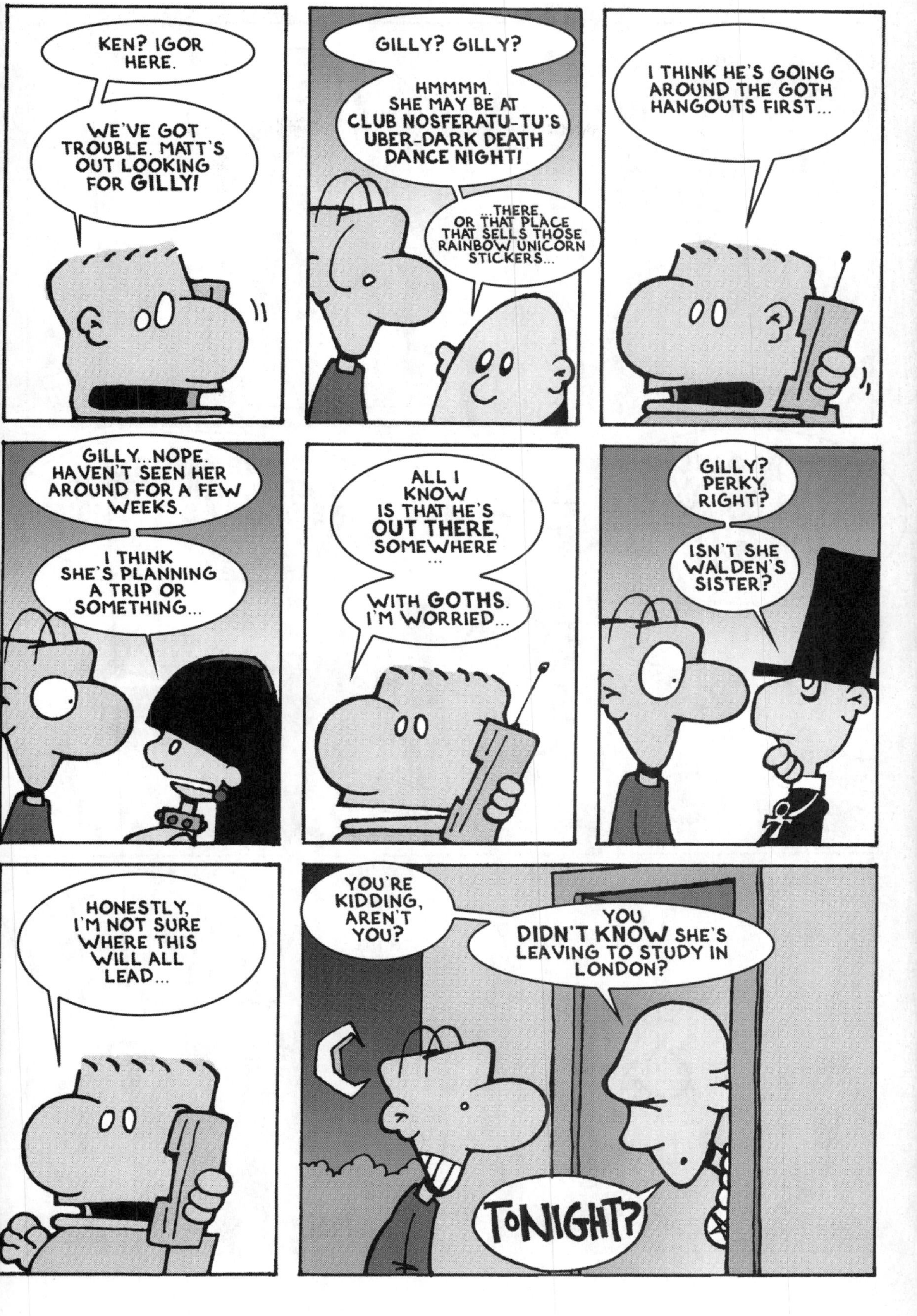
KEN? IGOR HERE.
WE'VE GOT TROUBLE. MATT'S OUT LOOKING FOR GILLY!
GILLY? GILLY?
HMMMM. SHE MAY BE AT CLUB NOSFERATU-TU'S UBER-DARK DEATH DANCE NIGHT!
...THERE. OR THAT PLACE THAT SELLS THOSE RAINBOW UNICORN STICKERS...
I THINK HE'S GOING AROUND THE GOTH HANGOUTS FIRST...
GILLY...NOPE. HAVEN'T SEEN HER AROUND FOR A FEW WEEKS.
I THINK SHE'S PLANNING A TRIP OR SOMETHING...
ALL I KNOW IS THAT HE'S OUT THERE, SOMEWHERE ...
WITH GOTHS. I'M WORRIED...
GILLY? PERKY, RIGHT?
ISN'T SHE WALDEN'S SISTER?
HONESTLY, I'M NOT SURE WHERE THIS WILL ALL LEAD...
YOU'RE KIDDING, AREN'T YOU?
YOU DIDN'T KNOW SHE'S LEAVING TO STUDY IN LONDON?
TONIGHT?

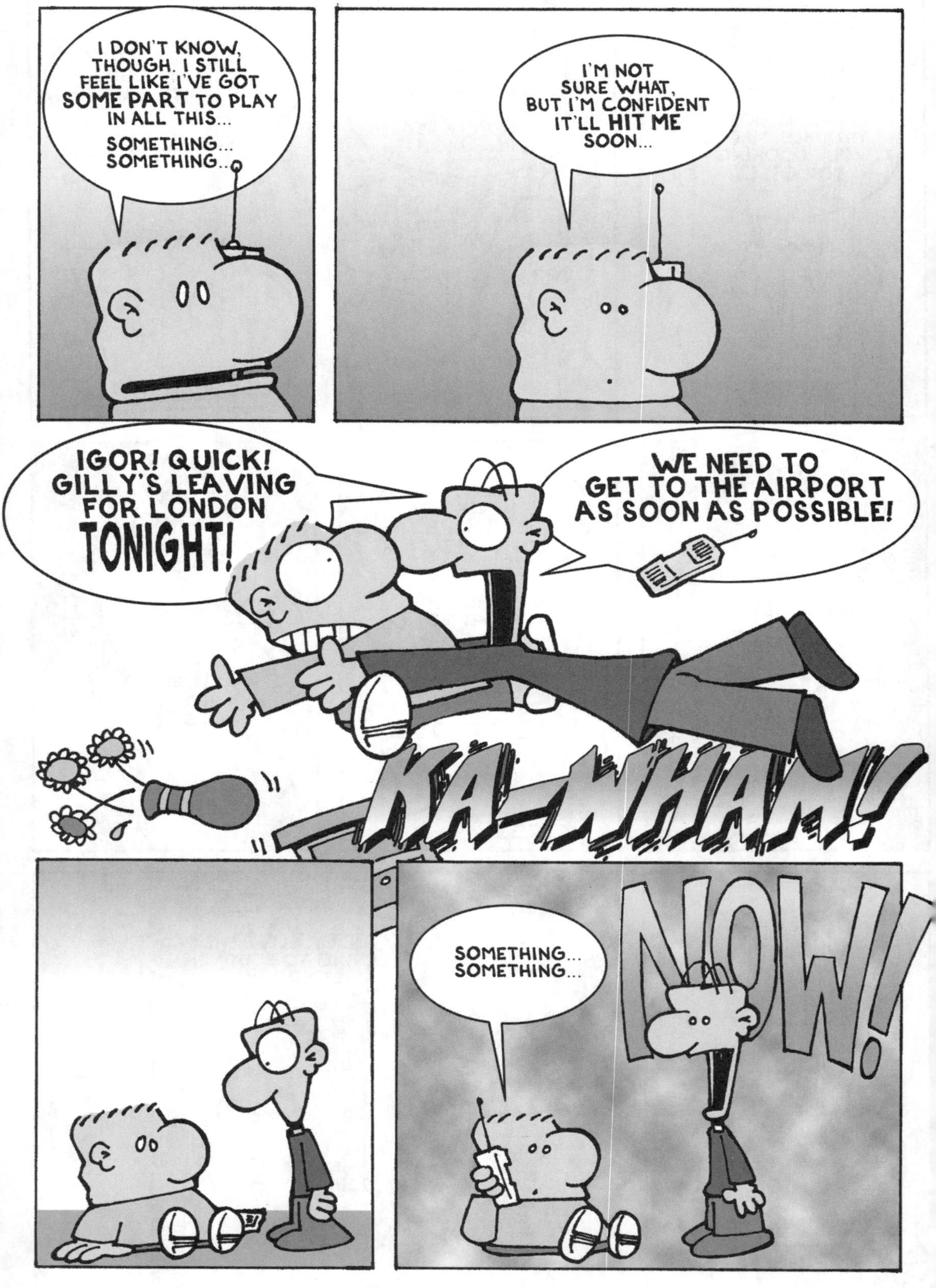
I DON'T KNOW, THOUGH. I STILL FEEL LIKE I'VE GOT SOME PART TO PLAY IN ALL THIS...
SOMETHING... SOMETHING...
I'M NOT SURE WHAT, BUT I'M CONFIDENT IT'LL HIT ME SOON...
IGOR! QUICK! GILLY'S LEAVING FOR LONDON TONIGHT!
WE NEED TO GET TO THE AIRPORT AS SOON AS POSSIBLE!
KA-WHAM!
SOMETHING... SOMETHING...
NOW!!

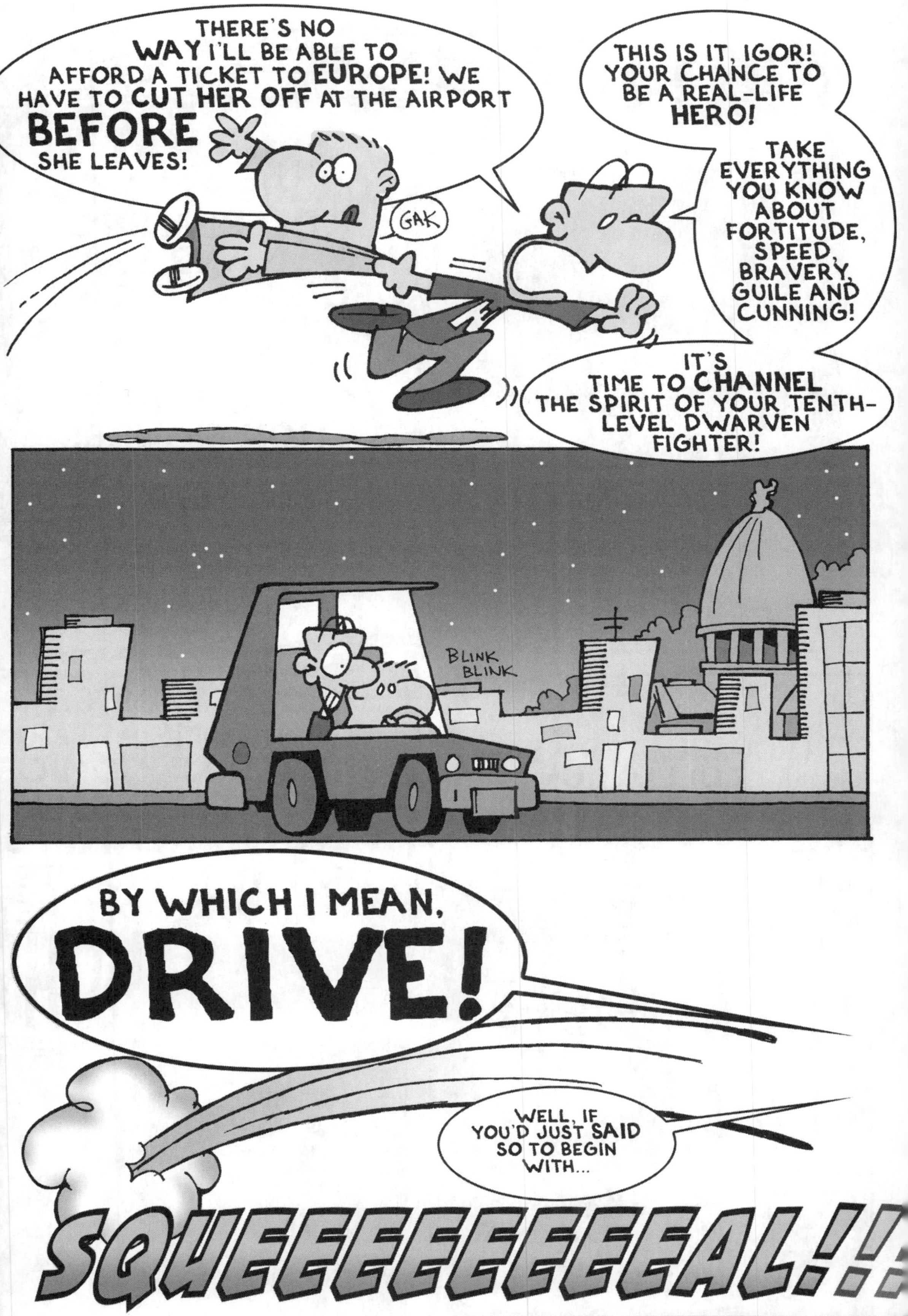
THERE'S NO WAY I'LL BE ABLE TO AFFORD A TICKET TO EUROPE! WE HAVE TO CUT HER OFF AT THE AIRPORT BEFORE SHE LEAVES!
GAK
THIS IS IT, IGOR! YOUR CHANCE TO BE A REAL-LIFE HERO!
TAKE EVERYTHING YOU KNOW ABOUT FORTITUDE, SPEED, BRAVERY, GUILE AND CUNNING!
IT'S TIME TO CHANNEL THE SPIRIT OF YOUR TENTH-LEVEL DWARVEN FIGHTER!
BLINK BLINK
BY WHICH I MEAN, DRIVE!
WELL, IF YOU'D JUST SAID SO TO BEGIN WITH...
SQUEEEEEEEEEAL!!

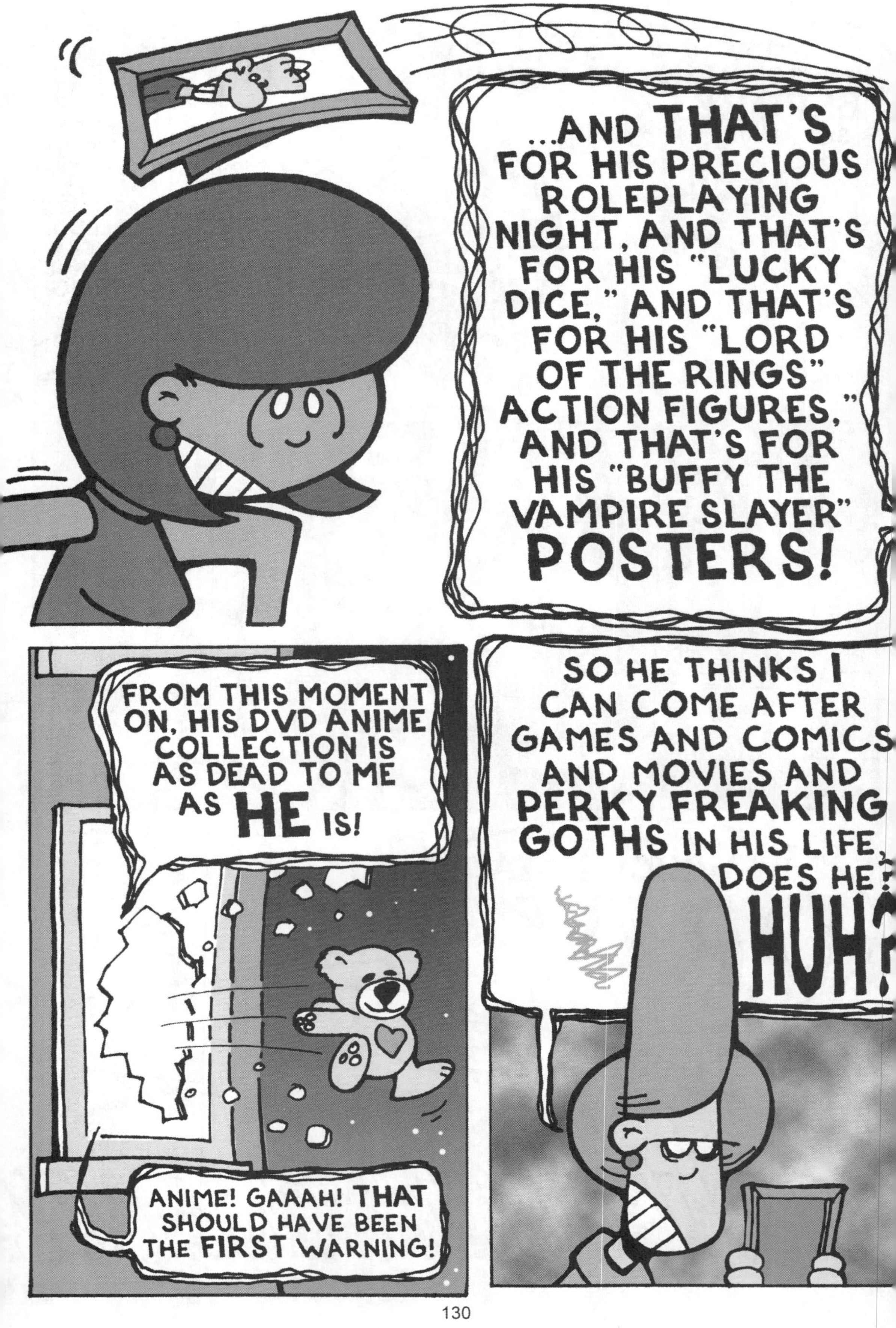
...AND THAT'S FOR HIS PRECIOUS ROLEPLAYING NIGHT, AND THAT'S FOR HIS "LUCKY DICE," AND THAT'S FOR HIS "LORD OF THE RINGS" ACTION FIGURES," AND THAT'S FOR HIS "BUFFY THE VAMPIRE SLAYER" POSTERS!
FROM THIS MOMENT ON, HIS DVD ANIME COLLECTION IS AS DEAD TO ME AS HE IS!
ANIME! GAAAH! THAT SHOULD HAVE BEEN THE FIRST WARNING!
SO HE THINKS I CAN COME AFTER GAMES AND COMICS AND MOVIES AND PERKY FREAKING GOTHS IN HIS LIFE, DOES HE? HUH?

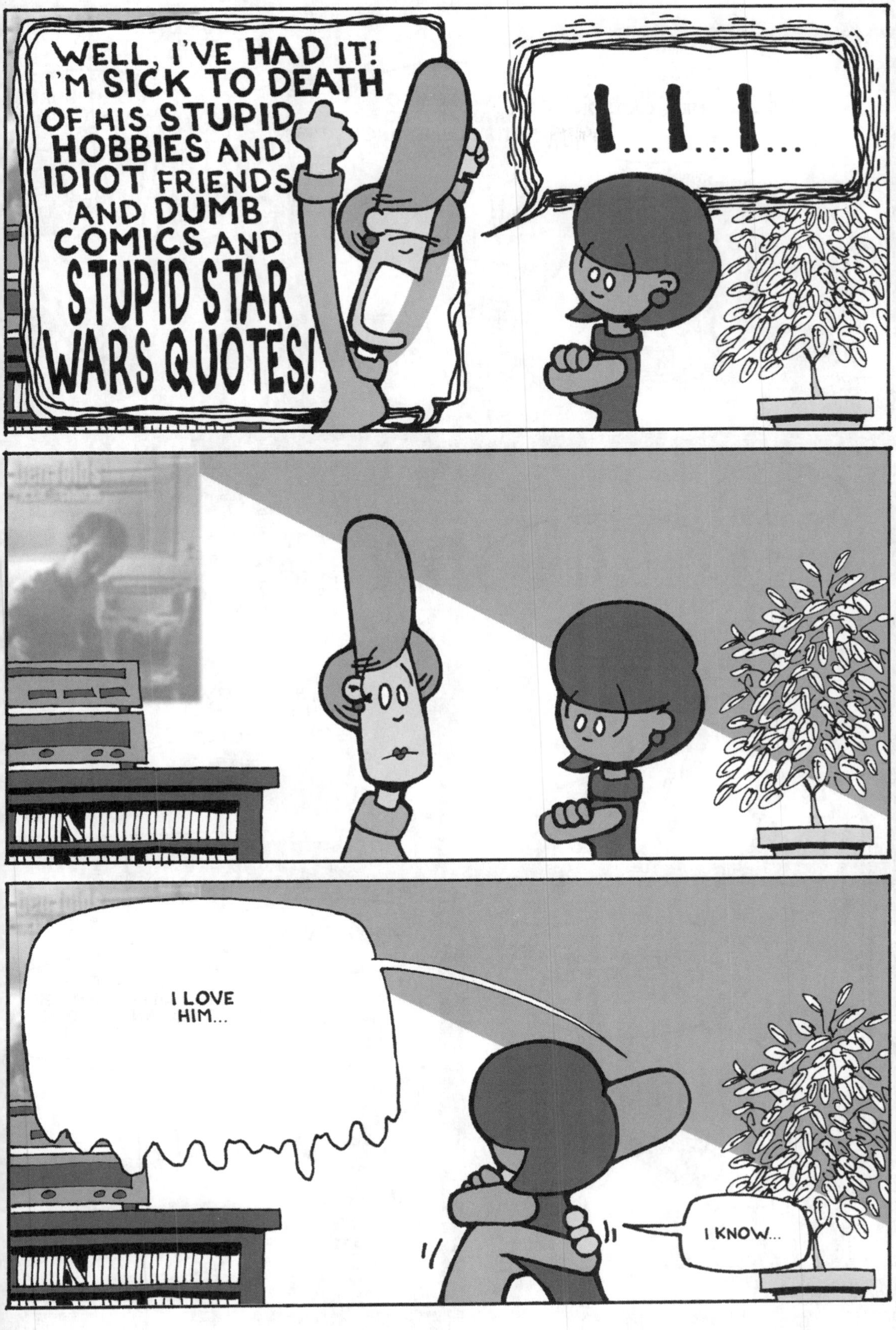

WELL, I'VE HAD IT! I'M SICK TO DEATH OF HIS STUPID HOBBIES AND IDIOT FRIENDS AND DUMB COMICS AND STUPID STAR WARS QUOTES!
I... I... I...
I LOVE HIM...
I KNOW...

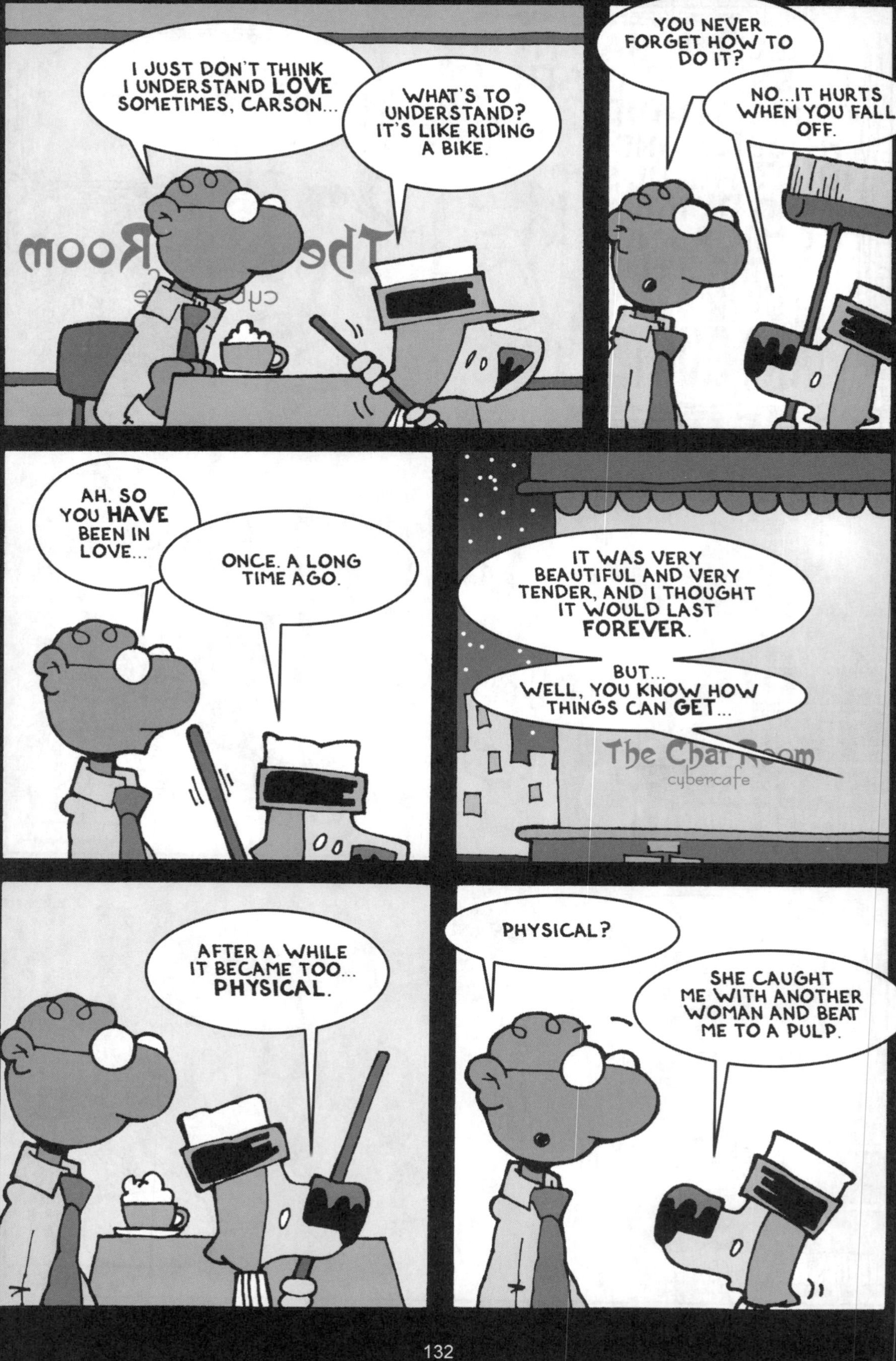
I JUST DON'T THINK I UNDERSTAND LOVE SOMETIMES, CARSON...
WHAT'S TO UNDERSTAND? IT'S LIKE RIDING A BIKE.
YOU NEVER FORGET HOW TO DO IT?
NO...IT HURTS WHEN YOU FALL OFF.
AH. SO YOU HAVE BEEN IN LOVE...
ONCE. A LONG TIME AGO.
IT WAS VERY BEAUTIFUL AND VERY TENDER, AND I THOUGHT IT WOULD LAST FOREVER.
BUT... WELL, YOU KNOW HOW THINGS CAN GET...
The Chat Room
cybercafe
AFTER A WHILE IT BECAME TOO... PHYSICAL.
PHYSICAL?
SHE CAUGHT ME WITH ANOTHER WOMAN AND BEAT ME TO A PULP.

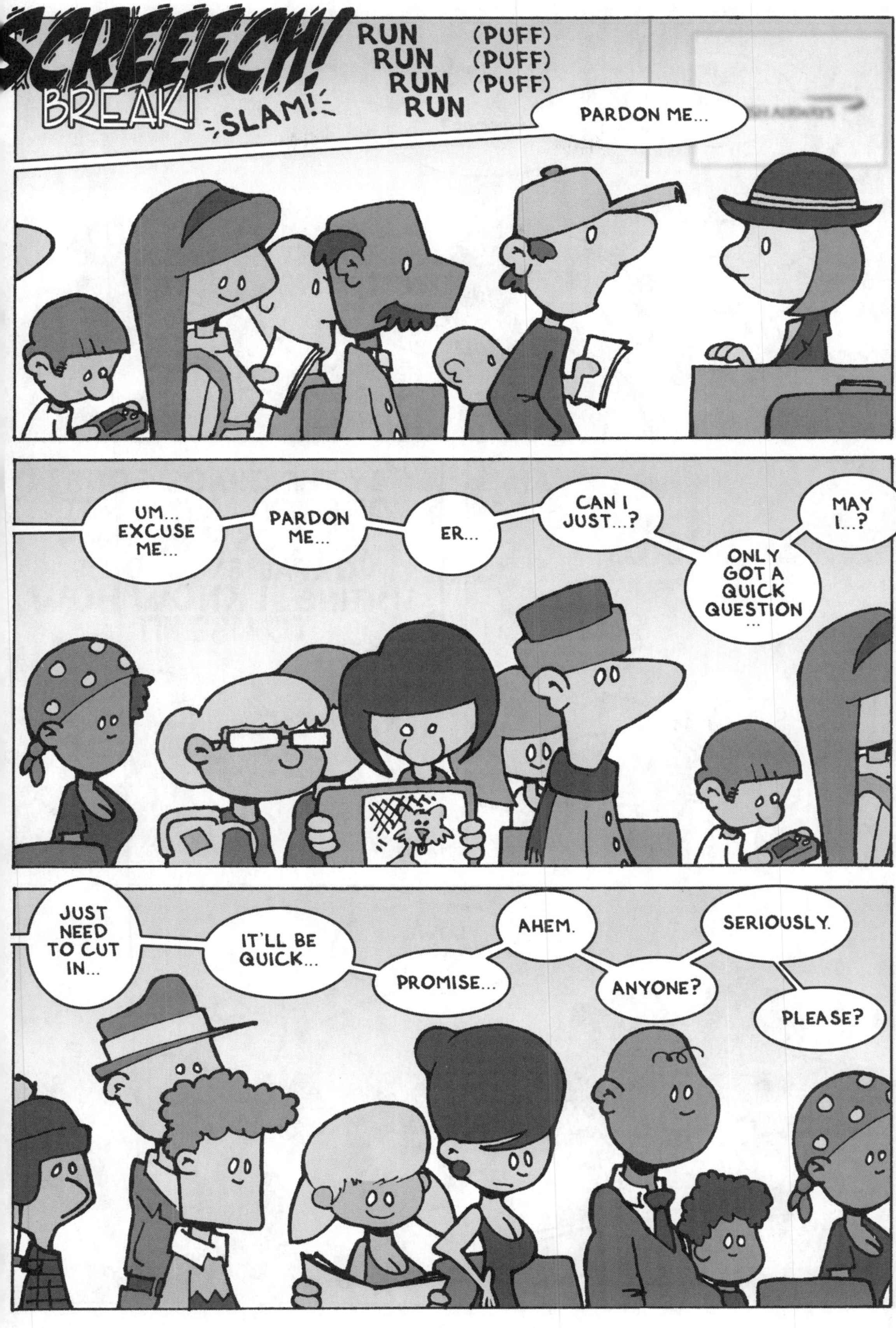
SCREEECH!
BREAK!
SLAM!
RUN (PUFF)
RUN (PUFF)
RUN (PUFF)
RUN
PARDON ME...
UM... EXCUSE ME...
PARDON ME...
ER...
CAN I JUST...?
MAY I...?
ONLY GOT A QUICK QUESTION...
JUST NEED TO CUT IN...
IT'LL BE QUICK...
PROMISE...
AHEM.
ANYONE?
SERIOUSLY.
PLEASE?

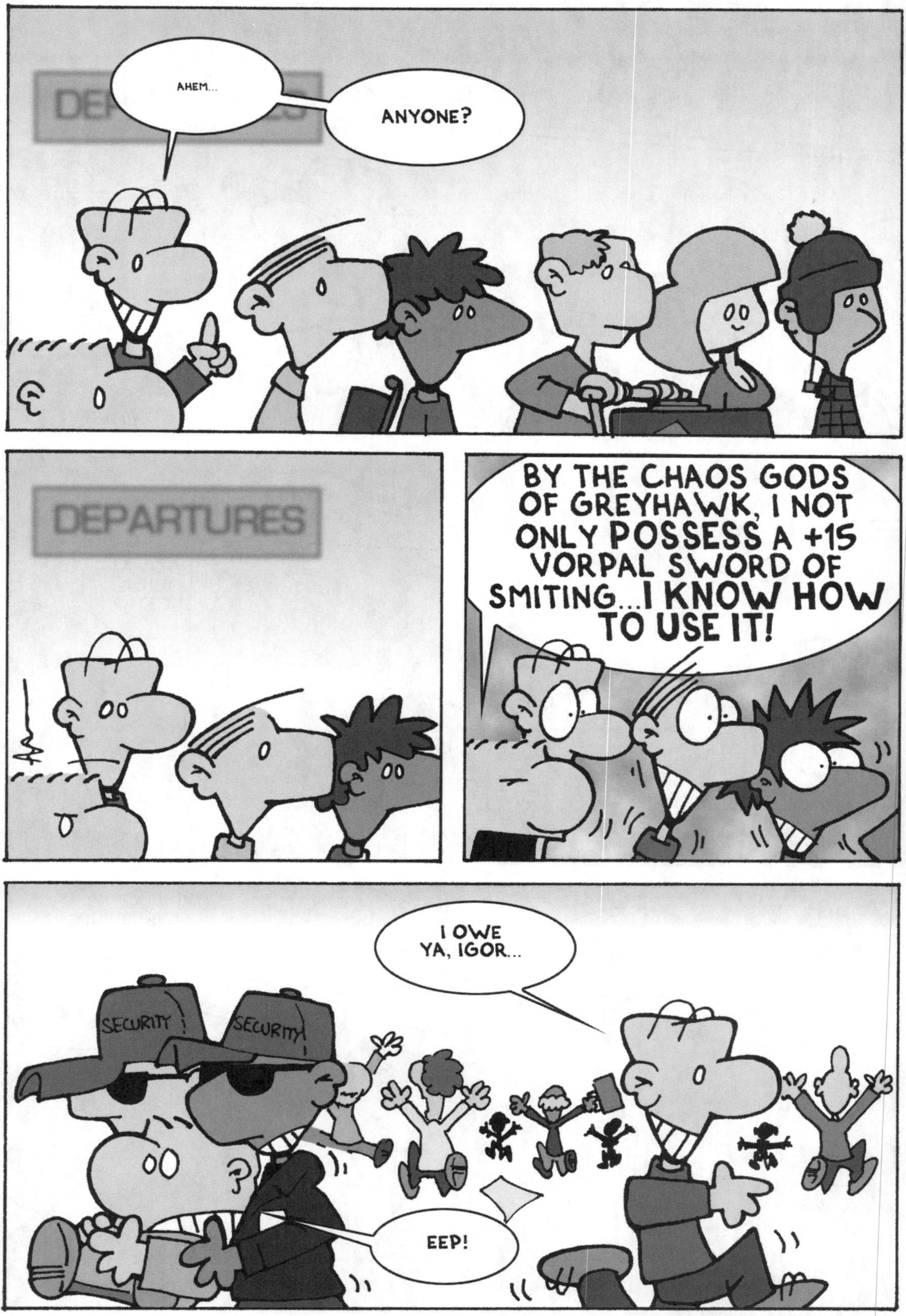
AHEM...
ANYONE?
DEPARTURES
BY THE CHAOS GODS OF GREYHAWK, I NOT ONLY POSSESS A +15 VORPAL SWORD OF SMITING...I KNOW HOW TO USE IT!
I OWE YA, IGOR...
SECURITY
SECURITY
EEP!

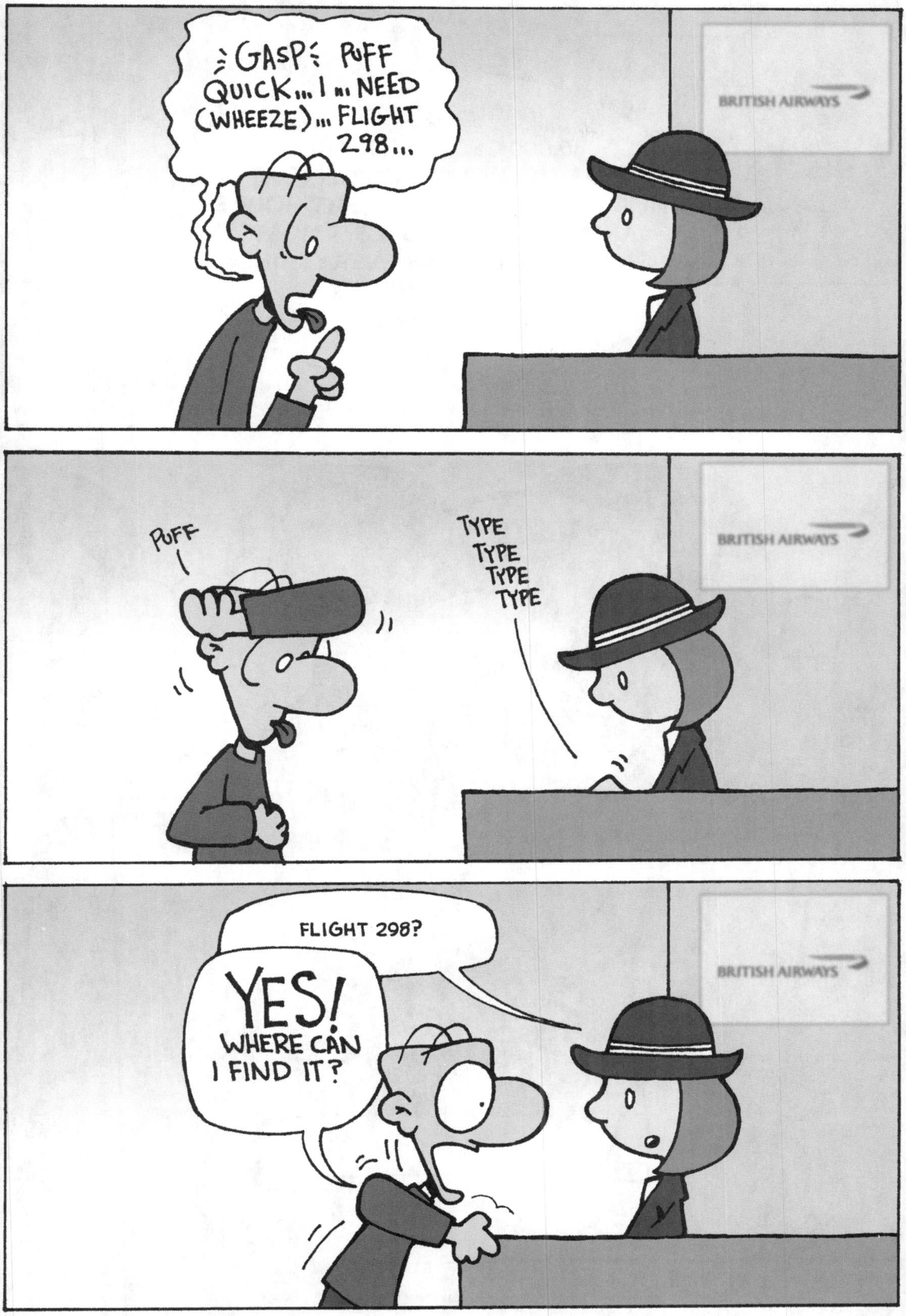
GASP PUFF QUICK... I ... NEED (WHEEZE)... FLIGHT 298...
BRITISH AIRWAYS
PUFF
TYPE TYPE TYPE TYPE
BRITISH AIRWAYS
FLIGHT 298?
YES! WHERE CAN I FIND IT?
BRITISH AIRWAYS

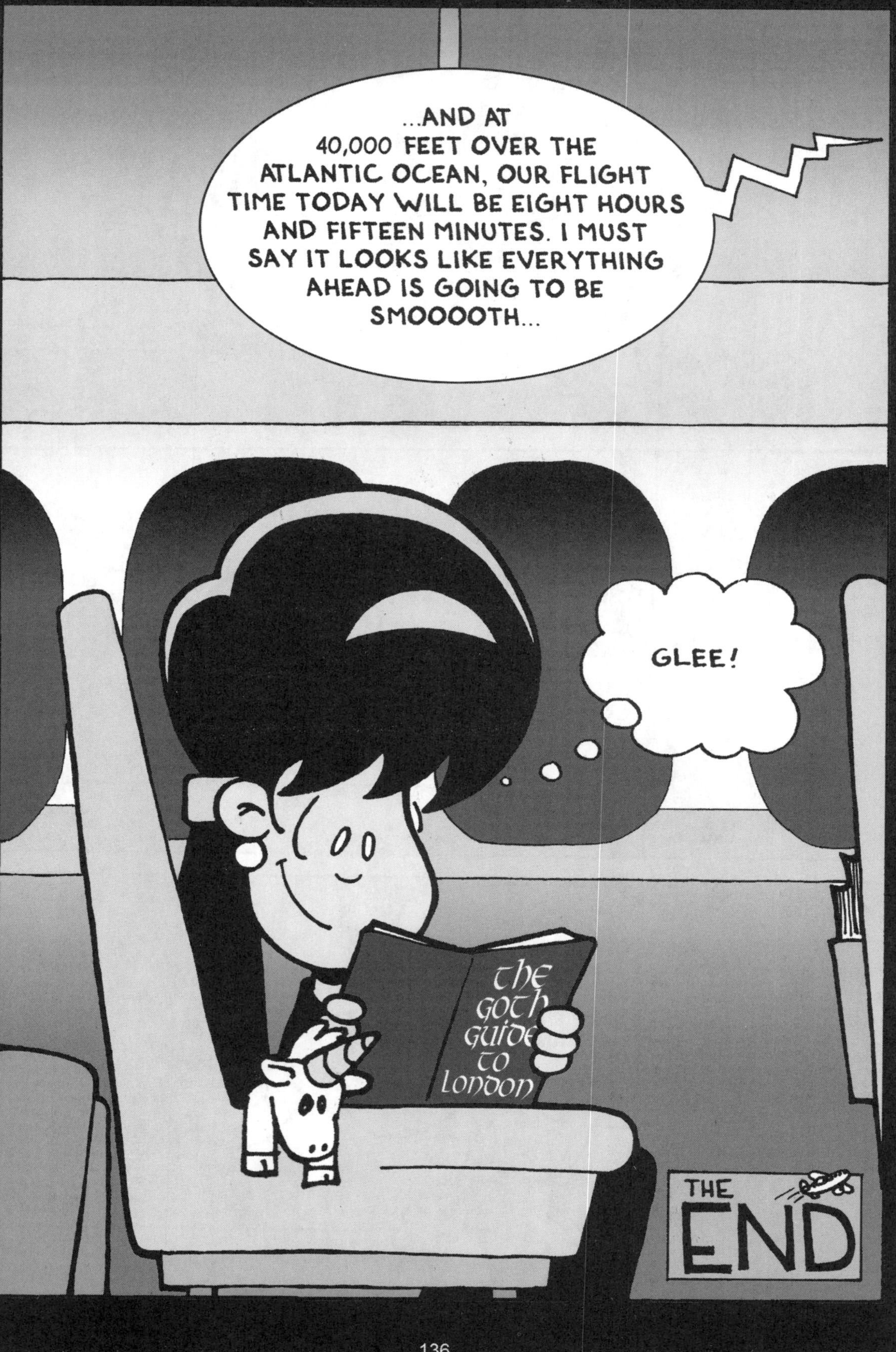
...AND AT 40,000 FEET OVER THE ATLANTIC OCEAN, OUR FLIGHT TIME TODAY WILL BE EIGHT HOURS AND FIFTEEN MINUTES. I MUST SAY IT LOOKS LIKE EVERYTHING AHEAD IS GOING TO BE SMOOOOTH...
GLEE!
THE GOTH GUIDE TO LONDON
THE END

It doesn't matter if we ever meet again.
What we have said will always remain.
- The Jam

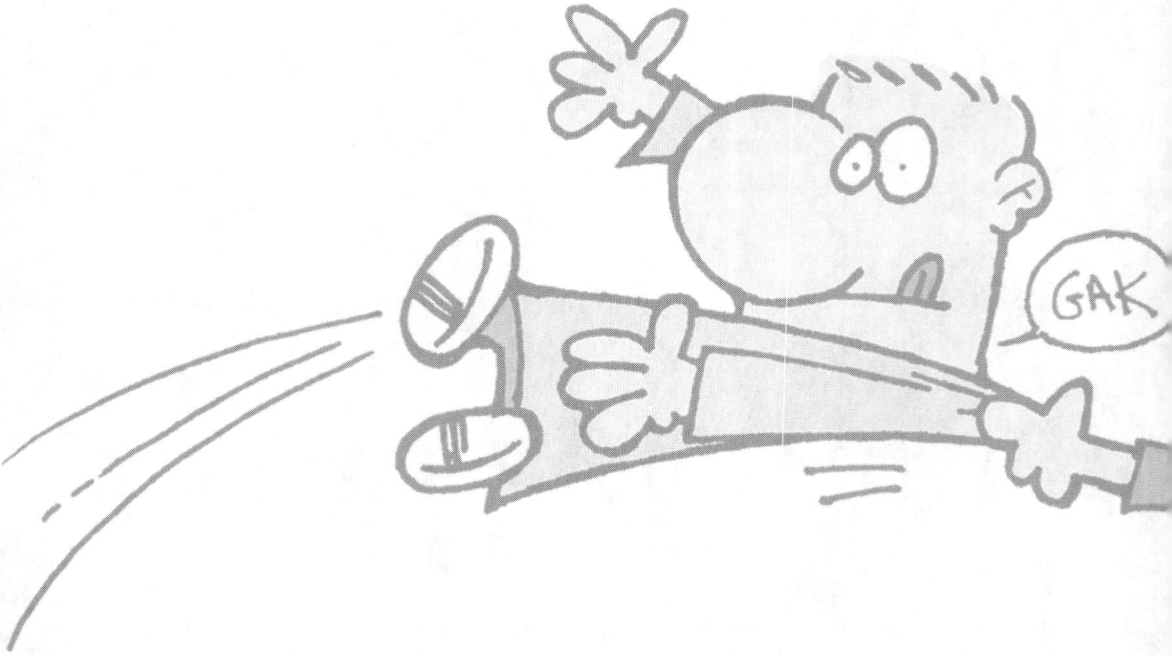
GAK

Igor's Last Date: The Legend of Serape Bob

by Michael A. Stackpole

Ken actually could recall a time when Matt had looked worse, but that time had been following too little sleep, too much tequila, and a long walk through a sleet-storm that, in their worm-serum wisdom, was too dangerous to drive through. The red nose and the kleenex rash on the cheeks mixed with the rheumy eyes and slumped shoulders made Matt look as if he'd gone ten rounds with Jack Frost.

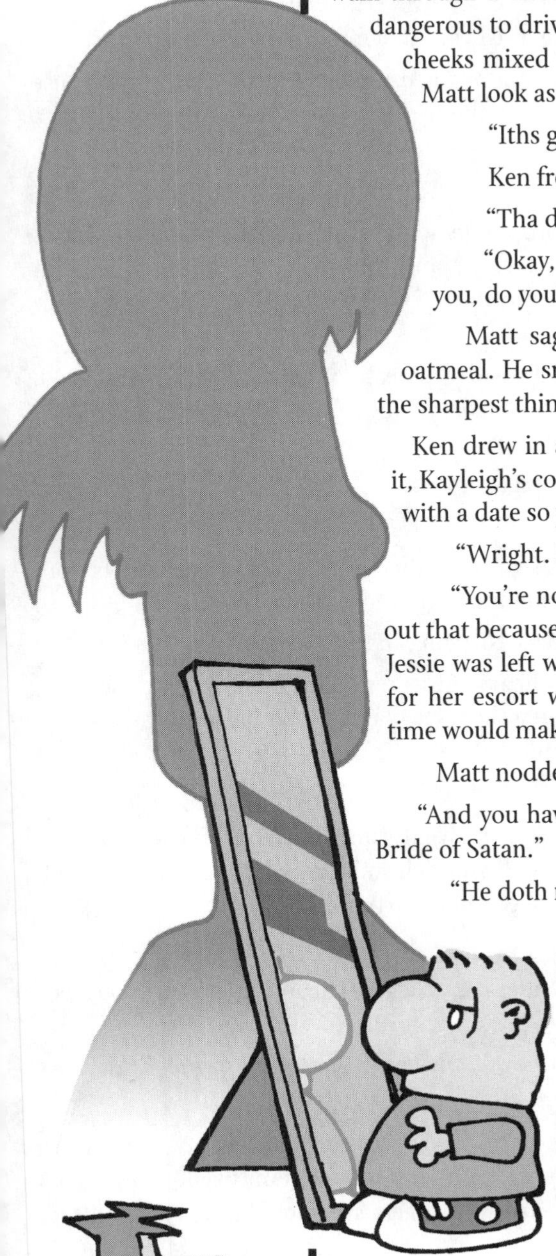

"Iths gobba be okay, wright?"

Ken frowned. "The cold, or the date?"

"Tha date."

"Okay, Matt, sit down. You don't have any sharp objects on you, do you?"

Matt sagged onto the couch like a sack full of overcooked oatmeal. He sneezed and proved beyond a shadow of a doubt that the sharpest thing he had on him was soggy tissue. "How bab?"

Ken drew in a deep breath and sighed. "Well, as you've explained it, Kayleigh's cousin Jessie is visit and you were supposed to fix her up with a date so you and Kayleigh could double with her."

"Wright. Kayleigh's weird cousin Jessie."

"You're not making it any better." Ken refrained from pointing out that because Matt and Kayleigh has shared a communicable virus, Jessie was left without someone to do things with, and Matt's choice for her escort was without adult supervision. "Jessie having a good time would make Kayleigh happy. Right?"

Matt nodded slowly, horror slowly blossoming in his eyes.

"And you have her dating someone who thinks of Kayleigh as the Bride of Satan."

"He doth not."

"You should see the fantasy wedding pictures of you he's photoshopped up."

"Oh no!" Matt glanced at his watch. "Iths too late to stop him."

Ken squatted, getting face to face with his friend. "I don't want to freak you out, but Igor is getting advice."

"Bwess you, Ken."

"Not from me." Ken sighed. "From Carson."

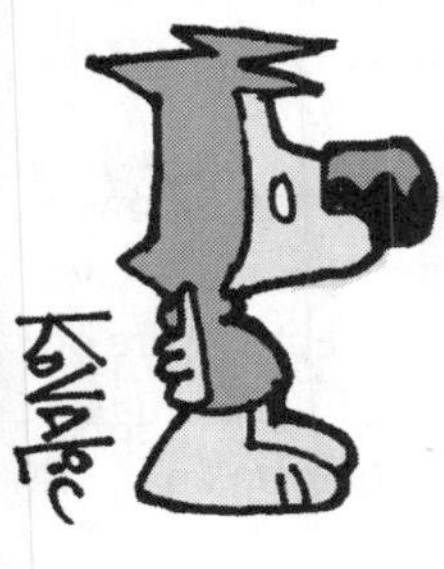

Matt closed his eyes. "No chance this is Ebowa and not a cowd?"

"Sorry, Matt. You're going to survive." Ken couldn't help a smile forming on his face. "At least until Kayleigh gets her hands on you."

Igor stood before the mirror, giving his reflection a steely glare. "Yes, Carson, I agree. Matt did say she was Kayleigh's weird cousin, which means she has to be some sorority queen and cheerleader or something. Undoubtedly she's the Bridesmaid of the Bride of Satan. It's going to be tricky to handle."

The muskrat sitting on the dresser shrugged. "I still think having to place a last minute bid on a pair of Claudia Christian's underwear on Ebay is a legitimate excuse for breaking the date."

Igor forced himself to raise an eyebrow coolly, which gave him a moment to make sure his voice would not break. "Huzzah, little friend, but few would truly understand that."

Carson's head came up. "That tone in your voice. I've heard it before."

"You have." Igor turned fluidly, tightening his eyes. "You'd understand the bidding because you're a gamer, but that's not a gamer solution. I have to be true to myself, and deal with this as a gamer would."

"Be yourself?"

"Are you kidding?" Igor shook his head. "Carson, we spend days and weeks crafting characters that we hone through a variety of adventures. This develops our problem solving skills to the point where few people in the civilized world can match our acumen. I have to take all this vast experience and apply it to the current situation."

"Um, Igor, the last time one of your characters had a date...." Carson scratched his head. "Actually, *none* of your characters has ever had a successful date. That's not really experience you can parlay here."

"HA!" Igor's eyes became slits. "How soon they forget."

"Huh?"

"You've forgotten the one character who was the scourge of the West. He left broken hearts from the Mississippi to the coast, from border to border, and then over each border, too."

Carson raised his hands to ward off the inevitable. "No, you can't. That's not fair."

"Yes, it is. Extraordinary times require extraordinary measures." Igor opened his closet and, standing on tiptoes, rescued a black cowboy hat from a shelf. He planted it on his head then tugged the brim with his right hand. "Serape Bob rides again!"

Carson shivered. "But, Igor, this Jessie, she may be Kayleigh's cousin, but she's only human."

"Serape Bob, frontier gentleman and devil-may-care-adventuring-hunka-burning-love doesn't mean to break their hearts. It just happens." Igor didn't let himself smile, but did allow a Serape Bob smirk to tug at the corner of his mouth. "Kayleigh won't be able to complain..."

"Like that will stop her."

"Ahem, be that as it may, I will be the perfect gentleman." He gave the muskrat a curt nod. "For Jessie it will be a night to remember."

Carson covered his eyes with his hands. *And her therapist will buy a boat getting her to forget.*

As per their agreement, Igor met Jessie in the central courtyard of Mud Bay's Megamall. He almost missed her at first glance. He'd given her a test, telling her to meet him twenty paces from the multiplex's entrance. She was five feet from the exact spot where she should have been but that mistake was natural: she had long legs.

Igor noticed the legs first, since they were clad in jeans that fit them very nicely. As he followed his gaze upward, he reached the hip-huggers' waist then noted a gap between it and the hem of her t-shirt. The t-shirt itself was black and had been knotted at the back. It had a Bradstreet vampire on it and the short sleeves had been torn off, giving Igor a good look at strong shoulders. Continuing up past her neck, he found himself looking at a green-eyed goddess who wore her dark hair up and had on some glasses with thick lenses and librarian frames.

Igor's heart fluttered for a moment, for Jessie was everything he could have imagined desiring in a woman. His mouth began to go dry. His hands shook. His toes began to tingle. He was waiting to sprout wings so he could fly around the mall's atrium. He began to vibrate and that proved to be his salvation.

A violent jerk tipped his hat down, eclipsing his view of her. The moment he stopped looking at her he could feel the saliva dripping from the corner of his mouth and he regained control. He got in touch with his inner Serape Bob and blushed fiercely—not because of his reaction to her, but because of how close he came to falling into the trap.

His nostrils flared. *Serape Bob will not be mocked.*

In that moment of clarity it became, well, very clear. Kayleigh's hand was clearly evident and obvious. Kayleigh had mocked him when he gave her one of his favorite characters and ran her through *Sheep on the Borderlands*. She had punished him and here, she used her cousin against him. She'd clearly dressed her up and instructed her how to be everything he desired. Kayleigh had clearly pushed Matt to set things up, then deliberately infected him with the cold from hell so she and her cousin could have this laugh on him.

Igor almost bolted, but his inner Serape Bob tightened the reins. *Serape Bob runs from no danger.* Igor let those words echo through his head, then slitted his eyes and tipped his hat back. She was still there, and his toes tingled again, but the stamp of a foot took care of that.

Clearing his throat, he gave her a Bob-smirk. "Hi, I'm Igor. You must be Jessie."

She looked over and then down, smiling widely. "Yes, I'm Jessie. I'm sorry I got here early. I don't know Mud Bay and didn't want to be late. I didn't mind waiting."

Sure, but you have logged how long you waited to tell Kayleigh. Igor shook his head, refusing to let that beguiling smile blind him to the predatory nature of her mission. *Serape Bob is more than a match for you and your evil Mistress.*

"Yeah, sorry about not being here sooner. Ready to go to the movie?"

Jessie nodded. "I checked the times of the films here. Nothing starts for an hour. Did you want to eat first?"

"Oh, we're not going here. This is just an easy place to meet." Igor pointed to the side entrance and, across a vast expanse of parking lot, to a strip mall with a little theatre. "Mud Bay Dollar Cinema is playing *The Matrix Reloaded*."

Jessie clasped her hands to her breastbone. "Really?!"

Igor had to admire how he managed to inject what seemed to be a genuine note of enthusiasm into her squeal. "Really."

"Oh, that's so great. I've only seen the movie four times. I wanted to see it more, but grad school takes up a lot of time."

Igor nodded and led the way, holding the door for her. He marveled at how she managed to mock him, since he'd seen it eight times. The little scourge about how graduate school kept her from seeing it more had been employed with exquisite skill. *Kayleigh may have prepped her, but she's very good. Must be a professional actress.*

As they walked to the cinema, Jessie went on and on about how she liked the sequel, couldn't wait for the completion of the trilogy, and could understand why the filmmakers had reduced the violence of the second film. She even mentioned she'd heard rumors of a trading card game that never somehow got released, and she even sounded sad that it hadn't come out.

"Oh, Igor, I bet you think I'm just silly."

"No, not at all, Jessie." *I'm wise to your game.* "I actually agree with you."

"You do?" Green eyes flashed behind the horn-rims. "You're actually listening to me?"

"Of course." *As a hunter stalking a lion listens to roars.*

She smiled. "Thank you. You don't know how hard it is to be a woman studying genetics. So many men think I'm only good for autoclaving instruments. Just don't let me talk too much, okay? I spend so much time being quiet, I can just run on when I get going."

Igor wanted to scream that he knew what 'autoclaving' meant, but he stopped himself. She was getting under his skin. He needed to re-exert control. It was time to do something Kayleigh never would have expected. He was going to throw Jessie a curve.

Reaching the theatre, he held a hand up and left her standing shy of the box office. "My treat, I insist."

"But Kaye said it was dutch-treat. I expected that. I agreed."

"Pish-tosh." Igor waved her protest away. "You were waiting for me. It is the least I can do."

"Why, Igor, that's sweet of you." Jessie approached while he was fishing the money from his pocket—fishing quarters from that little change pocket in the jeans being tough at the best of times. She bent down and kissed him on the cheek. "Thank you."

"Um, well, yeah." He turned his face to hide his blush, then spilled the sixteen-bits on the counter. "Two for Matrix, please."

He took the tickets back and had recovered his composure. He could feel Jessie following closely and desperately invoked his Serape-bobness. Tipping his hat back, he smiled and handed the tickets to the usher. "I know, in theatre three, to the right."

The usher grunted something as they swept past. Igor took another step Kayleigh couldn't have predicted. "Would you like some popcorn? A soda? Candy?"

"Are you kidding?"

"Ah, no." Visions of his getting a hernia carrying all the stuff she wanted danced through his head. "Anything you want, my treat."

"No, Igor, thank you, I couldn't." She patted her flat, smooth tummy. "I had a late lunch. Besides...," her voice dropped into a whisper, "what they charge here is ridiculous. At a warehouse store could fill a wheelbarrow with malted milk balls for what they want for a box here."

Igor flushed crimson. *Matt promised he'd never tell anyone about the wheelbarrow and milk balls thing!* For an instant he was furious with Matt, then realized Kayleigh had gotten it out of Matt using all her feminine wiles. He betrayed me in pillow-talk.

"Would you like anything Igor?"

A wave of nausea washed over him as the idea of Kayleigh and pillow-talk refused to leave his mind. "Nope, not hungry."

"Okay, lead the way."

Igor did, taking the time to let Serape Bob flow back into him. He also reached into his back pocket and pulled out a small notebook and a pencil.

"What's that for?"

"Um, I hope you don't mind, but I had an ulterior motive for wanting to see this movie."

"You're multitasking?" Jessie laughed lightly. "That's cool. What's up?"

Mock me if you will, I don't care. Serape Bob doesn't care. "In the start of the movie, when the numbers cascade..."

"That's a cool effect, yes."

"Well, see, Ken and I are arguing about the numbers. They're a code, I know it, and if you can decrypt it, it will tell you about the next movie. So I have to get the numbers down."

She looked at him, her eyes wide. "Why didn't I think of that?"

Because you share blood with Kayleigh. You are incapable of thinking that.

Jessie smacked the heel of her hand against her forehead. "If you want to lend me your data, I can get time on the mainframe at State and see if we can break it down."

"Oh, that would be nice." Igor was glad the dim theatre allowed him to hide his face. He could read her like a book. She'd take his notes and share them with all the other cheerleaders in the sorority and they'd tell their boyfriends who all played football or basketball or some other tall sport, and they would find him and mock him. The very thought would have been unendurable save for his quick reflecting on the Serape Bob adventure where a gang of Robber Barons had tried to do just that, incited by the town's dancing girls.

Jessie, Igor had to admit, had done her homework. She moved down the aisle toward the front. "I hope you don't mind if we sit close. I'd rather not have to use these." She removed her glasses and tucked one earpiece into the t-shirt's neckline.

Oh, very nice. You know from the Antichrist that I sit close so no one will sit in front of me. "This is great."

As they settled into their seats, Igor braced himself for the next great test. Judging by the one time Kayleigh had gone to the movies with them, the probability of Jessie reconsidering the need for food rose with every second that ticked down to the start of the movie. He was ready to get up and fetch things fast, assuming that since he'd told her he needed the number cascades up front, she'd wait until the last moment to strike.

A different emergency popped up. Four college kids came and sat in the seats in front of them. The tallest positioned himself smack between Jessie and the screen. Moving right or left wasn't an option since the other seats were sprung. Silently he offered to switch with her, but she shook her head.

Then the kids started talking. On cell phones. Apparently to each other. Jessie sighed aloud, which made them just talk louder. And then they started fidgeting and tossing popcorn. Kernels flew like shrapnel and one bounced off Jessie's glasses.

From the depths of his soul, Serape Bob rose and took possession of Igor. He lowered his voice and leaned forward, keeping the tone sepulchral. "You're ending your calls. You're begging this lady's pardon. You're moving to the back of the theatre. Now!"

The phone conversations stopped immediately. The biggest of the kids—which meant the one who o'er-topped the others by an inch and Igor by a yardstick, looked down. "You think you're man enough to do something about it?"

Part of Igor wanted to invoke the better part of valor and Igor Olman would have, but Igor Olman had already left the building. Serape Bob, on the other hand, was there with spurs on. With his voice buzzing like a rattlesnake, he spoke slowly. "Son, there are four of you, and you're bigger than me. Now I'd have to be a damned fool to brace you if I couldn't mop the deck with you. So, why don't we have pity on emergency room doctors and let them practice needlework on folks who couldn't avoid trouble."

The big guy kept staring at Igor, but it was Serape Bob who stared back with viper-flat eyes. The big guy's right eye twitched. Serape Bob didn't move a muscle. The tension began to thicken. Igor absorbed it and let it flow back into his stare.

The other guy blinked. "Yeah, okay, man, be cool." He and his buddies began to move off.

"Hey, you forgot something."

"Yeah?"

Igor couldn't stop Serape Bob from speaking. "The apology."

"Oh, yeah." The tall guy bowed his head to Jessie. "Sorry about that, just having fun. No harm meant."

Jessie smiled. "No blood, no foul."

"Enjoy the movie." The frat boys moved to the back row and kept their discussions to a minimum.

Igor took his seat again and began trembling. All the while Serape Bob had been speaking, Igor had been having visions of taking the next year's worth of meals through a tube.

Jessie's hand descended on his. "Oh, Igor, you're still trembling with rage. It's okay. I've forgiven them. It's cool."

"Well, yes, if you say so." Igor smiled meekly. He took it as a small victory she couldn't tell terror from rage.

"No, really, you were great." She gave him a soft smile. "Most guys I date would have had me take care of that myself."

"Huh?"

"After seeing the first Matrix movie, I started studying some of the martial arts. Grad school has taken its toll on my training schedule, but could have decked him. Thanks to you, I didn't have to. What do you study?"

"What?"

"Martial arts." Jessie narrowed her eyes. "Probably aikido, right? Smooth as you are, you'd go for that, not power."

"Ah, um...."

The theatre darkened, saving him. Jessie put a finger to her lips then slumped down in her seat, keeping her head the same height as his. She shared the same opinions of the previews with him with a nod or shake of the head, then got very quiet and still as the numbers cascaded. Igor scribbled intently, then settled back and watched the movie.

Igor was still lost in flashbacks of the scene where Carrie Anne Moss was riding on the motorcycle when the lights came up in the theatre. As he came out of things he felt Jessie's hand on his again. He began to get flustered, but then Serape Bob took over, and saved him from the embarrassment of falling for so transparent a stratagem.

"What did you think, Jessie?"

"Is it possible for a film to keep getting better and better?"

"A select few."

She nodded. "Fellowship, Lost Ark, Star Wars and Empire, of course."

He listened for a hint of ridicule. "Time Bandits."

"Okay, guilty pleasure, Buckaroo Banzai."

But for having his heart armored with Bobness, Igor might have been lost then. *Kayleigh is even more evil than I could have imagined.* "That's a good movie, too. It's on DVD."

"Maybe we could watch it some time."

Oh, the old 'hold out hope of a second date that will never happen' trick. "That would be fun. Are you hungry?"

"Yes, famished." She followed him to the aisle and from the theatre. "You bought the tickets for the movie, so dinner is on me, I insist."

"Oh no, my dear." Stealing a trick from her, Igor took her hand in his and patted it. "A gentleman could never allow that."

"Dutch treat, as we planned."

"As you wish." Igor guided her from the cinema along the strip mall to Peppo's Pizza. Being as how it was only around the corner from Pegasaurus Games, he half-expected to see some familiar faces in there, but none of the regs were in sight.

Smiling, Igor paused inside the door and fished a hole-punched discount card from his wallet. "I recommend the meatball subs."

"Oh, I've not had one of them in ages, you're on."

Of course you haven't. When cheerleaders are really hungry they eat the whole rice cake.

Jessie took the card from Igor, ordered and got it punched. She moved to the left, tucked her change into her pocket and waited for her order to come up. Igor took the card, gallantly said, "I'll have what she had."

Elaine, at the register, took his card and squinted at it. "Hey, thirteen punches. Your sub is free."

Jessie laughed-clearly covering her disappointment at how well he'd lured her into the trap of getting him his dinner for nothing. "That's cool, a free sandwich."

Igor shrugged. "No biggie."

Elaine snorted. "Once a week occurrence for Igor. What's with the hat?"

He gave her a Serape Bob stare, which ricocheted off her +2 Shield of Disdain. He was about to lose the staring contest, but Jessie leaned over and purred, "I think it's cute."

That comment went through Elaine faster than Teflon-coated, depleted-uranium rounds from a Vulcan mini-gun. She staggered back for a second then her expression sharpened. "Time to get those glasses checked, deary."

Jessie straightened up. "I don't need glasses to look past the exterior."

Elaine again recoiled then hand-carried the order slips into the kitchen.

Serape Bob covered for Igor. "Much obliged."

"De nada, pardner." Jessie winked at him. "Food's good here, huh?"

"Yeah."

"Must be, if you put up with that shrew and keep coming back." Real venom poured through Jessie's voice, and again Igor found himself drifting toward a trap. "I am sick and tired of folks judging others based on how they look. It's stupid."

He expected her to follow with, "Don't hate me because I'm beautiful," but she didn't.

Jessie shook her head. "I'm sorry, pet peeve. I didn't mean to lose it."

Lose your temper, or slip out of character? "It's okay. Elaine is just having a bad day. It's lasted a couple of years, but..."

She laughed and gathered napkins, forks and straws for them, then picked out a table. Somehow she knew it was his table. Kayleigh had really trained her well. *I bet they came in here before. Elaine is in on it. This conspiracy is vast. No wonder Matt couldn't escape.*

Igor got the subs and brought them over to the table, then returned with the sodas. He settled in to tuck himself into his sandwich, then looked up, half-horrified. He'd almost started eating before her. Experience from the few meals he'd taken with Matt and Kayleigh had alerted him to the danger that situation provided. If he had his mouth full when she started talking, he'd surrender initiative to her. She'd be able to ask things like relationship questions, which were a deadly trap. Second only to the dreaded, "Do I look fat in this dress?" relationship questions were enough to curdle the courage of any man. Igor was pretty sure Ulysses stayed away from Penelope for as long as he did because of such questions.

Jessie blushed, her mouth full of meatball, her cheeks dabbed with tomato sauce.

Igor hesitated. It was a perfect chance for him to deploy the male counter-battery fire to relationship questions. Half a dozen sports stats questions were ready to go, but he stopped. Kayleigh would have prepped her for that. *And for gaming. I can't go there.*

He lost his chance as she wiped her face and swallowed. "Oh, I am such a pig. I'm sorry, but it tastes soooo good."

Igor nodded. "Yeah, it does."

"You must hang in the area a lot."

"I do." He began to nibble, taking small bites so he could answer quickly.

"What's around here? The movies, right?"

Panic raced through him. He'd not seen it coming, a classic move: the Dork-fork. If he said it wasn't the movies, he'd have to explain the game store was nearby. If he didn't admit to gaming, he'd admit to being someone who spent a lot of time at the dollar movies watching the same film over and over again. Either way he lost. He was trapped. He was doomed.

Nonsense. Serape Bob asserted himself again. Kayleigh had prepped Jessie for Igor, but she couldn't prepare her for everything. Even Kayleigh's evil had limits. Just as he had bluffed the guys in the movie, Serape Bob slid easily into an explanation. *If she wants to follow up, it's her funeral.*

"You see, Jessie, there's a game store nearby."

"Really?" She frowned for a moment. "Oh, of course, you're in the group Kaye plays with. Oh my god...."

"What?"

"You're the one who ran her through her first scenario."

Even Serape Bob could not stop Igor from stiffening at that mention. "Uh, yeah."

"Oh, she told me all about it." Jessie set her sandwich down, wiped her hands then took his trembling hands in hers. "I know what went on there."

"Yeah?" His voice quailed as his humiliation drained all color from his face.

"Yes, you were so kind to her and took it easy on her. You knew having her in the group was important to Matt and, being a true friend, you let her win." Jessie smiled and squeezed his hands. "I wish I'd been there to see that."

"I'm sorry you missed it."

"Maybe you could run me through a game some time?"

The hopeful note in her voice—worthy of an Academy Award—gave him the moment's respite he needed to let Serape Bob return. "I think that could be arranged. In fact, if you wish, after this, we could go to the store."

"Really? Wow." She glanced at her watch. "I'd like that, but I do have to drive back to State in the morning. It would have to be quick."

Oh, it will be, though you'll think it's forever. "Yes, an early night would be good." Igor grasped his sandwich in both hands to stop himself from rubbing them together. Jessie, the poor thing, tore into her sub with gusto—clearly so confident she had him that she didn't even bother with any relationship questions while his mouth was full.

Rising to leave, Igor looked at Elaine and offered a burp. Jessie laughed quickly, and Igor watched her carefully. "You know, in China, burping is a sign you liked the meal."

"I've heard that before." She jerked her head toward Elaine. "I don't think she gets it, though."

Igor knew the burp would be reported back to Kayleigh, but he didn't mind. His doing that had irritated her before, and it would be just a hint to her that he'd figured out her nefarious plot. *She trained her minion well, but roleplaying has prepared me for anything.*

Dusk had thickened while they ate, so they walked from pool to pool of light to the only illuminated storefront visible. Pegasaurus Games, home away from home, sanctuary, Mecca, Heaven—Igor thought of it in many ways. *Tonight it becomes the site of my greatest victory.*

He opened the door with a flourish and heard Jessie gasp. This did not surprise him, for the store was packed with gaming groups that thought of each other with the same bonhomie as the Crips and the Bloods. The Cards in the corner had a couple of Lord of the Rings holdouts, but Yu-Gi-Oh players had them surrounded. The opposite corner had the Click-basers, and their factions glowered at each other. Clearly the ages-old feud over which was tougher, the Incredible Hulk or a MadCat had become hot again. The RPGers in the center were holding their own, but Igor could see by the notebooks full of scribbled notes that folks were once again thinking—foolishly, nay, *heretically*—that Warhamster could stand improvement. (Beyond those changes which Igor himself had made and freely distributed, but were clearly being ignored.)

Igor never let Jessie catch her breath—in part to prevent any of the sizzling bon mots Kayleigh had prepared from issuing forth. He conducted her on a whirlwind tour of the store, starting with miniatures and historical games—as befitting the industry's history—on through the roleplaying games. He included the necessary discussion of the D20 revolution, which caused a couple players to kibitz until he gave them a Serape Bob glare. From there it was on to card games, then click games.

For the first time that evening, Igor shed Serape Bob's identity and let his passion for gaming come through. He refrained from war stories, since he knew Kayleigh would have prepared Jessie for that. Instead he let her know all the ins and outs of gaming, from the earliest conventions to the long, twisted path SPI took to be engulfed time and again. He dismissed the rumor that Hasbro was buying Decipher so Lucasfilm could go back to the original Star Wars CCG without losing face. He even gave her a taste of the Origins/GenCon battle for dominance, without bogging down in details.

He watched for that tell-tale moment when her eyes began to glaze over, then he stopped. "I'm not boring you, am I?"

Jessie hesitated for a moment, then shook her head. "No, I just, well, you know so much about gaming. I just never realized there was so much to it. And you tell it all so well."

"Thanks." Igor blushed a little, then smiled. "I guess you have to be going now."

Jessie looked at her watch, then nodded slowly enough that Igor could almost imagine she was reluctant to go. "It's a long drive."

"I'll walk you back to your car." Serape Bob slid back into place and he offered her his arm. "I know you can take care of yourself, but a gentleman would not let you go alone."

"Thank you, sir." Her hand fell lightly in the crook of his elbow. "I had a lot of fun tonight."

"Really?"

"Yes, Igor."

He was glad he hat hid his face in shadows, for she was very good and likely could have read the surprise there. She managed to make her enjoyment seem genuine. Despite that, he knew she and Kayleigh would be up all night laughing over every facet of the date. Try though he had, Igor wasn't certain he'd succeeded in doing enough to spoil Kayleigh's fun. *It would be better she's told nothing of the evening. But how to seal Jessie's lips?*

All too quickly they reached Jessie's Beetle. Knowing what he must do, Igor summoned up the core of Serape Bob's being. Tipping his hat back, he looked up at Jessie. "It has been my great pleasure, Miss Jessie, to be your escort this evening." He raised an eyebrow and pursed his lips every so slightly, letting the lower one quiver just a bit. With that very look Serape Bob had driven women wild, rendering them uncontrollable with desire.

Jessie smiled and raked her fingers back through her hair, freeing it to flow over her shoulders. "The pleasure was all mine, Igor." With her left hand she swept his hat off, then leaned down a kissed him full on those pursed lips.

And quite a kiss it was. Igor's toes curled and his hair stood on end. Serape Bob might have been the most powerful kisser west of the continental divide, but this kiss was something more than a natural 0-0 on matched gemstone dice. His pulse roared in his ears and his cheeks burned where her palms touched them.

After an eternity he felt her soft, warm lips leave his. He staggered back, readjusting his hat as she slipped it back on his head. He wanted to shout and to gasp and to beg for another kiss,

but everything fought for control of his tongue, so he said nothing. He remained silent, brim of the hat down, his thumbs hooked into the pockets of his jeans to keep his hands under control.

She pressed a hand to her lips. "That was quite a kiss."

Igor could do nothing but nod.

Jessie sighed, then smiled and opened her car's door. "It's going to be a real long ride tomorrow."

Her use of the word ride saved him. He clutched at it and focused on it. *Ride. Ride. Serape Bob rides...*

Igor let his eyes narrow and noticed she looked a little sad. It was too much for to hope that she'd not noticed how her kiss had gotten to him. It had blasted clean through him, doing critical damage even. He'd been holding it together until then and—yes, that was it, the nod! The silent nod in reply to the kiss. He'd covered himself and not let her see how his heart had been fluttering.

One more kiss and it would have been over. He would have gloated, but Serape Bob was always gallant. He gave her the hint of a smile, then handed his hat to her through the car's open window. "Something to remember me by."

She parked the hat on her head, and her smile broadened. "There will be no forgetting you, Igor, thank you."

"Happy trails, Jessie."

"You, too, Igor."

Igor stared after the retreating taillights for a long time, then wandered over to his car. He patted it on the flank. Jessie would have had him with that kiss but for a stroke of luck that tied his tongue up in knots. Now she'd never tell much of anything to Kayleigh because her last ditch effort, her most powerful tool, that kiss, had failed to break him.

"Of course, there's no breaking Serape Bob." Igor smiled as he climbed into his car. His lips still tingled and his heart still raced. *Kissing her was better than kissing a horse.*

Smiling, thinking lots of things and being able to concentrate on none of them, Igor drove off.

And his was a long ride, too.

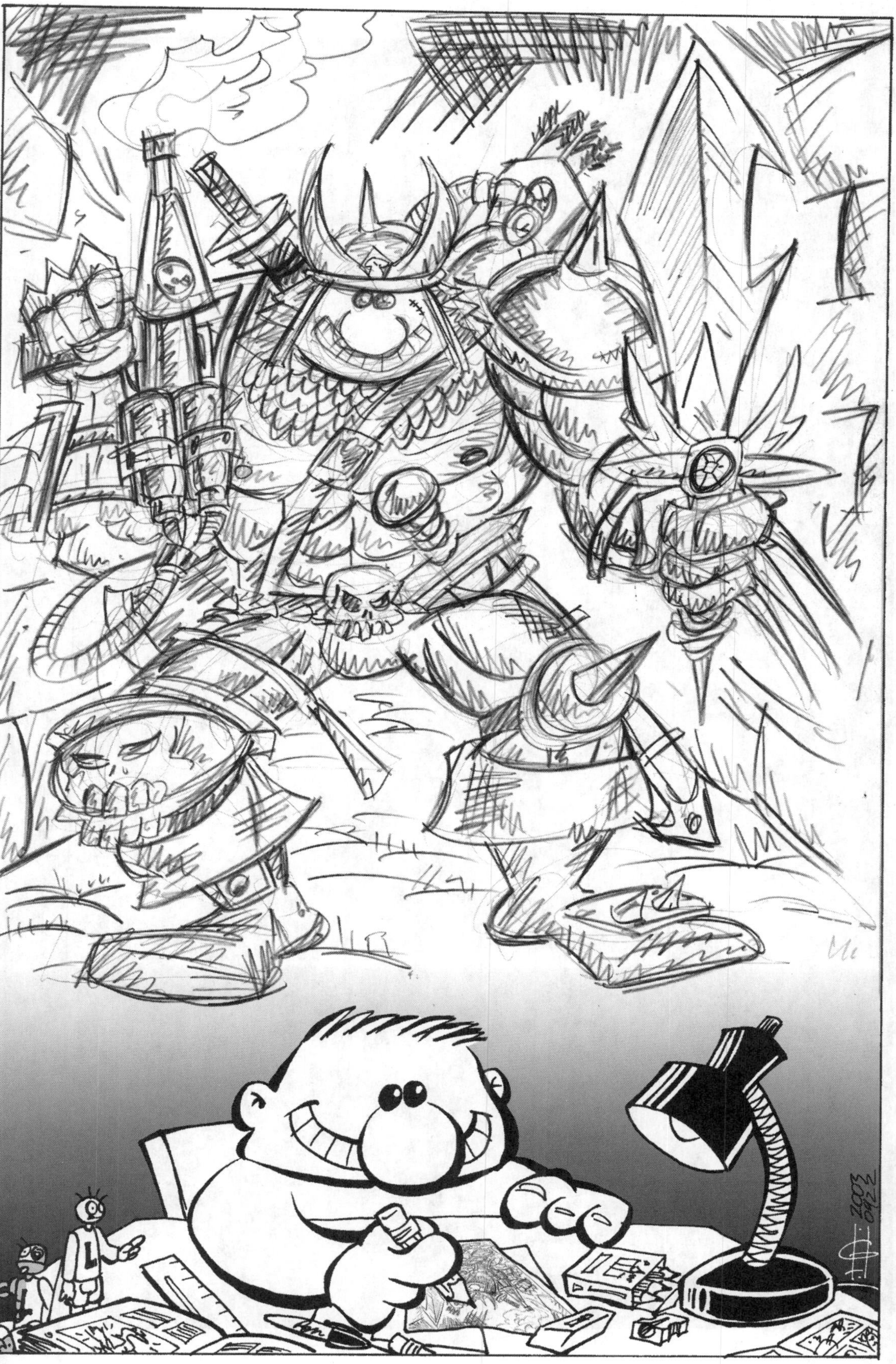

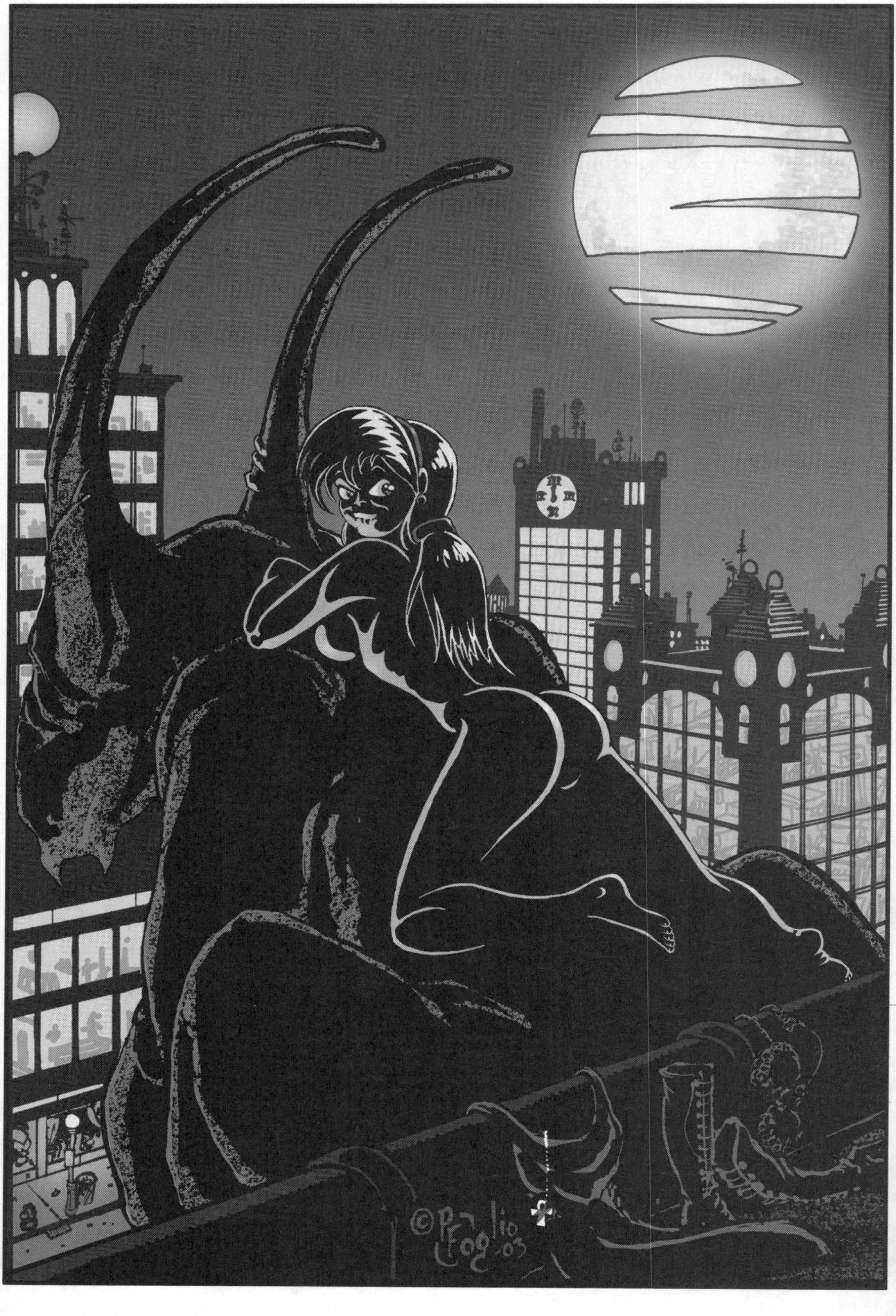

CLANBOOK:

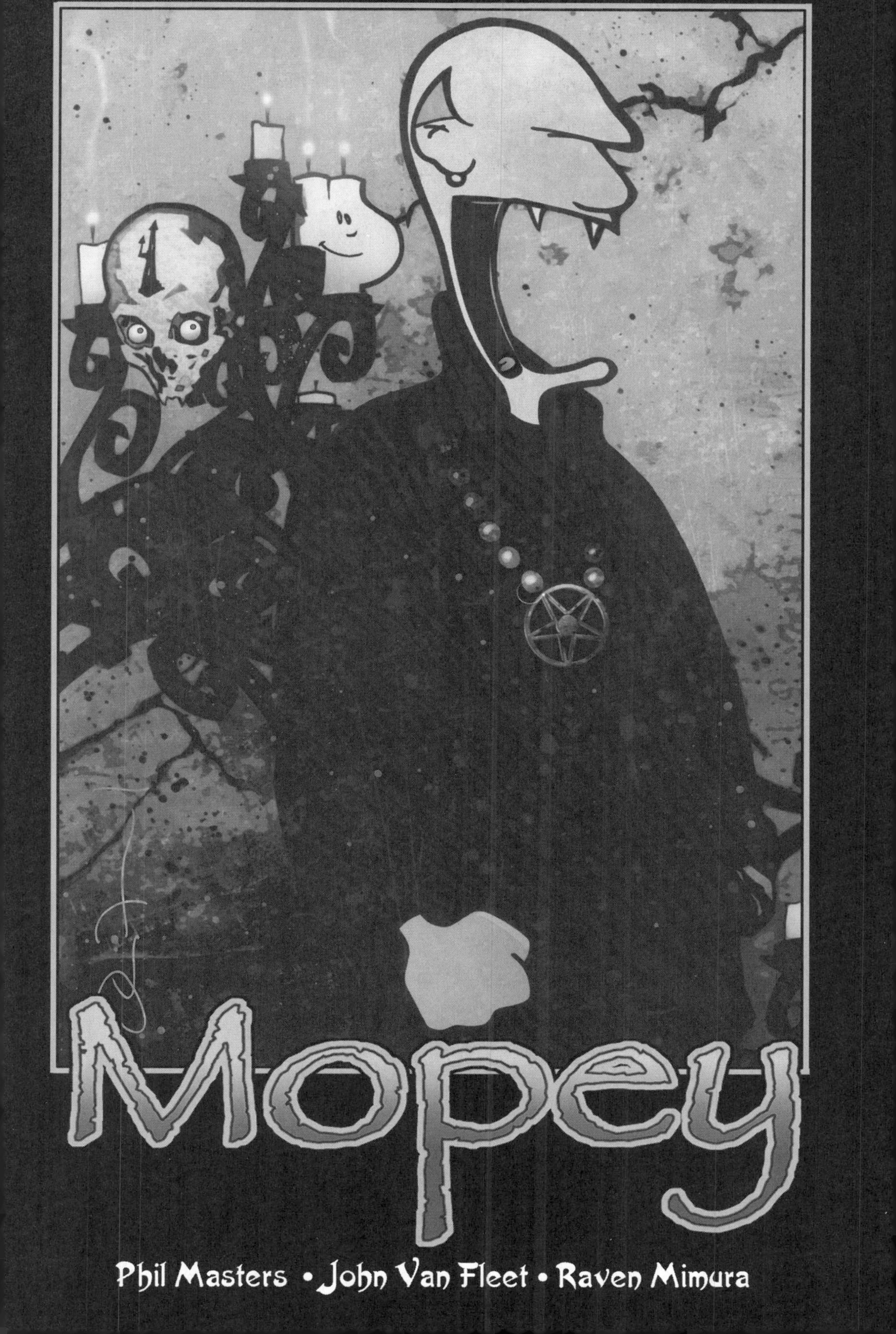

Mopey

Phil Masters • John Van Fleet • Raven Mimura

CLANBOOK MOPEY

The neon light from the sign over the front of the club reflected off the windows of the run-down vinyl, PVC, and real naughahyde goods shop opposite, glittered through the rusted ironwork of the fire escape, and reflected again off the puddle which filled the center of the back alley. The two figures standing either side of the back entrance to the club said nothing, but the waft from the cigarette which one of them was smoking carried the tones of the kitchen spice rack and the medicine chest up through the city gloom.

Then the cigarette burned down, and with an exasperated sigh, the smoker flicked the stub away. It fell into the puddle, and with a faint hiss, almost went out.

The door opened, and a third figure emerged. Pausing to straighten her skirt, feather boa, stocking seams, and dog collar, the newcomer totally failed to notice the first two. She did notice her own reflection in the puddle, and stared at it in nauseated fascination for a long moment. Then, it seemed, she reached a conclusion.

"Blurry min" she declared. Then she thought for a moment more. "Thee yall make me blurry sick."

Then, turning to one side, she demonstrated the literal truth of the statement, all over the shoes of one of the other figures. After which, with a final "Blurry s'ree...", she slumped onto the fire escape and began to snore softly.

With a sigh, her accidental victim began to swirl his shoes in the puddle, in an attempt to restore their prior pristine state. His friend looked at him and the sleeping newcomer, and raised an eyebrow in enquiry.

"One of ours, perhaps?"

The shoe-rinser looked at the subject of the question, and shrugged. "Might as well be," he said. "After all, what's the point of arguing with fate?"

Introduction

Always be sincere, even if you don't mean it.

– attrib. President Harry S. Truman.

There is purity, even among the accurséd. Or so some people like to think. Mostly those who think of themselves as (a) pure and (b) accurséd, funnily enough.

That Clan amongst the Kindred which is known as the Mopeys sees itself as pure. Whatever explanation one accepts for the origin of the Kindred in general – and let's face it, there are as many of those as there are Kindred wannabe cult leaders who've read about the importance of explanatory creation myths in books about folklore – it's generally agreed that being one of the Kindred is something to get depressed about. Most people solve this problem the old-fashioned ways, with hedonistic pleasure or refined art or mindless violence (and it's terribly unfair to imply that they all default to the mindless violence the moment that the other options get difficult), but the Mopeys take a simpler, more honest approach. They get on with being miserable.

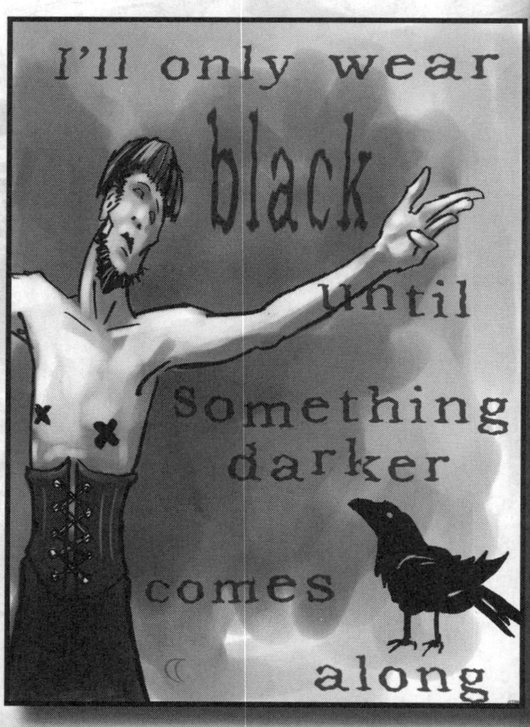
I'll only wear
black
until
Something
darker
comes
along

(Yes, some of them see being miserable as a pleasure or an art form or an excuse for mindless violence. Now will you please stop quibbling and let me get on with the splatbook? These things are traditionally *short*, though we were hoping to swing another 32 pages this time.)

It might seem that moping a lot is a poor strategy or recruiting tool, but don't underestimate it. What it lacks in motivation, dynamism, or excuses to wear Hawaiian shirts, it makes up in simplicity. You never have any problems deciding what to wear in the morning – certainly, you know what *color* you'll be going for – and you know how you'll feel about anything even before it happens. Plus, there are always members of the opposite sex who'll read it as mysterious sincerity.

So Clan Mopey not only endures, but does okay for itself. Now, let's get on with the crunchy bits.

Chapter 1: Lifestyles of the Bitch and Fatuous

And furthermore, I don't like your trousers – your appalling taste in women – and what about your mind? Your insipid record collection...

– The Pretenders, "Pack It Up"

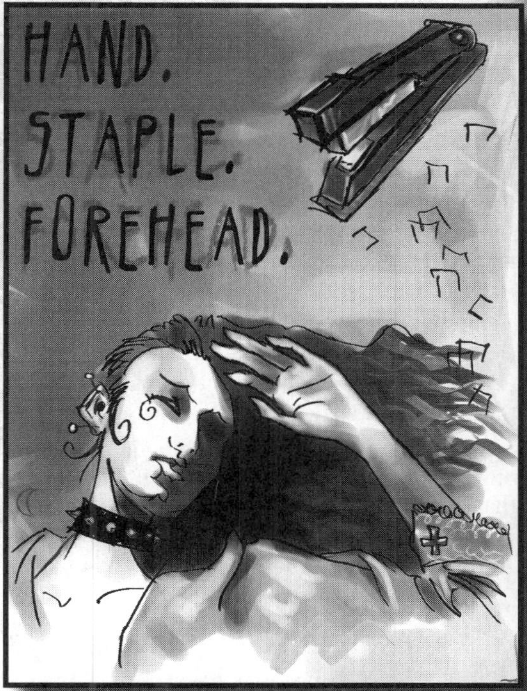
HAND.
STAPLE.
FOREHEAD.

"We are what we are! We will not change! Not mockery, not fortune, not the wiles of others can make us!"

"Coooool. Ah. What are we?"

"We are Clan Mopey!"

At this point, the instructor's energy seemed to lapse for a moment. The new recruit took the opportunity to venture a careful response. "Yes, you said. But what does that mean, really?"

"Oh, nothing means anything, really – never forget that. But I suppose that you could say that this is about philosophy. Except without the boring logic stuff."

Attitudes (Oh Woe!)

You know what this section is going to say already, don't you? I mean, the big heading at the top doesn't say "Clanbook Variable Moods" or "Clanbook Subtle Psychology."

Still, there is one thing to point out here; even moping can vary. Some Mopeys lurk in corners and don't say very much; some explain their position in calm, level, boring tones; some rant about it. Okay, the last have a slight problem, in that moping as such isn't supposed to be loud – but the projected, highly audible mope is part of the Clan mystique.

And when you look closely, there are variations in form as well as style. Admittedly, these can usually boil down to any one of "my parents (or sire) suck," "my former significant other sucks," or "the world sucks," and once the Mopey realizes that his or her parents (or sire) are going to say that they tried to warn him or her about that former significant other, he or she usually concludes that the world sucks – but still, there can be some variation.

Anyway, just *try* not to play *all* your characters as Clan stereotypes, why don't you?

Relations With Other Kindred

The nightclub was shaking to the sound of Bauhaus, as every male in the place worked at looking like Bowie and every female thought Catherine Deneuve. The new recruit entered cautiously, looking to left and right before turning to her companion.

"Is this okay?" she asked.

"Well," he said, "it's a bit passé, and..."

Before he could finish the sentence, there was a strange and unmistakable sound from the other side of the room. The sound of laughter.

"No," he said darkly, "it's not really okay."

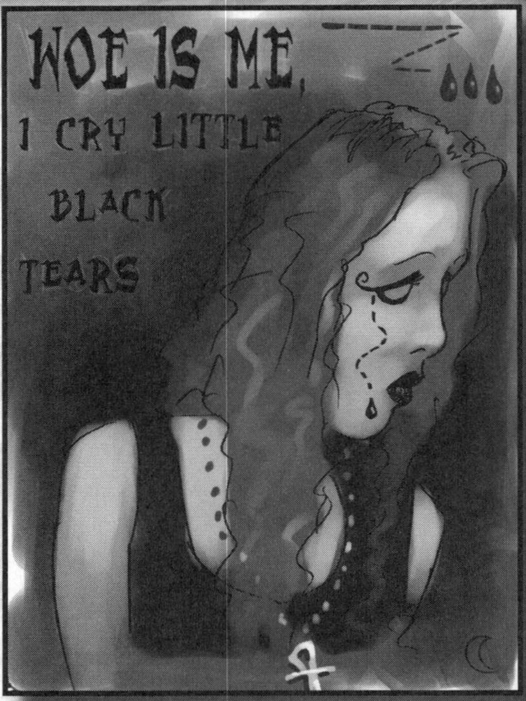
WOE IS ME,
I CRY LITTLE
BLACK
TEARS

To the true Mopey, there is but one other group among the Kindred. It's not that they aren't aware of other Clans, bloodlines, or subdivisions, or that they feel that anyone who isn't for them is against them; it's just that anyone who isn't Mopey is clearly off in the same direction from themselves. The signpost pointing in that direction says "Perky." Well, it's as good a term as any other.

And to the true Mopey, the Perky is trouble. It's not that Mopeys generally *dislike* any individual Perky – indeed, the less than perfectly embittered Mopey may even admit that some Perkies are almost okay, really, and at least they get the color scheme right – but, well, it's a *credibility* thing, isn't it? Image is all, and so long as the Perkies are out there, being Perky, the Mopeys are going to have trouble getting the respect they know they deserve.

But open warfare is out of the question. In the end, the Kindred must hang together, because otherwise they wouldn't have enough places to hang out. But it's nothing to do with the possibility that some Mopeys think some Perkies are sort of cute. Really.

Views of Other Supernaturals

"It's so depressingly predictable, isn't it?"

"Yessss..." The new recruit nodded sadly and stared at the remnants of her clove cigarette. Then, slowly, carefully, she asked. "What is?"

"Oh, you'll find out soon enough. Not only is the world laden down with problems and woes, but there's more than one way to fend off the abysmal depths of existential despair by exertion of metaphysical and paranormal power. Or so I've been told, by some loser who cared. I mean, to begin with, there's the puppies."

"Oh, cute puppies make me really..."

"No no no, these aren't cute. Not really. Well, I suppose that if you wanted to annoy them, you could say that they were. That would be a good way to be sure of being confronted by the unrelenting hostility and incomprehension of an uncaring world, certainly. But they're more, sort of, big and hairy. With teeth."

"Ugh. Sound like football players."

"But with teeth. Then there's the wizards. I mean, just because reality bends to their every whim, and by the mere contemplation of the words and symbols encoded in certain ancient texts they can command the elements, they think that they're something special."

"Okay, I'm beginning to see the problem. Is there anybody who really gets how life... Y'know..."

"Sucks? Yeah, well, there are the ghosts. Being dead is pretty instructive. Lucky sods. They'd be our sort of people, if some of them didn't pointlessly hang on to a futile delusion from their lifetimes concerning the most elementary of aesthetic realities."

"You mean..."

"Yeah. Not all of them wear black. They say it doesn't go with being transparent."

"Right." There was a pause before the new recruit ventured another question. "Anyone else I should know to avoid?"

"Well... There's... Ah..."

"Yeah?"

"Fairies."

"Oh."

CHAPTER 2:
THINGS WE CAN'T AVOID DOING (DESPITE OUR BEST EFFORTS)

And all the world is football shaped

It's just for me to kick in space

And I can see, hear, smell, touch, taste –

And I've got one, two, three, four, five, senses working overtime...

> – XTC, "Senses Working Overtime"

As any Mopey will explain, without even being asked, the Kindred thing is nothing to do with power for them. It's about attitude and a recognition of the Truth About the World, and maybe some really bloody depressing music.

However, despite not looking for it, some Mopeys do wind up with power. In fact, strangely enough, there are a couple of special abilities which are kind of specific to the Clan, except when other Kindred use them anyhow. Just like there are for every other Clan. Funny, that.

MISERICORD

Misericord represents the uncanny ability, essential to Mopey philosophy, to find something to get miserable about. A character with this power can assess a situation and determine what the most depressing problem is about it. At low levels, he or she may also come up with suggested solutions, but that little problem goes away with more splodges.

ONE SPLODGE, ☹: The character can always look on the dark side of any normal situation. Of course, almost anyone can do this, but with a bit of Misericord, a character can do it with intensity and conviction.

TWO SPLODGES, ☹☹: The character can see the problem with any bit of good news, without even trying. Winning the lottery will just lead to hard decisions and make the winner suspicious of old friends, any new love affair is bound to end in tears, and so on and so forth, forever.

THREE SPLODGES, ☹☹☹: At this point, the character no longer needs a situation to see the dark side *of*. Mere existence or inaction imply untold depths of mopeworthiness.

FOUR SPLODGES, ☹☹☹☹: No one ever tells the character to cheer up, it may never happen. Just by looking at him or her, you can see it already has – only slightly worse.

FIVE SPLODGES, ☹☹☹☹☹: What's the point of explaining this stuff? It's just too, too horribly depressing.

DECLIVITY

While some Mopeys just sit in corners and, well, mope, many have a last vestigial sense that it is their duty to make the rest of the world aware of the sheer futility and depressing unreliability of it all. The art of Declivity assists in this, by enabling the possessor to convey his, her, or its thoughts and feelings to everyone around. Over a very large distance, in fact, in some cases.

ONE SPLODGE, ☹: This ability adds to any other form of persuasion, rhetoric, or logic when describing a problem – even if the character has no actual skill in the ability in question. Which is just as well, because a committed Mopey will never actually learn any sort of skill if it can possibly be avoided.

TWO SPLODGES, ☹☹: It's in the voice. At this level, the character has got the dragging bass tones exactly right.

THREE SPLODGES, ☹☹☹: With this level of accomplishment, the character no longer needs to shout – although if he or she chooses to, his rants of depression and annoyance are things of wonder. A murmur, even a mumble, will carry the message of negativity across a crowded room.

FOUR SPLODGES, ☹☹☹☹: Further progress grants the ability to project without words at all. A wave of the hand, a half-hearted shrug, a slightly cocked eyebrow – all can speak volumes, at a volume which mere sound can never match.

FIVE SPLODGES, ☹☹☹☹☹: The highest expertise in Declivity is persuasion by inaction. A look, a sigh – even these feel excessive, implying energy in contradiction to the message. The character radiates negativity. Indeed, it is said that true adepts can be depressing even in their absence. (Which is bad news for those who wish that they'd just go away when they are around.)

Chapter 3:
We, the Purple

Listen while I tell of a secret life

Clandestine lives entwined like vines

You may already know where when and how

If I tell ya then . . . it's no secret

– Debbie Harry, "Secret Life"

The irregular click of overly high heels was counterpointed by the shuffle of worn leather soles as the new recruit and her mentor made their way through the clammy yet chilly night. Eventually, the former ventured a question.

"So – where we going now? Ah, if it matters, of course."

"It doesn't." There was a pause, then the mentor shrugged. "Well, we might as well round off the whole depressing night by meeting some people."

"Friends?"

"Friends? Friends? You've forgotten – we're all ultimately alone in the night!" Then the mentor paused and shrugged forlornly. "But these are people we can hang with, without it all getting too much worse too quickly."

The new recruit nodded, and secretly smiled as she deliberately misaligned her feather boa one last time. Everything was going to plan!

And somewhere else, someone else smiled even more. Because as usual, there was a lot more plotting going on in the background than mere readers would ever be permitted to know. Which would guarantee sales for a long time to come, especially if the world blew up a couple of times in the next few months.

Archetypes

Nightclub Philosopher

I get no kick from champagne,

Mere alcohol doesn't thrill me at all...

– Cole Porter, "I Get a Kick Out of You."

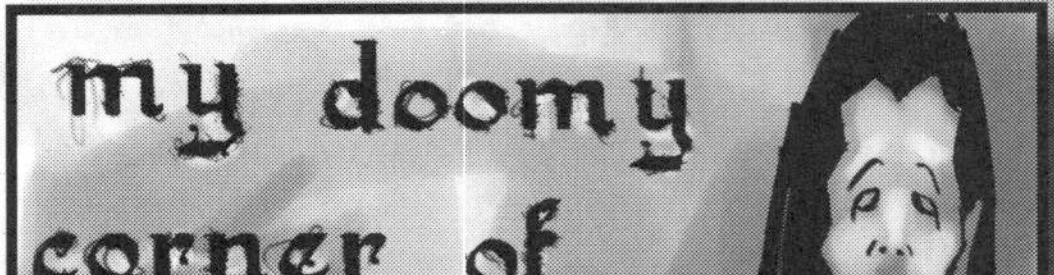
my doomy
corner of
darkness
beckons
to
me

Quote: *Look at them all, dancing and drinking and thinking that they're having fun. If only they knew how little pleasure they are really experiencing – if only they were aware of the futility of… Oh, sorry – red wine, please.*

Prelude: Your ascent to a position of power – for that is what you occupy, in truth – was gradual but inexorable. A name dropped here, a reputation for knowing the next band to listen to there – it doesn't take much, really, if your timing is perfect. And yours was.

But the rep you've so carefully cultivated is that of a nascent leader among Mopeys, which meant that your progress was also a voluntary entry into a trap. Now, you're a prisoner of others' expectations, your mastery of nihilism preventing you from ever taking any other approach.

But we're all prisoners, aren't we? You explained that to your coterie only last week.

Concept: You have status, and that's the important thing about your place in your world. Oh, it's strictly local, and beyond the clubs where you rule, you are ignored or even laughed at – but you value what you've got. After all, its saves you from having to chase your own drinks.

Roleplaying Hints: Sit in that corner seat, with a bitter half-smile playing about your lips and a glass of what seems to be red wine in front of you – no, of course you don't *have* to drink it, the important thing is that someone else provided it for you – and make it look like a throne. Pass trenchant and deeply pained comments just often enough to maintain your rep. Remember, you're an alpha among omegas.

Possessions: A set of black silk shirts and black leathers. These are all identical, and subtly stylish; you have to look good, and you mustn't be seen to be suffering from wear or grime, but equally, you mustn't give the impression that you *care* about your appearance.

Movie Buff

There is only one thing that can kill the movies, and that is education.

– Will Rogers, Autobiography.

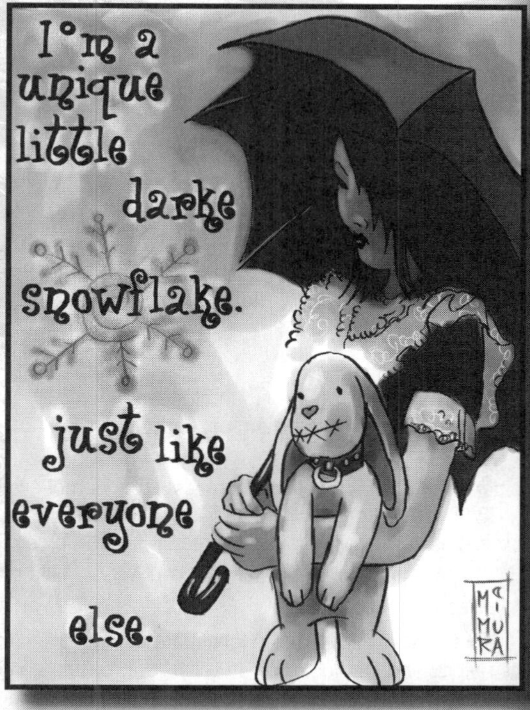
I'm a
unique
little
darke
snowflake.
just like
everyone
else.
MCMURA

Quote: *But have you seen the '72 Hammer Drac? It's totally pathetic. They clearly had no idea about realistic Transylvanian vampire psychology. Of course, the third assistant director has done better work since, and the actress who gets bitten in the second reel has gone into production work and knows a salvageable script when she sees one...*

Prelude: Once, you were as other students, surely bound for a life in suburbia, the 2.4, and all that. Then, one night, you passed through darkness and came forth forever changed and beyond hope.

You went to see a movie.

Oh, you'd seen movies before, of course, and even on this occasion, you were not at first aware of the change which had destroyed your former identity forever. Not, at least, until you awoke the next day with terrible cravings – the urge to identify that actor in the last scene who you'd seen in some other film, and the need to tell your friends about how good the movie would have been, if only the editor had paid a bit more attention to pacing in the final half-hour.

The descent after that was rapid and uncontrollable. You soon shed your former friends, as you left their tastes and standards far behind and beneath you. You have new friends now – pale creatures with refined sensitivities and aggressively judgmental natures...

Concept: You are a true creature of darkness, to whom real daylight is anathema – although you could write whole books about the use of daylight in the cinema. Many people think that your haunts are limited to your home, the local arts cinema, and one or two coffee shops, but they're wrong; you're acquainted with dozens of *different* cinemas, and also some specialist movie bookshops.

Roleplaying Hints: You are obsessive and subtle, and somewhat competitive – although you regard other movie buffs of proven alertness as your peers, and all other folk with a casual and amused disdain. But never forget that you are a Mopey. You can't ever let anyone believe that you enjoy any of this stuff. It never meets your ruthlessly high standards, and everything always has fatal flaws and crippling compromises. Your particular obsession with obscure horror films is especially useful here, as most of them are obscure because they're so lousy – as you can and will explain at every opportunity, but at vast length and using your own deeply arcane vocabulary.

Possessions: Plain clothes, an excellent home cinema system, a DVD and video collection of phenomenal breadth – and an even larger collection of books *about* the cinema and copies of early-draft scripts.

I.T. Support Techie

Do not expose your LaserWriter to open fire or flame.

– The Apple LaserWriter user's manual.

Quote: *No, I will deal with this call, as I have dealt with so many others – for only by confronting my darkest fears may I achieve true freedom. And this one mocks me not, but truly and justly seeks repair for his broken cup-holder.*

they'd all be
unhappy
if only
they
took
the time
to
realize
it.

Prelude: Once upon a time, you were as other mortals, save only that you nursed that most poisonous of all vipers; an ambition to work with computers. And indeed, you possessed the talent and wisdom to enter that career, and for a while, all was well.

But somewhere, you had an enemy; or you caught the attention of a being with a malevolent wit; or Dark Fate simply turned against you. You know not, although you may still sometimes seek to discover the truth. For you received a "temporary" assignment to the help desk.

As a route to falling among the Mopey Kindred, it may seem unusual – but it is most terribly reliable.

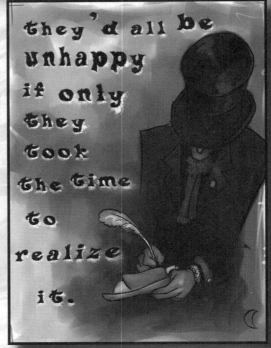

Concept: You have become a creature of routine, bitter irony, and minimal expectations. For much of every day, you are bound, Prometheus-like, to a desk and a PC, forced to deal with whatever questions are brought to you. Occasionally, you may go forth to provide on-site assistance, and strange creatures, dark forces, and worst of all, users, all strike at you in person with great glee. But you can survive, for by now, you have seen the worst that this life has to offer.

Or so you hope.

Roleplaying Hints: Sit upright, stare at that screen, and accept whatever you hear on your headset 'phone as natural and inevitable. Whatever human beings do or say can no longer surprise or anger you, although it may provoke varying levels of irony or sarcasm. When away from your desk, try to avoid mentioning what your job is, despite all the problems which this causes. Resort to violence only in extreme circumstances or when attempting to open recalcitrant PC base units.

Possessions: Hands-free 'phone headset, a vast collection of plain black T-shirts, a smaller collection of PC games.

Famous Mopeys

Hamlet, Prince of Denmark: The quintessential black-clad mopester. Any comments about him being fictional are, like, totally missing the point, okay?

Edgar Allan Poe: We are not worthy! We are not worthy!

Queen Victoria: Moped continuously for forty years. Respect.

Rasputin: Look, if you were poisoned, shot, chained up, and then dropped in a frozen river, wouldn't you mope a bit, too?

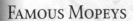

Clanbook Mopey

Written by Phil Masters, Cover by John Van Fleet, Illustrations by Raven mimura

THE GREAT WALL OF VIENNA

Vienna Fantasy Gaming Con 2004 is now history, and Judith and I had a spectacular time at it

What was an added bonus, though, was the warmth and friendship we were shown by our hosts. We stayed with a family in Vienna's sixth district, a short walk away from the main historic and shopping centers. Julia and Clemens (our hosts) made us feel completely at home, and on top of everything, fed us like you couldn't believe. Apart from being just great, great people, Julia is also a terrific cook.

They have a fantastic apartment, very modern and cool, and our room had a fabulous view of the rooftops of the old city. We spent a day traipsing around downtown Vienna, visiting various Habsburg palaces, drinking great coffee and really good beers.

Well, the day we were to take the train to leave, Julia approached me with a question, and a couple of pairs of giant Magic Markers.

"Would you draw on our walls?"

DRAW on your WALLS? Those gorgeous, giant white walls? You're kidding?

She wasn't kidding.

I was happy to do it...but petrified, at the same time. Especially when I realized the scope of the project. I just didn't want to ruin their beautiful apartment. So I started sketching Igor, Carson and Gilly in a small corner, out of sight of everything. Just, y'know, in case I messed up....

"No, no, no," Julia laughed. "We want you to draw THERE"

She was pointing to the very center of the room, on the stairway wall leading upstairs.

I panicked.

But how can you say no to such neat people? People who, apparently, had no idea that a single mis-step with a pen would send their property values plummeting?

So I made sure I did a LOT of pencil work first. But you know what? It didn't turn out too badly, if I do say so myself. I think the gods of cartooning knew that these were great people who did NOT deserve to have their walls ruined. Grin.

So anyhoo, here is the World's Largest Dork Tower, located in Vienna, courtesy of Julia and Clemens...two of the coolest people Judith and I have ever met!

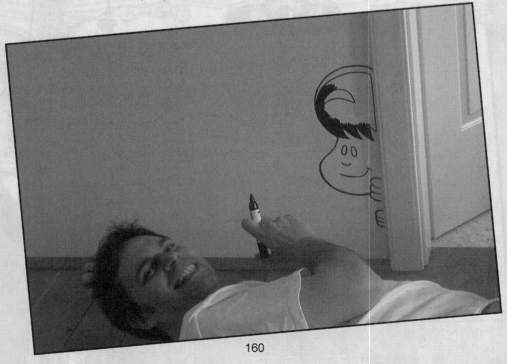

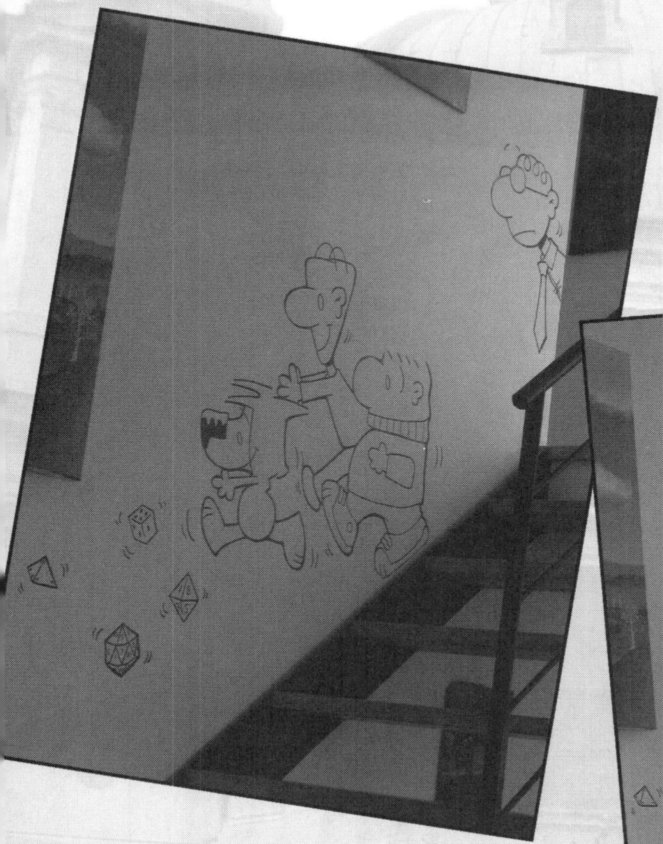

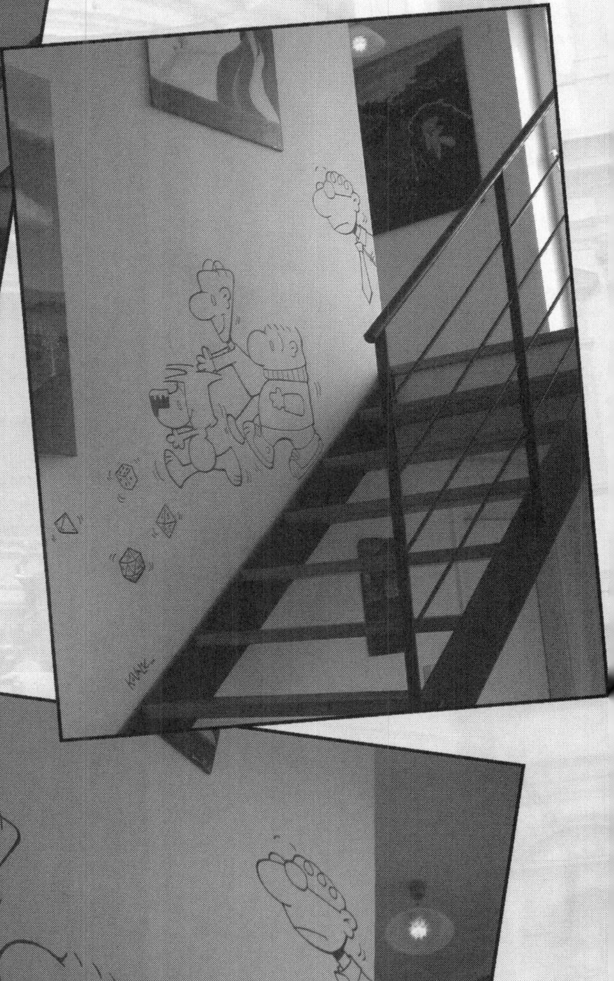

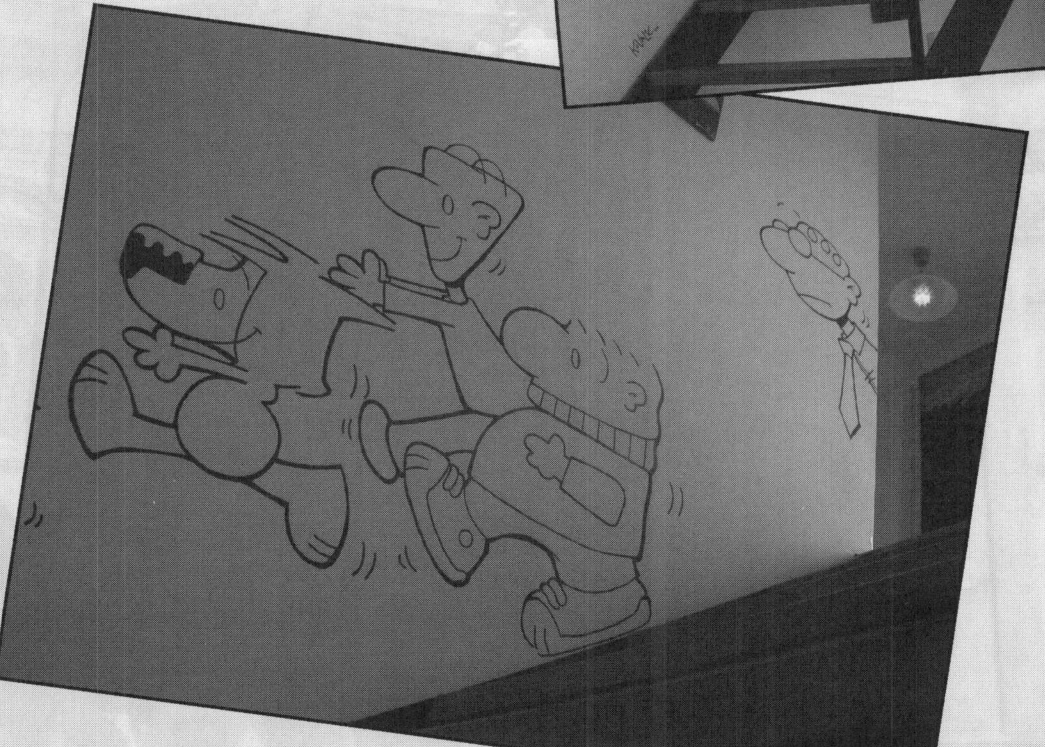

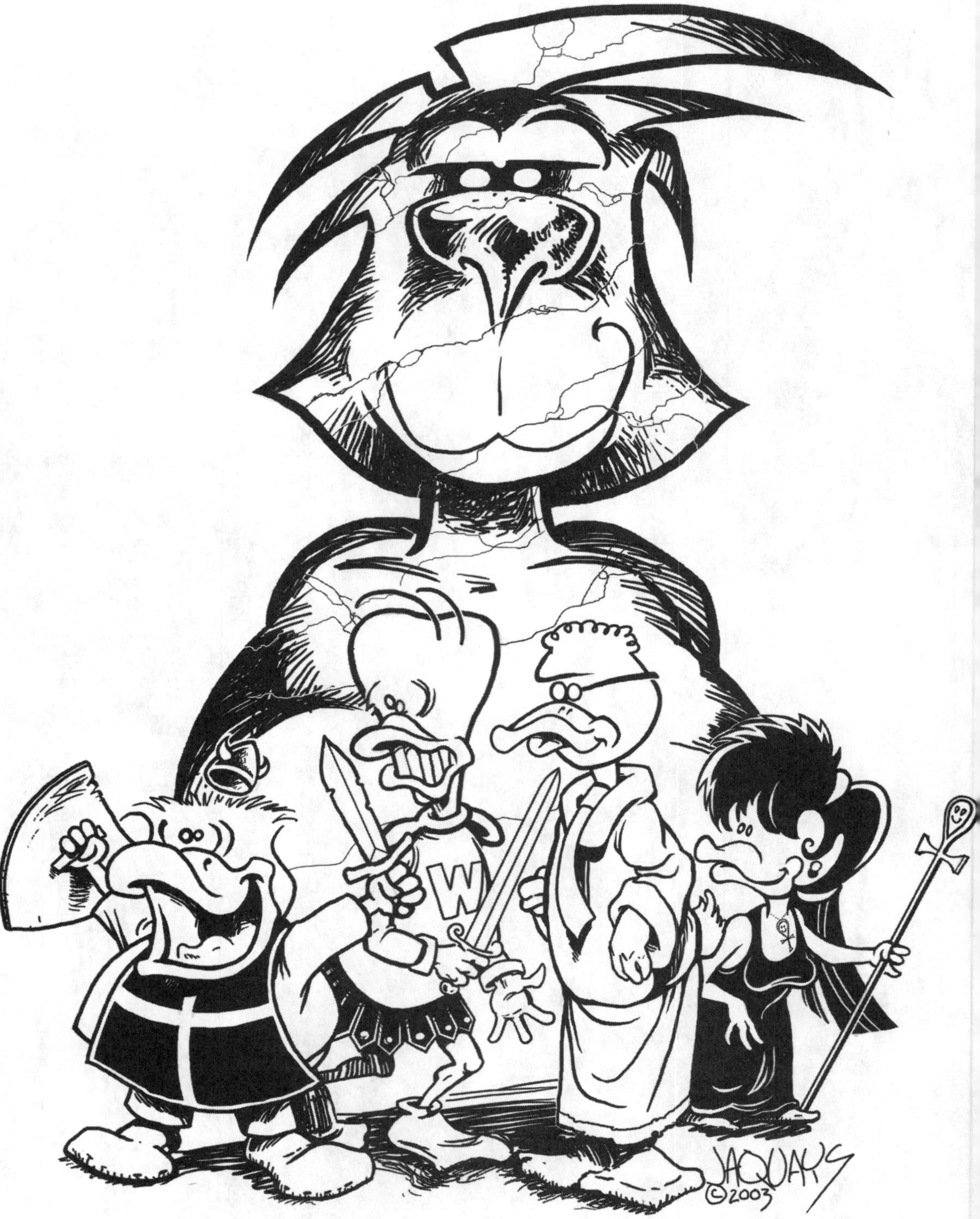
W
JAQUAYS
©2003

WHAT IF THE DORK TOWER CHARACTERS *DIDN'T* LIVE IN SUCH A GREAT BUIDING?

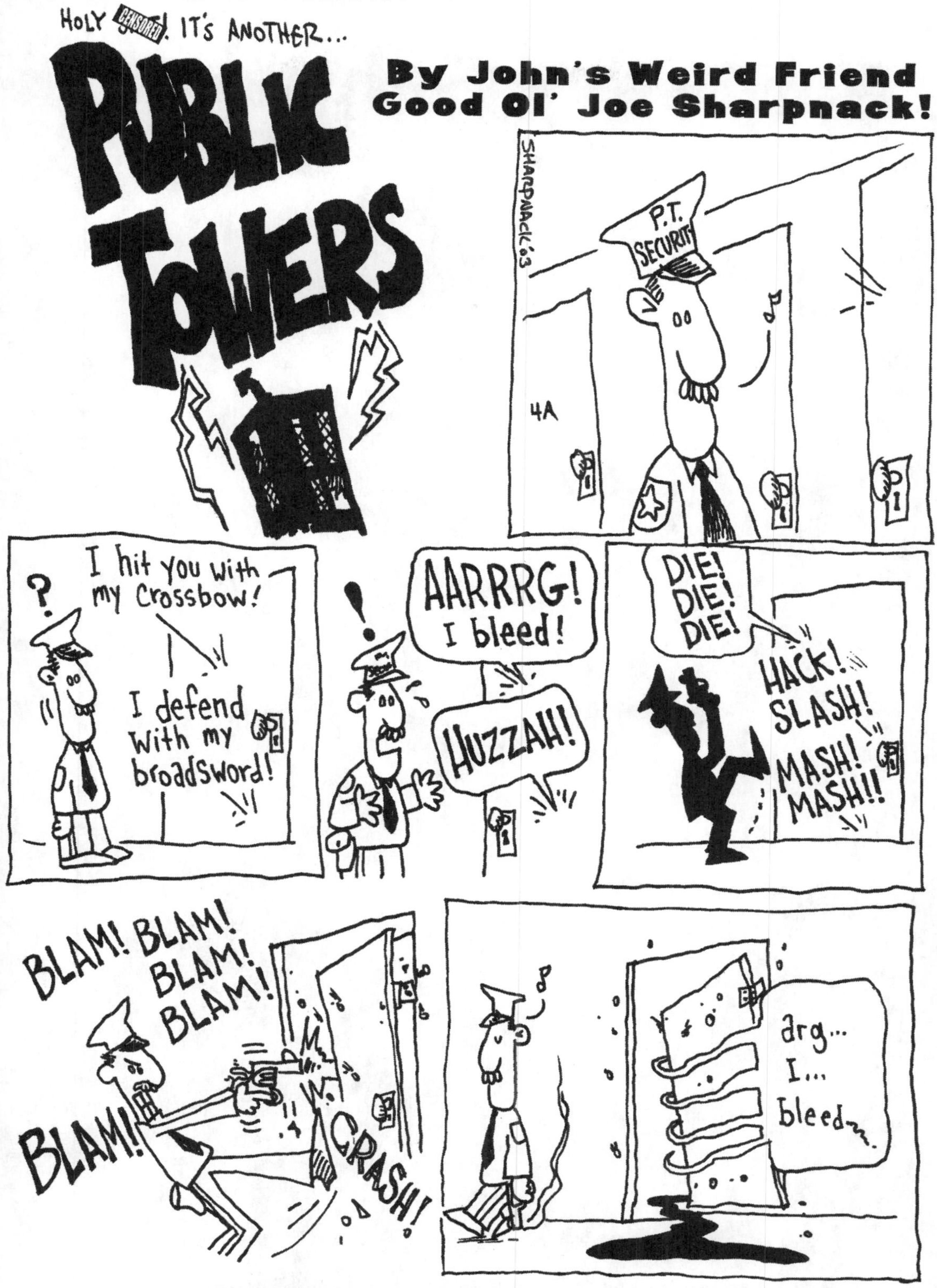
HOLY CENSORED. IT'S ANOTHER...
PUBLIC TOWERS
By John's Weird Friend Good Ol' Joe Sharpnack!
SHARPNACK '03
P.T. SECURITY
4A
I hit you with my Crossbow!
I defend with my broadsword!
AARRRG! I bleed!
HUZZAH!
DIE! DIE! DIE!
HACK! SLASH! MASH! MASH!!
BLAM! BLAM! BLAM! BLAM!
BLAM!
CRASH!
arg... I... bleed

JOE@SHARPTOONS.COM WWW.SHARPTOONS.COM

*D*ork *W*anderings

The Board Game of Wandering in the Dork

Courtesy of James Ernest and Cheapass Games

STORY:

Welcome to the Dungeon of No Return. You and your friends are a party of wily adventurers who have stumbled upon this dungeon through the machinations of your superlative game master. Luckily, you live in a world where it's perfectly okay to kill other creatures and take their stuff, so you will win the game by killing other creatures and taking their stuff.

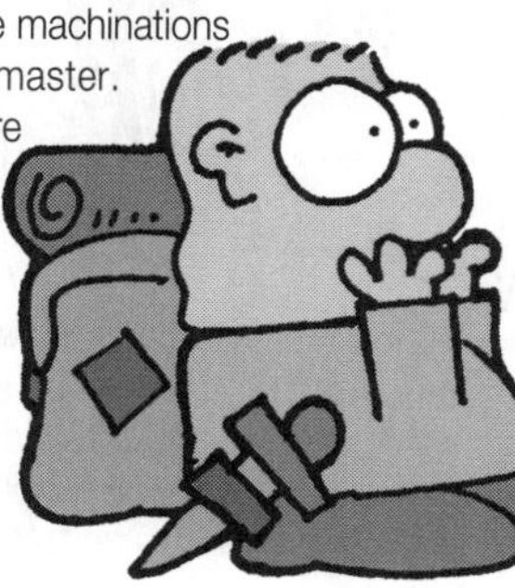

Players: 3 to 6

Playing Time: 45-90 Minutes.

EQUIPMENT:

You will need one **pawn** for each adventurer, at least three six-sided **dice**, and a few decks of **playing cards** without the jokers. The more decks you have, the better; we play with six. You will also need about twenty **stones** or counters for each player, of no particular color.

BEFORE THE GAME:

Each player starts by building a "character," which is made up of three cards: a Heart, a Club, and a Spade. Hearts represent your **Health**, Spades represent your **Speed**, and Clubs represent your **Strength**. Collectively, these three attributes are called "Skills." Aces and Face cards can't be used as Skill cards, and your character's starting Skill total must equal 16 points or less. (You don't want less.)

Speed (Spades): Speed helps characters dodge traps and use Weapons.

Power (Clubs): Power is your strength in combat.

Health (Hearts): Health represents the amount of damage you can take before you die

Spread the cards face up on the table and let each player take whatever cards he needs to construct his character. If you have at least as many decks as players, there are enough cards for everyone to have whatever they want. If not, be nice.

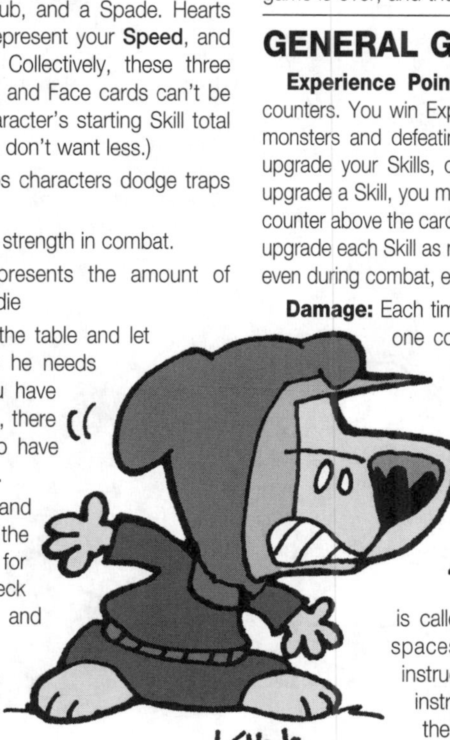

Shuffle the remaining cards and place the deck face down in the middle of the table, with space for a discard pile beside it. If the deck runs out, reshuffle the discards and replace it.

Put everyone's pawn on the "Start" space. If John Kovalic is playing, he'll take the first turn. Otherwise, determine randomly who will go first, and proceed to the left.

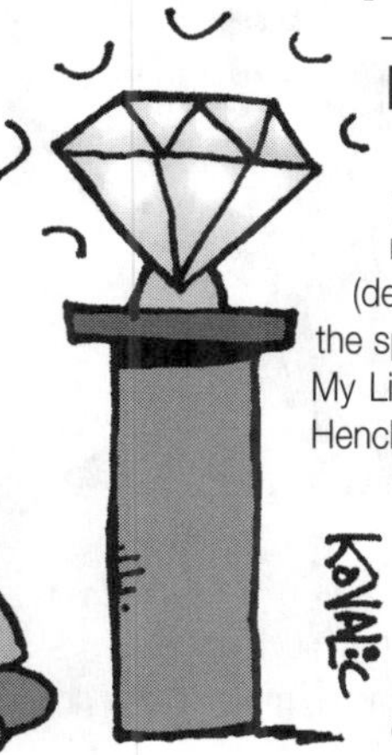

MOVEMENT:

Roll one 6-sided die to see how far you move. You must move the entire roll unless you want to join a combat (described below). You react only to the space where you stop. (If you land on My Life Hurts and jump back to Wizard's Henchman, you do fight the Henchman.)

If you would walk past a player who is engaged in combat, you can choose to stop there and join in the combat. If you start on a space where a combat is taking place, you can't move and must participate in the combat.

The map (page 44/53) is composed of five zones. Each zone has a locked door at the end. A player can't pass through the door into the next zone until the **all** the players are in the current zone. If you get to the end of a zone before the entire party has made it into the zone, the path loops back to the first space in the zone.

There is not a locked door at the Finish space. Players **do not** have to wait for their friends to enter the last zone before they can escape the dungeon. When the first player exits, the game is over, and the player with the highest score wins.

GENERAL GAME DEFINITIONS:

Experience Points: Experience Points are tracked with counters. You win Experience during your adventure by killing monsters and defeating traps. You may use these points to upgrade your Skills, or keep them for points at the end. To upgrade a Skill, you must spend three experience points. Put a counter above the card and treat it as a +1 to that Skill. You can upgrade each Skill as much as you like, whenever you like. Yes, even during combat, even after you've rolled the dice. Why not.

Damage: Each time you take a point of damage, you put one counter on your Heart card. (Be sure to keep your damage distinct from your upgrades to Health!) If you ever take more damage than the value of your Heart, you die and leave the game. You can heal damage by finding Food.

Board Spaces: Most spaces are marked with a card. These make you draw one card, which is called finding cards "in the open." Other spaces have specific cards or special instructions written on them. If the space has instructions, you follow them when you land there. Exception: You **do not** draw a card if you stop on a card space where a combat is taking place. Instead, you join the combat.

CARDS:

You can find cards in two different places: In the open (on the board) and in a Treasure Pile. You will find a Treasure Pile after you kill a Big Monster.

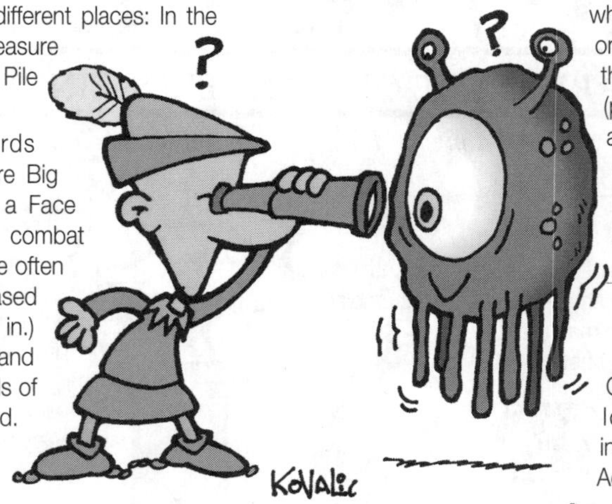

Face Cards: Face Cards (Jacks, Queens, and Kings) are Big Monsters. Whenever you find a Face Card in the open, you enter combat with it. (Note that face cards are often treated as different monsters based on the rules of the zone you're in.) The Health value, Power value, and Treasure value of the three kinds of monsters is printed on the board.

To represent the Monster's health, place a number of counters on the card equal to its heart value, shown on the board. Putting all the hit points on the card makes tracking the combat much easier.

The player who discovers the Monster immediately fights the first round of combat with it. Both the player and the Monster roll three dice, and add their Power. Whoever rolls higher wins. In a tie, the player wins.

If you win the roll, take a health counter off the monster and keep it as an Experience Point. If you lose, add a counter to your own Heart card, representing one point of damage.

When you are in combat with a Monster, you can't move away. When your turn comes, you will take another swing at the beast. If there are other players in the same space, they are stuck in the same combat and will swing at the monster on their turn.

When the Monster loses its last health counter, you have killed it. Discard the Monster and create a Treasure Pile as described below. Whoever killed the monster gets first draft of the treasure.

Combat continues until either the Monster, or the whole group fighting it, is dead. If everyone in the combat dies, the Monster and all its treasure go away.

Treasure: The player who kills the Monster turns over the Monster's loot, called the Treasure Pile.

The Treasure Pile includes Diamonds that were recently found out in the open (see below), plus a number of cards from the deck: 2 for a Jack, 3 for a Queen, and 4 for a King.

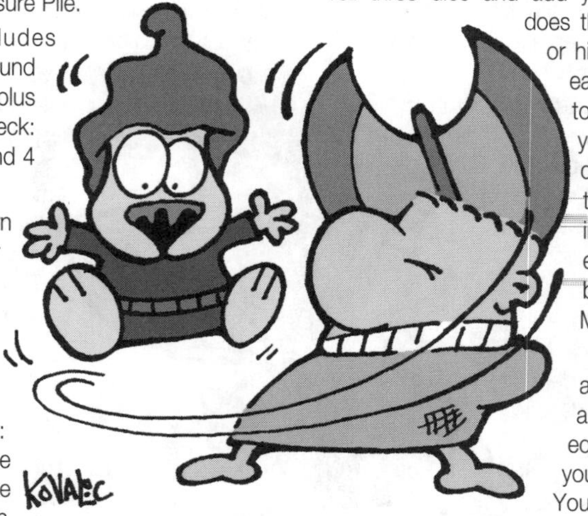

To build a Treasure Pile, turn over the appropriate number of cards in the deck. If any of them are face cards, discard them and draw replacements. If any of them are traps (small Spades), they will affect the player who killed the Monster: he can disarm them for one Experience point each, or take one point of damage for each one he can't disarm. Discard the traps but don't draw replacements.

The Treasure Pile should now be composed of some number of small Diamonds, Clubs, and Hearts. The player who killed the Monster takes one card from that pile, then the next player in the combat (proceeding left), and so on around the table until all the cards are distributed. Note that some cards act differently when found in Treasure Piles than when found "in the open," i.e., as a card on a board space.

Small Cards: "Small Cards" means everything lower than Face cards, including Aces. In this game, Aces are valued at one.

Ace through Ten of Diamonds: Small Diamonds are Gold. Gold is worth points, assuming you live long enough to spend it. If you find Gold in the open, you must set it aside. It will be added to the Treasure Pile of the next monster anyone finds.

When you encounter a Big Monster, immediately give all the diamonds that were recently found in the open to that Monster. They will go into its Treasure Pile, along with its normal cards. If new Diamonds are found after the combat begins, those will wait for the next Monster.

Ace through Ten of Spades: Small Spades are Traps. If you find a Trap in the open, compare it to your Speed. If the Trap is equal to or lower than your Speed, you disarm the Trap and earn one Experience Point. If it is higher, you take one point of damage. For example, if your Speed is 4 and you find a 7 of Spades, you take 1 damage. Disarmed or not, discard the Trap.

If you find a small Spade in a Treasure Pile, it's still a Trap. The player who killed the Monster finds all the traps in the pile.

Ace through Ten of Clubs: Small Clubs are either Monsters or Weapons. Found in the open, Small Clubs are Monsters with no treasure. When you meet a Small Monster, roll three dice and add your Club value. The Monster does the same. If your total is equal or higher, you kill the Monster and earn an experience point. If your total is lower, the Monster deals you one point of damage and disappears. Clubs printed on the board act the same, though in this case each player who enters the same space on the board will have to fight the same Monster.

In a Treasure Pile, Small Clubs are Weapons. You only pick up a Weapon if it is smaller than or equal to your Skill (this means you're talented enough to use it). You can hold only one Weapon at a time. When you have a Weapon, you add the Weapon's value to all your combat rolls. If you already hold a Weapon, you must discard it when you take a new one. This means that if you wish to prevent a companion from taking a weapon from a Treasure Pile by picking it up yourself, you must throw away whatever weapon you're currently holding.

If no one is able (or willing) to pick up a weapon, discard it.

Ace through Ten of Hearts: No matter where you find them, Small Hearts are Food. Food let you remove Damage Counters, one counter for each point of Food.

You can only carry one Food at a time, but you can eat a new one and still hang on to an old one. For example: Suppose you are carrying a 10 Food, and have taken 4 points of damage. You find a 2 Food in a Treasure Pile. You can eat the 2 Food, discard it, and heal 2 points of damage, and still hold on to your 10 for later.

Food can be eaten at the moment it's needed, so you can die from a Monster attack, then discard your Food and heal the damage.

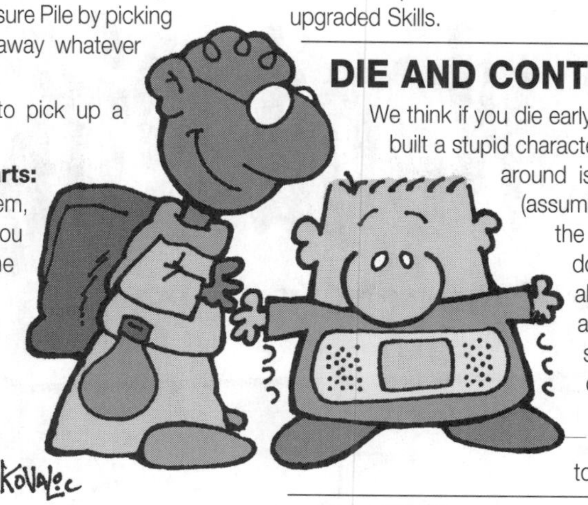

SCORING:

The game ends when one player reaches the "Finish" space. You must be alive at the end of the game to score. Your score is equal to the face value of your Diamonds, the face value of your Weapon, the number of experience points you have, and the total points you've added to your Skills. Note that raw experience is therefore worth 3 times as much as upgraded Skills.

DIE AND CONTINUE OPTION:

We think if you die early, you deserve it because you built a stupid character. But if you feel that sticking around is the only way to have fun (assuming you don't mind making the game take longer) you can do this: when you die, you lose all your experience, upgrades, and collected cards, and restart the game with the same character in the same place you died. If you can catch up and still win, more power to you.

QUESTIONS?

This is a free game and we probably left something out. What's worse, we've probably stated something ambiguously that will keep you and your friends up all night arguing. Think of it as an opportunity to learn more about the mysterious vicissitudes of game design, not as an opportunity to send us incoherent emails at three in the morning.

QUICK REFERENCE CHART:

Card	Suit	In The Open	In Treasure Pile
A-10	Spades	Trap	Trap
A-10	Clubs	Small Monster	Weapon
A-10	Diamonds	Gold in next Treasure Pile	Gold
A-10	Hearts	Food	Food
J-K	Any	Big Monster	Ignore and Replace

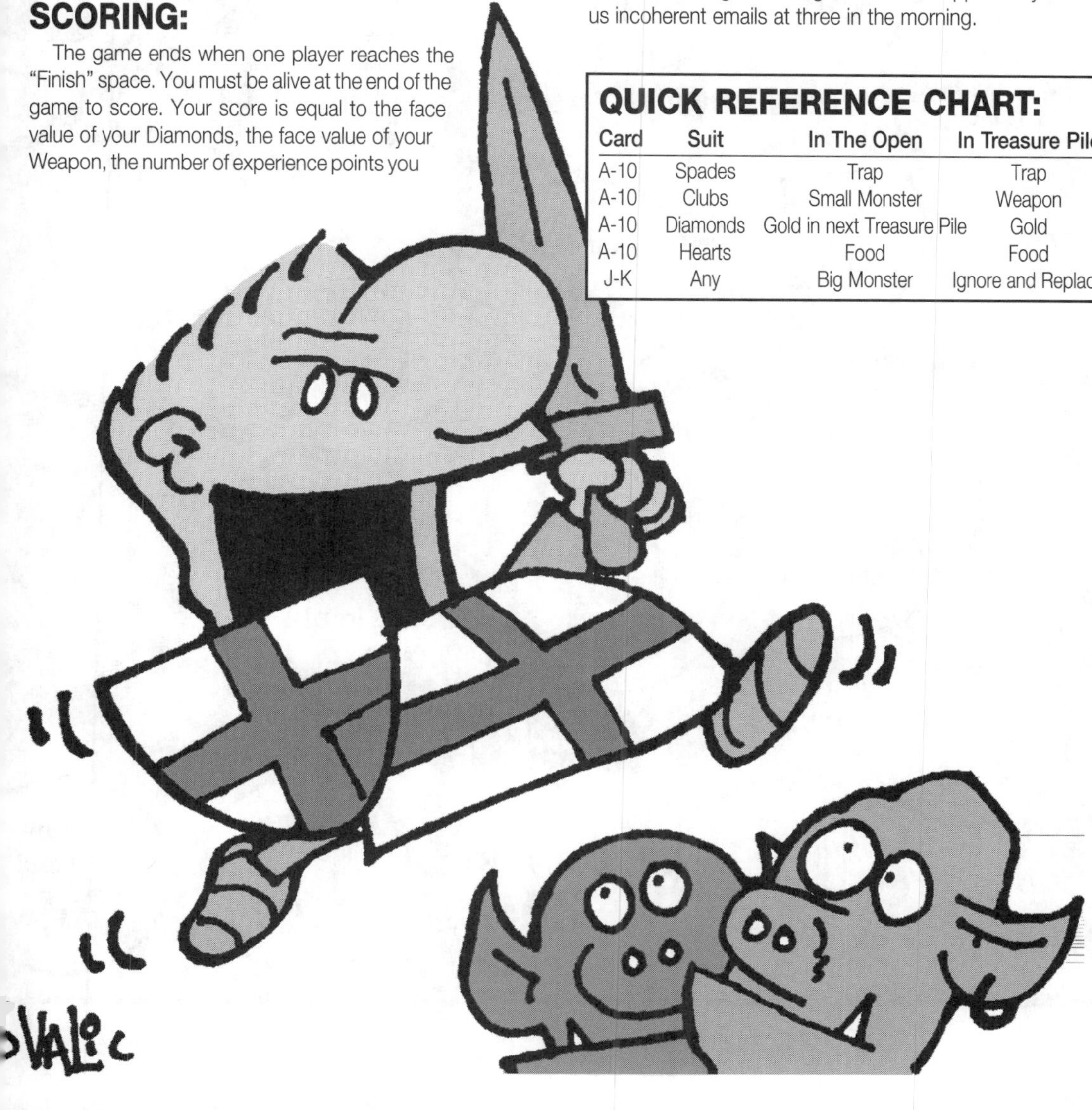

Dork Wanderings

The Board Game of Wandering in the Dork

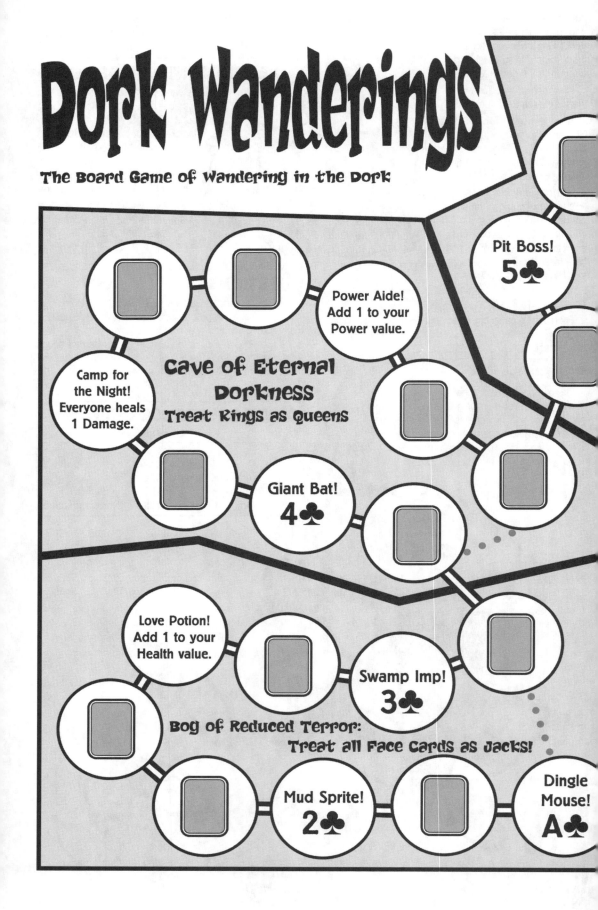

Pit Boss!
5♣

Power Aide!
Add 1 to your
Power value.

Camp for
the Night!
Everyone heals
1 Damage.

Cave of Eternal Dorkness
Treat Kings as Queens

Giant Bat!
4♣

Love Potion!
Add 1 to your
Health value.

Swamp Imp!
3♣

Bog of Reduced Terror:
Treat all Face Cards as Jacks!

Mud Sprite!
2♣

Dingle
Mouse!
A♣

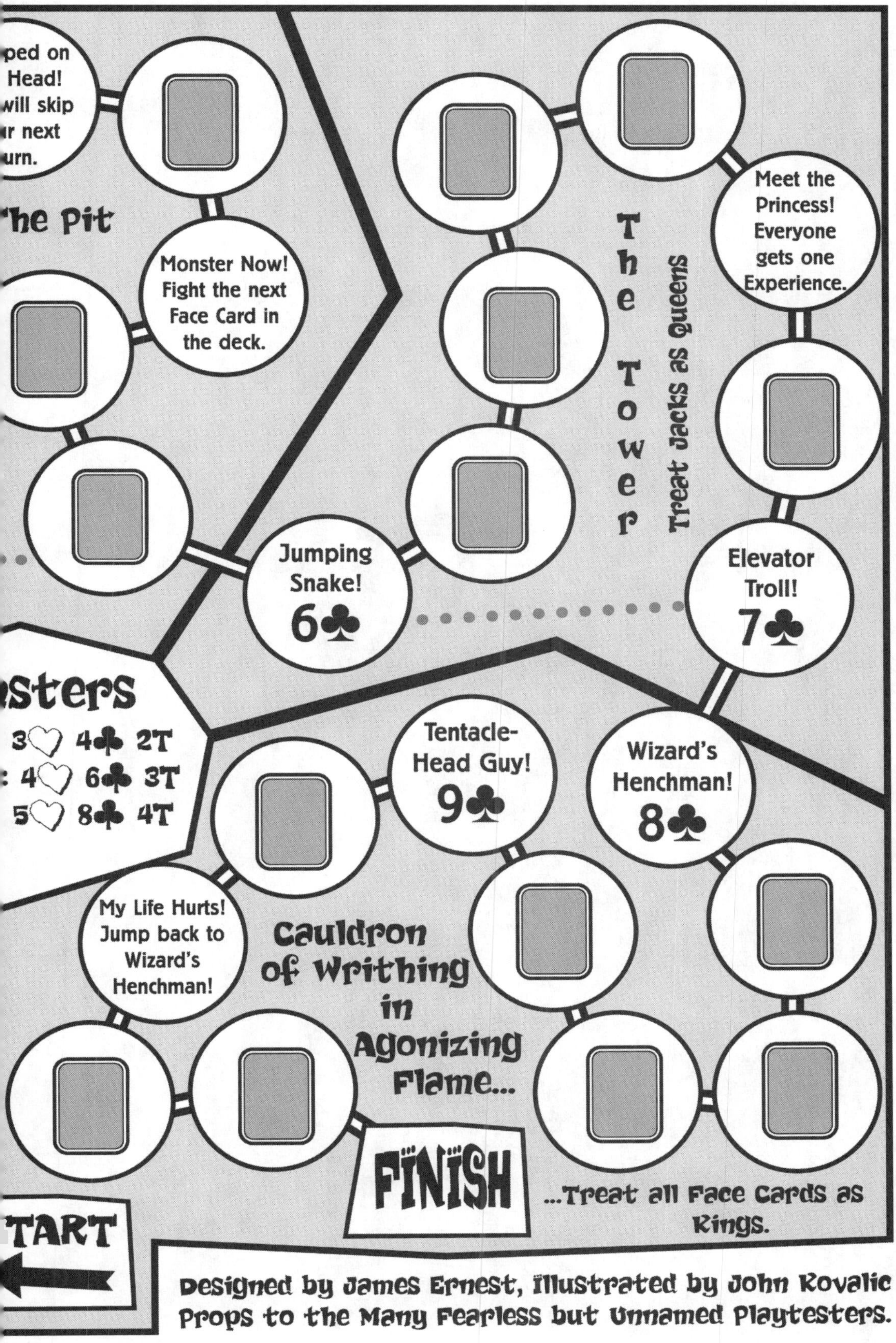

...ped on ... Head! ... will skip ...r next ...urn.
...he Pit
Monster Now! Fight the next Face Card in the deck.
Jumping Snake! 6♣
The Tower
Treat Jacks as Queens
Meet the Princess! Everyone gets one Experience.
Elevator Troll! 7♣
...sters
3♡ 4♣ 2T
4♡ 6♣ 3T
5♡ 8♣ 4T
Tentacle-Head Guy! 9♣
Wizard's Henchman! 8♣
My Life Hurts! Jump back to Wizard's Henchman!
Cauldron of Writhing in Agonizing Flame...
...Treat all Face Cards as Kings.
FINISH
...TART

Designed by James Ernest, Illustrated by John Kovalic
Props to the Many Fearless but Unnamed Playtesters.

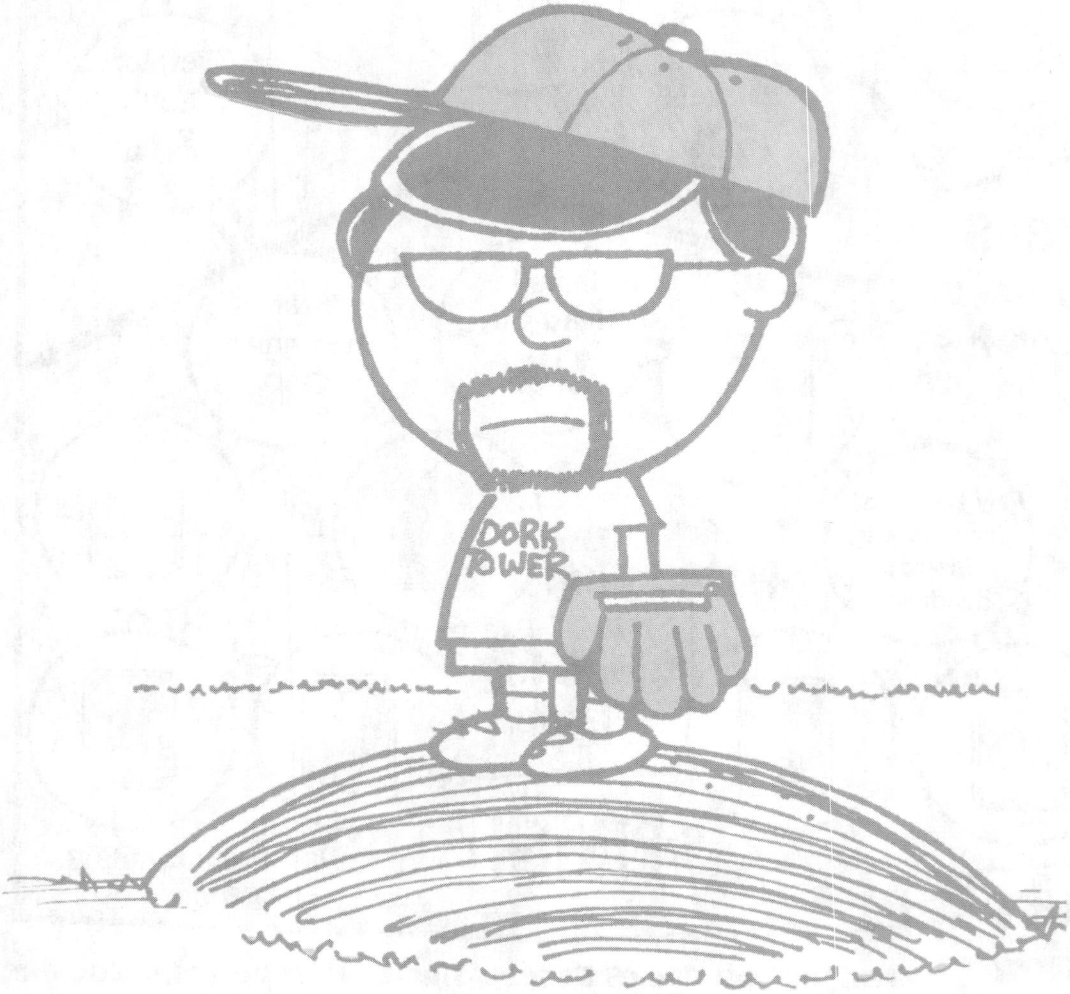
DORK
TOWER

About the Author

John Kovalic was born in Manchester, England in 1962, although he's carefully cultivated a Wisconsin accent in the last few years. USA TODAY called the Madison resident a "Hot Pick," and his award-winning cartoons have appeared everywhere from Dragon magazine to the NEW YORK TIMES and the WASHINGTON POST.

The five-time Origins award-winning Dork Tower comic book was launched in June 1998, with its first issue selling out within a matter of weeks. "Dork Tower may just be the perfect comic book," raved Diamond Comics Distributors. Dork Tower is now printed in German, Italian, Portuguese, Spanish, and French editions, proving geekdom is universal.

John was a co-founder and is Art Director of Out of the Box Games (where he's worked on such massive hits as Games Magazine's 1999 Party Game of the Year, "Apples to Apples," among many other award-winning games), and his artwork has graced smashes such as Chez Greek and Munchkin. Along with his SnapDragons partner Liz Rathke, John's warped creations can now be found on WizKids' Creepy Freaks game.

In 2003, John became the first cartoonist ever inducted into the Academy of Adventure Gaming Arts and Design Hall of Fame. Also that year, he created the party quiz game "Whad'Ya Know?" (Out of the Box), winner of the prestigious Games Magazine Games 100 award.

John's degree was in Economics with a minor in Astrophysics. He's never used either. But if you ask him nicely, he may even tell you how he once ended up in the pages of the National Enquirer.

In his spare time, John searches for spare time.

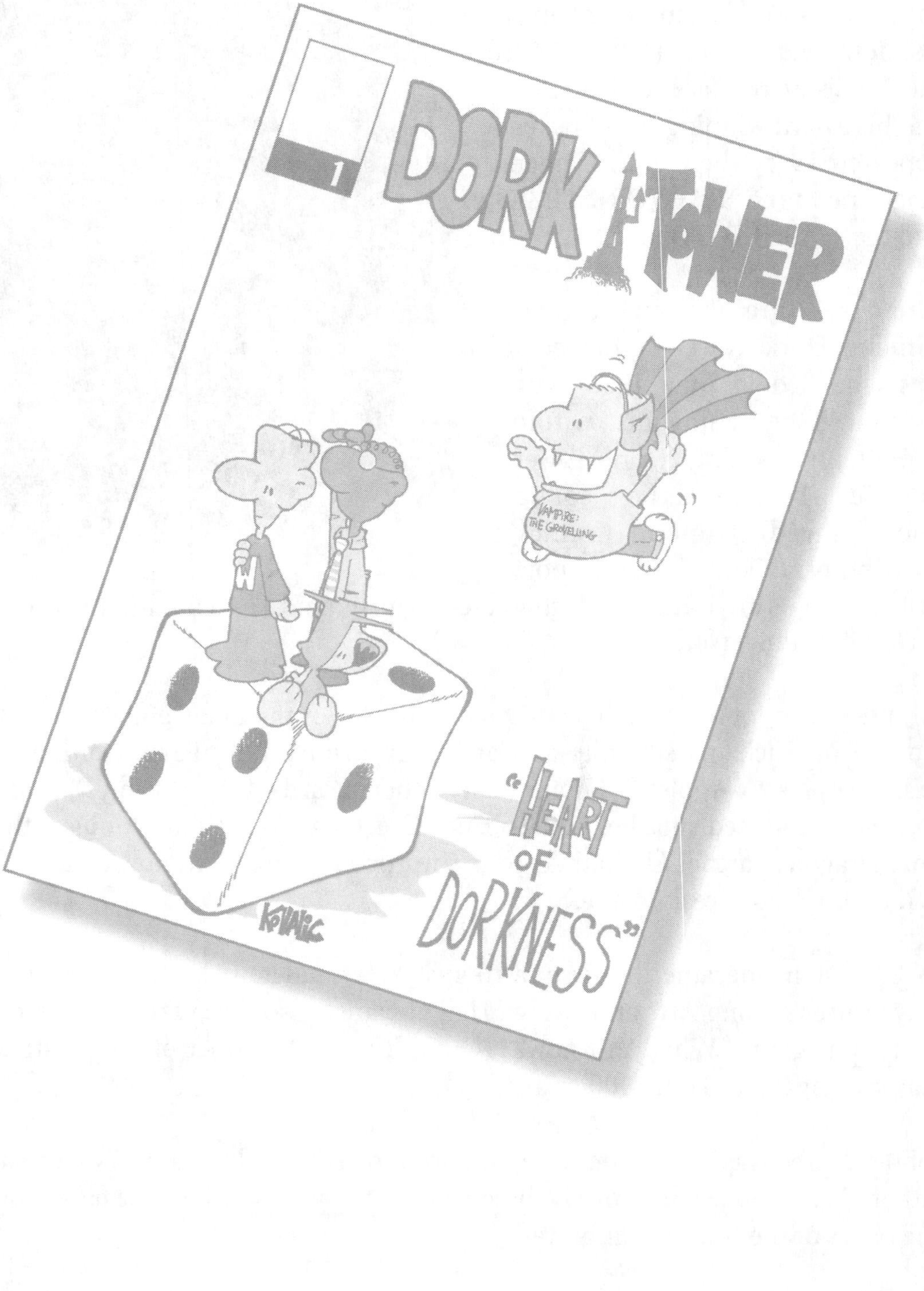
1
DORK TOWER
VAMPIRE: THE GROVELLING
W
"HEART OF DORKNESS"
KOVALIC

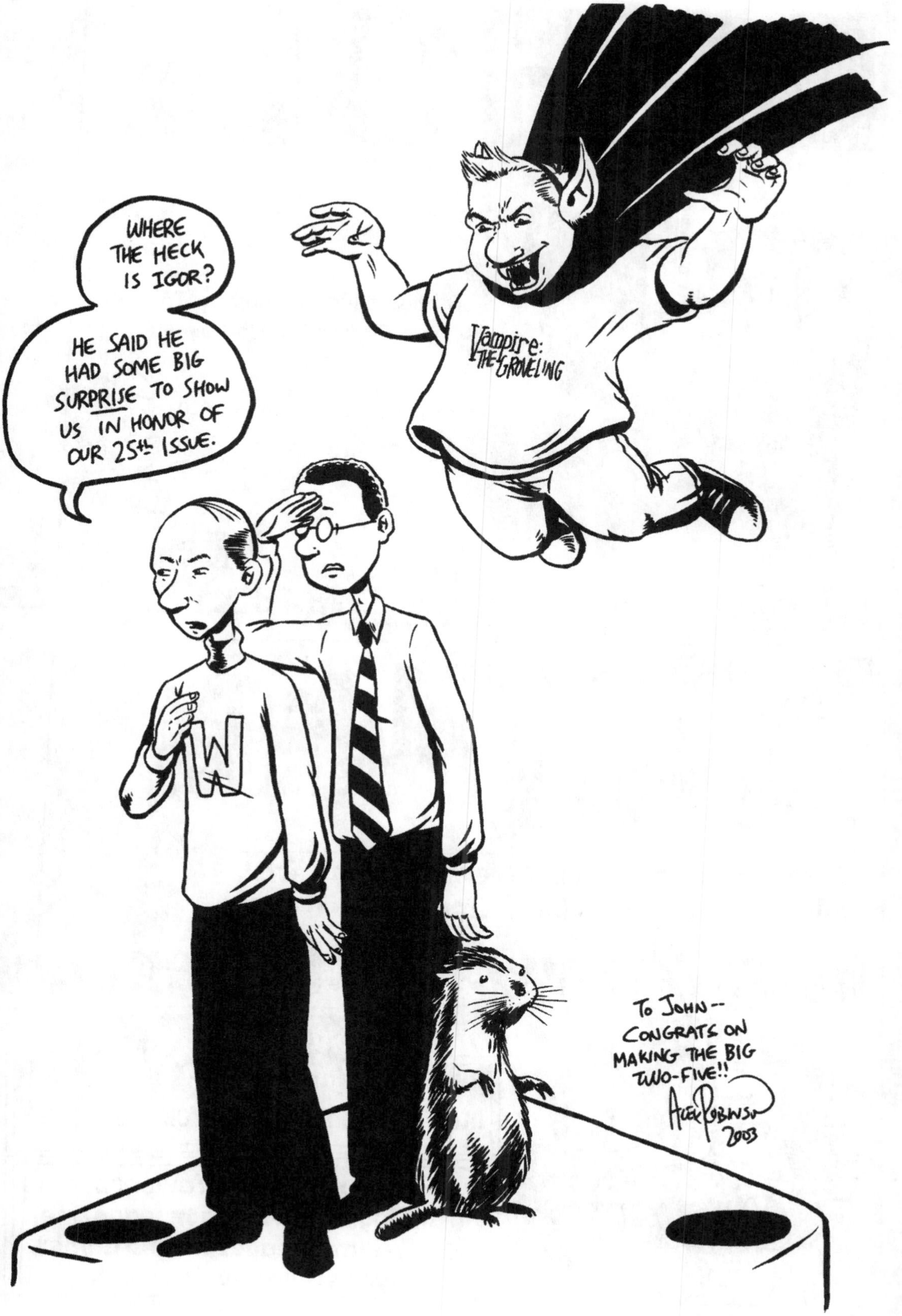
WHERE THE HECK IS IGOR?
HE SAID HE HAD SOME BIG SURPRISE TO SHOW US IN HONOR OF OUR 25th ISSUE.
Vampire: THE GROVELING
W
TO JOHN -- CONGRATS ON MAKING THE BIG TWO-FIVE!!
ALEX ROBINSON 2003

BEHOLD.

56 New Illustrations by John Kovalic.
(Oh, yeah. They're on cards that work with your d20 game.)

See for yourself at:
www.atlas-games.com/dork20

 'd20 System' and the d20 System logo are trademarks of Wizards of the Coast, Inc. in the United States and other countries, and are used with permission. Dork Tower is a trademark of John Kovalic, used under license by Trident, Inc. d/b/a Atlas Games. Dork20 is a trademark owned by Trident, Inc. d/b/a Atlas Games. The Atlas Games logo is a trademark of John Nephew and Trident, Inc. d/b/a Atlas Games.

Three cartoons a week! News! Mailing lists! FAQs! Downloads! Links! Stores! Muskrats!

http://www.dorktower.com

Join the Army of Dorkness Mailing List!
http://groups.yahoo.com/group/dorktower/

...and, of course, Dork Tower appears in analog form in Dragon magazine, Scrye, Games magazine and Comics Buyer's Guide every month!

DORK TOWER

Now you can play John Kovalic's *Dork Tower* characters . . . as they play their characters . . . in a magical quest for glory. Adventure through the land of Aurora, smiting monsters and growing in power, until you are strong enough to challenge the evil wizard in his tower. Slay him and you win . . . fail, and be cast from the heights . . . **Dork Tower** is a fast-moving game for 2 to 6 players. It features a full-color game map with a 3-D central tower, over 100 monster and character disks, pretty dice, spell cards, rules, and character sheets . . . all illustrated, of course, by John Kovalic!

Dork Tower Miniatures

The *Dork Tower* gang as you've never seen them before – in 3-D!

John Kovalic's great characters are now 28mm metal miniatures. The stars of the wildly popular *Dork Tower* comic book are brought to life by legendary sculptor Tom Meier. They're dressed up in their best adventuring gear, and ready to tackle any challenge, even the dread Turbonium Dragon! (Dragon not included . . .)

In the **Dork Tower Miniatures** set you get Ken as a cleric, Matt as an archer, Kayleigh as a knight, Igor as an armored Munchkin . . . er, warrior, Gilly as a seductive sorceress, and Carson as a hairy-footed rogue.

One look, and you'll know what Igor means when he says, "It must be mine!"

STEVE JACKSON GAMES
www.sjgames.com